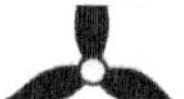

HUNGRY
ORTHODOX CHRISTIAN
READER

The "Hidden" Writings of Orthodox Christianity

OLGA
Press

Orthodox Literary Growth Advocates
Chicago, Illinois

ISBN: 978-0-9966441-0-5
LCCN: 2015913957

Acknowledgements
Much gratitude to the long-suffering draft readers.

See Also
www.OrthodoxReader.com

CONTENTS

An Alternative Order for Reading

Orientation

Ellipses

The larger works represented in this book are sampled in a way that makes them short enough for general consumption but long enough to provide a real sense of the quoted sources. Some abridgement has been necessary. Small gaps in the text are indicated with ellipsis points (. . .), larger lacunae with asterisks (* * *).

Footnotes

Footnotes from the original source appear normally. [Editorial footnotes are enclosed in square brackets].

Psalm References

Psalm quotations are referenced using Septuagint numbering. Generally, Psalms 9 to 148 are numbered one less than the Hebrew (Masoretic) numbering, e.g., Psalm 50 in the Septuagint is Psalm 51 in Western Bibles.

Saints' Days and Dates

Most references to saints are followed by [† *year of repose*, *day of commemoration*], e.g., Saint Symeon the New Theologian [†1022, March 12].

The year of the saint's falling asleep gives the reader a chronological context for the saint. When compared with other saints, it confirms the consistency of their teaching over the centuries.

The commemoration day allows for easy reference. The volumes of the Lives of Saints are ordered by commemoration day, not by alphabet. Follow-up reading is encouraged.

Preface

This Reader is not spiritual guidance but practical direction. It is less about *what* Orthodox believe and more about *how* Orthodox believe. Most important, it is about the *sources* currently available in English. This book should leave you unsatisfied, appetite whetted. It is intended to expose the hungry reader to various types of Orthodox nourishment and to provide a key to the pantry.

At the end of each chapter is a note regarding its source as well as a box full of Miscellanea: books, specimens, oddments related (usually) to that particular topic or type of writing. Many of these Miscellanea include **Parent Friendly** tips for busy parents (or relatives or friends) who are concerned to pass on their Orthodoxy to their children. One may not be inspired by each and every article, but wherever one feels a special resonance would be a good place to launch into further study (and practice/*praxis*).

As with so many Orthodox books, it may be expedient to skip the Introduction and begin immediately with the real text. The Introduction might be more useful to the reader after getting a sense of the book. That is, rather than politely (and perhaps yawningly) accept the Introduction's (pre)suppositions, wrestle them armed and witting.

In the same vein, the Alternative Order for Reading is provided for those who prefer a less "intellectual," more "hands-on" approach or who are weary (wary) of Academia. Or, if reading or interest bogs down in the first few chapters, switch to the alternative. The Alternative Order is especially recommended for people whose available time and attention for reading is stressfully tight; for others who, though hungry for Orthodoxy, feel they don't know enough about Orthodoxy to read about Orthodoxy; and for those for whom reading is not yet (or is no longer) a normal, natural, enjoyable activity.

Bon Appétit!

Introduction

For He satisfies the empty soul, and fills the hungry soul with good things.—Psalm 106 [1]

Establish Thy Church in Orthodoxy, O Christ, and bring peace to our life, in that Thou art good and lovest mankind.—"Lord, I have cried" sticheron, Saturday Evening, Tone I [2]

The "Hidden" Writings of Orthodox Christianity

This Reader is a sampler of books and types of Orthodox writings that are "hidden." Although traditional, everyday reading and currently available in English, they are hidden either through unfamiliarity or, surprisingly, a seeming too much familiarity. Many writings are hidden away in multi-volume sets of books, daunting by their size, sheen of scholarship, and prohibitive cost—an unfortunate deterrent from what is normal, everyday reading. Other staples of Orthodox reading have only recently arrived in English. Older Orthodox in America, inured to their too-long absence, stopped looking for them; younger generations never learned of their existence and major role in Orthodox life. Certain others are avoided as though proscribed: *for priests only*. Those obscured by ostensible over-familiarity—the services, for example, with their expansive beauty and depth—are simply taken for granted and too often become burdensome obligation.

This collection provides an encouraging glimpse into and introduction to these "hidden"—though widely available—texts and sources. One cannot *read* one's way into salvation, but through reading one finds instruction, example, encouragement. The various selections in this anthology point toward a more Orthodox world view, way of life, living culture.

---

1 *The Septuagint with Apocrypha: Greek and English*, trans Sir Lancelot C.L. Brenton, originally published by Samuel Bagster & Sons, 1851; reprinted in US by Hendrickson Publishers (1986–2013), 764.

2 *The Octoechos: The Hymns of the Cycle of the Eight Tones for Sundays and Weekdays*, vol 1 (Tones I & II), trans Reader Isaac E. Lambertsen (Liberty, TN: Saint John of Kronstadt Press, 1999), 4; SJKP.org. Used with permission.

To say it another way, the emphasis of this book is not so much *what* Orthodox believe, but rather *how* Orthodox believe. The *how* answers the "so what?" of *what* Orthodox believe. For example, "I believe" that the sun rises and sets every day. So what? So, I plan my outdoor activities during the daytime. "I believe" that the doctor and physical therapist know better than I do about healing and rehabilitation, so I follow their prescribed regimen, even if I do not understand why, even if it is painful. *How* I believe is the *what* I believe—*in action.*

The Symbol of Faith is said in both the morning and the evening prayers. "I believe in one God, the Father Almighty, Maker of Heaven and Earth." So what? What behavior does this "I believe" entail? How do I give ortho (right) doxy (glory, praise, worship) to God? How do I conduct myself so that "Hallowed be Thy Name"? The answer is not a one-size-fits-all sound bite, yet is vital to a genuine Orthodoxy.

> Let us glorify God, not by our faith alone, but also by our life, since otherwise it would not be glory, but blasphemy. For God is not so much blasphemed by an impure heathen as by a corrupt Christian.[1]

Hunger

Much of contemporary Orthodox literature is *about* Orthodoxy. It is often presented as a sanitary Orthodoxy: pre-digested, post-analyzed, and pretty much explained away. Orthodoxy easily becomes a museum piece. The Holy Fathers speak directly to our very own personal, serious, ailing, practical spiritual life. Yet in the hands of academics, the works of the Holy Fathers can become little more than objects of speculation, conjecture, wrangling: authors, dates, influences, variant texts—the life-blood of academics, but not practically (spiritually) useful to living, breathing, working, praying, *hungry* Orthodox. Often a reader will put down a book before finishing the introduction, sapped of gumption and no longer interested in the actual text.

Another malnourishing factor may be our contemporary American mindset that is attuned, for example, to headlines with no substance: we hear snippets and think that we know something. In like manner, we take basic, introductory "101" courses and then assume that we understand *enough*, as much as anyone would need to know, enough to get by at coffee hour and cocktail parties, never again to approach the

1 St John Chrysostom [†407, Nov 13], *Homily LXVII on the Gospel of St John* in *Nicene and Post-Nicene Fathers* (First Series) 14:250.

subject. Hence, we celebrate our would-be graduation "commencement" as an ending rather than as a beginning. In such an atmosphere, works intended to make Orthodoxy comprehensible—that is, to distill two thousand years of a living thing of such depth and breadth into a two-gulp draft—even the best of these works can, rather than instill Orthodoxy, inoculate us against it. Orthodoxy becomes separate and other—not as in "holy" but as in not-applicable-to-us.

The purpose of this Reader is to point readers to Orthodox sources that are currently available in English, to open up new resources, new vistas, new understanding. It does not pre- or post-analyze each article, but encourages readers to discover for themselves the original writings, without the filters, the obfuscations, the dilutions, and the plethora of explanations of why Orthodoxy is not really relevant to us twenty-first century sophisticates.

To be sure, many contemporary Orthodox works are extraordinarily helpful. For example, Father Alexander Schmemann's *Great Lent: Journey to Pascha*[1] is an excellent overview of and introduction to Great Lent. Some people read it year after year. There comes a time, however, to take off the training wheels. Instead of reading *about* the *Lenten Triodion*,[2] why not read, why not *experience*, the *Triodion* itself? That is, rather than simply tick off the themes of the passing Sundays—Publican and Pharisee, Prodigal Son, and so on—why not bask, to some degree, in their spiritual illumination?

This is easily accomplished by reading the services. In our Lenten example, if time is tight, one could read through the *Triodion* Sunday service in small parts during the preceding week. Or on Lenten weekdays, one might read the hymns of Sixth Hour (half a page) or Vespers (less than two pages) along with their prescribed Scripture readings.[3] This is only one possible approach, and can be applied not only to Lent but year-round.[4]

The point is to get at the meat of the matter, to listen to the saints and to embrace the original sources that have delivered Orthodoxy—the

1 Crestwood, NY: St Vladimir's Seminary Press, 1969.

2 South Canaan, PA: St Tikhon's Seminary Press, 2002.

3 Lenten weekdays are in the *Triodion Supplement*.

4 Reading the services does not replace attending them—at every opportunity. Neither does one read *during* the services, but participates undistracted. If the chanter or choir cannot be understood, say the Jesus Prayer.

Faith of the Apostles—to us in our own day. This is real nourishment. We are hungry, after all.

> I remember an elderly monk at Esphigmenou Monastery on Mount Athos who was so simple that he thought "Ascension" was the name of a female saint. He prayed to her on his *komboschoini*, "Saint of God, intercede for us!" Once, he had to feed a sick Brother in the infirmary but there was no food. He immediately went down the stairs, opened a window overlooking the sea, stretched out his arms and said, "Ascension, my Saint, give me a little fish for the Brother." And right away—what a miracle—a big fish jumped out of the sea and into his hands. The others who saw him were astonished, but he simply looked at them smiling, as if he were saying, "What's so strange about what you've just seen?" Now look at us. We may know everything about the life and martyrdom of the saints, or about when and how the Ascension took place, and yet we cannot even catch a tiny little fish! These are the strange and paradoxical things of the spiritual life. These are things that the minds of intellectuals who are centered on themselves and not on God cannot explain because their knowledge is of this world; it is sterile. Their spirits are ill with secularism, and their minds are void of the Holy Spirit.[1]

The Need for Reading

Read assiduously, says Saint Isaac the Syrian [†c.700, Jan 28]. If this is good advice for monks in the desert, where there is nearly no material distraction even for the asking, how much better advice for twenty-first century Americans, where there is nearly no escape from distraction. Images, idiocy, idolatry are constantly spewed into our eyes and ears; pride, pleasure, and forgetfulness are endlessly hawked by the blaring media that surround us. Reading is a way to teach us—and constantly to remind us—of what (Who) is true, what is truly valuable, the one thing needful.

That there is no time to read, we know. Consider, however, Saint Macrina [†c.380, July 19, sister of Saints Basil the Great, Gregory of Nyssa, *et al!*]. Educated in Holy Scripture, she psalmodized tenaciously:

---

1 Elder Paisios [St Paisios the New of Mt Athos, †1994, July 12], *Spiritual Counsels*, vol 1, *With Pain and Love for Contemporary Man*, trans Cornelia A. Tsakiridou, Maria Spanou, 3rd ed (Souroti, Thessaloniki: Holy Monastery "Evangelist John the Theologian," 2011), 237–8. Used with permission.

arising from bed in the morning, before and after any work, before and after meals, before bed and again arising for her nighttime prayers. Saint Macrina emphasized that the soul is self-determining, that is, the soul itself *chooses* salvation. Or not. The tenor of the soul's actions and its utter dependence on God demonstrate its desire to receive God's gifts and God Himself. This kind of understanding finds time to read. With our busy schedules, this will more likely happen little by little rather than all at once.

Again with an eye to Saint Macrina, the idea of reading expands. It is not a constant reading of new material, which is often no more than a compulsion for novelty or a desire to be fashionably in-the-know. Reading also includes revisiting works we have already read. The writing doesn't change, but we do. We see things in a new light. Reading also includes, for example, our daily prayers. Rather than scramble to meet our daily quota, we read with as much attention as we can muster in the time at our disposal. As these prayers become internalized, along with memorized psalms and Scripture and other helps, we read directly from the heart.

An especial need for reading is that Orthodox Christians must know and nourish their faith in order to remain Orthodox. Where the fullness of Orthodoxy is not proclaimed, preached, and practiced—not for the sake of super-correctness but simply to get beyond the shallows of Anything-Goes America—where the fullness of Orthodoxy is not sought out, apprehended, and embraced, there heterodoxy, distortion, and division creep in to fill and fester in the gaps. It is not a game of pick-and-choose-whatever-you-like-and-call-it-Orthodoxy.

There are many and constant temptations to compromise, a little here, a little there, often in the name of love, to get along, to be "a Good Christian." This is exemplified in the life of Saint Mark Eugenikos, Metropolitan of Ephesus [†1444, Jan 19]. At that time, the emperor[1] sincerely desired the reunion of the Orthodox Church with the Latin Church of Rome—though not quite as sincerely as he desired to appease the pope and secure military support for his tottering empire. When the Orthodox and the Latins met in council,[2] Saint Mark humbly yet clearly, unequivocally, and unwaveringly refuted the Latin errors. Eventually, however, due to pressure applied by the emperor, bribes from the pope,

1 Emperor John VIII Palaeologos, 1425–48.
2 Ferrara/Florence, 1438–39.

and month after month of ill-treatment, the Eastern delegation capitulated to Rome's demands. All of the patriarchal delegates, bishops, abbots, priest-monks, priests, deacons, scholars, laymen, and even the baggage-handlers signed the Decree of Union—except for Saint Mark of Ephesus. Returning to their homes, the unionists were shunned, repudiated, disowned by the Orthodox people, *people who knew their faith* and did not blindly accept the errors of their hierarchy. The emperor strangely admired Saint Mark for his faith and integrity, but imprisoned him nonetheless. The people lionized him.

Today the Uniates in America seem to think they are Orthodox: their master, the pope, as much as tells them so. Protestants pride themselves on the orthodoxy of their multi-sectarian beliefs. Catholics proclaim the orthodoxy of their ancient yet ever-innovative doctrine. At the same time, so few Orthodox have an inkling of the immense spiritual treasure within their grasp.

Reading

The case might be made that, in addition to the morning and evening prayers, a Christian's minimum dietary requirement includes daily reading from the Bible, if only the lectionary readings on the calendar, more if possible. The aim is not rigidity, but consistency. And of course, one prays throughout the day as one is able.

As for the rest, some reading comes easily and naturally: topics that interest, indulge, or pleasantly distract in familiar formats and styles. Other types of writing may seem strange ("You call that poetry?"), off-putting ("That book is *huge!*"), or ever so dreadfully dreary ("How many beheadings do we celebrate today?"). All right, then, some tastes are acquired. Acquiring them, however, is neither difficult nor burdensome. As the Valentine writer points out (chapter 8 of this book), when beginning to read the Lives of Saints, it feels a little weird to read many martyrs in succession—but all that soon changes, and one can't get enough. This is true for other types of writing as well.

By the end of this book, you will have sample-tasted many types and styles of writing. Pick up where your interest draws you and branch out from there. The Miscellanea sections that follow each chapter may give you further ideas and directions.

For example. If you have a penchant for Bible study, make sure you get the Orthodox interpretation (see Saint Theophylact's commentary, chapter 6, or rummage through the lists of chapter 17). Then one might expand into Scriptural exegesis found in homilies (see Saint Gregory Palamas, chapter 10).

From homilies that deal with specific passages of Scripture, one might move on to those that present specific ideas with references drawn from throughout the Bible, like Saint Symeon the New Theologian (chapter 1).

From there, one might explore the *Great Canon* of Saint Andrew of Crete, which covers the entire Old and New Testaments, to unveil "new" interpretations of familiar passages. (Scripture references are noted in most editions.)

From there one might read the services, for example, the Service of The Great Blessing of Waters at Theophany, to see how the Church plucks passages of Scripture and plaits them into a fragrant bouquet (see Annunciation Canon, chapter 9, for the Theotokos in the Old Testament).

From there one might read lives of saints to find out how holy people applied Scripture to their lives.

From there one might read the desert fathers to discover how Scripture is distilled in action.

Another example. *The Evergetinos* (chapter 18) states, "Discussing matters of Faith and reading books about dogma cause a man's compunction to wither and disappear; by contrast, the lives and sayings of the Elders enlighten the soul, filling it with spiritual tears."[1] Nevertheless, if dogmatics attracts you—and this is quite understandable for those eager to pin down "What is Orthodoxy?"—then go ahead and read dogmatics. Then move on to the ancient theological treatises and famous orations. For example, try *On the Incarnation* by Saint Athanasius the Great [†c.373, Jan 18] or *On the Holy Spirit* by Saint Basil the Great [†379, Jan 1].

> The divine physicians of souls [Saints Basil the Great, John Chrysostom, and Gregory the Theologian], with the wise charms and arts and graces of their words, made sweet the bitterness and astringency of the medicines [e.g., asceticism] that bring salvation. Be enchanted, ye pious, and be saved as ye take delight.[2]

---

1 *The Evergetinos: A Complete Text*, trans Archbishop Chrysostomos, et al (Etna, CA: Center for Traditionalist Orthodox Studies, 2008), Book II:256–7. Used with permission.

2 Canon to the Three Hierarchs, by St John (Mauropos) of Euchaita [†c.1100, Oct 5], *The Menaion* (Boston: Holy Transfiguration Monastery, 2005), 5:265 (Jan 30, Ode 5).

A dogma-minded person often wishes to study the canons—the laws—of the Church, because they seem clear, defined, unquestionable. This is not such a good idea.[1] A much better direction is toward the canons—the liturgical poetry—of the Church, the canons that are sung in the services.[2]

Plunging from the logical theological heights of rhetoric into the depths of worship-filled canons, one discovers that sacred logic and sacred art have a great deal in common. For example, in the exceedingly joyous celebration of Pascha Matins, the *Pentecostarion* instructs us to read the *Oration on Easter*[3] by Saint Gregory the Theologian [†390, Jan 25]. What is heard? The same words that are in the Paschal Canon by Saint John of Damascus [†c.749, Dec 4]. This is true again at Pentecost with Saint John's canon and Saint Gregory's oration. It is solid Orthodox theology.

A smaller illustration that fits the page. Saint Gregory of Nyssa [†c.395, Jan 10] writes in his treatise *On the Making of Man*:

> If reason . . . assumes sway over such emotions [from the irrational parts of the soul], each of them is transmuted to a form of virtue: for anger produces courage, terror caution, fear obedience, hatred aversion from vice, the power of love the desire for what is truly beautiful; high spirit in our character raises our thought above the passions, and keeps it from bondage to what is base. The apostle praises such a form of mental elevation when he bids us constantly to mind the things above.[4]

Saint Theophanes the Hymnographer [the Branded, †845, Oct 11] makes the same point in his canon to Saint Theodore the Studite [†826, Nov 11]:

> Thou madest thy mind to shine with knowledge, and thy desire with chastity; and girding the incensive part of thy nature with virtue, O all-wise Theodore, thou didst sacredly direct the faculties of thy soul by righteousness, while harmoniously singing: Bless Christ, O ye priests; supremely exalt Him, O ye people, unto the ages.[5]

---

1 Canon Law should not be approached casually. It requires not only extreme humility, but also extensive knowledge of history, theology, law, scripture, lives of saints, etc.

2 To reiterate: the same word, "canon," is used both for Church Law (the canons of the Church) as well as for a particular form of liturgical poetry used in Church services.

3 Greek (Holy Transfiguration Monastery) calls for his First Oration (available in *Nicene and Post-Nicene Fathers*, 2nd series, 7:203f); Slav (St John of Kronstadt Press) calls for his Second Oration (ibid, 422f).

4 NPNF 2nd series, 5:408; apostle, Phil 4:8.

It is solid Orthodox anthropology.

Again, there are rhetorical expositions on the Holy Trinity—and the poetic canons to the Holy Trinity, sung at the Midnight Service early Sunday morning.[1] The rhetoricians and the poets say the same thing, but in a significantly different way. Logical expositions are absorbed, typically, in studious, secluded cerebration at a scholar's desk; the canons are pronounced in prayerful, communal celebration from the prayer desk—or in our own icon corner. They do not compete but complement each other.

From treatises and canons, the dogmatic person may do well to read the Lives of Saints, to learn that Orthodoxy is not just about "the right ideas," as important as they are, but about right living. Dare we say it? that one must live in a God-pleasing manner before one can even begin to understand what all those dogmas mean. *That* is Orthodoxy. By then, perhaps, one will come to understand "the lives and sayings of the Elders enlighten the soul, filling it with spiritual tears." God's gift of salvation is so great, as the Fathers say, that it takes a lifetime to assimilate.

For all this talk of diversity of reading: caution. It will take time to understand the readings. The reader should look forward to applying what is read, but not necessarily immediately. In contemporary America, one does not rise from the baptismal waters in a hair shirt. It will take time to understand what is read, it will take time to understand how to apply it to oneself. And one must absolutely resist that all-too-common disaster of applying it *to everyone else.* Small steps are indicated.[2]

> The course of your reading should be parallel to the aim of your way of life. Not all books, however, are profitable for the concentration of the mind. Most books that contain instruction [*in doctrine*] are not useful for purification. The reading of many diverse books lets loose upon you distraction of mind. Know, then, that not every

5 *The Menaion* (Holy Transfiguration Monastery), 3:82 (Nov 11, Ode 8).

1 Available in *The Octoechos* from St John of Kronstadt Press.

2 Besides historical and cultural considerations, there are the complexities of individual souls. St Paisios the New of Mt Athos was careful that his specific spiritual instructions were not recorded for general consumption—for the very reason that the instructions he gave were for specific individuals. The teachings and practices of the Church, e.g., prayer, fasting, almsgiving, study of Holy Scripture and the Fathers, are applicable to all. The Church, however, and her spiritual elders in particular, recognize that every person is different. The goal remains ever the same, but the path to that goal may vary according to the individual—though always within the context, culture, and direction (protection) of the Orthodox Church.

> book that teaches about religion is useful for the purification of the conscience and the concentration of thoughts.[1]

As a helpful digression concerning large books and occasional reading, we point to the "Reading Calendar for *Saint Gregory Palamas: The Homilies*," the last page in the appendix to this Reader. This simple chart coordinates each homily with the Sunday or Feast on which it was preached, rendering that fat (and quite wonderful) book much less intimidating. The reader can always go directly to *today's* reading.[2]

To generalize, thick books do not need to be read in their entirety, nor do they need to be read at one sitting. Hence, instead of pressure and panic, we have "occasional reading." From there we discover profitable re-reading to find treasures overlooked or under-appreciated in things we think we have already read.

Sources

Having come to America from all over the world, Orthodox often congregate "with their own kind," as the saying goes, and confine themselves to what they have grown up with, to what is familiar. This sometimes promotes a sort of parochialism, a narrow view of Orthodoxy. By contrast, the wide-ranging selections in this anthology visit many nationalities and time periods. Its sources cross jurisdictional lines, mingle with "schismatics," and even stoop to Protestant purveyors. "But they're schismatics!" Perhaps, but they translate the ancient texts sufficiently well. Consider how easily and happily Orthodox in America adopt Protestant attitude, thought, and practice—in their personal lives as well as importing them into Orthodox churches and services. Even the most staunchly ethnic, Old World, traditions-filled congregations cling to their American pews and Sunday-only services. We strain off Orthodox gnats and swallow American camels! In these penurious times, we would do well to grab all the Orthodoxy we can.

---

1 St Isaac the Syrian, *The Ascetical Homilies of Saint Isaac the Syrian*, 2nd ed (Boston: Holy Transfiguration Monastery, 2011), 450. Copyright © Holy Transfiguration Monastery, Brookline, MA, used by permission. All rights reserved.

2 Obviously, this is not the only way to read *The Homilies*. With its thorough indexes of Scripture References, Names and Subjects, and Greek Words, it is a great help for Bible study, research on particular topics, and learning the Orthodox understanding of Greek terms as they are translated into English.

Omissions

The Western mindset knows *about* God and concerns itself with proving or disproving His existence. Orthodoxy takes His existence as an inescapable fact and knows Him experientially, personally, face-to-face. An explicit exploration of this topic, this *knowing*, is beyond the scope of this book, though the referenced titles and authors point in that direction. It is not something that happens overnight ... usually.

Another and related "hole" in this book is a discussion of the Jesus Prayer. This would seem to border on spiritual direction, which this book definitely is not. Besides which, priests across America are "all over the map" in regard to when and how and by whom this practice should be employed. Saint Theophan the Recluse [†1894, Jan 10] in *The Path to Salvation*[1] has some discussion of it, expanding on it last while urging its primary importance. Saint Ignatius Brianchaninov [†1867, Apr 30] claims that this praying in the name of Jesus was so well known and generally practiced by the ancients that there was no need to mention it in the New Testament and early writings of the Church.[2] Yet, as Saint Ignatius recommends the Jesus Prayer everywhere and always, by lay people as well as monastics—as mental prayer or said with the lips—at the same time he warns of the very serious dangers, with quotes from the Holy Fathers, of attempting to achieve the prayer with the mind in the heart without qualified spiritual direction. In any case, the Prayer belongs within the context, culture, mindset of Orthodoxy, not in a loosey-goosey American believe-and-do-whatever-you-want.

In addition to Saints Theophan and Ignatius, four books on the Jesus Prayer are recommended here for a general Orthodox audience: *The Way of a Pilgrim*,[3] *Blessed Paisius Velichkovsky*,[4] *The Art of Prayer*,[5] and *Unseen Warfare*.[6] A word of caution regarding American rugged individualism

---

1 St Theophan the Recluse, *The Path to Salvation: A Manual of Spiritual Transformation*, trans Fr Seraphim Rose and the St Herman of Alaska Brotherhood (Platina, CA: St Herman of Alaska Brotherhood [St Herman Press], 1996).

2 See Ignatii Brianchaninov, *On the Prayer of Jesus: from the ascetic essays of Bishop Ignatius Brianchaninov* (Worcester: Elements Books Ltd, 1987). Other editions are available.

3 *The Way of a Pilgrim and The Pilgrim Continues His Way*: many editions are available.

4 Schema-monk Metrophanes, *Blessed Paisius Velichkovsky: The Life and Ascetic Labors of Our Father, Elder Paisius, Archimandrite of the Holy Moldavian Monasteries of Niamets and Sekoul. Optina Version* (Platina, CA: Saint Herman of Alaska Brotherhood, 1976).

5 Igumen Chariton of Valamo, *The Art of Prayer: An Orthodox Anthology*, trans E. Kadloubovsky and E.M. Palmer (London: Faber and Faber, Inc., 1966).

6 *Unseen Warfare*, the *Spiritual Combat* and *Path to Paradise* of Lorenzo Scupoli, ed [St]

("I'll do it myself, by myself"): it is worth remark that at Saint Paisius's monastery, which centered its entire existence on the Jesus Prayer, the monks spent fourteen hours each day in communal church services.

For similar reasons, *The Philokalia* is barely referenced. It is not the place to start. One may note, however, that *The Way of a Pilgrim* recommends, for those who are not instructed in theology, an alternative order for reading from *The Philokalia*. In the English edition, one would start with Volume Four.[1]

Time

It cannot be overemphasized that this Reader is not spiritual guidance but practical direction. It is not intended to teach but merely to point to authentic Orthodox teachers (people, books, types of writing) that may be unfamiliar, perhaps frightening, or seem, from outside, completely uninteresting. After a polite introduction to these teachers, the reader may warm to some and at least no longer fear the others. The buffet is amply laden. The banquet awaits you.

> Let us not put off our healing from day to day: so that death might not creep upon us unawares and take us suddenly; so that we would not be proved incapable of entering the habitations of unending rest and festival; so that we would not be cast down as useless chaff into the fires of hell that burn eternally but do not consume. The healing of old illnesses does not happen so quickly and conveniently as ignorance might imagine.
>
> There is a reason why God's mercy grants us time for repentance; there is a reason why all the saints begged God to give them time for repentance. Time is needed to erase the sinful impressions; time is needed for us to be marked by the impressions of the Holy Spirit; time is needed to cleanse us from defilement; time is needed to clothe ourselves in the garments of virtue, to adorn ourselves in the God-beloved qualities that adorn all those who dwell in heaven.[2]

Nicodemus of the Holy Mountain and revised [St] Theophan the Recluse, trans E. Kadloubovsky and G.E.H. Palmer (Crestwood, NY: St Vladimir's Seminary Press, 1987).

1 The pilgrim's friend recommends starting with Nicephorus the monk, Gregory of Sinai, and Simeon the New Theologian.

2 St Ignatius Brianchaninov, "Homily on the Sunday of the Myrrh Bearing Women. On Spiritual Deadness," trans m. Cornelia Rees, April 29, 2012. www.pravoslavie.ru/english/53230.htm [pravoslavie.ru/english *aka* OrthoChristian.com]. Used with permission.

Finally, the compilers of this Reader ask you to pray for them.

> O Nicholas, accept as a worthy hymn this little work, as Christ accepted the widow's two mites. Abhor not mine undertaking, O thrice-blessed, for I have made bold with longing, not with boasting.[1]

If the book is useful to you, well and good, and glory to God! If not, forgive and pray for us as you would for your enemies. As we are all in this together, perhaps a prayer by an American bishop, now deceased, would be worth daily offering:

> O Lord, have mercy on Thy Church in this land: on our Holy Synod of Bishops, the clergy, monastics, and all the faithful. Fill us with Thy grace. Send us a spirit of wisdom and discernment, that all the members of Thy Holy Body may serve Thee in all truth, love, integrity, and peace, as befits those called by Thy Name. For Thou art a merciful God, and unto Thee we ascribe glory: to the Father, and to the Son, and to the Holy Spirit, now and ever, and unto ages of ages. Amen.

---

1 Canon to St Nicholas the Wonderworker, Archbishop of Myra in Lycia, *The Menaion*, (Holy Transfiguration Monastery), 4:44 (Dec 6, 2nd Canon, Ode 9).

1. Spiritual Anthropology

Despite our advanced science, "societal evolution," and ubiquitous electronic gizmos, our human condition—indeed, our human predicament—remains the same. We are separated from God by our sins and passions.

"Sins are one thing and passions another. The passions are anger, idleness, desire for pleasure, hate, evil desire, and others. Sins, on the other hand, are the acting out of passions, that is to say, someone puts them into practice when using his body to enact everything dictated by the passions. It is expected for someone to have passions but not to carry them out. Thus, as we have said, [God] gave us commandments which purify us even from our passions, from the evil disposition which is contained within us."[1]

In the following article, **Saint Symeon the New Theologian** *[†1022, commemorated March 12] describes our spiritual condition, how it came about, and how God, in His great mercy, uses it—if we turn to Him—to confer upon us even greater blessings and benefactions in salvation.*

In the beginning God made man king of all the things that are on the earth [Gen 1:26,28]; indeed of all things that are under the vault of the sky. In fact sun, moon, and stars were brought into being for man. What then? When he was king of all these visible objects, did they harm him with regard to virtue? In no way whatever. On the contrary, had he continued to give thanks to God, who had made him and given him all things, he would have fared well. Had he not transgressed the commandment of his Master, he would not have lost this kingship, he would not have deprived himself of the glory of God. Since, however, he did this, it was with good reason that he was cast out and exiled, and so spent his life and died. I will tell you something that no one, I think, has clearly

1 St Dorotheos of Gaza [†Sixth century, Aug 13], *Abba Dorotheos: Practical Teaching on the Christian Life*, trans Constantine Scouteris (Athens: Constantine Scouteris, 2000), 72.

explained, though it has been said in a somewhat obscure way. What is it then? Listen to the divine Scripture as it speaks [Gen 3]: "And God said to Adam" (that is, after his Fall) "'Adam, where are you?'" Why does the Maker of all things speak in this way? Surely it is because He wishes to make him conscious [of his guilt] and so call him to repent that He says, "Adam, where are you?" "Understand yourself, realize your nakedness. See of what a garment, of how great glory, you have deprived yourself. Adam, where are you?" It is as though He spoke to encourage him, "Yes, come to your senses, poor fellow, come out of your hiding place. Do you think that you are hidden from Me? Just say, 'I have sinned.'" But he does not say this! (Or rather, it is I, miserable one, who do not say this, for I am in this position!) But what does he say? "I heard the sound of Thee as Thou wast walking in the garden, and I realized that I was naked and I hid myself." What then does God say? "Who told you that you were naked? Unless you ate of the tree of which I commanded you not to eat."

Do you see, dear friend, how patient God is? For when He said, "Adam, where are you?" and when Adam did not at once confess his sin but said: "I heard the sound of Thee, O Lord, and realized that I am naked and hid myself," God was not angered, nor did He immediately turn away. Rather, He gave him the opportunity of a second reply and said, "Who told you that you are naked? Unless you ate of the tree of which I commanded you not to eat." Consider how profound are the words of God's wisdom. He says: "Why do you say that you are naked, but hide your sin? Do you really think that I see only your body, but do not see your heart and your thoughts?" Since Adam was deceived he hoped that God would not know his sin. He said something like this to himself, "If I say that I am naked, God in His ignorance will say, 'Why are you naked?' Then I shall have to deny and say, 'I do not know,' and so I shall not be caught by Him and He will give me back the garment that I had at first [cf. Lk 15:22]. If not, as long as He does not cast me out, as long as He does not exile me!" While he was thinking these thoughts—as indeed many do even now (and I myself am the first) when they hide their own evil deeds—God, unwilling to multiply his guilt, says, "How did you realize that you are naked? Unless you ate of the tree of which I commanded you not to eat." It is as though He said, "Do you really think that you can hide from Me? Do I not know what you have done? Will you not say, 'I have sinned'? Say, O wretch, 'Yes, it is true, Master, I have transgressed Thy command, I have fallen by listening to the woman's counsel, I am greatly at fault for doing what she said and disobeying Thy word, have mercy upon me!'" But he does not say this. He does not humble himself, he does not bend. The neck of his heart is like a sinew of iron [Is 48:4], as is mine, wretch as I am! For had he said this he might have stayed in paradise. By this one word he might have spared himself that whole cycle of evils without number that he endured by his expulsion and in spending so many centuries in hell.[1]

This, then, is what I have promised to tell. Now listen to the sequel and realize that the discourse is true and no lie whatever is in it. God said to Adam, "At the hour when you eat from the tree of which alone I commanded you that you must not eat, you will surely die" [Gen 2:17, 3:11]. Obviously this is the death of the soul, and this is what took place the same hour. By this Adam was stripped of the robe of immortality. God predicted no more than this, and no more happened. For God had foreknowledge that Adam would sin, and wished to pardon him when he repented. So, as we have said, He made no further pronouncement against him. But he denied his sin and did not repent even when God reproved him, for he said, "The woman whom Thou gavest me, she deceived me." "Whom Thou gavest me"—how thoughtless a soul, as though it said to God, "Thou hast made a mistake; the woman whom Thou gavest me, she has deceived me." I, wretched and miserable man, do the same, and I am unwilling ever to be humbled and to say with my heart that I am to blame for my undoing. Rather I say, "Such and such a person has urged me on to do and to say such and such things; this or that person has advised me to do this or that." O wretched soul that utters words full of sin! So as Adam speaks thus, God says to him, "In toil and sweat you shall eat your bread, and the earth shall bring forth to you thorns and thistles," and, finally, "You are earth, and to earth you must return." In other words, "I have told you to repent and return to your former state. But since you are so hardened, from henceforth depart from Me. Your apostasy will be a sufficient chastisement for you, because you are earth and to earth you will return." [2]

---

1 ["Hell" should be read as Hades, the place of the Dead before Christ's Resurrection, to distinguish it from Gehenna after His Second Coming and Judgement.]

2 ["[Adam] died this death [of the soul] as soon as he tasted the forbidden tree, and it was of this death that both Adam and Eve were warned of God before their disobedience, for He said, 'In the day that thou eatest of the tree, thou shalt surely die.' (cont'd)

Now you have known that Adam was condemned after his transgression because he did not repent and say "I have sinned." He was exiled and commanded to spend his days in toil and sweat and to return to the earth from which he had been taken. The sequel will make this clear. When He had left him God came to Eve. He wanted to show her that she too would justly be cast out, if she was unwilling to repent. So He said, "What is this that you have done?" so that she at least might be able to say, "I have sinned." Why else did God need to speak these words to her, unless indeed to enable her to say, "In my folly, O Master, I, a lowly wretch, have done this, and have disobeyed Thee, my Master. Have mercy upon me!" But she did not say this. What did she say? "The serpent beguiled me." How senseless! So you have spoken with the serpent, who speaks against your Master? Him you have preferred to God who made you; you have valued his advice more highly and held it to be truer than the commandment of your Master! So, when Eve too was unable to say, "I have sinned," both were cast out from the place of enjoyment. They were banished from paradise and from God. But consider how deep are the mysteries of God's love for men. Learn and be instructed that had they repented, they would not have been expelled. They would not have been condemned, they would not have been sentenced to return to the earth from which they had been taken. How? Listen further.

After they had been cast out they were at once subject to sweat and bodily toil. They began to hunger and thirst, to be cold and shiver and to suffer the same things that we daily suffer. As they perceived more vividly their misfortune and fall, they realized their own perversity and God's unspeakable mercy. While they were walking about and sitting down outside paradise they repented. They wept, they groaned, they beat their faces, they tore their hair and plucked it out and bewailed their

---

We were condemned to physical death after the transgression, when God said to Adam, 'Dust thou art, and unto dust shalt thou return.' Physical death is when the soul leaves the body and is separated from it. The death of the soul is when God leaves the soul and is separated from it, although, in another way, the soul remains immortal. Once separated from God, it becomes more ugly and useless than a dead body, but unlike such a body, it does not disintegrate after death...." St Gregory Palamas, Homily Sixteen, "About the Dispensation according to the Flesh of our Lord Jesus Christ and the Gifts of Grace Granted to Those Who Truly Believe in Him, also teaching that God was able to redeem man from the devil's tyranny in many different ways but rightly preferred this dispensation," *Saint Gregory Palamas: The Homilies*, trans Christopher Veniamin (Waymart, PA: Mount Thabor Publishing, 2009), 118. Used with permission.]

own hardness of heart. Believe me! They did not do this for a day or two, or even ten, but all their lives. How could they lack occasion always and constantly to weep? They would think of that gentle Master, that unutterable delight, the unspeakable beauties of those flowers, that life free from cares and toil, and how the angels ascended and descended to them. As long as servants of a great lord of this present world, whom he has chosen to serve in his presence, observe, respect and honor him with genuine submission as their master and love him and their fellow-servants, they enjoy familiarity with him, his benevolence and love, and live in great ease and luxury. If, however, they fall into presumption and act proudly against their own master and haughtily toward their fellow-servants [cf. Mt 24:49], they can no longer be on familiar terms with him or enjoy his love and favor. He banishes them into a distant land, and by his orders they undergo thousands of trials; as they suffer weariness and are worn out they appreciate more and more how they have lost their former ease and have been deprived of the good things they once enjoyed. In the same way those who were first formed suffered after they had fallen from the blessings and enjoyment of paradise and been sent into exile. When they realized their downfall they wept constantly and called on their Master's loving-kindness.

But how did God act, who is "rich in mercy" [Eph 2:4] and slow to punish? When He saw them humbled He did not as yet cancel their sentence. He had pronounced it on them for their correction, and to prevent anyone from setting himself up against the Maker of all things. But being God He foreknew man's fall and his repentance. So, before creating all things, He foreordained the occasion and the time that He would recall man from his exile, judgments unutterable and unsearchable [Rom 11:33] for all that breathes. Were these judgments to be revealed to such as would record them time, paper, and ink would not suffice, nor would the whole world be able to contain the very volumes [cf. Jn 21:25]. As He foreordained and predicted in His loving-kindness, so He acted. Once those whom He had cast out of paradise for their shamelessness and impenitence heard and had shown proper penitence, worthily humbling themselves by weeping and mourning, He Himself came down to them. He who is the Only One begotten of the Only One, the only-begotten Son and Word, came from His Father who has no beginning, as you all know. Not only did He become like them, becoming Man, He undertook to die like them and chose for Himself a violent and most shameful death.

He descended into hell and raised them thence. Would not He, then, who as you hear every day suffered such great things for them in order to recall them from that long exile, have had compassion on them if they had repented in paradise? How would He have failed to do so? By nature He loves man and has created him for the end of enjoying His blessings in paradise and of glorifying his Benefactor. Indeed, I believe this would have happened! But listen to what follows in order that you may learn the rest and be yet more persuaded by my word.

Had they repented while they were still within paradise, they would have received that paradise and nothing else. But they were cast out because of their impenitence, and afterwards repented with great weeping and tribulation. As I have said, they would not have undergone this if they had repented inside paradise. So God their Master wished to honor and glorify them on account of these toils, sweat, and labors. And more than that, he also wished to make them forget all these evils. What does He do? Consider the greatness of His love for man! When He went down into hell He raised them up from there and restored them, not to paradise whence they had fallen, but to the very heaven of heavens. When the Master had sat down on the right hand of God His Father, who is without beginning, what do you think He did to him who by nature is His slave, but has become His ancestor by grace? Have you seen how lofty is the height to which the Master has raised him because of his repentance, humiliation, mourning, and tears?

How great the power of penitence and tears! How great, brethren, the ocean of ineffable and unsearchable loving-kindness! For it is not only Adam whom God has honored and glorified. All his seed, that is, we who are his sons—if we imitate his confession, his repentance, his mourning, his tears, and the rest that we have mentioned above—share in this glory; so also those who have done so until now and will do so in the future, whether they are seculars or monks. "Verily," says the God of truth, "I will never forsake them" [Heb 13:5], but will show that they are my brothers and friends, fathers and mothers [cf. Mt 12:50], my kinsmen and fellow-heirs [cf. Rom 8:17], and I have glorified and will glorify them [cf. Jn 12:28] both in heaven above and on the earth below [cf. Deut 4:39], and there will never be an end of their life, their joy and glory.

Tell me, what profit would it have been to our first-formed [parents] if they had remained in the life in paradise, which had no pain and care, once they had become careless and by their unbelief despised God and transgressed His commandment? If they had believed Him Eve would not have trusted the serpent more than God, nor would Adam have trusted Eve more. They would have kept themselves from eating from the tree. But since they ate and failed to repent they were cast out. Nor did their exile harm them, but they reaped the greatest benefits from it, and this turned out for the salvation of us all. When our Master descended from on high He by His own death destroyed the death that awaited us. The condemnation that was the consequence of our forefather's transgression he completely annihilated. By Holy Baptism He regenerates and refashions us, completely sets us free from the condemnation, and places us in this world wholly free instead of being oppressed by the tyranny of the enemy. By honoring us with our original free will He gives us strength against our enemy, so that those who are willing may overcome him more readily than could all the saints who lived before Christ's coming. Unlike them, when they die they will not be brought down to hell, but enter into heaven with its delight and pleasure. At this present time they enjoy these in part. But after the resurrection from the dead they will be granted the fullness of eternal joy.

As for those who make excuses for themselves [cf. Ps 140:4], let them not say that we are totally under the influence of Adam's transgression and so dragged down into sin. Those who think and speak to this effect claim that the coming of our Master and our God was to no purpose and in vain. These are words fit for heretics, not believers! Why did He come down, and for what purpose did He taste death? [Heb 2:9] Was it not that He might altogether cancel the condemnation of sin and set our race free from the slavery and oppression of our adversary and enemy? True independence consists in being in no way under the dominion of another. Because of him who had committed sin we were sinners, because of the transgressor we too were transgressors, because of the slave of sin we ourselves became slaves of sin [cf. Rom 6:17,20]. Because he was accursed and died, we became accursed and dead. Because he was influenced by the counsel of the evil one and was enslaved and lost his independence, so we, as his children, were influenced, dominated, oppressed, and tyrannized. But God came down and was incarnate and became man like us, "but without sin" [Heb 4:15], and destroyed sin. He hallowed conception and birth and, as He grew up, bit by bit blessed every age. When He had reached mature manhood He began His preaching and taught us that we, especially those who are mere youths and not mature men, should not leap ahead in any way or surpass those who are aged in understanding and virtue [cf. Wis4:8f.]. He assumed that which was enjoined on us and kept all the commandments of His own God and Father [Jn15:10]. Thus He canceled the transgression and set the transgressors free from their sentence [cf. Rom 8:2]. He became a slave and "took on himself the form of a slave" [Phil 2:7] and restored us slaves to the dignity of masters in that he made us masters of him who had been our tyrant. To this the saints bear witness, for even after their death they drive him and all his servants away like weaklings. He became a curse by being crucified; as it is said, "Accursed is everyone who hangs on a tree" [Gal 3:13; Deut 21:23]. He destroyed altogether the curse of Adam. He died, and by His own death He destroyed death. He rose, and did away with the power and activity of the enemy [cf. Lk 10:19], who had held sway over us through death and sin [cf. Heb 2:14]. As He applied the ineffable and life-giving power of His Godhead and His flesh to the deadly venom and poison of sin, He completely delivered all our race from the action of the enemy. Through Holy Baptism and the Communion of His undefiled Mysteries, His Body and His precious Blood, He cleanses us and gives us life and restores us to holiness and sinlessness [cf. 1Jn 5:18]. More than that, He sends us forth to enjoy the honor of liberty, so that we may not appear to serve our Master by compulsion, but out of free choice. In the beginning Adam was free and without sin and violence; yet of his own free will he obeyed the enemy and was deceived [by him] and transgressed God's commandment. So we have been born again in Holy Baptism and have been released from slavery and become free, so that the enemy cannot take any action against us unless we of our own will obey him. Before the Law and before Christ's coming many people, countless people, were able to please God without these aids and were found without reproach [Heb 11]. Among these God translated and thus honored righteous Enoch [Gen 5:24]. He took up Elijah into heaven in a fiery chariot [4Kg 2:11]. If this is so, what excuse have we, who live after [the coming of] grace, who have enjoyed such great and wonderful benefits, who live after death and sin have been destroyed? After the regeneration of Baptism, the protection of the holy angels, and the overshadowing and descent of the Holy Spirit, shall we not be found equal to those who lived before grace? Are we to be slothful, despisers of God's commandments who transgress them? But that we, if we persist in evil, are liable to greater punishment than those who sinned under the Law, Saint Paul made clear when he said, "If the message declared by angels was valid, and every transgression or disobedience received a just retribution, how shall we escape if we neglect so great a salvation?" [Heb 2:2–3]

The Source

Excerpts from *Symeon the New Theologian: The Discourses*, "On Penitence," from The Classics of Western Spirituality series, trans C.J. deCatanzaro, copyright © 1980 by The Missionary Society of St Paul the Apostle in the State of New York, Paulist Press, Inc., New York/ Mahwah, N.J. Used with permission of Paulist Press. www.paulistpress.com [pp 94–102]

Saint Symeon urgently and continually exhorts his monks of the eleventh century: This is *real!* How much greater need have we to hear this, to be reminded of this, in the twenty-first century.

Miscellanea

Reality Check

"How did we get here?" is the flip side of "Where are we going?" A good reminder of the latter is an occasional re-reading of the funeral services. These can be found in the *Service Book* by Isabel Hapgood,[1] a good resource for all parish services. A reflective walk in a cemetery can also have a salutary effect.

Remember Death, Judgement, Hell, and Eternal Life

Remember death often, and the judgement of Christ, eternal torment, and eternal life, and inevitably the world with all its lusts and enticements will become abhorrent to you. You will not desire to become rich, to be glorified, or to make merry in this world. Your only care will be to please God, to have a blessed end, not to be put to shame in the judgement of Christ, to escape eternal torment, and to enter into the Kingdom of God. This is truly a great and powerful means by which a man may escape enticement by the vanity of this world and remain in true repentance and contrition of heart, which is absolutely necessary to every Christian. Truly, this remembrance and steadfast consideration by everyone is able to raise up the most depraved man and keep him in fear.

The very mention of eternal misfortune or torment, brings a man to trembling and horror. It truly so happens that people become attached to vanity, and they sin because they have forgotten about eternity. O eternal torment, how bitter is your very memory! It is a fearful and bitter thing to fall into that torment, but it is also a fearful and bitter thing to be deprived of God and eternal life! Remember these last things, then, and you will never sin.[2]

—Saint Tikhon of Zadonsk

1 *Service Book of the Holy Orthodox-Catholic Apostolic Church*, 7th ed (Englewood, NJ: Antiochian Orthodox Christian Archdiocese of North America, 1996).

2 St Tikhon of Zadonsk [†1783, Aug 13], *Journey to Heaven: Counsels on the Particular Duties of Every Christian*, trans Fr George D. Lardas (Jordanville, NY: Holy Trinity Monastery, 1991), 166. Used with permission.

Parent Friendly

As important as remembering our first parents—how we got here—is remembering (learning) our spiritual history and inheritance, that is, the knowledge of the Old and New Testaments and our life in the Church. The catechetical *The Law of God: For Study at Home and School*,[1] compiled by Archpriest Seraphim Slobodskoy, covers Church basics, provides short prayers with explanations (good for starting children—or anyone), and has an extensive section explaining the Faith. Much of the information is conveyed by visual illustration: nearly every page displays photos, icons, drawings, and diagrams. These grab and hold the attention of the reader—and of the pre-literate student in the reader's lap.

Father Slobodskoy escaped from communist Russia and is especially attuned to answering questions asked from a materialistic, skeptical, "scientific" mindset. He conscripts science to bolster biblical claims. This book is a good first step (and refresher course) in establishing Scripture as one's native language and culture.

Digging Deeper

Genesis, Creation, and Early Man: The Orthodox Christian Vision[2] by Father Seraphim Rose may not be for the casual reader (1143 pages), but it is a storehouse of information. It explains "How to Read Genesis" and provides extensive patristic textual commentary. It also confronts the scientific theories of—and more important, the "philosophy" of—evolution. It is replete with resources, both scientific and theological, even for young people and home-schoolers.

The Homilies on Genesis by Saint John Chrysostom are available in the Fathers of the Church series.[3] In his usual fashion, Saint John in each homily expounds on the Scripture and closes with a moral exhortation. When he talks about horse races, theater, and the marketplace, think modern day sports, television, shopping sprees and the press of business.

The *Hexameron* (the six days of creation) might also be of interest, though its style is not for people in a hurry. There is one by Saint Basil the Great [†379, Jan 1] in *Nicene and Post-Nicene Fathers* (Second Series); and one by Saint Ambrose of Milan [†397, Dec 7] in the Fathers of the Church series. They are more leisurely, meditative glorifications of God through the Six Days (Creation, not the Fall), Scripture, and the science of antiquity.

For more on the consequences of sin and what to do about it (the ascetic Fathers), keep reading....

1 Jordanville, NY: Holy Trinity Monastery, 1996.
2 Platina, CA: St Herman of Alaska Brotherhood (St Herman Press), 2011.
3 Three volumes, Washington, DC: Catholic University of America Press, 1986–92.

2. The Path to Salvation

Working out one's own salvation is not simply having the right ideas, but actually living them. **Saint Theophan the Recluse** *[†1894, Jan 10] was a Russian monk and bishop, as well as a prolific writer and translator of the works of the Holy Fathers. From his book* The Path to Salvation, *the following excerpt encourages the reader to zeal for God and a life according to His commandments. It also emphasizes the necessary interworking of grace and individual effort in the work of salvation; that is, you cannot do it by your own efforts alone (without grace), but neither can you sit and wait for grace to do it for you.*

It is possible to describe the feelings and inclinations which a Christian must have, but this is very far from being all that is demanded for the ordering of one's salvation. The important thing for us is a real life in the spirit of Christ. But just touch on this, and how many perplexities are uncovered, how many guideposts are necessary, as a result, almost at every step!

True, one may know man's final goal: communion with God. And one may describe the path to it: faith, and walking in the commandments, with the aid of divine grace. One need only say in addition: here is the path—start walking!

This is easily said, but how to do it? For the most part the very desire to walk is lacking. The soul, attracted by some passion or other, stubbornly repulses every compelling force and every call; the eyes turn away from God and do not want to look at Him. The law of Christ is not to one's liking; there is no disposition even to listen to it. One may ask, how does one reach the point when the desire is born to walk toward God on the path of Christ? What does one do so that the law will imprint itself on the heart, and man, acting according to this law, will act as if from himself, unconstrained, so that this law will not lie on him, but will as it were proceed from him?

But suppose someone has turned toward God, suppose he has come to love His law. Is the very going toward God, the very walking on the path of Christ's law, already necessary and will it be successful merely because we desire it to be? No. Besides the desire, one must also have the strength and knowledge to act; one must have active wisdom.

Whoever enters on the true path of pleasing God, or who begins with the aid of grace to strive toward God on the path of Christ's law, will inevitably be threatened by the danger of losing his way at the crossroads, of going astray and perishing, imagining himself saved. These crossroads are unavoidable because of the sinful inclinations and disorder of one's faculties which are capable of presenting things in a false light —to deceive and destroy a man. To this is joined the flattery of satan, who is reluctant to be separated from his victims and, when someone from his domain goes to the light of Christ, pursues him and sets every manner of net in order to catch him again—and quite often he indeed catches him.

Consequently it is necessary for someone who already has the desire to walk on the indicated path to the Lord to be shown in addition all the deviations that are possible on this path, so that the traveller may be warned in advance about this, may see the dangers that are to be encountered, and may know how to avoid them.

These general considerations which are unavoidable to all on the path of salvation render indispensable certain guiding rules of the Christian life by which it should be determined: how to attain to the saving desire for communion with God and the zeal to remain in it, and how to reach God without misfortune amidst all the crossroads that may be met on this path at every step—in other words, how to begin to live the Christian life and how, having begun, to perfect oneself in it.

The sowing and development of the Christian life are different in essence from the sowing and development of natural life, owing to the special character of the Christian life and its relation to our nature. A man is not born a Christian, but becomes such after birth. The seed of Christ falls on the soil of a heart that is already beating. But since the naturally born man is injured and opposed by the demand of Christianity—while in a plant, for example, the beginning of life is the stirring of a sprout in the seed, an awakening of as it were dormant powers—the beginning of a true Christian life in a man is a kind of re-creation, an endowing of new powers, of new life.

Further, suppose that Christianity is received as a law, i.e., the resolution is made to live a Christian life: this seed of life (this resolution) is not surrounded in a man by elements favorable to him. And besides this, the whole man—his body and soul—remain unadapted to the new life, unsubmissive to the yoke of Christ. Therefore from this moment begins in a man a labor of sweat—a labor to educate his whole self, all his faculties, according to the Christian standard.

This is why, while growth in plants, for example, is a gradual development of faculties—easy, unconstrained—in a Christian it is a battle with oneself involving much labor, intense and sorrowful, and he must dispose his faculties for something for which they have no inclination. Like a soldier, he must take every step of land, even his own, from his enemies by means of warfare, with the double-edged sword of forcing himself and opposing himself. Finally, after long labors and exertions, the Christian principles appear victorious, reigning without opposition; they penetrate the whole composition of human nature, dislodging from it demands and inclinations hostile to themselves, and place it in a state of passionlessness and purity, making it worthy of the blessedness of the pure in heart—to see God in themselves in sincerest communion with Him.

Such is the place in us of the Christian life. This life has three stages which may be called: 1) Turning to God; 2) Purification or self-amendment; 3) Sanctification.

In the first stage a man turns from darkness to light, from the domain of satan to God; in the second, he cleanses the chamber of his heart from every impurity, in order to receive Christ the Lord Who is coming to him; in the third, the Lord comes, takes up His abode in his heart, and communes with him. This is the state of blessed communion with God—the goal of all labors and ascetic endeavors.

To describe all this and determine its laws will mean—to indicate *the path to salvation.*

Complete guidance in this matter takes a man standing on the crossroads of sin, leads him along the fiery path to purification, and leads him up to the degree of perfection attainable to him, according to his level of maturity in Christ. Thus, it should show:

1) how Christian life begins in us;
2) how it is perfected, ripened and strengthened; and
3) how it manifests itself in its perfection.

How the Christian Life Begins in Us

We must make clear for ourselves when and how the Christian life truly begins in order to see whether we have within ourselves the beginning of this life. If we do not have it, we must learn how to begin it, in so far as this depends upon us.

It is not yet a decisive sign of true life in Christ if one calls himself a Christian and belongs to the Church of Christ. *Not every one that saith unto Me, Lord, Lord, shall enter the kingdom of heaven* [Mt 7:21]. *And they are not all Israel, which are of Israel* [Rom 9:6]. One can be counted as a Christian and not be a Christian. This everyone knows.

Christian Life begins with Ardor of Zeal

There is a moment, and a very noticeable moment, which is sharply marked out in the course of our life, when a person begins to live in a Christian way. This is the moment when there began to be present in him the distinctive characteristics of Christian life. Christian life is zeal and the strength to remain in communion with God by means of an active fulfillment of His holy will, according to our faith in our Lord Jesus Christ, and with the help of the grace of God, to the glory of His most holy name.

The essence of Christian life consists in communion with God, in Christ Jesus our Lord—in a communion with God which in the beginning is usually hidden not only from others, but also from oneself. The testimony of this life that is visible or can be felt within us is the ardor of active zeal to please God alone in a Christian manner, with total self-sacrifice and hatred of everything which is opposed to this. And so, when this ardor of zeal begins, Christian life has its beginning. The person in whom this ardor is constantly active is one who is living in a Christian way. Here we will have to stop and pay more attention to this distinctive characteristic.

I am come to send fire on the earth, the Saviour said, *and what will I, if it be already kindled!* [Lk 12:49]. He is speaking here of Christian life, and He says this because the visible witness of it is the zeal for the pleasing of God which is in the heart by the Spirit of God. This is like fire because, just as fire devours the material which it takes hold of, so also does zeal for the life in Christ devour the soul which receives it. And just as during the time of a fire the flame takes hold of the whole building, so also the fire of zeal, once it is received, embraces and fills the whole being of a man.

In another place the Lord says, *For every one shall be salted with fire* [Mk 9:49]. This also is an indication of the fire of the spirit which in its zeal penetrates our whole being. Just as salt, penetrating decomposable matter, preserves it from decomposition, so also the spirit of zeal, penetrating our whole being, banishes the sin which corrupts our nature both in soul and body; it banishes it even from the least of the places where it has settled in us, and thus it saves us from moral vice and corruption.

The Apostle Paul commands, *Quench not the Spirit* [1Thess 5:19], to be *not slothful in business; fervent in spirit* [Rom 12:11]. He commands this to all Christians so that we might remember that the fervor of the spirit, or unslothful striving, is an inseparable attribute of Christian life. In another place he speaks of himself thus: *Forgetting those things which are behind, and reaching forth unto those things which are before, I press toward the mark for the prize of the high calling of God in Christ Jesus* [Phil 3:13–14]. And to others he says, *So run, that ye may obtain* [1Cor 9:24]. This means that in Christian life the result of the fervor of zeal is a certain quickness and liveliness of spirit, with which people undertake God-pleasing works, trampling upon oneself and willingly offering as a sacrifice to God every kind of labor, without sparing oneself.

Having a firm basis in such an understanding, one may easily conclude that a cold fulfillment of the rules of the Church, just like routine in business, which is established by our calculating mind, or like correct and dignified behavior and honesty in conduct, is not a decisive indicator that the true Christian life is present in us. All this is good, but as long as it does not bear in itself the spirit of life in Christ Jesus, it has no value at all before God. Such things would then be like soulless statues. Good clocks also work correctly; but who will say that there is life in them? It is the same thing here. Often *thou hast a name that thou livest, and art dead* in reality [Rev 3:1].

This good order in one's conduct more than anything else can lead one into deception. Its true significance depends upon one's inward disposition, where it is possible that there are significant deviations from real righteousness in one's righteous deeds. Thus, while refraining outwardly from sinful deeds, one may have an attraction for them or a delight from them in one's heart; so also, doing righteous deeds outwardly, one's heart may not be in them. Only true zeal both wishes to do good in all fullness and purity, and persecutes sin in its smallest forms. It seeks the good as its daily bread, and with sin it fights as with a mortal enemy.

An enemy hates an enemy not only personally, but he hates also relatives and friends of this enemy, and even his belongings, his favorite color, and in general anything that might remind one of him. So also, true zeal to please God persecutes sin in its smallest reminders or marks, for it is zealous for perfect purity. If this is not present, how much impurity can hide in the heart!

The Fire of Zeal

What success can one expect when there is no enthusiastic zeal for a Christian pleasing of God? If there is something that involves no labor, one is ready to do it; but as soon as one is required to do a little extra labor, or some kind of self-sacrifice, immediately one refuses, because one is unable to accomplish it oneself. For then there will be nothing to rely on that can move one to good deeds: self-pity will undermine all the foundations. And if any other motive besides the one mentioned becomes involved, it will make the good deed into a bad deed.

The spies under Moses were afraid because they spared themselves. The martyrs willingly went to death because they were kindled by an inward fire. A true zealot does not do only what is according to the law, but also what has been advised and every good suggestion that has been secretly imprinted on the soul; he does not only what has been given, but he is also an acquirer of good things; he is entirely concerned with the one good thing which is solid, true, and eternal.

Saint John Chrysostom says that everywhere we must have fervor and much fire of the soul, prepared to be armed against death itself. For otherwise it is impossible to receive the kingdom.[1]

The work of piety and communion with God is a work of much labor and much pain, especially in the beginning. Where can we find the power to undertake all these labors? With the help of God's grace, we can find it in heartfelt zeal.

A merchant, a soldier, a judge, or a scholar has work which is full of cares and difficulties. How do they sustain themselves in the midst of their labors? By enthusiasm and love for their work. One cannot sustain oneself by anything else on the path of piety. Without this we will be serving God in a state of sluggishness, boredom, and lack of interest. An animal like the sloth also moves, but with difficulty, while for the swift

---

1 Cf. St John Chrysostom, *Homilies on the Acts of the Apostles* in *Nicene and Post Nicene Fathers*, Homily 31.

gazelle or the nimble squirrel movement and getting about are a delight. Zealous pleasing of God is the path to God which is full of consolation and gives wings to the spirit. Without it one can ruin everything.

One must do everything for the glory of God in defiance of the sin which dwells in us. Without this we will do everything only out of habit, because it seems "proper," because this is the way it has always been done, or the way others do it. We must do all we can, otherwise we will do some things and neglect others, and this without any contrition or even knowledge of what we have omitted. One must do everything with heedfulness and care, as our *chief* task; otherwise we will do everything just as it comes.

And so, it is clear that without zeal a Christian is a poor Christian. He is drowsy, feeble, lifeless, neither hot nor cold—and this kind of life is not life at all. Knowing this, let us strive to manifest ourselves as true zealots of good deeds, so that we might truly be pleasing to God, having neither stain nor spot, nor any of these things.

Therefore, a true witness of Christian life is the fire of active zeal for the pleasing of God. Now the question arises, how is this fire ignited? Who produces it? Such zeal is produced by the action of grace. However, it does not occur without the participation of our free will. Christian life is not natural life. This should be the way it begins or is first aroused: as in a seed, growth is aroused when moisture and warmth penetrate to the sprout which is hidden within, and through these the all-restoring power of life comes. So also in us, the divine life is aroused when the Spirit of God penetrates into the heart and places there the beginning of life according to the Spirit, and cleanses and gathers into one the darkened and broken features of the image of God. A desire and free seeking are aroused (by an action from without); then grace descends (through the Mysteries) and, uniting with our freedom, produces a mighty zeal. But let no one think that he himself can give birth to such a power of life; one must pray for this and be ready to receive it. The fire of zeal with power—this is the grace of the Lord. The Spirit of God, descending into the heart, begins to act in it with a zeal that is both devouring and all-active.

To some the thought arises: should there be this action of grace? Can we ourselves really not do good deeds? After all, we have done this or that good deed, and, if we live longer, we will do some more. Perhaps it is a rare person who does not ask this question. Others say that of ourselves we can do nothing good. But here the question is not only of separate good deeds, but of giving rebirth to our whole life, to a new life, to life in its entirety—to such a life as can lead one to salvation.

As a matter of fact, it is not difficult to do something which is even quite good, as the pagans also did. But let someone intentionally define a course for himself of a continuous doing of good, and define the order of it according to what is indicated in the word of God—and this not for one month or for a year, but for one's whole life—and place as a rule to remain in this order unwaveringly; and then, when he remains faithful to this, let him boast of his own power. But without this it is better to close one's mouth. How many cases there have been in the past and in the present of a self-trusting beginning and building of a Christian life! And they have all ended and continue to end in nothing. A man builds a little in his new order of life—and then throws it away. How can it be otherwise? There is no strength. It is characteristic only of the eternal power of God to support us unchanging in our disposition in the midst of the unceasing waves of temporal changes. Therefore one must be filled abundantly with this power; one must ask for and receive it in order—and it will raise us up and draw us out of the great agitation of temporal life.

In the Face of Temptation

Let us turn now to experience and see when it is that such thoughts of self-satisfaction come. When a man is in a calm condition, when nothing is disturbing him, nothing is deceiving him or leading him into sin—then he is ready for every kind of holy and pure life. But as soon as the movement of a passion or a temptation comes, where are all the promises? Does a man not often say to himself as he leads an unrestrained life, "Now I will no longer do this"? But once the passions again become hungry, a new impulse arises, and again he finds himself in sins.

It is all well and good to reflect on the bearing of offenses when everything is going according to our will and not against our self-love. In fact, here it would be rather strange to have a feeling of offense or anger such as others might give themselves over to. But just find yourself in the opposite condition, and then a single glance—not even a word—will make you beside yourself! Thus you may well dream, trusting in yourself, about leading a Christian life without any help from above—as long as your soul is calm. But when the evil that lies in the depths of the heart is roused up like dust by the wind, then in your own experience you will find the condemnation of your own presumption. When thought after thought, desire after desire—one worse than the other—begin to disturb the soul, then everyone forgets about himself and involuntarily cries out with the prophet: *The waters are come in unto my soul. I am stuck fast in the mire of the deep* [Ps 68:1–2]. *O Lord, save now; O Lord, send now prosperity* [Ps 117:25].

Often it happens in this way: someone dreams of remaining in the good, trusting in himself. But a face or a thing comes to the imagination, desire is born, passion is aroused: a man is attracted and falls. After this one need only look at oneself and say: How bad that was! But then an opportunity for distraction comes, and again he is ready to forget himself.

Again, someone has offended you, a battle begins, there are reproaches and judgment. Some unjust but convenient way of looking at it presents itself to your mind, and you seize it. You belittle one, spread the tale to others, confuse someone else—and all this after you were boasting of the possibility of leading a holy life by yourself, without special help from above. Where was your strength then? *The spirit indeed is willing, but the flesh is weak* [Mt 26:41]. You see good and do evil: *When I would do good, evil is present with me* [Rom 7:21]. We are in captivity. Redeem us, O Lord!

One of the first tricks of the enemy against us is the idea of trusting in oneself: that is, if not renouncing, then at least not feeling the need for the help of grace. The enemy as it were says: "Do not go to the light where they wish to give you some kind of new powers. You are good just the way you are!" And a man gives himself over to repose. But in the meantime the enemy is throwing a rock (some kind of unpleasantness) at one; others he is leading into a slippery place (the deception of the passions); for yet others he is strewing with flowers a closed noose (deceptively good conditions). Without looking around, a man strives to go further and further, and does not guess that he is falling down lower and lower until finally he goes to the very depths of evil, to the threshold of hell itself. Should one not in such a case cry out to him as to the first Adam: "Man, where are you? Where have you gone?" This very cry is the action of grace, which compels a sinner for the first time to look about himself.

Therefore, if you desire to begin to live in a Christian way, seek grace. The minute grace descends and joins itself to your will is the minute when the Christian life is born in you—powerful, firm, and greatly fruitful.

Where can one obtain and how can one receive the grace which gives the beginning of life? The acquisition of grace and the sanctification by its means of our nature is performed in the Mysteries. Here we offer to God's action, or present to God, our own worthless nature; and He, by His action, transforms it. It was pleasing to God, in order to strike down our proud mind, to hide His power at the very beginning of true life beneath the covering of simple materiality. How this happens we do not understand, but the experience of all Christianity testifies that it does not happen otherwise.

The Source

The Path to Salvation: A Manual of Spiritual Transformation by St Theophan the Recluse, trans Fr Seraphim Rose and the St Herman of Alaska Brotherhood (Platina, CA: St Herman of Alaska Brotherhood [St Herman Press], 1996), 21–35. © St Paisius Monastery (Safford, AZ, 2002). Reprinted with permission.

Miscellanea

Parent Friendly

In this book, *The Path to Salvation*, Saint Theophan describes and explains the Christian experience: 1) How it begins—with a helpful discussion of what a truly Christian upbringing would look like, 2) Repentance and turning to God, and 3) How to live and maintain a God-pleasing life.

Zeal

"Zeal," "zealous," "zealot" are words that make people nervous. As Saint Theophan uses the word, zeal is an essential trait for salvation, the ardent love for God that propels us through the difficulties, obstacles, and just plain laziness that incessantly confront us. On the other hand, we all know people with an inordinate or misdirected sort of zeal or fanaticism (how often ourselves!), or zeal without knowledge [cf. Rom 10:2].

> A zealous man never achieves peace of mind; but he who is a stranger to peace is a stranger to joy. If, as it is said, peace of mind is perfect health, and zeal is opposed to peace, then the man who has a wrong zeal is sick with a grievous disease. Though you presume, O man, to send forth your zeal against the maladies of other men, you have expelled the health of your own soul; be assiduous, rather, in laboring for your own soul's health. If you wish to heal the infirm, know that the sick are in greater need of loving care than of rebuke. Therefore, although you do not help others, you expend labor to bring a grievous disease upon yourself. Zeal is not reckoned among men to be a form of wisdom, but as one of the maladies of the soul, namely narrow-mindedness and deep ignorance.
>
> The beginning of divine wisdom is clemency and gentleness, which arises from greatness of soul and the bearing of the infirmities of men. For, it is said, "We that are strong ought to bear the infirmities of the weak" [Rom 15:1], and "Restore the transgressor in the spirit of meekness" [Gal 6:1]. The Apostle numbers peace and patience among the fruits of the Spirit [Gal 5:22].[1]
>
> — Saint Isaac the Syrian

Ascetic Shortlist (Introduction/Refresher)

Way of the Ascetics by Tito Colliander, St Vladimir's Seminary Press. This thin volume is a succinct introduction to asceticism as normal Orthodox life.

The Joy of the Holy: Saint Seraphim of Sarov and Orthodox Spiritual Life by Harry M. Boosalis, St Tikhon's Seminary Press. This book contains the saint's Spiritual Instructions as well as "The Conversation with Motovilov"—an inspiring *why* of asceticism.

Abba Dorotheos: Practical Teaching on the Christian Life trans Constantine Scouteris, also available as *Dorotheos of Gaza: Discourses and Sayings* trans Eric P. Wheeler, Cistercian Publications.

See also the writings of Hierotheos, Metropolitan of Nafpaktos, who emphasizes the Church as a hospital and asceticism as therapy for the sick soul.

1 St Isaac the Syrian [†c.700, Jan 28], *The Ascetical Homilies of Saint Isaac the Syrian*, 2nd ed, Homily 51 (Boston: Holy Transfiguration Monastery, 2011), 378.

Jesus answered them and said, "My doctrine is not mine, but His that sent me. If any man will do His will, he shall know of the doctrine, whether it be of God, or whether I speak of myself." [Jn 7:16,17]

One of the differences between the eloquent philosophy of the Greeks and the Christian Faith is that Greek philosophy can be clearly expressed with words and comprehended by reading, while the Christian Faith cannot be clearly expressed by words, and still less can it be comprehended by reading alone. When you are expounding the Christian Faith, the example of the one who expounds it is indispensable; and for its understanding and acceptance, both reading and the practice of what is read are necessary. When Patriarch Photius read the words of Saint Mark the Ascetic on the spiritual life, he noticed a certain lack of clarity in the author, about which he wisely said: "It does not proceed from the obscurity of expression but from the truth which is expressed there; it is better understood by means of practice (rather than by means of words) and cannot be explained by words only. And this," the great patriarch added, "is the case not only with these homilies, and not only with this man, but rather with all of those who attempt to expound the ascetic rules and instructions, which are better understood by deeds (in practice)."[1]

This incident helped me to understand the power of the word of the elders, who—according to Abba Pimen and Abba Dorotheus—conceal within themselves the power and operation of grace, as a sign of their personal state and experience. Like so many other elders in the patristic hierarchy, those two luminaries base their advice and instruction on patristic texts rather than the Bible—the patristic tradition being in essence the Bible analysed.[2]

---

1 St Nikolai Velimirovic [†1956, Mar 5], *The Prologue of Ohrid*, trans Fr T. Timothy Tepsic (Alhambra, CA: Serbian Orthodox Diocese of Western America, 2002), 1:649. Used with permission.

2 *Elder Joseph the Hesychast: Struggles, Experiences, Teachings (1898-1959)*, trans Elizabeth Theokritoff (Mount Athos: The Great and Holy Monastery of Vatopaidi, 1999), 130. Used with permission.

3. The Shepherd of Hermas

The Shepherd of Hermas *was written in the first or second century, author (which Hermas?) undetermined. It was well-known and revered in the early Church and was nearly included in the Bible.*[1] *Saint Athanasius the Great [†373, Jan 18] placed it on his list of books "for instruction in the word of godliness."*[2] The Shepherd *is frequently referenced by authors ancient and modern. The excerpts that follow give a heavenly perspective on our earthly life.*

Now a revelation was given to me, my brethren, while I slept, by a young man of comely appearance, who said to me, "Who do you think that old woman is from whom you received the book?"

And I said, "The Sibyl."

"You are in a mistake," says he; "it is not the Sibyl."

"Who is it then?" say I.

And he said, "It is the Church."

And I said to him, "Why then is she an old woman?"

"Because," said he, "she was created first of all. On this account is she old. And for her sake was the world made."

* * *

Falling down at her feet, I begged her by the Lord that she would show me the vision which she had promised to show me. And then she again took hold of me by the hand, and raised me, and made me sit on the seat

---

1 Part of *The Shepherd* was found the Codex Sinaiticus, a fourth-century volume of the Holy Scriptures.

2 Festal Letter XXXIX, in *Nicene and Post-Nicene Fathers*, 2nd Series, 4:551–2. Of that list, only this *Shepherd* and the *Teaching of the Apostles* (also known as *The Didache*) are not in the Orthodox Bible.

The Didache is **available in** *Ante-Nicene Fathers*, vol 7; **also in** a Penguin paperback, *Early Christian Writings: The Apostolic Fathers*, which includes the epistles of Clement, Ignatius, Polycarp, and Barnabas; **and in** *Early Epistles*, vol 6 of the Ancient Christian Writers series from Paulist Press.

to the left; and lifting up a splendid rod, she said to me, "Do you see something great?"

And I say, "Lady, I see nothing."

She said to me, "Lo! do you not see opposite to you a great tower, built upon the waters, of splendid square stones?" For the tower was built square by those six young men who had come with her. But myriads of men were carrying stones to it, some dragging them from the depths, others removing them from the land, and they handed them to these six young men. They were taking them and building; and those of the stones that were dragged out of the depths, they placed in the building just as they were: for they were polished and fitted exactly into the other stones, and became so united one with another that the lines of juncture could not be perceived. And in this way the building of the tower looked as if it were made out of one stone. Those stones, however, which were taken from the earth suffered a different fate; for the young men rejected some of them, some they fitted into the building, and some they cut down, and cast far away from the tower. Many other stones, however, lay around the tower, and the young men did not use them in building; for some of them were rough, others had cracks in them, others had been made too short, and others were white and round, but did not fit into the building of the tower. Moreover, I saw other stones thrown far away from the tower, and falling into the public road; yet they did not remain on the road, but were rolled into a pathless place. And I saw others falling into the fire and burning, others falling close to the water, and yet not capable of being rolled into the water, though they wished to be rolled down, and to enter the water.

On showing me these visions, she wished to retire. I said to her, "What is the use of my having seen all this, while I do not know what it means?"

She said to me, "You are a cunning fellow, wishing to know everything that relates to the tower."

"Even so, O Lady," said I, "that I may tell it to my brethren, that, hearing this, they may know the Lord in much glory."

And she said, "Many indeed shall hear, and hearing, some shall be glad, and some shall weep. But even these, if they hear and repent, shall also rejoice. Hear, then, the parables of the tower; for I will reveal all to you, and give me no more trouble in regard to revelation: for these revelations have an end, for they have been completed. But you will not cease praying for revelations, for you are shameless. The tower which you see building is myself, the Church, who have appeared to you now and on the former occasion. Ask, then, whatever you like in regard to the tower, and I will reveal it to you, that you may rejoice with the saints."

I said unto her, "Lady, since you have vouchsafed to reveal all to me this once, reveal it."

She said to me, "Whatsoever ought to be revealed, will be revealed; only let your heart be with God, and doubt not whatsoever you shall see."

I asked her, "Why was the tower built upon the waters, O Lady?"

She answered, "I told you before, and you still inquire carefully: therefore inquiring you shall find the truth. Hear then why the tower is built upon the waters. It is because your life has been, and will be, saved through water. For the tower was founded on the word of the almighty and glorious Name, and it is kept together by the invisible power of the Lord."

In reply I said to her, "This is magnificent and marvellous. But who are the six young men who are engaged in building?"

And she said, "These are the holy angels of God, who were first created, and to whom the Lord handed over His whole creation, that they might increase and build up and rule over the whole creation. By these will the building of the tower be finished."

"But who are the other persons who are engaged in carrying the stones?"

"These also are holy angels of the Lord, but the former six are more excellent than these. The building of the tower will be finished, and all will rejoice together around the tower, and they will glorify God, because the tower is finished."

I asked her, saying, "Lady, I should like to know what became of the stones, and what was meant by the various kinds of stones?"

In reply she said to me, "Not because you are more deserving than all others that this revelation should be made to you—for there are others before you, and better than you, to whom these visions should have been revealed—but that the name of God may be glorified, has the revelation been made to you, and it will be made on account of the doubtful who ponder in their hearts whether these things will be or not. Tell them that all these things are true, and that none of them is beyond the truth. All of them are firm and sure, and established on a strong foundation.

"Hear now with regard to the stones which are in the building. Those square white stones which fitted exactly into each other, are apostles, bishops, teachers, and deacons, who have lived in godly purity, and have acted as bishops and teachers and deacons chastely and reverently to the elect of God. Some of them have fallen asleep, and some still remain alive. And they have always agreed with each other, and been at peace among themselves, and listened to each other. On account of this, they join exactly into the building of the tower."

"But who are the stones that were dragged from the depths, and which were laid into the building and fitted in with the rest of the stones previously placed in the tower?"

"They are those who suffered for the Lord's sake."

"But I wish to know, O Lady, who are the other stones which were carried from the land."

"Those," she said, "which go into the building without being polished, are those whom God has approved of, for they walked in the straight ways of the Lord and practised His commandments."

"But who are those who are in the act of being brought and placed in the building?"

"They are those who are young in faith and are faithful. But they are admonished by the angels to do good, for no iniquity has been found in them."

"Who then are those whom they rejected and cast away?"

"These are they who have sinned, and wish to repent. On this account they have not been thrown far from the tower, because they will yet be useful in the building, if they repent. Those then who are to repent, if they do repent, will be strong in faith, if they now repent while the tower is building. For if the building be finished, there will not be more room for anyone, but he will be rejected. This privilege, however, will belong only to him who has now been placed near the tower.

"As to those who were cut down and thrown far away from the tower, do you wish to know who they are? They are the sons of iniquity, and they believed in hypocrisy, and wickedness did not depart from them. For this reason they are not saved, since they cannot be used in the building on account of their iniquities. Wherefore they have been cut off and cast far away on account of the anger of the Lord, for they have roused Him to anger. But I shall explain to you the other stones which you saw lying in great numbers, and not going into the building. Those which are rough are those who have known the truth and not remained in it, nor have they been joined to the saints. On this account are they unfit for use."

"Who are those that have rents?"

"These are they who are at discord in their hearts one with another, and are not at peace amongst themselves: they indeed keep peace before each other, but when they separate one from the other, their wicked thoughts remain in their hearts. These, then, are the rents which are in the stones. But those which are shortened are those who have indeed believed, and have the larger share of righteousness; yet they have also a considerable share of iniquity, and therefore they are shortened and not whole."

"But who are these, Lady, that are white and round, and yet do not fit into the building of the tower?"

She answered and said, "How long will you be foolish and stupid, and continue to put every kind of question and understand nothing? These are those who have faith indeed, but they have also the riches of this world. When, therefore, tribulation comes, on account of their riches and business they deny the Lord."

I answered and said to her, "When, then, will they be useful for the building, Lady?"

"When the riches that now seduce them have been circumscribed, then will they be of use to God. For as a round stone cannot become square unless portions be cut off and cast away, so also those who are rich in this world cannot be useful to the Lord unless their riches be cut down. Learn this first from your own case. When you were rich, you were useless; but now you are useful and fit for life. Be ye useful to God; for you also will be used as one of these stones.

"Now the other stones which you saw cast far away from the tower, and falling upon the public road and rolling from it into pathless traces, are those who have indeed believed, but through doubt have abandoned the true road. Thinking, then, that they could find a better, they wander and become wretched, and enter upon pathless places. But those which fell into the fire and were burned, are those who have departed for ever from the living God; nor does the thought of repentance ever come into their hearts, on account of their devotion to their lusts and to the crimes which they committed. Do you wish to know who are the others which fell near the waters, but could not be rolled into them? These are they who have heard the word, and wish to be baptized in the name of the Lord; but when the chastity demanded by the truth comes into their recollection, they draw back, and again walk after their own wicked desires."

She finished her exposition of the tower. But I, shameless as I yet was, asked her, "Is repentance possible for all those stones which have been cast away and did not fit into the building of the tower, and will they yet have a place in this tower?"

"Repentance," said she, "is yet possible, but in this tower they cannot find a suitable place. But in another and much inferior place they will be laid, and that, too, only when they have been tortured and completed the days of their sins. And on this account will they be transferred, because they have partaken of the righteous Word. And then only will they be removed from their punishments when the thought of repenting of the evil deeds which they have done has come into their hearts. But if it does not come into their hearts, they will not be saved, on account of the hardness of their heart."

When then I ceased asking in regard to all these matters, she said to me, "Do you wish to see anything else?" And as I was extremely eager to see something more, my countenance beamed with joy. She looked towards me with a smile, and said, "Do you see seven women around the tower?"

"I do, Lady," said I.

"This tower," said she, "is supported by them according to the precept of the Lord. Listen now to their functions. The first of them, who is clasping her hands, is called Faith. Through her the elect of God are saved. Another, who has her garments tucked up and acts with vigour, is called Self-restraint. She is the daughter of Faith. Whoever then follows her will become happy in his life, because he will restrain himself from all evil works, believing that, if he restrain himself from all evil desire, he will inherit eternal life."

"But the others," said I, "O Lady, who are they?"

And she said to me, "They are daughters of each other. One of them is called Simplicity, another Guilelessness, another Chastity, another Intelligence, another Love. When then you do all the works of their mother, you will be able to live."

"I should like to know," said I, "O Lady, what power each one of them possesses."

"Hear," she said, "what power they have. Their powers are regulated by each other, and follow each other in the order of their birth. For from Faith arises Self-restraint; from Self-restraint, Simplicity; from Simplicity, Guilelessness; from Guilelessness, Chastity; from Chastity, Intelligence; and from Intelligence, Love. The deeds, then, of these are pure, and chaste, and divine. Whoever devotes himself to these, and is able to hold fast by their works, shall have his dwelling in the tower with the saints of God."

* * *

First of all, believe that there is one God who created and finished all things, and made all things out of nothing. He alone is able to contain the whole, but Himself cannot be contained. Have faith therefore in Him, and fear Him; and fearing Him, exercise self-control. Keep these commands, and you will cast away from you all wickedness, and put on the strength of righteousness, and live to God, if you keep this commandment.

* * *

"There are two angels with a man—one of righteousness, and the other of iniquity."

And I said to him, "How, sir, am I to know the powers of these, for both angels dwell with me?"

"Hear," said he, "and understand them. The angel of righteousness is gentle and modest, meek and peaceful. When, therefore, he ascends into your heart, forthwith he talks to you of righteousness, purity, chastity, contentment, and of every righteous deed and glorious virtue. When all these ascend into your heart, know that the angel of righteousness is with you. These are the deeds of the angel of righteousness. Trust him, then, and his works. Look now at the works of the angel of iniquity. First, he is wrathful, and bitter, and foolish, and his works are evil, and ruin the servants of God. When, then, he ascends into your heart, know him by his works."

And I said to him, "How, sir, I shall perceive him, I do not know."

"Hear and understand," said he. "When anger comes upon you, or harshness, know that he is in you; and you will know this to be the case also, when you are attacked by a longing after many transactions, and the richest delicacies, and drunken revels, and divers luxuries, and things improper, and by a hankering after women, and by overreaching, and pride, and blustering, and by whatever is like to these. When these ascend into your heart, know that the angel of iniquity is in you. Now that you know his works, depart from him, and in no respect trust him, because his deeds are evil, and unprofitable to the servants of God.

* * *

"I told you," said he, "that the creatures of God are double, for restraint also is double; for in some cases restraint has to be exercised, in others there is no need of restraint."

"Make known to me, sir," say I, "in what cases restraint has to be exercised, and in what cases it has not."

"Restrain yourself in regard to evil, and do it not; but exercise no restraint in regard to good, but do it. For if you exercise restraint in the doing of good, you will commit a great sin; but if you exercise restraint so as not to do that which is evil, you are practising great righteousness. Restrain yourself, therefore, from all iniquity, and do that which is good."

"What, sir," say I, "are the evil deeds from which we must restrain ourselves?"

"Hear," says he: "from adultery and fornication, from unlawful revelling, from wicked luxury,[1] from indulgence in many kinds of food and the extravagance of riches, and from boastfulness, and haughtiness, and insolence, and lies, and backbiting, and hypocrisy, from the remembrance of wrong, and from all slander. These are the deeds that are most wicked in the life of men. From all these deeds, therefore, the servant of God must restrain himself. For he who does not restrain himself from these, cannot live to God. Listen, then, to the deeds that accompany these."

"Are there, sir," said I, "any other evil deeds?"

"There are," says he; "and many of them, too, from which the servant of God must restrain himself—theft, lying, robbery, false witness, overreaching, wicked lust, deceit, vainglory, boastfulness, and all other vices like to these."

"Do you not think that these are really wicked?"

"Exceedingly wicked in the servants of God. From all of these the servant of God must restrain himself. Restrain yourself, then, from all these, that you may live to God, and you will be enrolled amongst those

---

1 [cf. "Every act of a man which he performs with pleasure is an act of luxury; for the sharp-tempered man, when gratifying his tendency, indulges in luxury; and the adulterer, and the drunkard, and the back-biter, and the liar, and the covetous man, and the thief, and he who does things like these, gratifies his peculiar propensity, and in so doing indulges in luxury. All these acts of luxury are hurtful to the servants of God." This is excerpted from later in the text.]

who restrain themselves in regard to these matters. These, then, are the things from which you must restrain yourself.

"But listen," says he, "to the things in regard to which you have not to exercise self-restraint, but which you ought to do. Restrain not yourself in regard to that which is good, but do it."

"And tell me, sir," say I, "the nature of the good deeds, that I may walk in them and wait on them, so that doing them I can be saved."

"Listen," says he, "to the good deeds which you ought to do, and in regard to which there is no self-restraint requisite. First of all there is faith, then fear of the Lord, love, concord, words of righteousness, truth, patience. Than these, nothing is better in the life of men. If any one attend to these, and restrain himself not from them, blessed is he in his life. Then there are the following attendant on these: helping widows, looking after orphans and the needy, rescuing the servants of God from necessities, the being hospitable—for in hospitality good-doing finds a field—never opposing anyone, the being quiet, having fewer needs than all men, reverencing the aged, practising righteousness, watching the brotherhood, bearing insolence, being long-suffering, encouraging those who are sick in soul, not casting those who have fallen into sin from the faith, but turning them back and restoring them to peace of mind, admonishing sinners, not oppressing debtors and the needy, and if there are any other actions like these."

The Source

Reprinted from the American Edition of *Ante-Nicene Fathers,* vol 2, originally published in the United States by the Christian Literature Publishing Company, 1885 (Peabody, MA: Hendrickson Publishers, reprint 2004).

Also on Saint Athansius's list, and included in the (Orthodox) Bible, are *Tobit, Judith, Esther, Wisdom of Solomon,* and *Wisdom of Sirach* [a.k.a. *Ecclesiasticus*]. All are well worth (re)reading.

Miscellanea

Virtues, Vices, Passions

The cardinal virtues are four: courage, sound understanding, self-restraint and justice.[1] There are eight other moral qualities that either go beyond or fall short of these virtues. These we regard as vices, and so we call them; but non-spiritual people regard them as virtues and that is what they call them. Exceeding or falling short of courage are audacity and cowardice; of sound understanding are cunning and ignorance; of self-restraint are licentiousness and obtuseness; of justice are excess and injustice, or taking less than one's due. In between, and superior to, what goes beyond or what falls short of them, lie not only the cardinal and natural virtues, but also the practical virtues.[2]

* * *

Just as the virtues are begotten in the soul, so are the passions. But the virtues are begotten in accordance with nature, the passions in a mode contrary to nature. For what produces good or evil in the soul is the will's bias: it is like the joint of a pair of compasses or the pivot of a pair of scales: whichever way it inclines, so it will determine the consequences. For our inner disposition is capable of operating in one way or another, since it bears within itself both virtue and vice, the first as its natural birthright, the second as the result of the self-incurred proclivity of our moral will.

* * *

There are eight ruling passions: gluttony, avarice and self-esteem—the three principal passions; and unchastity, anger, dejection, listlessness and arrogance—the five subordinate passions. In the same way, among the virtues opposed to these there are three that are all-embracing, namely, total shedding of possessions, self-control and humility, and five deriving from them, namely, purity, gentleness, joy, courage, and self-belittlement—and then come all the other virtues.[3]

— Saint Gregory of Sinai

1 [Courage is often translated as fortitude; sound understanding as prudence or wisdom; self-restraint as temperance or self-control or chastity; justice as righteousness.]

2 [cf. 1. sin = αμαρτία, to miss the mark; 2. the "royal road," neither to the left (negligence) nor to the right (overdoing, zeal without knowledge).]

3 St Gregory of Sinai [†1346, Apr 6], Sections 87, 89, and 91, "On Commandments and Doctrines, Warnings and Promises; on Thoughts, Passions and Virtues, and also on Stillness and Prayer: One Hundred and Thirty-Seven Texts" from *The Philokalia: The Complete Text*, compiled by St Nikodimos of the Holy Mountain [†1809, July 14] and St Makarios of Corinth [†1805, Apr 17], trans G.E.H. Palmer, Philip Sherrard, and

Sin Oblivion

As Saint Theophan the Recluse observed in a previous chapter, "Good order in one's conduct more than anything else can lead one into deception. Its true significance depends upon one's inward disposition, where it is possible that there are significant deviations from real righteousness in one's righteous deeds." With all our distractions, it is easy for us to think that, as long as we are not in jail, we are obviously doing just fine. We may need help to see ourselves more clearly: O Lord, "sanctify our souls, make chaste our bodies, correct our thoughts, *purify our intentions.*"[1]

The following "Daily Confession of Sins" from the Prayers before Sleep suggests a few things we may daily overlook.

> I confess to Thee, my Lord, God and Creator, to the One glorified and worshipped in Holy Trinity, to the Father, Son and Holy Spirit, all my sins which I have committed all the days of my life, at every hour, in the present and in the past, day and night, in thought, word and deed; by gluttony, drunkenness, secret eating, idle talking, despondency, indolence, contradiction, neglect, aggressiveness, self-love, hoarding, stealing, lying, dishonesty, curiosity, jealousy, envy, anger, resentment, and remembering wrongs, hatred, mercenariness; and by all my senses: sight, hearing, smell, taste, touch; and all other sins, spiritual and bodily, through which I have angered Thee, my God and Creator, and caused injustice to my neighbours. Sorrowing for this, but determined to repent, I stand guilty before Thee, my God. Only help me, my Lord and God, I humbly pray Thee with tears. Forgive my past sins by Thy mercy, and absolve me from all I have confessed in Thy presence, for Thou art good and the Lover of Mankind. Amen.[2]

A first reaction might be, "None of that applies to me." Our spiritual anthropology tells us differently: "If we do not know what we are like when God makes us, we shall not realize what sin has turned us into."[3] Calling to mind, then, not only our sins and passions, but also the virtues we have

Kallistos Ware, 4:230–231.

1 From the Prayer of the Hours, in *A Prayer Book for Orthodox Christians* (Brookline, MA: Holy Transfiguration Monastery, 1995), 24 (emphasis added). Copyright © Holy Transfiguration Monastery, Brookline, MA, used by permission. All rights reserved.

2 *Prayer Book* (Jordanville, NY: Holy Trinity Monastery, 1979), 54–55. Used with permission.

3 St Gregory of Sinai, Section 50, *The Philokalia*, vol 4:221.

failed to achieve, we have double reason to weep over ourselves. At the same time, remembering the virtues, coming to love the virtues, striving to embrace (with God's help) the virtues, and knowing that the Lover of Mankind is eager to forgive and to help us, we do not despair but arise again with thankfulness and resolve, striving again with complete trust in and dependence on God, to do and to become what is pleasing to Him.[1]

THEM!

He who busies himself with the sins of others, or judges his brother on suspicion, has not yet even begun to repent or to examine himself so as to discover his own sins, which are truly heavier than a great lump of lead; nor does he know why a man becomes heavy-hearted when he loves vanity and chases after falsehood [cf. Ps 4:2]. That is why, like a fool who walks in darkness, he no longer attends to his own sins but lets his imagination dwell on the sins of others, whether these sins are real or merely the products of his own suspicious mind.[2]

—Saint Maximos the Confessor

1 "What do you do at the monastery?" "We fall down and get back up, fall down and get back up."

2 St Maximos the Confessor [†662, Jan 21], Section 55, "Third Century on Love" from "Four Hundred Texts on Love," from *The Philokalia: The Complete Text*, compiled by St Nikodimos of the Holy Mountain and St Makarios of Corinth, trans G.E.H. Palmer, Philip Sherrard, and Kallistos Ware, 2:92. Translation copyright © 1981 by the Eling Trust. Reprinted by permission of Farrar, Straus and Giroux, LLC, and Faber and Faber Ltd.

Also available in *Maximus Confessor: Selected Writings*, trans George C. Berthold (New York: Paulist Press [Classics of Western Spirituality series], 1985), 68–9.

4. The Unity of Christ's Ideal

How do we see ourselves in the world? How do we see ourselves as Christians? And what is monasticism about? The author of the following letter, ***Saint Hilarion Troitsky****, Confessor and Holy New Martyr [†1929, Dec 28], was consecrated vicar bishop*[1] *in 1920 by Saint Tikhon [Apostle to America, Patriarch of Moscow and All-Russia, †1925, Mar 25 (24)]. Continually harassed and imprisoned, he died in a Communist prison hospital at age 44.*

A year ago, my dear friend, in one of my letters to you, I briefly—in two pages or so, as I recall—touched on the question of monasticism and Christianity, of their unity in essence. This was followed by an even briefer reply from you. You didn't go so far as to argue with me, yet all the same you didn't agree. But I would like to establish a friendly oneness of mind with you on this particular question . . . namely, the idea that the Christian ideal in all its loftiness is binding and needful only for monks, while for laymen—well, laymen need something more reasonable, something easier. "We're not monks!" For laymen, this explains and excuses everything. I even read in a report of a sensational trial this curious detail: A gentlemen is being questioned whether he was unfaithful to his wife, and, if so, often? He answers, "Of course! I did not live like a monk!" Really, doesn't that seem typical to you?

We have come to have two Christianities, two Christian ideals: one for monks, another for laymen. I consider this division of Christ's ideal to be absurd in principle and extremely harmful in practice. That's

1 A vicar bishop is an auxiliary bishop. He extends the ruling bishop's effectiveness by attending to matters, in the bishop's absence, that require episcopal authority. It often includes extensive travel, as with St Tikhon's auxiliary bishop in America, St Raphael of Brooklyn [†1915, Feb 27 or Saturday before the Synaxis of the Archangels (Nov 8)]. See *Our Father among the Saints Raphael of Brooklyn: Good Shepherd of the Lost Sheep in America* (Wichita, KS: Antakya Press, 2000). As for St Tikhon, see (among other things) the Church Trials in Aleksandr Solzhenitsyn's *The Gulag Archipelago*.

why I'm grieved to realize that my good and intelligent friend is inclined to share this prejudice, sprung from the soil of human thoughtlessness. This harmful prejudice does not suit you, my friend. Again I invite you to think through together the question I posed.

So, one Christianity or two? Is Christ's ideal indivisible or differentiated? I think you will agree with me without debate that there is one Christianity and that Christ's ideal is indivisible. But perhaps in that ideal there are differing degrees of perfection? Friend! You know this is an absurdity! Really, in an ideal, can there be higher and lower degrees? An ideal is infinity, you see, and infinity is always equal to itself. You know where the ideal of Christianity is expressed in a nutshell? In the forty-eighth verse of the fifth chapter of the Gospel according to Saint Matthew: "Be ye perfect, as your heavenly Father is perfect." Are any degrees permitted in this ideal? Of course, in the attainment of this "be ye perfect," there might be a countless multitude of degrees, but the ideal itself always remains indivisible and it is the same for all. Christ didn't teach monks, you know, but all people—and taught one thing. Truly, my friend, it's rather awkward for me to be opening the Gospel and proving what is clear in and of itself. Alas, in our time, hostility toward monasticism has blinded many to such an extent that they are ready to reject even self-evident truths.

In order to stop the mouths of those who divide the indivisible ideal of Christ, I will quote the remarkable words of Saint John Chrysostom [†407, Nov 13], which I advise you to ponder so as to agree with me. Saint John Chrysostom writes:

> You do greatly err and deceive yourself, if you think that one thing is required of a layman and another of a monk. The difference between them is that one marries and the other does not. In everything else they bear the same responsibility. So, whoever is angry with his brother without a cause, be he a layman or a monk, offends God just as much, and whosoever looks on a woman to lust after her, be he one or the other, will be punished just as much for this adultery [Mt 5:22, 28]. If I might add something from my own understanding, then a layman is less to be excused for this passion, because it is not the same if he who is tempted by the beauty of a woman has a wife and enjoys this consolation as if he who is captured by this sin has no such help (against passion).

Likewise, he who swears, be he one or the other, will be judged just the same, because Christ, when He gave the commandment and the law concerning this, did not make any such distinction. He did not say, if the one who swears is a monk, then his oath is evil, but if he is not a monk, then it is not. He simply and to all alike said, "I say unto you, swear not at all" [Mt 5:34]. And further, having said, "Woe unto you that laugh now" [Lk 6:25], He did not add, "if you are monks," but laid down this rule for all alike.

This is how He treated all the other great and marvelous commandments. When, for instance, He says, Blessed are the poor in spirit, they that mourn, the meek, they which do hunger and thirst after righteousness, the merciful, the pure in heart, the peacemakers, they which are persecuted for righteousness' sake, they who are reviled by outsiders (unbelievers) in spoken and unspoken ways for His sake [Mt 5:3–11], He does not mention the word layman, nor monk. This distinction was introduced by the mind of man. The Scriptures are not acquainted with this distinction, but rather desire that all live the life of monks, even if they have wives.

Listen to what Saint Paul says (and when I say Saint Paul I speak again of Christ). Saint Paul, addressing himself in his epistles to people who have wives and are raising children, demands from them all the strictness of life characteristic of monks. So, dismissing every kind of luxury in clothing and in food, he writes these words: "In like manner also, that women adorn themselves in modest apparel, with shamefacedness and sobriety; not with braided hair, or gold, or pearls, or costly array" [1Tim 2:9]; and also "She that liveth in pleasure is dead while she liveth" [1Tim 5:6]; and further, "Having food and raiment let us be therewith content" [1Tim 6:8]. What more than this would it be possible to demand from one living as a monastic? And teaching people to restrain their tongues, he again establishes strict rules, hard even for monks to fulfill, for he dismisses not only shameless and foolish speech, but also jesting; he banishes from faithful lips not only bitterness and wrath and insults, but also shouting: "Let all bitterness, and wrath, and anger, and clamour, and evil speaking, be put away from you, with all malice" [Eph 4:31]. Or does that seem insignificant to you? Wait and you will hear much more about how he commands all about meekness. "Let not the sun go down upon your wrath" [Eph 4:26],

"See that none render evil for evil unto any man; but ever follow that which is good, both among yourselves, and to all men" [1Thess 5:15]; and further: "Be not overcome of evil, but overcome evil with good" [Rom 12:21]. Do you see that love of wisdom and long-suffering are carried to the utmost degree?

Listen likewise to what he commands about love, the chief of virtues: having placed it above everything and having told of its effects, he explained that he expects the same love from laymen as Christ expected from his disciples. The Saviour said the highest degree of love consists of laying down one's life for his friends [Jn 15:13]. Saint Paul expressed the same thing when he said, "Love seeks not its own" [1Cor 13:5], and he commands us to strive for that love. So if only this alone had been said, it would be enough to prove that the same is expected from laymen as from monks, because love is the bond and the root of many virtues, and Saint Paul expounds it in detail. What more could be expected than this true philosophy?

When he enjoins us to be above wrath, bitterness, shouting, covetousness, gluttony, luxury, vainglory and other worldliness and to have nothing in common with the world; when he commands us to mortify our members [Col 3:5], then obviously he is demanding from us the same strict life as Christ demanded from His disciples, and wishes that we were as dead to sin as those dead and buried. For this reason he says, "For he that is dead is freed from sin" [Rom 6:7]. And in other places he exhorts us to imitate Christ and not just His disciples. Thus when he tries to persuade us to love, to be forgiving and to be meek, then he gives Christ as an example. And so if he (Saint Paul) enjoins us to imitate not just monks and not even the disciples but Christ Himself, and for those who do not imitate Him prescribes the greatest punishment, then why do you call their height a greater one? All people should ascend to one and the same height.

This is precisely what has perverted the whole universe—that we think as though only those living as monastics need great strictness of life, while the rest can live carefree. No, no. This same true philosophy, he says, is expected from all of us, a love I would very much like to inspire, or rather not I, but the very One Who will judge us.

If you are still amazed and perplexed, then for your benefit we will draw on the same sources again, so that you may be completely cleansed of any impurity of unbelief. I offer as proof the punishments which will come to pass on that day (of judgment). The rich man was greatly punished, not because he was a cruel monk, but, if I may say a word or two in explanation, because being a layman and living in wealth and royal luxury, he despised Lazarus in his extreme poverty. Or rather, I won't dwell on these details, but simply will say that he was cruel and for this suffered the most grievous torments in the fire....

I will try now to prove that a monastic life doesn't lead to more grievous punishment, but that laymen face the very same punishment if they sin in the same way. Thus the man who was improperly dressed [Mt 22:1–13] and the man who demanded 100 denarii from his debtor [Mt 18:23–34] suffered the disasters which befell them not because they were monks, but the former perished because of prodigal behaviour and the latter for being unforgiving. If you look at others who will be punished on that day, then you will see that they face punishment only for their sins.

This can be noted not only about punishment but also in exhortations. Thus saying, "Come unto me, all ye that labor and are heavy laden and I will give you rest. Take my yoke upon you, and learn of me, for I am meek and lowly in heart: and ye shall find rest unto your souls," [Mt 11:28–29] the Lord addresses not only monastics but the whole human race. And when He enjoins (His disciples) to go by the narrow way [Lk 13:24], then He directs this saying not to them alone, but to all people. He commanded everyone alike to hate life in this world [Jn 12:25] and all such similar things.

And so, from now on, I think, that even the most argumentative and shameless person cannot deny that layman and monk should attain the same height and that both, if they fall, will receive the same condemnation.[1]

Don't be amazed, my friend, that I took such a big excerpt from Saint John Chrysostom. It seems to me that Saint John Chrysostom in the preceding words proves, perfectly clearly and convincingly, precisely

1 Source of the original Russian quotation: *To a Faithful Father.* Third Homily, ch. 14, *Works.* Published by the St Petersburg Spiritual Academy. Vol. I, pp. 107–110.

the unity of Christ's ideal. Before this ideal all are equal: both monks and laymen. And so to excuse oneself with that so-common phrase, "We are not monks," is the most utter misunderstanding of the essence of Christianity, simply a failure to think it through . . . .

On the whole, I believe the question of the unity of Christ's ideal has been explored and resolved quite sufficiently by the words of Saint John Chrysostom. The proposition that monasticism doesn't offer some kind of special ideal, different from the common Christian ideal, should be recognized as an axiom, as a starting point. No special ideal whatsoever can exist, because Christ's ideal is eternal, unchanging and infinite . . . .

In the moral system of the [Roman] Catholics, the teaching of Christ is divided into obligatory commandments and individual counsel. Everyone is bound to fulfill the commandments, but the counsel is directed to those who wish. Whoever fulfills the counsel has done more than is required, and he has surplus "merits" which he does not need. These merits go into the church treasury and the pope distributes from this church treasury stored-up "merits" to those who do not have enough merits of their own. This is how indulgences originated and, in general, the whole financial mechanism of the Vatican. "Checks are issued for good works and wire transfers are made from saints to sinners." The division of Christ's teaching into commandments and counsel is an unbreakable link in this heretical system of [Roman] Catholicism. Our Orthodox theology, although it paid some tribute to [Roman] Catholicism, always fought against this Roman scheme of virtue. In our theological literature, the very division of Christian moral teaching into commandments and counsel was rejected and refuted. So it is strange to think that monks take upon themselves some kind of special struggles, struggles which were not commanded by Christ.

For a Christian there exists no yardstick of any kind, beyond which he has no need to grow spiritually. His yardstick is infinite perfection, together with infinitely increasing blessedness, because we affirm that virtue and blessedness are one. "The measure of the stature of the fullness of Christ" [Eph 4:13]—this is the measure of a Christian. And this is his frame of mind: "So likewise ye, when ye shall have done all those things which are commanded you, say, we are unprofitable servants: we have done that which was our duty to do" [Lk 17:10]. What could any kind of human vows add to this? Add, I mean, in a moral ideal sense. What vow could surpass "the measure of the stature of the fullness of Christ?" Read, my friend, the service of monastic tonsure. You will see there a selection, as it were, of Gospel sayings; that is, of truths which are binding upon all.

"And what about renunciation of the world?" should be the question stirring in your mind. "You renounce the world and we don't."

I wouldn't like to hear this perplexity from you, my friend, because you need—and it wouldn't hurt you at all—to grasp something of theology. This is the talk of worldly people, who love to express decisive opinions, but don't consider it necessary to know anything, to think about anything or to understand anything. As for you, friend, such worldly lightmindedness doesn't at all become you as an intelligent person. In fact, what does it mean to renounce the world? It means to renounce the universe. A difficult task! Well, how do you renounce the universe? How do you leave it? Where do you go? To a monastery? But where is the monastery? Isn't it on this same earth? Yes, how easy it would be to renounce the world if for that it were enough to hide oneself behind monastery walls! But they say, "He brought the world to the monastery." It turns out that you can take the world with you. They say, "The world is chasing him." It turns out that the world can move. What kind of world is this?

On the other hand, the tonsurer asks of the one being tonsured, "Do you renounce the world and those in the world according to the Lord's commandment?" Do you hear, my friend—according to the Lord's commandment! Renunciation of the world is called the Lord's commandment; that is, without a doubt, something for all Christians. Yes, of course this commandment of God is for all Christians. Remember from the Gospel, "My kingdom is not of this world" [Jn 18:36]. "They are not of the world, as I am not of the world" [Jn 17:14,16]. "The world hateth you" [Jn 15:19]. "The world hath hated them" [Jn 17:14]. About whom is He speaking? About monks? No, of course not—about Christians in general. And remember the apostolic teachings. "Do not love the world or what is in the world" [1Jn 2:15]. "Friendship with the world is enmity with God" [Jas 4:4]. "Whatsoever is born of God overcometh the world" [1Jn 5:4]. "He that is in you is greater than he that is in the world" [1Jn 4:4]. Anyone who does not want to be at enmity with God must renounce the world—not only, consequently, monks, but all Christians. So then, what is the world and what does it mean to renounce it?

Here is how the greatest "teachers of monks" and best authorities on questions of Christian moral teaching—the Holy Fathers—the ascetics—answer that question. Listen to what Saint Basil the Great has to say, he who took so much care for the ordering of monastic life: "Withdrawing from the world consists not of being outside the world bodily, but of tearing oneself away in soul from the inclinations of the body." By "the world" the Holy Scriptures mean evil deeds, according to Chrysostom [On Ephesians, XXII, 3]. Saint Mark the Ascetic writes, "It is not commanded for us to love the world and all that is in the world. We have not received this command so that we should heedlessly hate God's creation, but so that we would cut off the causes for the passions." Saint Abba Esaias says, "The world is when we fulfill the desires of the flesh, when we take more care for the body than for the soul" [Homily 21]. But Saint Isaac the Syrian gives the most precise definition of "the world": "The world is a collective name, embracing in itself that which is called passions. When we want to name the totality of the passions, we call them the world. To put it more briefly—the world is the carnal way of life and the 'mind of the flesh,' when a Christian does not fulfill the requirement to live in the flesh, but not according to the flesh" [Homily 30].[1]

Here, my friend, is what the word "world" means in ascetic language. The "world" is the totality of the passions. Tell me, can it really be that only monks must renounce the passions? Of course not. Renunciation of the world is a commandment of the Lord for all Christians. You laymen also gave a vow to renounce the world. Where and when? At baptism we all were asked if we renounced Satan and all his works. Our godparents answered for us, "I do!" And we were asked again, had we renounced Satan, and our answer was, "I have!" Then we spit on Satan. We renounced, you see, precisely the one who is in the world, in the words of Christ. We united ourselves unto Christ. It's a pity that laymen, when they grow up, don't even look at the baptismal service. We have a very widespread prejudice among laymen that asceticism is a specialty of monks. We use the words "monk" and "ascetic" as synonyms. But this is an utter failure to comprehend. What is asceticism? In our theological literature there is a voluminous and very instructive essay by Prof. S.M.

---

1 In the English translation of *The Ascetical Homilies of St Isaac the Syrian* by Holy Transfiguration Monastery, these sentences are excerpted from different paragraphs in Homily 2, 14–15, except for the last clause.— Trans.

Zarin, "Asceticism in Orthodox Christian Doctrine" [St Petersburg, 1907]. These are the kind of books you laymen ought to be reading more! Then you wouldn't be saying the kind of things to which one can only open his eyes wide with amazement and shrug his shoulders with pity. Here is how asceticism is defined in that essay, on the grounds of philology, philosophy and patristic literature. "By 'asceticism' in the direct and proper sense one should understand the systematic use, the conscious application of expedient means to acquire Christian virtue, to attain religious-moral perfection." Think about that definition and tell me whether asceticism is exclusively a monastic affair. If we all need to struggle against the passions, then the struggle against them is, you see, asceticism, the renunciation of the world. This same learned specialist on questions of asceticism, Prof. S.M. Zarin, puts it well: "Orthodoxy, recognizing perfection as a requirement for all Christians, considers asceticism, practiced in various forms, as an obligation for all Christians."

* * *

"Your [ascetic] way," they say, "is against nature." Quit it, for God's sake! Christian life, if you like, is entirely against nature. Christ came to renew our nature, which had been corrupted by sin. The task of every Christian is to lay aside the former way of life of the old man, which is corrupt according to the deceitful lusts, to be renewed in the spirit of his mind, and to put on the new man, which after God is created in righteousness and true holiness [Eph 4:22–24]. It follows to resist unto blood, striving against sin [Heb 12:4] . . . . The renewal of nature is accomplished gradually. What is asceticism? Indeed, it is the struggle against the present condition of human nature. Laymen, my friend, have given very little thought to this point. All Christian life is against nature, because its goal is the creation of a "new creature."

* * *

Another detail. They say, "Monks have spoiled the joy of life." Utter falsehood! Monks do have joy—quiet, pure, the particular cheerfulness of a virtuous soul. Indeed, those noxious fumes, that intoxication with life, which is commonly called "the joy of life," all that is something dreary, consisting of surfeiting and a hangover. The intellectuals who have strayed from the Church are the ones who have really lost the joy of life. Tell me, my friend, have you seen very many laymen weeping for joy? But we monks, from joy, from compunction, weep and thank the Lord for His mercy. Every monk has experienced tears of compunction, and next to those tears, worldly joys seem pale and pathetic to him.

* * *

How strict is life in a monastery? They rise from sleep at two-thirty, and at three are already in church. They read morning prayers, the midnight service, and listen to matins. The morning services continue for three hours. At seven they are in church again for Liturgy, which ends around ten. After Liturgy they work at their "obediences." Until Liturgy is finished, they don't partake of food. At midday, they have trapeza [a common meal], during which the life of the saint of the day is read. Trapeza proceeds sedately, in silence. Before and after trapeza, prayers are sung. Every dish is served with prayer. After trapeza, there is an hour and a half of rest. After all, they got up long ago! After rest, some work, some read something spiritual, edifying. At 5 o'clock is the evening service, which lasts almost until 8 o'clock and ends in the trapeza, where the evening prayers are read with many prostrations. And at nine it is time to sleep, because tomorrow they will be waked at two-thirty again. Before sleep they also fulfill their rule, again with many prostrations. Thus it is day after day. During fasts, trapeza is very meager, and church services sometimes take 11–12 hours a day. I haven't dreamed up this daily schedule, just copied it from reality. In the majority of monasteries the day proceeds in exactly this way. Compare, my friend, this monastery "program for the day" with the "program for the day" of the people who surround you, and say which way of life is more adapted to the salvation of the soul. Doesn't it follow to agree for now with Saint Chrysostom, who says, "Here [in the world] there are more likely to be shipwrecks, from the fact that there are more waves, and those who have to struggle are defenseless; while there they do not have such waves, but great calm, and more zeal in those who should struggle."

The monastery way of life thus attains the goal of its existence. Salvation is the same for all people and the ideal of Christ is one, but he who lives in a monastery takes a beautiful road to the eternal dwelling, not one through a marshy swamp, as laymen do. How, actually, can sinful nature not be crushed here? Seven to eight hours a day spent in church, work as many more or read something edifying. When is there time to sin? Monastery life is arranged so that a monk has no idle time. All church, all salvific, all with prayer—in this way an inclination toward thoughts and feelings about church is created. Communal life and a communal striving bring people together, create a grace-filled atmosphere of communal brotherly love.

* * *

The sum is this. Monasticism does not create any kind of new Christianity. Christ's ideal is absolutely the same for all. All Christians alike may ascend all the steps of moral perfection. The idea that laymen might attain only to the middle steps, while the higher ones are only accessible to monks, I consider absurd. All monastic vows are the same as general Christian vows, because all should be saved, and for salvation it is necessary to renounce the world of the passions and to take up an ascetic struggle against sin. Monks are distinguished from laymen only by the vow of celibacy. But this vow carries nothing new in the moral sense, because celibacy is only one of the paths of life, on par with the path of marriage. Neither of these paths in and of itself makes a man holy or sinful. To subordinate one path to the other in a moral sense is extremely unwise. Each chooses the path which he considers more suitable for himself.

The Source

Written by Archbishop Hilarion Troitsky in 1915; translated by Diaconissa Maria Tseitlin. Reprinted from *The True Vine*, Issue Number 40 (Vol 10, No 4).

Miscellanea

We're Not Monks!

Other than a mention of an abbot and superior, what of the following list does not apply to non-monks?

WHAT ARE THE INSTRUMENTS OF GOOD WORKS

IN the first place, to love the Lord God with the whole heart, the whole soul and the whole strength.

Then one's neighbour as if oneself.

Then, not to kill.

Not to commit adultery.

Not to steal.

Not to covet.

Not to utter false witness.

To honour all men.

To do as one would be done by.

To deny oneself that one may follow Christ.

To chastise the body.

Not to embrace delights.

To love fasting.

To relieve the poor.

To clothe the naked.

To visit the sick.

To bury the dead.

To help in tribulation.

To console the sorrowing.

To become a stranger to worldly deeds.

To prefer nothing to the love of Christ.

Not to carry anger into effect.

Not to prolong the duration of one's wrath.

Not to retain guile in one's heart.

Not to make a false peace.

Not to abandon charity.

Not to swear, lest perchance one forswear.

To utter only truth from heart and mouth.

Not to return evil for evil.

Not to do injury, but to suffer it patiently.

To love enemies.

Not to curse in return those who curse one, but rather to bless them.

To bear persecution for righteousness.

Not to be proud.

Not to be given to much wine.

Not to be gluttonous.

Not given to much sleep.

Not to be sluggish.

Not to be given to grumbling.

Not to be a detractor.

To put one's hope in God.

When one sees any good in oneself to attribute it to God, not to self.

But to recognize that evil always comes from self and to refer it to self.

To have wholesome fear of the day of judgment.

With fear to shrink from hell.

To long for eternal life with all spiritual desire.

To have the expectation of death daily before one's eyes.

Hour by hour to keep guard over one's every act.
To know for certain that God sees one everywhere.
Forthwith to dash down upon the Rock, even Christ, any evil thoughts approaching the heart: and to lay them open before one's superior.
To keep one's mouth from evil or depraved speech.
Not to love to speak much.
Not to speak useless or mirth-provoking words.
Not to love much or excessive laughter.
To listen with goodwill to holy reading.
To be frequently occupied in prayer.
With tears and groaning daily to confess in prayer to God one's past sins and concerning those same sins to amend for the future.
Not to fulfil the desires of the flesh: to hate one's own will.
To yield obedience in all things to the abbot's precepts, even if he himself act contrary to their spirit, the which be far from him: being mindful of that precept of the Lord: "What they say, do ye; but what they do, do ye not."
Not to wish to be called holy before one is, but to be so first, whereby one would be so called the more truly.
By deeds daily to fulfil the precepts of God.
To love chastity.
Not to hate anyone.
Not to harbour jealousy.
Not to love contention.
To avoid elation.
To venerate seniors.
To love juniors.
In the love of Christ to pray for one's enemies.
In case of discord with anyone, to make peace before the setting of the sun.
And never to despair of the mercy of God.

Behold, these are the instruments of the spiritual art, the which, when they shall have been ceaselessly employed by us day and night and duly given back in the day of judgment, shall be recompensed to us by that reward from God which He promised: "That which the eye hath not seen, nor the ear heard, and that hath not entered into the human heart, the things which God has prepared for them who love Him" [1 Cor 2:9].

And the cloister of the monastery and stability in the community are the workshop wherein we may diligently effect all these works.[1]

— Saint Benedict of Nursia

[1] *Rule of* ***St Benedict*** [†c. 560, March 14], trans Anonymous (London: SPCK, 1931), 15–19.

Let us purify the senses, and with the unapproachable light of the resurrection we shall behold Christ, resplendent; and chanting a hymn of victory, we shall hear [Him] clearly saying: "Rejoice."
—*Troparion, Ode 1, The Canon of Pascha*[1]

Let us rise very early in the morning and offer hymnody to the Master instead of myrrh; and let us behold Christ, the Sun of righteousness, Who shineth forth life upon all.
—*Irmos, Ode 5, The Canon of Pascha*

Beholding Thee now not with our eyes, but with heartfelt love, and believing Thee to be God, O King of all, we magnify Thee in hymns.
—*Matins aposticha sticheron, Thomas Monday and Thursday*

Enlighten, O Lord, my noetic eyes which have been blinded by dark sin, instilling humility, O Compassionate One; and wash me with tears of repentance.
—*Exapostilarion of Wednesday of the Blind Man*

Blind in the eyes of my soul, I come to Thee, O Christ, like the man blind from birth, and cry out to Thee with repentance: Thou art the all-radiant Light of those in darkness.

Grant me a stream of ineffable wisdom and higher understanding, O Christ, Thou Light of those in darkness and Guide of the deceived, that, wretch that I am, I may be able to declare Thy wonders which the divine book of the Gospel hath taught the world: that is, the miracle of the blind man. For, blind from birth, he received material eyes as well as spiritual eyes, crying out with faith: Thou art the all-radiant Light of those in darkness.
—*Kontakion and Ikos of Sunday of the Blind Man*

[Perhaps those who suffer from "post-Pascha blues" are unaware of the joy of the *Pentecostarion*....]

1 All hymns from the *Pentecostarion*, trans Isaac E. Lambertsen (Liberty, TN: Saint John of Kronstadt Press, 2010), 6, 7, 69, 77, 202, 225; SJKP.org. Used with permission.

5. The Samaritan Woman at the Well

This commentary on the Samaritan woman by ***Saint Theophylact of Ohrid*** *[†c.1126, Dec 31] demonstrates several types of Orthodox scriptural interpretation. Saint Theophylact received an excellent education in Constantinople and, consecrated bishop, was sent to Ohrid, where he governed the Bulgarian Church for twenty-five years. This chapter is from his Explanation of the entire New Testament, itself a distillation of the Holy Fathers.*

[The Gospel According to John: Chapter 4:] 5–6a. Then cometh He to a city of Samaria, which is called Sychar, near to the parcel of ground that Jacob gave to his son Joseph. Now Jacob's well was there. It would be worthwhile to explain the origin of the Samaritans and how they got their name. Ambri, a king of Israel, bought the mountain Semeron from its owner, Semer, and built a city on it which he named Samaria [3Kgs 16:23–25]. At first, Israelites, not Samaritans, lived in this city. Later, when they sinned against God, these Israelites were chastised at the hands of the Assyrians on various occasions [4Kgs 17:6–7]. Finally the Assyrian king [Tiglath-pileser III] attacked them as they were plotting a rebellion, took them captive, and to forestall future revolts exiled them to the country of the Babylonians and Medes. He settled their former home with Gentiles brought from various places in his realm. After this, God showed the barbarians that He had delivered the Jews into their hands, not because He was unable to defend His people, but because the Israelites had sinned. At His command, lions attacked the Gentiles of Samaria, devouring many. When the king learned of this, he sent for certain elders of the Jews in captivity and asked them what could be done to prevent further attacks by the lions. The elders explained that the God of Israel watched over that place and would not allow anyone ignorant of His laws to dwell there. Therefore, if the king was concerned about the settlers, he should send Jewish priests to teach them the laws of God, and thus the Lord would be appeased. The king did as they suggested and sent a Hebrew priest to Samaria to teach the new inhabitants the law of God [4Kgs 17:24–28]. However, they did not accept all the divine books, but only the five books of Moses: Genesis, Exodus, Leviticus, Numbers, and Deuteronomy. Neither did they at first completely renounce impiety; but later they did give up their idols and worshipped God alone.

After the Jews returned from captivity, they were always suspicious of the newcomers, considering them to be Assyrian by race, and called them "Samaritans" after the mountain, Semeron. But the Samaritans reckoned themselves descendants of Abraham and Jacob: for Abraham was from Chaldea, as were they; and Jacob they considered to be their own because they possessed his well. To the Jews, then, the Samaritans were an abomination, as were all Gentiles. When the Jews wished to revile the Lord, they said, *Thou art a Samaritan* [Jn 8:48]; and the Lord Himself commanded His disciples, *Into any city of the Samaritans enter ye not* [Mt 10:5]. Why does the Evangelist provide these details about Jacob's ground and well? So that you will understand the woman's startling statement: *Our father, Jacob ... gave us this well* [Jn 4:12]. Sychar is another name for the town of Sykima [Shechem], whose inhabitants were massacred by Simeon and Levi, sons of Jacob, because their sister Dinah had been ravished by the son of the Sykimite ruler [Gen 34]. From all this we learn that the rejection of the Jews began long ago. When the Jews sinned against God, the Gentiles [i.e., the Samaritans] took possession of their land; and what the patriarchs had acquired through faith in Christ, their descendants—the Jews—lost through impiety. So it is nothing new that Gentiles have now entered into the kingdom of heaven in their place.

6b–8. Jesus therefore, being wearied with His journey, sat thus on the well: and it was about the sixth hour. There cometh a woman of Samaria to draw water. Jesus saith unto her, Give Me to drink. For His disciples were gone away unto the city to buy food. By saying that the Lord was *wearied with His journey*, the Evangelist shows us his humility and simplicity, for Christ did not use even a donkey on his journey, but walked on foot, teaching us to make do with less. He also indicates that the Lord did not journey in a leisurely manner, but purposefully. From this we should learn to labor diligently and attentively at God's work. The words *He sat thus* indicate that He sat unpretentiously on the ground by the well. He did so because it was *about the sixth hour*, high noon, and the Lord needed rest and refreshment from the intense heat of the day. Lest anyone accuse the Lord of inconsistency—forbidding His disciples to go near the Gentiles while He Himself went to the Samaritans—the Evangelist explains that He stopped there and conversed with the woman because He was tired and thirsty, in accordance with His human nature. When He asked the woman for drink, she showed her eagerness to learn. Was He to shun this woman so eager to learn, who thirsted to resolve her perplexity? Of course not! God, the Lover of man, could never act thus. Again, the Lord's utter simplicity is in evidence here. He is left all alone on the road, while His disciples have gone into the city to buy food. They gave so little attention to the demand of the stomach that they were out buying food at a time when most people are napping after dinner. They bought loaves of bread only, from which we too may learn to limit the variety of what we eat. Note the preciseness of the Evangelist. He did not assert, "It was the sixth hour," but instead, *It was about the sixth hour*, so careful was he to ensure the accuracy of every word of his Gospel.

9–11. Then saith the woman of Samaria unto Him, How is it that Thou, being a Jew, asketh drink of me, who am a woman of Samaria? For the Jews have no dealings with the Samaritans. Jesus answered and said unto her, If thou knewest the gift of God, and Who it is that saith to thee, Give Me to drink, thou wouldest have asked of Him, and He would have given thee living water. The woman saith unto Him, Sir, Thou hast nothing to draw with, and the well is deep: from whence then hast Thou that living water? The Samaritan woman concluded that the Lord was a Jew—presumably because of His appearance, dress, manner, and speech. This led her to ask, *How is it that Thou, being a Jew, asketh drink of me?* See how circumspect she is. If either of them had need of caution, it was the Lord, not her. For it was not the Samaritans who were forbidden to have contact with the Jews, but, as she says, *the Jews* who *have no dealings with the Samaritans*. Nonetheless, the woman attempted to correct Him out of concern that He would do something not permitted by His own Jewish law. The Lord does not reveal Who He is until the woman's virtue, prudence, and conscientiousness have all been manifested. Then He begins to speak of more profound things: *If thou knewest the gift of God....* This means, "If you knew what eternal and incorruptible blessings God bestows, and if you comprehended that I, being God, am able to give you these things, you would have asked for and received living water." The Lord calls the gift of the Holy Spirit *water* because it cleanses and refreshes those who receive it. It is not still, like the water in ponds and wells, but *living* and continuously gushing upwards. For the grace of the Holy Spirit makes the soul constantly active in doing good, and always ready for spiritual ascents. Of such living and active water did the Apostle Paul drink, causing him to forget *those things which are behind, and reach forth unto those which are before* [Phil 3:13]. Then *the woman saith unto Him, Sir.* She quickly discards her perception of Him as a lowly person and addresses Him as Sir. However, she has not yet perceived the depth of Christ's words. He means one thing by *water*; she understands something quite different.

12–15. Art Thou greater than our father Jacob, who gave us the well, and drank thereof himself, and his children, and his cattle? Jesus answered and said unto her, Whosoever drinketh of this water shall thirst again: but whosoever drinketh of the water that I shall give him shall never thirst; but the water that I shall give him shall be in him a well of water springing up into everlasting life. The woman saith unto him, Sir, give me this water, that I thirst not, neither come hither to draw. The woman claims Jacob as her ancestor, insisting that she shares the noble lineage of the Jews, and from the difference between the two kinds of water, at once infers the difference between the two who give them. "If You can give such water as You claim, truly You would be greater than Jacob who gave us this water." Behold, an astute woman indeed! She approves the sweetness of the water from Jacob's well, saying that the patriarch *drank thereof himself, and his sons*, and she praises its abundance, adding that there was enough for all *his cattle*. Then the woman asks, *Art Thou greater than our father Jacob?* Not having given any indication of His power, the Lord does not wish to appear boastful by stating plainly, "Yes, I am." But His answer implies that He is indeed greater. "*Whosoever drinketh of this water shall thirst again, but whosoever drinketh of the water that I shall give ... shall never thirst*. If you marvel at Jacob who gave you this water, much more should you be amazed at Me. For the water I give is far superior, and becomes a spring continuously abounding." The saints do not merely lay up the gifts of grace they receive from God. Rather, having accepted these gifts as seeds of virtue, they put them to use and thus increase them. The Lord teaches us to do the same in His parables of the talents and of the Good Samaritan.

The man who had been given two talents earned another two by putting them to work [Mt 25:17]; and to the innkeeper who received the man wounded by thieves the Lord promised, "Whatever more you have spent of your own, I will repay" [Lk 10:35]. This is what the Lord implies here: "I, too, give water to the thirsty, but what I give does not remain the same in quantity. Instead, it increases to overflowing and becomes a spring." The Lord gave Paul a small amount of water, namely, the teaching given by Ananias [Acts 9:17]; but Paul increased it, and it became a fountain pouring out torrents of preaching that flowed *from Jerusalem ... unto Illyricum* [Rom 15:19]. And how does the woman respond to the Lord's words? Still in a lowly manner, for she thought He was speaking about actual water. Yet she also shows signs of spiritual progress. Before, when she could not understand, she asked dubiously, *Whence then hast Thou that living water?* Now, without doubting she accepts Christ's words and begs, *Give me this water.* She shows herself to be wiser than Nicodemus, to whom the Lord gave a much lengthier explanation, but who still objected, *How can these things be?* [Jn 3:9] Already she esteems the Lord more highly than Jacob and his well, and says: "If You have such water, give it to me, and I will no longer come here to draw."

16–22. Jesus saith unto her, Go, call thy husband, and come hither. The woman answered and said, I have no husband. Jesus said unto her, Thou hast well said, I have no husband: for thou hast had five husbands; and he whom thou now hast is not thy husband; in that saidst thou truly. The woman saith unto Him, Sir, I perceive that Thou art a prophet. Our fathers worshipped in this mountain; and ye say, that in Jerusalem is the place where men ought to worship. Jesus saith unto her, Woman, believe Me, the hour cometh, when ye shall neither in this mountain, nor yet at Jerusalem, worship the Father. Ye worship ye know not what: we know what we worship; for salvation is of the Jews. Seeing the woman eager to receive what He offers and insistent that He give it, the Lord asks her to *call* her *husband*, as if bidding her to share His gift with him. She answers, *I have no husband*, striving at once to hide her sin and to receive the gift without delay. The Lord now discloses His prophetic power: He tells her how many husbands she has had, and reveals she is now living in sin. Does she become vexed at His rebuke? Does she flee from Him in shame? No, she marvels at Him, and becomes even more attentive, saying, *Sir, I perceive that Thou art a prophet*. Because her soul is filled with longing for wisdom and virtue, she then questions the Lord about divine doctrines and not about worldly things like health and money. *Our fathers worshipped in this mountain*. Here she refers to Abraham and Isaac; for the Samaritans believed it was on this mountain that Isaac was taken to be sacrificed [Gen 22]. "And how is it," she asks, "*ye say that in Jerusalem is the place where men ought to worship?*" Do you see how her thoughts are moving to a higher plane? Moments earlier her concern was how to avoid the daily trouble of satisfying her thirst; now she questions the Lord on issues of doctrine. Christ knows her capacity to understand spiritual things, but does not yet address her question. Instead He reveals a loftier teaching than He had disclosed to either Nicodemus or Nathaniel: "The time is coming when God will be worshipped neither here nor in Jerusalem. You are trying to prove that the worship of the Samaritans is superior to that of the Jews. But I say to you that neither one is the best: there will be another way, superior to both. Nonetheless, the worship of the Jews is holier than that of the Samaritans. *For ye worship ye know not what: we*, the Jews, *know what we worship*." Here Christ counts Himself a Jew, speaking in terms the woman can understand. She thinks of Him as a Jewish prophet, so He says, *We worship*. In what way did the Samaritans not know what they worshipped? They thought that God was limited to one location, their holy mountain. This is why, when the lions were attacking them, as related above, they sent word to the king of the Assyrians that the God *of that place* did not accept them. For this same reason, they continued a long time to worship idols and not God Himself. Most, but not all, of the Jews were free of this misconception and knew God to be the Lord of all; thus, *salvation is of the Jews*. This has two meanings for us. First, God's truth was revealed to the world through the Jews. The Jews were the first to know God and reject idols. Moreover, even many erroneous doctrines (such as the Samaritan notions about the worship of God) are merely distortions of Jewish teaching. Second, the Lord's advent, which was *from the Jews*, He calls "salvation." For the Lord—Who came *from the Jews* according to the flesh—is Salvation.

23–24. But the hour cometh, and now is, when the true worshippers shall worship the Father in spirit and in truth: for the Father seeketh such to worship Him. God is spirit: and they that worship Him must worship Him in spirit and in truth. "We Jews have a form of worship superior to yours; nevertheless, the worship of the Jews will also come to an end. Not only will the places of worship change, but the manner of worship as well. This change is at the very door, and *now is*; the statutes taught by the prophets will not last much longer." By *true worshippers* the Lord means those who live according to His law, who neither confine God to one place, as do the Samaritans, nor serve Him with a material worship, as do the Jews, but who worship Him *in spirit and in truth*, that is, with their soul and with purity of mind. Because God is *spirit*, which means He is bodiless, He must be worshipped in an incorporeal manner appropriate to the soul, which is both spiritual and bodiless. The Lord knew that many heretics would soon appear, seeming to worship Him incorporeally, but not holding to the Orthodox doctrine regarding His person. With this in mind, the Lord adds the words *and in truth*. For one must do both: worship God noetically, and hold to true doctrine regarding the nature of His being. By a different interpretation, some say that "spirit and truth" refer to the two aspects of our Christian philosophy: active virtue (πράξις, praxis) and divine vision (θεωρία, theoria). *In spirit* means "by activity." The Apostle Paul writes, *As many as are led by the Spirit of God ... mortify the deeds* (τάς πράξεις) *of the body* [Rom 8:13–14]. And again, *The desires of the flesh are against the spirit, and the desires of the spirit are against the flesh* [Gal 5:17]. Therefore, to worship the Father in spirit implies the active practice of the virtues (to subdue the flesh). To worship Him in truth implies contemplation of the divine. This is what Paul means when he writes, *Therefore let us keep the feast ... with the unleavened bread of sincerity and truth* [1Cor 5:8]. *Sincerity* refers to purity of life, which is active virtue; *truth* refers to divine vision (θεωρητιχου), which is, contemplation of the true dogma of the divine Word. By yet a third interpretation, *spirit* and *truth* may also be understood as follows. On the one hand, the Samaritans viewed God as a divinity limited to a particular location, and believed He must be worshipped only "in this place." On the other, all the religious observances of the Jews consisted of types and figures of things to come. Thus the words *in spirit* are addressed to the Samaritans: "You Samaritans offer to God a kind of worship that limits Him to one location. True worshippers will not be limited by locality; they will worship *in spirit*, which means, with mind and soul. Neither will they worship by means of types and figures, as do the Jews. Instead, they will worship *in truth*, in full reality, when the Jewish customs and observances have come to an end." Since the Judaic law, understood according to the letter, was a type and shadow, perhaps the words *in spirit* are contradistinctive to the letter of the law. (For the law of the letter no longer prevails among us, but in its place, the law of the spirit, *for the letter killeth, but the spirit giveth life* [2Cor 3:6].) And the words *in truth* are contradistinctive to the types and foreshadowings. Therefore the Lord proclaims that *the hour cometh, and* indeed *now is*. He is referring to the time of His advent in the flesh, when true worshippers will not worship in one place only, like the Samaritans, but in every place will offer immaterial worship according to the Spirit. Paul expresses the same thought when he writes, *God is my witness, Whom I worship with my spirit* [Rom 1:9]. Nor will true worshippers offer service to God that is a type and shadow of things to come, as did the Jews. Instead, they will offer true worship, containing nothing obscure. Such are the worshippers whom God seeks: spiritual, because He is spirit, and true, because He is truth.

25–27. The woman saith unto him, I know that the Messiah cometh, Who is called Christ: when He is come, He will tell us all things. Jesus saith unto her, I that speak unto thee am He. And upon this came His disciples, and marvelled that He talked with a woman: yet no man said, What seekest Thou? or, Why talkest Thou with her? How did the woman know *that the Messiah cometh*, *Who is called Christ?* From the writings of Moses, for the Samaritans accepted the five books of Moses, as we have already explained. Reading these, they knew the various prophecies concerning Christ, which tell that He is the Son of God. For example, when God said at the creation, *Let us make man* [Gen 1:26], the Father was speaking to the Son. When the three Angels visited Abraham, it was the Son Who spoke with Abraham in the tent [Gen 18]. When Jacob prophesied, *A ruler shall not fail from Judah … until there come the things stored up for Him, and He is the expectation of the nations* [Gen 49:10], he was referring to the Son. When Moses stated, *The Lord thy God shall raise up to thee a Prophet of thy brethren, like me; Him shall ye hear* [Dt 18:15], he was also speaking about the Son. From these and many other prophecies pointing to the coming of the Christ, the woman knew that *the Messiah cometh*. Having reached the opportune moment in their conversation, the Lord reveals himself to her. If He had said from the start, "I am the Christ," He would have put her off by appearing arrogant and presumptuous. Instead He leads her step by step to the point where she remembers that the Messiah will come; then He reveals Himself. But why to this woman, and not to the Jews who repeatedly demanded,

"Tell us if Thou art the Christ"? He said nothing to the Jews because the purpose of their questions was not to learn, but to have as many charges as possible to bring against Him. The Lord reveals Himself to this woman because she is honest and questions Him with a sincere intent: she desired simply to know the truth. This is clear from what follows: hearing His words, she at once believed, and led others into the net of faith, showing that her mind was both probing and believing. At just the right moment, when the Lord had finished teaching and conversing with the woman, the disciples returned. They were astounded at His humility when they saw Him, a man acclaimed by all, speaking meekly and compassionately with a poor woman, and moreover, one who was a Samaritan. But though astonished, they were not so presumptuous as to ask what He had been discussing with her, for they usually maintained the proper respect of disciples for their teacher. On certain other occasions they did act more boldly: for instance, when John leaned on His breast and inquired who would betray Him [Jn 13:23–25], or when they asked Him which of them would be the greatest in the kingdom of heaven [Mt 18:1], or when the sons of Zebedee requested that one of them sit at His right hand and the other at His left [Mk 10:35]. They were outspoken on these occasions because they wanted to know about seemingly important matters of direct concern to themselves. Here, however, such boldness would have been out of place. They had no need to ask about what did not pertain to them.

28–30. The woman then left her waterpot, and went her way into the city, and saith to the men, Come, see a man, who told me all things that ever I did: is not this the Christ? Then they went out of the city, and came unto Him. The Lord's words kindled such zeal in her heart that she *left her water pot*, straightway choosing Christ's water over that of Jacob's well. Ordained to the rank of apostle by the faith taking hold of her heart, she teaches an entire city and draws it to Christ.[1] *Come, see a man*, she says, *who told me all things that I ever did.* Her soul aflame with divine fire, she disregards all earthly consequences, even

---

1 The Church honors many great saints with the title "Equal of the apostles," including lay men and women who brought to Christ entire cities or kingdoms. Among them are: Mary Magdalene; Nina, Enlightener of Georgia; Constantine and Helena, Enlighteners of the Roman Empire; Cyril and Methodius, Enlighteners of the Slavs; and Vladimir and Olga, Enlighteners of Russia. [The Samaritan woman, Holy Martyr Photine, is commemorated Feb 26 Greek, March 20 Slav, and on the Fifth Sunday of Pascha.]

shame and dishonor. Behold, she is not afraid to declare her sins: *See a man who told me all things that ever I did.* She could have spoken more guardedly by saying, for instance, "Behold a prophet." Instead, she disregards her own reputation and thinks only to proclaim the truth. Nevertheless, she does not state categorically, "This is the Christ," but rather, *Is not this [perhaps] the Christ?* making the truth easier for the others to accept and encouraging them to reach the same conclusion themselves.[1] If she had insisted, "This is the Christ," they may have scoffed at her and rejected her proclamation out of hand as merely the opinion of a fallen woman.

Now there are some who understand the five husbands of the woman to represent the five books of Moses, the only part of the Old Testament that she, as a Samaritan, accepted. They also interpret Christ's words, *He whom thou now hast*, to mean, "The word which you have now received from Me *is not thy husband*," that is, "You have not yet been yoked to My teaching." The Samaritan woman may also be understood as a type of human nature, which formerly dwelt on a mountain, symbolizing the human mind originally filled with grace. Before he sinned, Adam was adorned with every divine gift, and was even a prophet. When he was raised from sleep he spoke prophetically of the fashioning of the woman and the husband's relationship to her: *This now is bone of my bones* and, *Therefore shall a man leave his father and his mother...* [Gen 2:23–24]. Our nature, then, was on this mountain; the human mind was exalted. But when it rebelled against God and transgressed, it was led away captive; and the devil, who had taken us prisoner, also took our nature's holy offspring, by which I mean all divine thoughts, and led them away to Babylon, that is, he subjected them to the confusion of this world. In their place the devil planted barbarous thoughts. These in turn were assailed by lions (symbolizing the noble thoughts which should exercise dominion over us) until these vile thoughts accepted divine truth. But they did not accept truth in its entirety, for the evil which had once settled on the mountain of our lofty mind was not altogether transformed into good: having accepted the law of Moses, it remained under the curse.

---

1 Μήτι οὗτός ἐστιν ὁ Χριστός; *Is not this [perhaps] the Christ?* The interrogative particle μήτι is used in Greek "by one asking doubtfully yet inclined to believe what he asks." (Thayer's Greek-English Lexicon of the New Testament.) This exactly describes the attitude so artfully adopted by the Samaritan woman in order to persuade her fellow citizens, according to the interpretation of Blessed Theophylact.

Therefore Jesus journeyed to us, that is, He took many paths and employed many stratagems to bring us salvation—sometimes issuing threats and warnings, sometimes striking us with calamities, sometimes showering us with blessings, sometimes promising us good things to come. When He had grown weary from His journey and employing all the methods devised for our correction, He found the final means for our salvation; being well-pleased, He sat down and rested. What was the final method? The font of Baptism, by which He brought salvation to our nature, as He did to the Samaritan woman. This spring may rightly be called the well of Jacob, that is, the well of him who seized the heel of his brother Esau and supplanted him.[1] For in the font of Baptism, where the Lord crushed the head of the dragon and gave him as food to the Ethiopian people, a man can trip up and vanquish the devil [see Ps 73:15]. By the dragon, understand the devil, who is the food and joy of those whose souls are black and have no share in the divine light. Five "husbands" have been yoked to our nature, namely, the various laws which God gave her: to Adam in paradise, to Noah, to Abraham, to Moses, and lastly, to the prophets. For Noah received a commandment after the flood, and Abraham received the law of circumcision [Gen9:1–17;17:10f.]. After our nature was wedded to these five laws, she took to herself a sixth, who was not her husband and whom she had not yet wedded—the law of the New Testament. But by a different interpretation, one might also understand this sixth, which was not our nature's husband, to be the law of idolatry. Indeed God did not give her this law for a husband; instead, she joined herself to it as an adulteress. Therefore the prophet cries, *She hath committed adultery with wood*, and, *They have fornicated under every tree* [Jer 3:6,9], referring to the pagan carvings and trees which Judah and Israel worshipped. Man has fallen headlong to such depths of senselessness as to worship lovely trees like the cypress and the plane simply because they are beautiful. Therefore, when our nature loved and

1 See Gen 25:26 and 27:36. When Rachel, the wife of Isaac, gave birth to twins, the younger twin, Jacob, seized the heel (πτέρνα) of the older, Esau. As an adult Jacob tricked and supplanted (ἐπτέρνικε) Esau on two occasions, first cheating him out of his birthright, which he bought with a mess of pottage, and later cheating him of his last blessing from his father. On the latter occasion Esau cried out in exasperation, *Rightly was his name called Jacob, for lo! this second time has he supplanted* (ἐπτέρνικε) *me*. In the writings of the holy fathers, Jacob becomes a type of the Christian who is enlightened by the grace of Baptism to struggle against his sins and passions, and by so doing trips up and vanquishes Satan.

embraced this sixth law and succumbed to idolatry as an adulterer, the Lord came and delivered us. This is why He says, *he whom thou now hast*; for by the time of Christ's appearing the wisest even of the Jews had been tainted by paganism. Thus the Pharisees believed in fate and practiced astrology. The Samaritan woman also represents every soul which, being yoked irrationally to the five senses, afterwards falls into the fornication of heresy, erring grievously in doctrine. On such a soul Jesus bestows blessings, whether through Baptism or through the font of tears. Tears may likewise be called *Jacob's well*, for they spring from a mind in which repentance has supplanted wickedness. From this water of repentance the mind drinks, together with *his children* (his thoughts) *and his cattle* (the powers of the soul, such as anger and desire, not endowed with reason). For tears bring refreshment to the soul, its thoughts, and its faculties.

The Source

Chapter Four, *The Explanation of the Holy Gospel According to John*, vol 4 of the series *Blessed Theophylact's Explanation of the New Testament*, by Blessed Theophylact, trans Fr Christopher Stade (House Springs, MO: Chrysostom Press, 2007), 63–74. Reprinted with permission.

The *Explanation* series covers the entire New Testament. So far, all of the Gospels and a few of the epistles have been translated into English.

Miscellanea

Font of Tears

An unconfirmed rumor has it that the first book assigned to novices on Mount Athos is Charles Dickens's *David Copperfield*. It softens up the heart and unclogs the tear ducts: a preparation for the work of repentance.

Rogues' Gallery

Heresies persist. After seemingly eradicated, they arise again and again in slightly different forms. In the fourth volume of *The Explanation* series (from which this selection is taken), Saint Theophylact uses Saint John's gospel to refute the major heresies, many of which had re-appeared in different guises by the time Saint Theophylact was writing (twelfth century). The editors at Chrysostom Press have conveniently appended to this volume useful descriptions of these heresies.

Contemporary heresies, or rather, the current re-packaging of old heresies, can be found in *Orthodoxy and Heterodoxy: Exploring Belief Systems through the Lens of the Ancient Christian Faith* by Andrew Stephen Damick.[1]

Christ is Preached?

Saint John Chrysostom, Patriarch of Constantinople [†407, Nov 13], led the Church at a time when older heresies were still thriving and newer ones burgeoning. Orthodox people were being snagged by the subtle, deviously crafted marketing of the heterodox.

In his homily titled "Concerning Lowliness of Mind,"[2] Saint John expands on a sentence from that day's particular reading: "Whether in pretense or in truth, Christ is preached; and I therein do rejoice, yea, and will rejoice" [Phil 1:18]. Saint John points out that people use this verse as an excuse to observe without qualm or concern the promulgation of heterodoxy. In our own day, we might take it even a step further, rally around the ubiquitous, non-Orthodox preachers, and cry, "But Christ is being preached!"

The imprisoned Saint Paul writes, "Many of the brethren in the Lord, waxing confident by my bonds, are much more bold to speak the word without fear. Some indeed preach Christ even of envy and strife; and some also of good will" [Phil 1:14–15]. Saint John explains that those who were preaching from nefarious motives—in order to speed Saint Paul's execution—were nonetheless preaching the unadulterated Gospel.

Saint Paul could not have rejoiced were it otherwise, for he says to the Galatians, "If any one preaches to you a gospel besides what ye have received,

1 Chesterton, IN: Conciliar Media Ministries, 2011.

2 *Nicene and Post-Nicene Fathers* (First Series) 9:148–153.

let him be anathema, were it even I, were it even an angel from the heavens" [Gal 1:8–9]. Saint Paul rejoices in the furtherance of the true Gospel *and* zealously guards his flock from the slightest deviation.

How complacent, then, should Orthodox be about heterodox preaching?

Many Orthodox, eager to increase their knowledge of the Faith but unaware of the danger of heterodoxy or of the many trustworthy Orthodox resources currently available, turn to heterodox books and personalities for guidance and instruction. Rather, we need to immerse ourselves in Orthodoxy. By honing our Orthodox sensibility and sensitivity, we become gradually more adept at seeing, hearing, detecting non-Orthodox diversions. This is not a lifelong ban from interaction with useful heterodox resources, but we must wise up to avoid being derailed by either well-intentioned ignorance or malicious falsehood and misdirection.

Believed Everywhere, Always, by All

Saint Vincent of Lerins [†c.450, May 24] parallels this concern in *A Commonitory* ["calling to mind," a reminder or remembrancer].

> All possible care must be taken that we hold that faith which has been believed everywhere, always, by all. . . . This rule we shall observe if we follow universality, antiquity, consent. We shall follow universality if we confess that one faith to be true, which the whole Church throughout the world confesses; antiquity, if we in no wise depart from those interpretations which it is manifest were notoriously[1] held by our holy ancestors and fathers; consent, in like manner, if in antiquity itself we adhere to the consentient definitions and determinations of all, or at the least of almost all priests and doctors.

1 ["Notoriously" meaning "well-known," not the modern, pejorative sense of "well-known for being bad."]

* * *

But some one will say perhaps, Shall there, then, be no progress in Christ's Church? Certainly; all possible progress. For what being is there, so envious of men, so full of hatred to God, who would seek to forbid it? Yet on condition that it be real progress, not alteration of the faith. For progress requires that the subject be enlarged in itself, alteration, that it be transformed into something else. The intelligence, then, the knowledge, the wisdom, as well of individuals as of all, as well of one man as of the whole Church, ought, in the course of ages and centuries, to increase and make much and vigorous progress; but yet only in its own kind; that is to say, in the same doctrine, in the same sense, and in the same meaning.[1]

Saint Vincent also discusses stratagems used by heretics to deceive the faithful, why God allows bishops to go astray (and possibly lead their flocks to perdition), but also how to protect against error.

Immersion in Orthodoxy

And so I entreat you (not I, though, but the love of Jesus Christ) not to nourish yourselves on anything but Christian [Orthodox] fare, and have no truck with the alien herbs of heresy. There are men who in the very act of assuring you of their good faith will mingle poison with Jesus Christ; which is like offering a lethal drug in a cup of honeyed wine, so that the unwitting victim blissfully accepts his own destruction with a fatal relish.[2]

— Saint Ignatius of Antioch

1 *Nicene and Post-Nicene Fathers* (Second Series) 11:132, 147.

2 St Ignatius of Antioch [†c.110, Dec 20], "Epistle to the Trallians," in *Early Christian Writings: The Apostolic Fathers*, trans Maxwell Staniforth (London: Penguin Classics, 1968, Revised 1987), 80. Copyright © Maxwell Staniforth, 1968. Reproduced by permission of Penguin Books Ltd.

Also available in *The Epistles of St. Clement of Rome and St. Ignatius of Antioch* (New York: Paulist Press [Ancient Christian Writers series]), 77.

6. The Mystery of Knowledge

In the following essay, excerpted from "The Theory of Knowledge of Saint Isaac the Syrian," twentieth-century **Saint Justin Popovich** *[†1979, Mar 25/Apr 7] explains the Orthodox understanding of knowledge according to seventh-century* **Saint Isaac the Syrian** *[†c.700, Jan 28]. Like all the Holy Fathers, Saint Justin does not reinterpret Orthodox Tradition but simply re-articulates it for contemporary ears.*

Here he explains that Orthodox understanding differs radically from the fragmented and self-limiting Science, Realism, and Rationalism of the Western mindset. By healing and purification through asceticism and the practice of the virtues, the organs of human understanding apprehend knowledge in a different way—a truly different way of knowing.

Truth is objectively given in the person of Christ, the God-man. But the way in which this becomes subjective—that is, the practical side of the Christian theory of knowledge—was fully developed by the Fathers, those experienced, holy, and evangelical philosophers. Among the most outstanding of these holy philosophers was the great ascetic, Saint Isaac the Syrian. In his writings, with a rare understanding based on experience, he traces the process of the healing and purification of man's organs of knowledge, his growth in understanding and his progressive path through experience to the apprehension of eternal Truth. In the philosophy of Saint Isaac the Syrian, based on the experience of grace, the principles and methodology of the Orthodox theory of knowledge have found one of their most perfect expressions.

* * *

Analyzing man by his empirical gifts, Saint Isaac the Syrian finds that his organs of understanding are sick. "Evil is a sickness of soul,"[1] whence all

[1] [All quotations are from Saint Isaac's writings, translated here from the Serbian of

the organs of understanding are made sick. Evil has its perceptions, the passions, and "the passions are illnesses of the soul." Evil and the passions are not natural to the soul. . . .

A feeble soul, a diseased intellect, a weakened heart and will—in brief, sick organs of understanding—can only engender, fashion and produce sick thoughts, sick feelings, sick desires, and sick knowledge. . . .

Since the passions are a sickness of the soul, the soul can only be healed by purification from the passions and from evil. The virtues are the health of the soul, as the passions are its sickness. The virtues are the remedies that progressively eliminate sickness from the soul and from the organs of understanding. This is a slow process, demanding much effort and great patience.

* * *

"In what does purity of intellect differ from purity of heart? Purity of intellect is one thing, but purity of heart is another. For the intellect is one of the senses of the soul, but the heart contains the interior senses and governs them. It is their root. And if the root is holy, then the branches are also holy. If then, the heart is purified, clearly all the senses are purified."

The heart acquires purity by means of many trials, tribulations, and tears, and by the mortifying of all that is of the world. Tears cleanse the heart from impurity. To the question: what is the sign by which one can know if a man has achieved purity of heart, Saint Isaac replies: "When he sees all men as good, and no one appears to him to be unclean or profane."

Purity of heart and intellect are acquired through asceticism. "Asceticism is the mother of holiness."

* * *

The healing and purification of the organs of human knowledge are brought about by the common action of God and man—by the grace of God and the will of man. On the long path of purification and healing, knowledge itself becomes purer and healthier. At every stage of its development, knowledge depends on the ontological structure and the ethical state of its organs. Purified and healed by a man's striving in the evangelical virtues, the organs of knowledge themselves acquire holiness and

---

Saint Justin's article. For a complete English translation, see Saint Isaac the Syrian, *The Ascetical Homilies of Saint Isaac the Syrian* (Boston: Holy Transfiguration Monastery, 1984 [revised 2nd edition 2011]).]

purity. A pure heart and pure mind engender pure knowledge. The organs of knowledge, when purified, healed, and turned towards God, give a pure and healthy knowledge of God and, when turned towards creation, give a pure and healthy knowledge of creation.

According to the teaching of Saint Isaac the Syrian, there are two sorts of knowledge: that which precedes faith and that which is born of faith. The former is natural knowledge, and involves the discernment of good and evil. The latter is spiritual knowledge, and is "the perception of the mysteries," "the perception of what is hidden," "the contemplation of the invisible."

There are also two sorts of faith: the first comes through hearing and is confirmed and proven by the second, "the faith of contemplation," "the faith that is based on what has been seen." In order to acquire spiritual knowledge, a man must first be freed from natural knowledge. This is the work of faith. It is by the ascesis of faith that there comes to man that "unknown power" that makes him capable of spiritual knowledge. If a man allows himself to be caught in the web of natural knowledge, it is more difficult for him to free himself from it than to cast off iron bonds, and his life is lived "against the edge of a sword."

When a man begins to follow the path of faith, he must lay aside once and for all his old methods of knowing, for faith has its own methods. Then natural knowledge ceases and spiritual knowledge takes its place. Natural knowledge is contrary to faith, for faith, and all that comes from faith, is "the destruction of the laws of knowledge"—though not of spiritual, but of natural knowledge.

The chief characteristic of natural knowledge is its approach by examination and experimentation. This is in itself "a sign of uncertainty about the truth." Faith, on the contrary, follows a pure and simple way of thought that is far removed from all guile and methodical examination. These two paths lead in opposite directions. The house of faith is "childlike thoughts and simplicity of heart," for it is said: Glorify God "in simplicity of heart" [Col 3:22], and: "Except ye be converted and become as little children, ye shall not enter into the kingdom of heaven" [Mt 18:3]. Natural knowledge stands opposed both to simplicity of heart and simplicity of thought. This knowledge only works within the limits of nature, "but faith has its own path beyond nature."

The more a man devotes himself to the ways of natural knowledge, the more he is seized on by fear and the less he can free himself from it.

But if he follows faith, he is immediately freed and "as a son of God, has the power to make free use of all things." "The man who loves this faith acts like God in the use of all created things," for to faith is given the power "to be like God in making a new creation." Thus it is written: "Thou desiredst, and all things are presented before thee" [cf. Job 23:13 LXX]. Faith can often "bring forth all things out of nothing," while knowledge can do nothing "without the help of matter." Knowledge has no power over nature, but faith has such power. Armed with faith, men have entered into the fire and quenched the flames, being untouched by them. Others have walked on the waters as on dry land. All these things are "beyond nature"; they go against the modes of natural knowledge and reveal the vanity of such modes. Faith "moves about above nature." The ways of natural knowledge ruled the world for more than five thousand years, and man was unable to "lift his gaze from the earth and understand the might of his Creator" until "our faith arose and delivered us from the shadows of the works of this world" and from a fragmented mind. He who has faith "will lack nothing," and, when he has nothing, "he possesses all things by faith," as it is written: "All things, whatsoever ye shall ask in prayer, believing, ye shall receive" [Mt 21:22]; and also: "The Lord is near; be anxious for nothing" [Phil 4:5–6].

Natural laws do not exist for faith. Saint Isaac emphasizes this very strongly: "All things are possible to him that believeth" [Mk 9:23], for with God nothing is impossible. Natural knowledge constrains its disciples from "drawing near to that which is alien to nature," to that which is above nature.

This natural knowledge to which Saint Isaac refers appears in modern philosophy under three headings: realism based on the senses, epistemological criticism, and monism.[1] These three approaches all limit the power,

---

[1] ["On one hand, realism brings man down to the level of the senses, and then through the senses to things, to matter, so that a man is no longer his own master but scattered among things. On the other hand, rationalism separates man and his understanding, seeing the latter as the chief fount of truth and the highest measure of all that is, attributing all worth to it, making it an absolute and idolizing it, while at the same time belittling the other psychic and physical powers of man. Critical thought, for its part, is little more than an apologia for a rationalism and sensualism that drags the understanding, and man with it, down to the level of the senses. As for pantheism and all such monistic systems, they regard the world and man as a mass of contradictory opposites which can never be brought to a single, logical unity. All of these philosophical systems have the same result: a superficial, phenomenalist understanding both of man and of the world."—Excerpted from earlier in the original article.]

reality, force, worth, criteria, and extent of knowledge to within the bounds of visible nature—to the extent that these coincide with the limits of the human senses as organs of knowledge. To step beyond the limits of nature and to enter into the realm of the supernatural is considered to be against nature, as something irrational and impossible, forbidden to the followers of the three philosophical paths in question. Directly or indirectly, man is limited to his senses and dare not pass beyond them.

Nevertheless, this natural knowledge, according to Saint Isaac, is not at fault. It is not to be rejected. It is just that faith is higher than it is. This knowledge is only to be condemned in so far as, by the different means it uses, it turns against faith. But when this knowledge "is joined with faith, becoming one with her, clothing itself in her burning thoughts," when it "acquires wings of passionlessness," then, using other means than natural ones, it rises up from the earth "into the realm of its Creator," into the supernatural. This knowledge is then fulfilled by faith and receives the power to "rise to the heights," to perceive Him Who is beyond all perception and to "see the brightness that is incomprehensible to the mind and knowledge of created beings." Knowledge is the level from which a man rises up to the heights of faith. When he reaches these heights, he has no more need of it, for it is written: "We know in part, but when that which is perfect is come, then that which is in part shall be done away" [1Cor 13:9–10]. Faith reveals to us now the truth of perfection, as if it were before our eyes. It is by faith that we learn that which is beyond our grasp—by faith and not by enquiry and the power of knowledge.[1]

The works of righteousness are: fasting, almsgiving, vigils, purity of body, love of one's neighbor, humbleness of heart, the forgiveness of sins, pondering on heavenly good things, study of the mysteries of Holy Scripture, the engagement of the mind in the higher works—these and

[1] ["There exist three states of soul: natural, unnatural, and supernatural. 'The natural state of the soul is the knowledge of God's creation, both visible and spiritual. The supernatural state of the soul is the contemplation of the super-essential Divinity. The unnatural state of the soul is its involvement in the passions,' for the passions do not belong to its nature. Passion is an unnatural state of the soul, but virtue is its natural state. When the mind is fed by the virtues, especially that of compassion, the soul is then 'adorned with that holy beauty' through which man is indeed in the likeness of God. The 'holy beauty' of man's being is revealed in a pure heart, and the more a man develops this holy beauty within himself, the more he will see the beauty of God's creation." —Excerpted from later in the original article.]

all the other virtues are steps by which the soul rises to the highest realms of faith.

There are three spiritual modes [degrees] in which knowledge rises and falls, and by which it moves and changes. These are the body, the soul and the spirit. Although knowledge is a single whole by its nature, it changes the way and form of its action in relation to each of these three. "Knowledge is a gift of God to the nature of rational beings, given to them at the beginning, at their creation. It is naturally simple and undivided, like the light from the sun, but in its function in relation to the body, the soul, and the spirit it changes and becomes divided."

At its lowest level, knowledge "follows the desires of the flesh," concerning itself with riches, vainglory, dress, repose of body and the search for rational wisdom. This knowledge invents the arts and sciences and all that adorns the body in this visible world. But in all this, such knowledge is contrary to faith. It is known as "mere knowledge, for it is deprived of all thought of the divine and, by its fleshly character, brings to the mind an irrational weakness, because in it the mind is overcome by the body and its entire concern is for the things of this world." It is puffed up and filled with pride, for it refers every good work to itself and not to God. That which the Apostle said, "knowledge puffeth up" [1Cor 8:1], was obviously said of this knowledge, which is not linked with faith and hope in God, and not of true knowledge. True, spiritual knowledge, linked with humility, brings to perfection the soul of those who have acquired it, as is seen in Moses, David, Isaiah, Peter, Paul, and all those who, within the limits of human nature, were counted worthy of this perfect knowledge. "With them, knowledge is always immersed in pondering things strange to this world, in divine revelations and lofty contemplation of spiritual things and ineffable mysteries. In their eyes, their own souls are but dust and ashes." Knowledge that comes of the flesh is criticized by Christians, who see it as opposed not only to faith but to every act of virtue.

It is not difficult to see that in this first and lowest degree of knowledge of which Saint Isaac speaks is included virtually the whole of European philosophy, from naive realism to idealism—and all science from the atomism of Democrates to Einstein's relativity.

From the first and lowest degree of knowledge, man moves on to the second, when he begins both in body and soul to practice the virtues: fasting, prayer, almsgiving, the reading of Holy Scripture, the struggle with the passions, and so forth. Every good work, every goodly disposition of the soul in this second degree of knowledge, is begun and performed by the Holy Spirit through the working of this particular knowledge. The heart is shown the paths that lead to faith, even though this knowledge remains "bodily and composite."

The third degree of knowledge is that of perfection. "When knowledge rises up above the earth and the care for earthly things and begins to examine its own interior and hidden thoughts, scorning that from which the evil of the passions springs and rising up to follow the way of faith in concern for the life to come ... and in the seeking out of hidden mysteries—then faith takes this knowledge into itself and absorbs it, returning and giving birth to it from the beginning, so as to become itself 'from the beginning,' so as to become itself wholly spirit." Then it can "take wing and fly to the realm of incorporeal spirits and plumb the depths of the fathomless ocean, pondering on the divine and wondrous things that govern the nature of spiritual and physical beings and penetrating the spiritual mysteries that can only be grasped by a simple and supple mind. Then the inner senses awaken to the work of the spirit in those things that belong to that other realm, immortal and incorruptible. This knowledge has, in a hidden way, here in this world, received already spiritual resurrection so as to bear true witness to the renewal of all things."

These, according to Saint Isaac, are the three degrees of knowledge with which the whole of man's life is linked in body, soul and spirit. From the moment that he "begins to discern between good and evil to the moment of his leaving this world," the soul's knowledge is composed of one or all of these three degrees.

The first degree of knowledge "cools the soul's ardor for endeavors on God's path." The second "rekindles it for the swift path that leads to faith." The third is a "rest from toil," when the mind "feasts on the mysteries of the life to come." "But, as nature cannot as yet wholly rise to the level of deathlessness and overcome the weight of the flesh and perfect itself in spiritual knowledge, not even this third degree of knowledge is able to move towards total perfection, so as to live in the world of death and yet leave behind completely fleshly nature." While a man is in the flesh, therefore, he passes from one degree of knowledge to another. He has the help of grace, but is hindered by the demons, "for he is not totally free in this imperfect world." Every work of knowledge consists in "effort and constant practice," but the work of faith "does not consist in acts," but in spiritual thoughts and in purity of soul, and this is above the senses. For faith is subtler than knowledge, as knowledge is subtler than the senses. All the saints who attained to such a life "abide by faith in the delights of a life above nature." This faith is born in the soul through the light of grace which, "by the testimony of the mind, sustains the heart that it may not be uncertain in hope—in a hope that is far removed from all presumption." This faith has "spiritual eyes" which perceive "the mysteries hidden in the soul, hidden riches that are concealed from the eyes of sons of the flesh" but are revealed by the Holy Spirit, Who is received by the disciples of Christ [cf. Jn 14:15–17]. The Holy Spirit is "the holy power" that abides within a man of Christ, preserving and defending his soul and body from evil. This invisible power is perceived with the eyes of faith by those whose minds are enlightened and sanctified. It is known to the saints "through experience."

To explain yet more clearly the mystery of knowledge, Saint Isaac presents further definitions of both knowledge and faith. "The knowledge that is concerned with the visible and sensual is called natural; the knowledge that is concerned with the spiritual and incorporeal is called spiritual, for it receives its perception through the spirit, and not through the senses. The knowledge that comes by divine power, however, is known as supernatural. It is unknowable and is higher than knowledge." "The soul does not receive this contemplation from the matter that is outside it," as is the case with the first two kinds of knowledge, "but it comes unexpectedly by itself as an immaterial gift contained within itself, according to the words of Christ: 'The kingdom of God is within you' [Lk 17:21]. There is no point awaiting its appearance in some outward form, for it does not come 'with observation'" [Lk 17:20].

The first knowledge comes "from continual study and the desire to learn. The second comes from a proper way of life and a clearly held faith. The third comes from faith alone, for in it knowledge is done away, activity ceases, and the senses become superfluous." For the mysteries of the Spirit, "which are beyond knowledge and are not apprehended either by the bodily senses nor the rational powers of the mind, God has given us a faith by which we know only that these mysteries exist." The Savior calls the coming of the Comforter "the gifts of the revelation of the mysteries of the Spirit" [cf. Jn 14:16,26], and it is therefore seen that the perfection of spiritual knowledge consists "in the receiving of the Spirit, as did the apostles." "Faith is the gateway to the mysteries. As bodily eyes see material things, so faith looks with spiritual eyes on that which is hidden." When a man passes through the gate of faith, God leads him into "the spiritual mysteries and opens the sea of faith to his understanding."

All the virtues have a role to play in this spiritual knowledge, for it is the fruit of the practice of the virtues. Faith "engenders the fear of God," and from this fear of God follow repentance and the practice of the virtues, which itself gives birth to spiritual knowledge. This knowledge, "coming from long experience and practice of the virtues, is pleasant" and gives a man great power. The first and chief basis of spiritual knowledge is a healthy soul, a healthy organ of knowledge. "Knowledge is the fruit of a healthy soul," while a healthy soul is the result of long practice of the evangelical virtues. The "healthy of soul" are the perfect, and it is to them that knowledge is given.

It is very difficult, and often impossible, to express in words the mystery and nature of knowledge. In the realm of human thought, there is no ready definition that can explain it completely. Saint Isaac therefore gives many different definitions of knowledge. He is continually exercised in this matter, and the problem stands like a burning question mark before the eyes of this holy ascetic. The saint presents answers from his rich and blessed experience, achieved through long and hard ascesis. But the most profound, and to my mind the most exhaustive answer that man can give to this question is that given by Saint Isaac in the form of a dialogue:

"Question: What is knowledge?

"Answer: The perception of eternal life.

"Question: And what is eternal life ?

"Answer: To perceive all things in God. For love comes through understanding, and the knowledge of God is ruler over all desires. To the heart that receives this knowledge every delight that exists on earth is superfluous, for there is nothing that can compare with the delight of the knowledge of God."

Knowledge is therefore victory over death, the linking of this life with immortal life and the uniting of man with God. The very act of knowledge touches on the immortal, for it is by knowledge that man passes beyond the limits of the subjective and enters the realm of the trans-subjective. And when the trans-subjective object is God, then the mystery of knowledge becomes the mystery of mysteries and the enigma of enigmas. Such knowledge is a mystical fabric woven on the loom of the soul by the man who is united with God.

For human knowledge the most vital problem is that of truth. Knowledge bears within itself an irresistible pull towards the infinite mystery, and this hunger for truth that is instinctive to human knowledge is never satisfied until eternal and absolute Truth itself becomes the substance of human knowledge—until knowledge, in its own self-perception, acquires the perception of God, and in its own self-knowledge comes to the knowledge of God. But this is given to man only by Christ, the God-man, He Who is the only incarnation and personification of eternal truth in the world of human realities. When a man has received the God-man into himself as the soul of his soul and the life of his life, then that man is constantly filled with the knowledge of eternal truth.

What is truth? Saint Isaac answers thus: "Truth is the perception of things that is given by God." In other words: the perception of God is truth. If this perception exists in a man, he both has and knows the truth. If he does not have this perception, then truth does not exist for him. Such a man may always be seeking truth, but he will never find it until he comes to the perception of God, in which lie both the perception and knowledge of truth.

It is the man who restores and transforms his organs of knowledge by the practice of the virtues that comes to the perception and knowledge of the truth. For him faith and knowledge, and all that goes with them, are one indivisible and organic whole. They fulfill and are fulfilled by one another, and each confirms and supports the other. "The light of the mind gives birth to faith," says Saint Isaac, "and faith gives birth to the consolation of hope, while hope fortifies the heart. Faith is the enlightenment of the understanding. When the understanding is darkened, then faith hides itself and fear holds sway, cutting off hope. Faith, which bathes the understanding in light, frees man from pride and doubt, and is known as 'the knowledge and manifestation of the truth.'"

Holy knowledge comes from a holy life, but pride darkens that holy knowledge. The light of truth increases and decreases according to a man's way of life. Terrible temptations fall upon those who seek to live a spiritual life. The ascetic of faith must therefore pass through great sufferings and misfortunes in order to come to knowledge of the truth.

A troubled mind and chaotic thoughts are the fruit of a disordered life, and these darken the soul. When the passions are driven from the soul with the help of the virtues, when "the curtain of the passions is drawn back from the eyes of the mind," then the intellect can perceive the glory of the other world. The soul grows by means of the virtues, the mind is confirmed in the truth and becomes unshakable, "girded for encountering and slaying every passion." Freedom from the passions is brought about by the crucifying of both the intellect and the flesh. This makes a man capable of contemplating God. The intellect is crucified when unclean thoughts are driven out of it, and the body when the passions are uprooted. "A body given over to pleasure cannot be the abode of the knowledge of God."

True knowledge—"the revelation of the mysteries"—is attained by means of the virtues, and this is "the knowledge that saves." The chief characteristic—and "proof"—of this knowledge is humility. When the intellect "abides in the realm of knowledge of the truth," then all questioning ceases, and a great calm and peace descend upon it. This peace of mind is called "perfect health." When the power of the Holy Spirit enters into the soul, then the soul "learns through the Spirit."

The Source

St Justin Popovich, "The Theory of Knowledge of St Isaac the Syrian," trans Mother Maria (Rule), *Sourozh* Magazine no 15 (Feb 1984), no 16 (May 1984), and no 17 (Aug 1984). Used with permission.

Miscellanea

Magazines

Periodicals have their own charm for readers: the size and feel, the novelty, the occasional surprise in the mailbox. Although *Sourozh* Magazine, the source of the preceding article, is not currently in publication, its back issues demonstrate the enduring value of Orthodox periodicals. This article and the two other magazine samples (chapter 4, "The Unity of Christ's Ideal," and chapter 11, "Glory to God") give only a glimpse of the variety of topics and types and styles of writing that these magazines make available. Besides letters from saints and illuminating essays, as we have seen, there are also homilies, histories, lives of saints, book excerpts, and assorted theological and practical considerations. Moreover, subscriptions provide financial support to the monasteries that publish them.

As this book goes to press, highly recommended periodicals include:

Orthodox Life from Holy Trinity Monastery, Jordanville, New York;

The Orthodox Word from the St Herman of Alaska Brotherhood, Platina, California;

The True Vine from The Holy Orthodox Metropolis of Boston (Holy Transfiguration Monastery, Brookline, Massachusetts);

Living Orthodoxy from the St John of Kronstadt Press, Agape Community, Liberty, Tennessee; and

Orthodox Tradition from the Center for Traditionalist Orthodox Studies, Etna, California. Many of the editorial Questions & Answers from past issues of this magazine have been consolidated into a thin, two-volume set, *Orthodox Insights*. Volume I deals with liturgical matters, Volume II with theological, pastoral, and ecclesiastical concerns. For example, a reader inquires about the very distracting censing that takes place during the reading of the Apostle in the Divine Liturgy. The editor responds that the censing is to be done during the pre-Gospel Alleluias, obviating any competition with the Apostle. *Voilà*.

Saint Justin Books

The preceding excerpt is only a fourth of the original. The complete article can be found in two books of Saint Justin essays.[1] *Man and the God-Man* from Sebastian Press (2008) contains: Perfect God and Perfect Man; The God-man: The Foundation of the Truth of Orthodoxy; The Supreme Value and Infallible Criterion; Sentenced to Immortality; Humanistic and

1 A third book with St Justin essays is *The Struggle for Faith and Other Writings of Bishop Nikolai Velimirovich and Archimandrite Justin Popovich*, vol 4 of A Treasury of Serbian Orthodox Spirituality [Out-of-Print?], Diocese of New Gracanica (1989). Its selections overlap the other two books, but does not contain the Theory of Knowledge.

Theanthropic Culture; Humanistic and Theanthropic Education; The Theory of Knowledge of St Isaac the Syrian; A Deer in a Lost Paradise. The full article also appears in *Orthodox Faith and Life in Christ*, ed Father Asterios Gerostergios, Institute for Byzantine and Modern Greek Studies (1994). It contains: The Inward Mission of Our Church; Introduction to the Lives of the Saints; Humanistic and Theanthropic Education; Reflections on the Infallibility of European Man; The Theory of Knowledge of St Isaac the Syrian; Humanistic Ecumenism; and a Selective List of titles published 1922–1980.

Environmental Interference

In the commercially spectacular, entertainingly enthralling, technologically pervasive roar we inhabit, we are often influenced to buy things we don't need or want, to conform to fickle fads and fashions, and to "follow" people or issues—real or fictitious or somewhere in between—that really have nothing to do with us. In the same way, spurious, misleading, non-Orthodox concepts, assumptions, ways of thinking can become deeply engrained in us, deeply rooted. One frequently heard example: "Every other Sunday we go to the [your choice of non-Orthodox] church with the spouse's family. *It's all the same God, isn't it?*" So-called cradle Orthodox are as susceptible to these distortions as the increasing number of converts. Attention is required to recognize these erroneous notions, and effort to root them out. Without this watchfulness, Orthodoxy becomes mere veneer, an empty designation, just another believe-whatever-you-want denomination.

The following books may help to sort this out.

Common Ground: An Introduction to Eastern Christianity for the American Christian by Jordan Bajis.[1] Although intended for non-Orthodox, this book is actually useful for Orthodox. The author describes what Western denominations believe and how they arrived at their particular beliefs. Some Orthodox may discover that they agree with them. The author then explains, "But the Eastern Church believes...." This helps to sift out what we have absorbed from our atmosphere and to reinforce our right Faith. Despite the book's tragic ending, it is a straightforward read. It also provides lengthy, information-packed chapter endnotes for those who appreciate detailed

1 Minneapolis: Light and Life Publishing, 2006 (5th revised edition).

expansion and original-source quotations. For missionary-minded people, the book could additionally provide a bridge to Catholic or Protestant friends, co-workers, associates.

The Ancestral Sin by Fr John S. Romanides.[1] Originally a doctoral thesis, this book is neither turgid nor obscure. It clearly explains the difference between the Eastern and Western—the patristic and the scholastic—interpretations of the Fall of Man and how it affects everything built on these differing foundations. To start with, we do not inherit the *guilt* of Adam and Eve's disobedience, but only the consequences: the passions, corruption, and death.

Nihilism: The Root of the Revolution of the Modern Age by Eugene (Father Seraphim) Rose.[2] To emphasize again, many of our assumptions seep into us from our toxic environment, from the "spirit of the age." This book explains what nihilism is under its deceptive coverings, its origin, and its effect on individuals and society. Readers may wish to re-examine ideas, convictions, or mindsets that seem so obvious that they have never thought them through. Artists and academics may find this book especially germane.

Relativism: Feet Firmly Planted in Mid-Air by Francis J. Beckwith and Gregory Koukl.[3] Moral relativism is a complete lack of critical evaluation, yet it paralyzes many Christian individuals and communities. "Who are you to judge?" On the surface it sounds reasonable and may even echo for us the gospel teaching, "Judge not, that ye be not judged." The confusion, however, lies in the meanings of "judge." We are not to *condemn* our neighbor, but it is clearly incumbent upon us to *discern* between good and evil, which is more than "if it feels good, do it." When relativists cry, "Don't force your morality on me," they are actually forcing *their* morality on *us*. It is utter hypocrisy! or as the book's authors calmly explain, the argument is self-refuting. The authors develop their logical arguments within the Catholic/scholastic "morality for morality's sake." This can be interesting and even helpful, but the reader should not be derailed from the Orthodox "morality for Christ's sake" (orthopraxis, right action, right living). In any case, this practical book provides surer footing in the morass of contemporary discourse.

1 Ridgewood, NJ: Zephyr Publishing, 2002.
2 Platina, CA: St Herman of Alaska Brotherhood, 2009.
3 Grand Rapids, MI: Baker Books, 1998.

Much is said about the "Western captivity" of Orthodox theology in recent centuries; when will we realize that it is a far more drastic "Western captivity" in which every Orthodox Christian finds himself today, a helpless prisoner of the "spirit of the times," of the dominating current of worldly philosophy which is absorbed in the very air we breathe in an apostate, God-hating society? An Orthodox Christian who is not consciously fighting against the vain philosophy of this age simply accepts it into himself, and is at peace with it because his own understanding of Orthodoxy is distorted, does not conform to the patristic standard.[1]

When they are giving the teaching of the Church, the holy Fathers (if only they are genuine holy Fathers and not merely ecclesiastical writers of uncertain authority) do not contradict each other, even if to our feeble understanding there seem to be contradictions between them. It is academic rationalism that pits one Father against another, traces their "influence" on each other, divides them into "schools" and "factions," and finds "contradictions" between them. All of this is foreign to the Orthodox Christian understanding of the holy Fathers. For us the Orthodox teaching of the holy Fathers is one single whole, and since the whole of Orthodox teaching is obviously not contained in any one Father (for all the Fathers are human and thus limited), we find parts of it in one Father and other parts in another Father, and one Father explains what is obscure in another Father; and it is not even of primary importance for us who said what, as long as it is Orthodox and in harmony with the whole patristic teaching.[2]

---

[1] Fr Seraphim Rose [†1982], *Genesis, Creation, and Early Man: The Orthodox Christian Vision*, ed Hieromonk Damascene, 2nd ed (Platina, CA: St Herman of Alaska Brotherhood, 2011), 497. Used with permission.

[2] Ibid., 447.

7. The Communion of Saints

The Christian life is not lived alone. The lone, desert hermits understood as much. God is Our Father, across the planet and across time—and even in our own parish. Who are these people we see on Sundays? the people standing around? the people in the icons?

The three chapters of this section provide an example of the way in which what we believe translates into how we believe. This first article, "The Communion of Saints" by Metropolitan Kallistos (Ware), explains what *we believe about the saints. The second article, "Valentine," addresses the "so what?" that is, the what-we-do-about-it, the* how *we believe. The third article, the "Canon of the Annunciation," is the what and how* in action.

Members One of Another

"Imagine a circle marked out on the ground," writes Saint Dorotheus of Gaza (sixth century) in his *Instructions.*[1] "Suppose that this circle is the world, and that the centre of the circle is God. Leading from the edge of the circle to its centre are a number of lines, and these represent the paths or ways of life that men can follow. In their desire to draw near to God, the saints advance along these lines towards the middle of the circle, so that the further they go, the nearer they approach to one another as well as to God. The closer they come to God, the closer they come to one another; and the closer they come to each other, the closer they come to God.... Such is the nature of love: the nearer we draw to God in our love for Him, the more we are united together by love for our neighbour; and the greater our union with our neighbour, the greater is our union with God."

---

[1] *Doctrina VI (Patrologia Graeca* lxxxviii. 1696 b-c) [St Dorotheos of Gaza [†Sixth century, Aug 13]. Trans Constantine Scouteris, *Abba Dorotheos: Practical Teaching on the Christian Life* (Athens: Scouteris, 2000), 140; **also** trans Eric P. Wheeler, *Dorotheos of Gaza: Discourses and Sayings* (Kalamazoo, MI: Cistercian Publications, 1977), 138–9.]

This simple image of the circle and its centre provides a key to the Orthodox understanding of the Communion of Saints. Love for God and love for our fellow men, as Saint Dorotheus saw, are inseparable; and so if a man is united with God, he must also be united with all the others who love God. As he advances on the path to union with his Creator, he becomes aware to an ever increasing degree of his membership in a community—the community or communion of saints.

The Christian life, in other words, is not solitary, but essentially corporate and social. It is not just the isolated search of an individual for his God, but a life lived in and for other people. An Orthodox Christian is vividly conscious of belonging to a community: as the Russian theologian Alexis Khomiakov (1804–60) put it, "We know that when any one of us falls, he falls alone; but no one is saved alone. He is saved in the Church, as a member of her and in union with all her other members."[1] We are, in Saint Paul's words, "one body in Christ" [Rom 12:5], "members one of another" [Eph 4:25], called to "bear one another's burdens" [Gal 6:2]. The Desert Fathers in their teaching develop this idea: "We should each of us look upon our neighbour's experiences as if they were our own. We should suffer with our neighbour in everything and weep with him, and should behave as if we were inside his body; and if any trouble befalls him, we should feel as much distress on his account as we would for ourselves. For 'we are one body in Christ' [Rom 12:5], and 'the multitude of those who believed was one in heart and soul'"[2] [Acts 4:32]. According to the Macarian Homilies (late fourth century), "There is no other way to be saved except through our neighbour";[3] writing some fifteen centuries later, a Russian monk of Mount Athos says exactly the same: "Blessed is the soul that loves her brother, for *our brother is our life*.... As God is love, so the Holy Spirit in the saints is love."[4] This sense

---

1 "The Church is One," §9 (W.J. Birkbeck, *Russia and the English Church*, London, 1895, p. 216).

2 *Apophthegmata Patrum*, ed. Nau, 389. Compare a western source of the fourteenth century, *The Book of the Poor in Spirit*: "Love makes others' sufferings its own, not one, but all" (IV. iv. 2). [Cf. *The Sayings of the Desert Fathers*, trans Benedicta Ward.]

3 XXXVII. 3 (*Patrologia Graeca* xxxiv. 752 c). [St Macarius the Great [†391, Jan 19], Homily 37, can be found in Pseudo-Macarius, *The Fifty Spiritual Homilies and The Great Letter*, trans George A. Maloney, S.J. (New York: Paulist Press [Classics of Western Spirituality series], 1992), 207.]

4 Father Silvan [a.k.a. St Silouan the Athonite, †1938, Sep 11/24], in *The Undistorted Image*, ed by Archimandrite Sophrony, London, 1958, pp 123, 163. [Archimandrite Sophrony (Sakharov), *Saint Silouan the Athonite* (Maldon GB: Monastery of St John the Baptist,

of loving fellowship extends, indeed, beyond the Church, and even beyond the human race: it includes the irrational animals also, for they too are a part of God's creation. "What is a merciful heart?" asks Saint Isaac the Syrian (seventh century); and he answers, "It is a heart that burns with love for the whole of creation—for men, for birds, for beasts, for demons, for every creature."[1]

But the community to which as Christians we belong is not limited only to the world we see around us. It extends across time as well as space, embracing the departed along with the living. In God and in His Church there can be no division between the living and the dead, for both are one in the love of the Father. Christians, whether they are alive or not, as members of God's Church still belong to one and the same family: they are still members one of another, called to bear each other's burdens. The Church, a reality at once both visible and invisible, encompasses within herself earth and heaven, the living, the departed, and the saints, men and angels, joining them all in the one Body.

This is the basic principle which underlies the doctrine of the Communion of Saints. No one is saved alone: he is saved in and through others. And since for us Christians death does not constitute an impassable barrier or wall of separation, we look for help and companionship not only to the living but to those who have already completed their earthly course. They have not ceased to be our brothers, for in the unity of the Church we and they are still organically linked together.

The Saints and Their Intercession

To an Orthodox it seems a natural and obvious thing to ask the saints for their prayers. Here on earth we ask others to pray for us, and we believe that by God's grace these prayers are of benefit to us. Since the saints are not divided from us but still belong to the same family, why should we not ask them to pray for us likewise? This line of thought can be used, indeed, to explain not only the invocation of the saints but also prayer for the faithful departed. We pray for others while they are alive: why should we not continue to pray for them after their death? Do they cease to exist, that we should cease to pray for them? Perhaps we do not

---

1991); **also available** in two abridged volumes: *The Monk of Mount Athos* and *Wisdom from Mount Athos: The Writings of Staretz Silouan* (Oxford, 1975, both reprinted by St Vladimir's Seminary Press)].

[1] Ed. Wensinck, p. 341. [*The Ascetical Homilies of Saint Isaac the Syrian*, 2nd ed (Boston: Holy Transfiguration Monastery, 2011), 491.]

know precisely how such prayers benefit the dead, but we still go on praying, commending our intercessions to the loving mercy of God. Both types of prayer—*to* the saints, *for* the departed—spring from our sense of the integral unity of living and dead in the one Church. Such prayers are not to be regarded as an exotic form of devotion, as an optional "extra": they are on the contrary something *normal* in the experience of every Orthodox—a natural expression of our love for one another.

In theory there is a fairly sharp distinction between the saints and the rest of the departed. We do not pray *for* the saints but *to* them;[1] we do not in public worship pray *to* the rest of the departed but only *on their behalf*. In the official procedure for canonizing saints the point of division is clearly marked. A last memorial office is celebrated for the soul of the departed servant of God; then, for the first time, a service is held in his honour invoking his prayers, and after that no more memorial offices are sung for his soul. In practice, however, the line of demarcation is not quite so absolute as this. For in the first place, an Orthodox is free in his private prayer to ask for the intercessions of *any* departed member of the Church, whether officially canonized or not. Secondly, the public cult of a saint often arises before there has been any official canonization: indeed, in its public proclamation the Church authority is not so much "canonizing" a saint as setting the seal of official confirmation on a cult which *already* exists. In some cases the act of public proclamation is dispensed with altogether. During the Turkish period, for example, many "new martyrs" came to be venerated, who suffered for the faith at Mohammedan hands; but in order not to attract the notice of the Ottoman authorities the Ecumenical Patriarchate usually issued no public act of proclamation. An analogous situation has arisen in Russia in the present century: both within and outside the Soviet Union there is a widespread devotion to the myriads of new martyrs put to death (often with the greatest brutality) by the Bolsheviks, but political conditions at the present time obviously make it impossible for them to be formally canonized.[2] Thirdly, it must not for one moment be thought that there are no saints except those publicly honoured as such. Those who are mentioned in the calendar form but a small fraction of the whole Com-

---

[1] There are, it is true, certain liturgical texts which appear to be prayers *for* (not to) the saints; but most Orthodox theologians interpret these passages as thanksgiving for the lives of the saints, not as prayer on their behalf.

[2] [This essay was originally published in 1964.]

munion of Saints; besides them, there is a great host whose names are known to God alone, and these are venerated collectively on the Feast of All Saints.[1]

Because the saints pray for us, it does not therefore follow that they come between us and God. "There is one mediator between God and men—Christ Jesus" [1Tim 2:5]: any kind of prayer that loses sight of this fact is undoubtedly heretical. But while Christ is the one and only mediator, there is yet a sense in which every Christian is called to be a co-mediator and co-redeemer through and with Him. The Christian is saved not in isolation but as a member of the community; he is saved in and through others. We can only be saved when praying for the salvation of all and with the aid of the prayer of all.

Strictly speaking, no one is holy, no one is a "saint," except God alone. Strictly speaking again, all prayer is directed to God the Holy Trinity: we pray always to God the Father, through our Lord Jesus Christ, in the Holy Spirit. When, therefore, we call others besides God "holy," we do so only in a secondary and derivative sense. If the saints are so called, it is because they participate in the sanctity of God—because they have been "deified," becoming "gods by grace," "Christs in Christ Jesus." The light which shines from them is not their own: it is the Uncreated Light of God. And if we pray to the saints at the same time as God, it is because they possess the "mind of Christ" and are filled with the power of the Holy Spirit. Thus in praying to the saints we do not cease to pray to God.

But can the saints hear our prayers? To an Orthodox it would seem self-evident that they can. United as they are with Christ, our High Priest who never ceases to make intercession for us, the saints are full of love and personal concern for the world. Christ knows what our needs are, and so the saints who share the mind of Christ cannot but know this also. The point is expressed simply but graphically by a recent Russian writer—widely venerated as a saint, although not yet officially canonized—Father John of Kronstadt (1829–1908):[2]

> You say that you do not understand how the saints in heaven can hear us when we pray to them. Think, then, of the rays of the sun—

---

[1] In the Byzantine calendar, observed on the first Sunday after Pentecost.

[2] [St John was officially recognized as a saint by the Russian Church Abroad in 1964 and by the Patriarchate of Moscow in 1990.]

> how they come down from heaven to us, shedding light upon everything throughout the earth. The saints in the spiritual world are like the rays of the sun in the material world. God is the eternal, life-giving Sun, and the saints are the rays of this all-knowing Sun. Just as the eyes of the Lord look constantly upon the earth and its inhabitants, so also the eyes of the saints cannot but turn in the same direction....
>
> The heart is the eye of the human being. The purer the heart is, the quicker, further, and clearer it can see. But with the saints of God this spiritual eye is refined, even during their lifetime, to the highest degree of purity possible for man, and after their death, when they have become united with God, through God's grace it becomes still clearer and wider in the limits of its vision. Therefore the saints can see very clearly, widely, and far: they see our spiritual wants; they see and hear all those who call upon them with their whole heart.... How easy it is to communicate with the saints! [1]

Mary, the Mother of God

Pre-eminent within the Communion of Saints stands our Lady, the Blessed Virgin Mary. Her position, indeed, is not merely specially privileged but unique: since there is only one incarnate God, there can only be one woman who is God's Mother. Orthodox hold her in high honour, venerating her as "more honourable than the cherubim and incomparably more glorious than the seraphim" (Liturgy of Saint John Chrysostom), but combined with this sense of reverence and profound awe there is also a spontaneous *warmth* in their devotion to our Lady, an affection that is *homely* as well as full of respect.

"Behold, from henceforth all generations shall call me blessed" [Lk 1:48]. Faithful to the words of Scripture, Orthodoxy never ceases to call her blessed. To illustrate Orthodox devotion to the Mother of God, three passages may be given, taken more or less at random. First, the salutation with which Saint Cyril of Alexandria began his great sermon in praise of Mary at the Council of Ephesus (431):

> Rejoice, Mary, Mother of God, precious treasure of the whole world, light unquenchable, crown of virginity, sceptre of orthodoxy,

---

1 In G.P. Fedotov, *A Treasury of Russian Spirituality*, London, 1950, pp. 407–8. [See also St John's *My Life in Christ*.]

> temple which shall never be destroyed, place which contained Him whom nothing can contain, Mother and Virgin.[1]

Precious treasure of the whole world: more than anything else, Orthodox devotion stresses the joy which our Lady brings to mankind. A hymn sung at the Liturgy of Saint Basil calls her "the joy of all creation":

> Full of grace, in thee all creation rejoices, both the company of angels and the race of men. Hallowed temple, paradise of the Word, the glory of virginity, from thee God took flesh and became a little child—He who is from all eternity our God. Thy womb he took as throne, thy body he made wider than the heavens. Full of grace, in thee all creation rejoices: Glory be to thee!

In some hymns she is given a title of particular beauty, "the Joy of all who sorrow":

> Thou art the joy of all who sorrow, the champion of all who suffer wrong, food to the hungry, comfort to strangers, a staff for the blind, visitor of the sick, protection and aid to all in trouble, and helper of orphans: Immaculate Mother of the Most High God, we pray thee, make haste to deliver thy servants.

Such language, however, will strike some western Christians as extravagant and dangerous. What, then, is the theological basis and justification for the Orthodox devotion to the Virgin Mary? The answer lies in a title already used several times, "Mother of God," *Theotokos*. "The name Mother of God," Saint John of Damascus (? 675–749) observes, "contains the whole history of the divine economy in this world."[2] When the members of the Council of Ephesus—the third of the seven Ecumenical Councils—decreed that Mary was to be so addressed, it was not because they sought to honour her as an end in herself, apart from her Son, but because they were anxious to safeguard the right doctrine of the incarnation. Their purpose was to underline the unity of Christ's Person: therefore they called her "Mother of God," so that all might realize that what our Lady bore was not a man loosely linked to God, but a single and indivisible Person who is God and man at once. Those

---

1 *Patrologia Graeca* lxxvii. 992, b.

2 *De fide orthodoxa*, III. 12 (*Patrologia Graeca* xciv. 1029d–1032a). [*Exposition of the Orthodox Faith*, available in *Nicene and Post-Nicene Fathers*, Second Series, vol 9; also in *Writings* of St John of Damascus in the Fathers of the Church series.]

who deny Mary this title—those who just call her "Mother of Christ," "Mother of man," or "Mother of Jesus"—are in danger of dividing our Lord into two; and such division overthrows the doctrine of the incarnation, and with it the whole message of salvation that the Church is appointed to preach. What was involved at Ephesus was not some optional "title of devotion," but the salvation of man.

We honour Mary, then, because she is God's Mother: Mariology is a branch of Christology. We do not venerate her in isolation, but because of her relation to our Lord.[1] Furthermore, a clear distinction is drawn in Orthodox theology between the relative *honour* or *veneration* which is ascribed to Mary (and in a lesser degree to all the saints), and the *worship* which is due to God alone. The reverence which we feel for our Lady in no way detracts from the worship of Jesus Christ: on the contrary, it is precisely on account of the Son that we honour the Mother. If we show such respect for the Blessed Virgin, how much greater must be our sense of wonder and adoration towards Him who is her Lord and her God![2]

Besides *Theotokos*, there is another title of particular importance—"Ever-Virgin," *Aeiparthenos*: this was applied to Mary by the fifth Ecumenical Council (Constantinople, 553). Following the clear teaching of Holy Scripture, Orthodox of course believe that our Lady was a virgin at the time of the birth of Christ. When a child is conceived and born in the ordinary way, a new person comes into existence; but at Christ's birth no new *person* was created (for the Person of the Word had already existed from all eternity) but only a new *nature*—Christ's humanity—and for this reason it was fitting that Christ should have no human father. Orthodox believe, however, not only that Mary was a virgin when she bore Christ, but that she remained a virgin for the rest of her life. This is not in fact stated in the Bible, but it quickly became an accepted part of the tradition of the Church. Such a belief is not inconsistent with Mark 3:31 and other Scriptural passages which mention the "brothers" of Jesus, for the word used here in Greek can mean half-brother, cousin, or near relative, as well as brother in the strict sense.

---

[1] Most icons of the Mother of God do not show just the Virgin but the Virgin *and Child*: they are not icons of Mary only, but rather of the incarnation.

[2] [Simply by calling Mary "Theotokos," the Birth-giver of God, we confess the Faith: that God truly came into the world in the flesh. By venerating her icon, we confess the same so much more boldly, with reverence, gratitude, and affection. The same is true with icons of the saints.]

"A virgin before giving birth," says Saint John of Damascus, "a virgin in giving birth, and a virgin after giving birth, she and she alone remains ever a virgin, alike in mind and soul and body."[1] It is vital to note that this passage speaks not only of her bodily virginity, but also of her virginity in mind and soul. Certainly, the title "Ever-Virgin" involves a reality in the physical order, and is most definitely not to be understood solely in a figurative and symbolical sense. But her virginity is not merely physical: it implies an inner and spiritual attitude as well, and without this the physical fact would be deprived of its chief significance. The name "Ever-Virgin" is thus closely related to another title given to Mary by the Orthodox Church—"all-holy," *panagia*. Orthodoxy believes that Mary, more than any other among God's creatures, deserves to be called "saint" and holy: in mind and soul she was truly a virgin, for in her heart impurity could find no place. If God chose her to be His Mother, it was because she, more than any other, was fitted for this supreme task. She, more than any other human being, "heard the word of God and kept it" [Lk11:28]—a text read at the Gospel in the Liturgy at every feast of the Mother of God.

Nor is this all. At the incarnation Mary was not just a passive instrument but an active participant: "Behold the handmaid of the Lord; be it unto me according to your word" [Lk 1:38]. Mary could have refused the vocation assigned to her by God, for God always respects human freedom, and before becoming incarnate from her, He asked for her voluntary consent. The incarnation was the work not only of God's initiative, but of Mary's free and willing response. We honour her, therefore, not only because God chose her but because she herself chose aright.

* * *

The saints, and above all others Mary the Mother of God, mark out the path of transfiguration and glory which the Church on earth is called to follow. In the words of Father John of Kronstadt:

> Father of all, Thou knowest and Thou alone what cares, what labour and what sweat the saints endured, purifying themselves in order to please Thee. Thou alone knowest Thy saints. Teach us to imitate them in our lives, that we too may be in union with all, through love.[2]

---

1 *Sermon on the Nativity of Christ*, 5 (*Sources chrétiennes*, vol. 80, p.56). [cf. St John of Damascus, "An Oration on the Nativity of the Holy Theotokos Mary" in *Wider than Heaven: Eighth-century Homilies on the Mother of God*, trans Mary B. Cunningham (Crestwood, NY: St Vladimir's Seminary Press, 2008), 59.]

2 Fedotov, *op. cit.*, p. 410.

In union with all, through love: like Saint Dorotheus, Father John stresses the union of all Christians with God and with one another. This vivid sense of union, of "belonging together," underlies the Orthodox vision of the Communion of Saints, and it helps to explain why, in their life of prayer, Orthodox assign so important a place to the saints and the Mother of God.

The Source

"The Communion of Saints" by Metropolitan Kallistos Ware, originally published in *The Orthodox Ethos: Studies in Orthodoxy* (Oxford: Holywell Press, 1964), 140–149. Abridged and reprinted with permission.

This book is out-of-print.

Miscellanea

Permanently Out-of-Print

The preceding article is from a book that is out-of-print, presumably for ever. That this book is eternally unavailable demonstrates what kind of treasure a well-stocked church library might contain, free from the vagaries of the book market. That is, a church library preserves the gifts that our forebears have bequeathed to us; makes them available, along with whatever else we ourselves provide, to the entire parish; and safeguards and transmits what we wish to hand down to future generations.

Church School/Congregation Friendly

A well-stocked church library can be useful for every member of a congregation. If questions of saints or services or customs or who-said-what come up, instead of the usual shrugged shoulders and Who Knows? parishioners can easily locate the answer—without the time, expense, and frustration of buying books that may or may not answer the question.

Moreover, church school classes (adults as well as children) could, for example, base assignments on material available in the library. A saintly idea: if the library had a multi-volume Lives of Saints or many book-length Lives, each student could report on a different saint. This would expose the students to the library resources and introduce all in the class to saints that they might not already know.

Prayers for the Dead

Saturday is always dedicated to All Saints and the Dead. Hymns for the Dead are sung at Friday evening Vespers, sometimes a canon at Friday night Compline, and hymns and canons at Saturday morning Matins. The Divine Liturgy on Saturday commemorates the Dead in a quiet but powerful way, the Eucharist being the most effective help we can offer for the souls of the departed. Saturday is the most appropriate day for these commemorations because it is the day that our Lord and God and Savior Jesus Christ was Himself in Hades, liberating the captive souls and destroying the power of Death.

Sunday joyously celebrates the Resurrection of Christ. For this reason, although the Dead are subtly but surely commemorated within the Eucharist, Memorial Services (Panikhidas) are out of place on Sunday. Death has been conquered; the Resurrection of Christ, the cause and confirmation of the resurrection of all, is manifest. How can Christians mourn—in the form of Memorial Services—on Sunday? It is not appropriate and it is not allowed, by instruction and Tradition of the Church, since the Apostles.

To the present day, for whatever reasons, in America the Church has allowed Memorial Services on Sunday. Unfortunately, in many places this has come to be accepted and even expected as the normal practice of the Church. More egregious still, there are parishes where the Memorial Service is incorporated into the Sunday Divine Liturgy itself.

Is it true that people who desire to commemorate their dead—a laudable sentiment and pious deed—cannot be inconvenienced to come to the church on one or two Saturdays, or Monday through Friday, during the course of a year?

The gravity of this issue is fully presented in *Confession of Faith* by Saint Nikodemos the Hagiorite.[1]

Refreshing Courses

Orthodoxy is so broad that even old-timers may feel the need for a general refresher or re-introduction. Good basic books include:

The Orthodox Church by Timothy Ware (Metropolitan Kallistos);[2]

The Mystery of Faith: An Introduction to the Teaching and Spirituality of the Orthodox Church by Metropolitan Hilarion Alfeyev;[3]

The Orthodox Church: An Introduction to its History, Doctrine, and Spiritual Culture by John Anthony McGuckin.[4]

Another book that is truly refreshing is *Northopraxis* by Father Bohdan Hladio,[5] who currently serves in Canada. "Northopraxis" is Canadian for orthopraxis (right practice of the faith, right living). Taken from his newspaper columns, the book addresses, in a refreshingly practical spiritual way, various difficulties of parish and personal life. Sensitive to New World/Old World friction, the author speaks plainly of real problems and provides sensible, spiritual solutions. A delicious and nutritious read. The publisher, HDM Press (Holy Dormition Monastery), carries several other titles, most notably the books of Father Roman Braga.

1 St Nikodemos the Hagiorite [i.e., of the Holy Mountain. †1809, July 14]. *Confession of Faith*, trans Fr George Dokos (Thessalonica: Uncut Mountain Press, 2007).

2 Harmondsworth, England: Penguin Books, 1963; 2nd ed. 1993.

3 Yonkers, NY: St Vladimir's Seminary Press, 2011.

4 Chichester, England: Wiley-Blackwell, 2011.

5 *Northopraxis or From Pastoral Life*, Rives Junction, MI: HDM Press, 2009.

8. Valentine

In the same way that it takes some effort to meet and to get to know people round about, some effort is required to get to know the saints. But how that effort is repaid! The following contemporary letter suggests how to approach the Lives of Saints, the benefits of reading the longer versions, and strategies for making them a part of every day life.

November 16—Holy Apostle and Evangelist Matthew

Dear Valentine:

Glory to Jesus Christ!

I am glad to hear that you will soon have access to the *Lives of Saints* by Saint Demetrius of Rostov.[1] I know you've been reading some short Lives, and I think you will enjoy reading longer ones—especially in Saint Demetrius's style: real hagiography,[2] not just "bios."

I was looking at one of those books of shorter Lives the other day. The write-up on Saint Gregory, Bishop and Enlightener of Armenia [†328, Sep 30], mentions that he was thrown into a deep pit of murky ooze filled with venomous snakes, scorpions, and other odious, lethal reptiles —but that he was pulled out of the pit in order to heal the king of his supernatural disorders. What it failed to divulge was that Saint Gregory was in that pit *for fourteen years*. Hmmm.

The longer Lives are so filled with wonders that I hardly know where to begin. They contain theology, ethics, history, apologetics, scriptural exegesis, and much more. For example, there is the description of how the Trisagion (Holy God, Holy Mighty, Holy Immortal) came into the liturgy [Sep 25].[3] Again, the hymn to the Theotokos,

[1] [St Demetrius of Rostov [†1709, Oct 28], *The Great Collection of the Lives of the Saints*, trans Fr Thomas Marretta (House Springs, MO: Chrysostom Press, 1994–2012).]

[2] [*hagio* = holy, saint; *graphy* = writing, study]

[3] [This is commemorated in the first troparion of each ode of the first canon to St

"More honorable than the Cherubim," was composed by hymnographer Saint Cosmas of Maiuma [†c.750, Oct 12 Slav, Oct 14 Greek]. The Lives describe the introductory addition to it, "It is truly meet to bless Thee, O Theotokos," delivered by Archangel Gabriel to a monk on Mount Athos in 980 [June 11].[1]

The Lives also contain homilies for and explanations of the major feasts. The joy and wonder of Christmas through Theophany, for example, are sustained not only with homilies on those days, but in between those days are commemorations of the Adoration of the Magi, the Slaughter of the Holy Infants, the Flight into Egypt, as well as the lives of Saint Joseph the Betrothed, the holy Protomartyr Stephen the Deacon, Saints Theodore and Theophanes the Branded, and of course, the Circumcision of the Lord and the life of Saint Basil the Great. And don't forget the day after Theophany: the joyous feast of the Synaxis of Saint John, the Forerunner and Baptizer of Christ!

What I like best about the longer Lives is that they allow you to spend more time with the saints, to get to know them better. You get a better sense of their struggles and difficulties, how they worked out their own salvation, so to speak. They become more real. They *are real*, after all, not just dead people whose memory we honor, but living people who teach us by the example of their lives, and who actually and actively intercede for us and help us.

This realization—and the bond one develops with the saints—also makes their icons come alive. As you know, many people study the icons as works of art: symbolism, colors, styles, etc. This is commendable, of course, but they often know little of the saints portrayed, and thus continue to venerate the icons as impersonal objects rather than with the natural warmth and affection one feels for family, dearest friends, and benefactors.

We once had a Protestant convert in our church. When it came to venerating icons, he had that typical, knee-jerk reaction against "worshipping pictures and pieces of wood." (How is this infused into them?) He started reading the Lives, however, and after he got to know the saints, you couldn't keep him away from their icons. He read all the saints whose

---

Euphrosyne in the Holy Transfiguration Monastery *Menaion*.]

[1] [Or 982. This also is commemorated with a service in the *Menaion*. The icon is known as *Axion Estin*. St Cosmas's hymn is the hiermos of ode nine of the triode canon of Matins of Holy Friday, a.k.a. the Service of the Twelve Gospels on Holy Thursday night.]

icons adorned the walls and pillars, and before each service he would go all around the church venerating them. As you would expect, the Orthodox looked on him as a lunatic. But surely he was no more lunatic than Saint John of Shanghai and San Francisco [†1966, June 19/July 2], who would make full prostrations in front of each of the many icons whenever he left the cathedral, venerating his close friends, the saints.[1]

Reading the longer lives of saints also explains their incomprehensible actions—incomprehensible to the world, but perfectly sensible from an Orthodox perspective. For example, why did Saint Symeon the Stylite [Sep 1]—and those who emulated him—choose to stand on a pillar for most of his life? Why did the early monastics, and so many people thereafter, choose to live in the desert? [see Saint Eudokia the Samaritan, March 1, and many others.] Why did Saint Mary the Reader [found in the life of Saint Cyriacus, Sep 29] flee to the desert? (She is also an example of a female reader in the early Church.) And what's with those mysterious "tollhouses"? [see Saint Basil the New, March 26] Reading about the "customs demons"—not dogmatically, but spiritually—really motivates one to prepare for Confession and to seriously examine one's whole life.

There are many scriptural references in the Lives of Saints that give an Orthodox and often surprising interpretation of Scripture. Although you would not say that the Lives of Saints are Scripture, they are a natural extension of the *Acts of the Apostles*: God's continuing work through His disciples. As holy Apostle John the Theologian says, if all that Jesus did were written down, the world could not hold the number of books that would be written. How many times do we read in the Psalter, "I will tell of all Your marvelous works"? This is what we do when we read the lives of saints. It is the same as we do in the services: we chant of the works of God as given to us through Scripture, but also as we praise the saints each day, for "God is wondrous in His saints."

One of the saints I especially love—and whose Life caught me off-guard—is Saint Dositheus [Feb 29 Slav, Aug 13 Greek]. As a very young man he came to the monastery where Saint Dorotheus [Aug 13] was a monk. Saint Dorotheus later became (and still is, through his writings)

---

1 [See *Man of God: Saint John of Shanghai & San Francisco*, trans and ed Archpriest Peter Perekrestov (Redding, CA: Nikodemos Orthodox Publication Society, 1994), 40–41.]

a famous teacher and spiritual guide of monks and laity.[1] Dositheus was Dorotheus's first disciple—his guinea pig, you might say.

At one point, Dositheus asks about the meaning of a certain passage of Scripture. He is answered with a smack upside the head and a rebuke for wanting to know what is beyond him. This story was alarming to me. It still is, a little. He simply wanted to understand Scripture. That deserves a slap? I think what it exemplifies, however, besides its specific point of monastic obedience, is how seriously the Orthodox take purity and preparation: one must be *ready* to read or hear the Scriptures in order to understand them.

I highlight this particular episode since we live in a very *sola scriptura* environment—Scripture first and only!—and this incident seems to go against the grain. You will probably find many such disturbing things in the Lives, but don't let them become stumbling blocks for you. They make sense after a while. In fact, they often come to mind at opportune moments. Be rather like the Mother of God, who "pondered these things in her heart."

The Lives of Saints, you see, are really an immersion in Orthodox thinking, seeing, understanding, doing. From them one distills the "spirit of Orthodoxy." The saints themselves read Lives of Saints and considered them an essential element of Orthodox understanding and spirituality. It may take a while for these things to sink in, but as they do, both Orthodoxy and "the world" make more sense. There is a great joy and comfort in knowing the saints, remembering them, and praying to them. As for myself, I like to ask people who their patron saints are—*which* John? *which* Mary? (how shocking when they don't know, have never given it a thought!) Then, when I pray for the person, I remember to pray to the saint; and when I pray to the saint, I remember to pray for the person. It's too bad that we don't make more of Name Days.

* * *

[1] ["The Orthodox doctrine of human nature is set forth most concisely in the *Spiritual Instructions* of Abba Dorotheus. This book is accepted in the Orthodox Church as the 'ABC,' the basic textbook of Orthodox spirituality; it is the first spiritual reading which an Orthodox monk is given, and it remains his constant companion for the rest of his life, to be read and re-read. It is most significant that the Orthodox doctrine of human nature is set forth in the very first page of this book, because this doctrine is the foundation of the entire Orthodox spiritual life."—Fr Seraphim Rose, *Genesis, Creation, and Early Man: The Orthodox Christian Vision*, ed Hieromonk Damascene, 2nd ed (Platina, CA: St Herman of Alaska Brotherhood, 2011), 472. Used with permission.]

You should be aware that there is a certain resistance to the Lives of Saints in America. On the one hand, the longer Orthodox Lives have not been available in English until recently. People simply are not familiar with them. The older generations of Orthodox became inured to their too-long absence; the younger generations never learned of their existence and major role in Orthodox life. Later in those dry decades, brief collections of "Sayings of the Desert Fathers" [1] became available—which, unfortunately, can seem profoundly obscure, like zen koans. People often assume that the Lives of Saints will be like that: impenetrable, paradoxical, and completely impractical. But you have read a few of the longer lives, so you know that this is not the case. In fact, the opposite is true: the Lives give the context for the Sayings, actually flesh them out, and explain them.

On the other hand, Americans demand that the lives of saints be *relevant* to our modern existence. They *are* relevant, actually, but without all the electronic gadgets, the labor-saving devices, the engulfing distraction. There is so much noise in our lives—flashing, beeping mind-buzz, invading our thoughts at every turn, we are saturated with so much noise—that we don't hear what the Lives are telling us.

For example, when Saint Myrope [martyr, Dec 2] steals the tortured body of Holy Martyr Isadore [May 14] to give it reverent burial, she becomes entangled in the potential execution of the four soldiers who had been guarding it—guarding it specifically to prevent its burial, so that it would be desecrated, eaten by birds and beasts. She says to herself, "It will not go well with me before the judgment seat of God if these men are tortured and beheaded because of what I have done. My soul will be delivered to torment if I am the cause of their death." Certainly in our own lives we don't run into such dramatic events every day. Nevertheless, her attitude and consideration are relevant to us every day, every hour: "It will not go well with me at the judgment seat of God if I...."

Sometimes even if we *can* hear, we *don't want* to hear. Saint Theodore the Sanctified [May 16], at the age of twelve, regarded the festive meal prepared by his family for the feast of Theophany. He was pierced with compunction and cried: "If you enjoy all this food, you will not enter eternal life." Relevant? Hmmm. Maybe one of those things that need to sink in....

---

[1] [Cf. *The Sayings of the Desert Fathers: The Alphabetical Collection*, trans Benedicta Ward (Kalamazoo, MI: Cistercian Publications, 1975 [revised edition, 1984]).]

On yet a third hand, there is the pervasive "scientific" atmosphere in which we live. Many church leaders, priests, seminaries, and publishers cast an academic pall on things that should be spiritually enlivening. This is especially true when it comes to the Lives of Saints. Tradition becomes "Legend." Nothing is certain. Everything is suspect. Many martyrdoms, for example, were written down by eyewitnesses who incorporated the recorded court proceedings into their report. These have been handed down to us through the Church. Since, however, the "original documents" have not survived 1700 years of fire, flood, earthquake, decay, heresy, malice, civil war, invasion, bureaucracy, and chaos to corroborate them, the writings of the Church cannot be trusted. Hmmm.

It is true that some errors and confusions have entered the literature, but this does not invalidate the entire body of work, and certainly not the spirit of it. One synaxarion describes the Lives of Saints as a great river that carries along mud, stones, branches, and other debris picked up along the way, but its waters are nevertheless life-giving.[1] Why quibble with our parched, raspy throats rather than quench our burning thirst in its cool, salubrious streams?

At the same time that the academic, "scientific" mindset denigrates the Church's Lives, *false "Lives" are fabricated and published*. One example is an "Orthodox" publishing house that actually promotes "fictionalized lives of saints" for their catalog, books for children, teens, and adults.

Another example comes from a seminary press, a children's book marketed as the life of Saint George. The author explains in the book that we don't really know anything at all about Saint George. It has come down to us that Saint George was a soldier, but there is no reason to believe it. He is called "George," which translates as "farmer," so it is possible that he was a farmer. The author claims that the most untrue of all in the traditional Life is Saint George's battle with the dragon. He then writes his children's story entirely and exclusively about Saint George's battle with the dragon. He turns it into a Western, medieval romance, with the knight, the fair maiden, and all the trappings. He makes Samaritans of us: "Ye worship ye know not what" [Jn 4:22].

What will become of the children who read these things? who grow up immersed in this distorting, worldly mindset? Older Orthodox

---

1 [See Hieromonk Makarios of Simonos Petra, *The Synaxarion: The Lives of the Saints of the Orthodox Church*, trans Christopher Hookway, Mother Mary, et al (Mt Athos, Greece: Holy Monastery of Simonos Petra, 1998), xix.]

generations lost their American children by keeping Orthodoxy alien and incomprehensible in foreign tongues. The younger generations will be lost by specious "science," outright fabrications, and implanted distrust of all things Orthodox.

American ignorance of the saints is understandable, but it is regrettable that so many of our Church leaders have a dismissive attitude toward them, a *sophisticated* unbelief. Some of them, for example, grudgingly accept the miracles reported in *The Prologue* by Saint Nikolai Velimirovic [†1956, March 5]. Do they believe Saint Nikolai because he is a saint teaching what the Church has taught for two thousand years? No. They believe him (grudgingly) because he had *five doctorate degrees*. (Uhh!) Lay people become infected by the attitude, the heedlessness, the distortion.

Saint Sophronius says in his Life of Saint Mary of Egypt [Apr 1]: "As for those who have no faith and consider the miracles too remarkable to be true, in view of the weakness of human nature, may the Lord have mercy on them!" [1] Or compare Isaiah, "If ye believe not, neither will ye at all understand" [Is 7:9 LXX], or Saint Paul, "Your faith should not be in the wisdom of men, but in the power of God" [1Cor 2:5]. Hmmm.

Saint Demetrius of Rostov wrote, and is elegantly translated, to be read aloud. This is no hindrance to private reading, and a boon for reading to children—or adults! He also tries to keep the lives short enough to be read at one sitting.

If you don't already have a plan for how to read the Lives, here are some ideas. As busy as you are, some of the daily readings may be too long to keep up with every day. You shouldn't worry about it or allow yourself to become frustrated over it. If you're really busy, you might choose to read one long life per week. You could start with the famous saints, like Saint John Chrysostom [Nov 13], Saint Basil the Great [Jan 1], Saint Nicholas [Dec 6], Great Virgin Martyr Catherine [Nov 24 Slav, Nov 25 Greek], Saint Theodore the Studite [Nov 11], and so on. At the end of a year, you would know fifty saints fairly well. You might want to read first the saints whose icons are on the walls of your church—you worship with them every week, after all. Or ask your priest for the list

1 [St Demetrius of Rostov, *The Great Collection of the Lives of the Saints*, 8:7. Also found in a softbound edition by Holy Trinity Monastery (Jordanville) with the *Great Canon* of St Andrew of Crete (the Life of St Mary and the *Great Canon* are both read on the fifth Thursday of Great Lent).]

of saints invoked at the lity. You'll be delighted at how that part of the service brightens up!

By the way, one does not cotton to every saint encountered. As with the people you meet day to day: you simply connect with some more than others. And just so you know, reading many martyrs when you're just beginning can feel a little weird—but you'll be amazed at how your feelings toward them change.

You see how much you have to look forward to! A spiritual feast, a whole new circle of friends: benefactors who have cared for you long before you met them. I could say that I envy your fresh beginning, but no—*re*-reading the Lives brings fresh insight, encouragement, and joy, as well as the happiness of visiting old friends.

Another set of Lives that might interest you is *The Synaxarion: The Lives of the Saints of the Orthodox Church.*[1] The lives are shorter and less edifying than Saint Demetrius, but there are many more saints represented. Whereas Saint Demetrius includes saints of the Mediterranean, the East, and Slavic lands up to the sixteenth century, the *Synaxarion* has all of those, plus the New Martyrs of the Turkish Yoke, the Martyrs of the Soviet Yoke, and Western (Orthodox) saints from the first century to the present day. It also displays several icons for each day, and has a helpful section of maps in Volume I. Its introduction is a very good read. For *longer* longer Lives, there's the *Great Synaxaristes*, but—enough said.

After you start connecting with the saints, you may want to procure a *Great Horologion* (Book of Hours). It contains the troparia and kontakia for the main saint(s) of each day—as well as the unchanging parts of all the services, and akathists and canons. And who knows? You may soon be clamoring for a *Menaion!*

The *Menaion* is the book(s!) containing the changeable parts of the services for every calendar day: the "immoveable" feasts and the saints. Like the *Octoechos* (the stichera, hymns, and canons for each day of the week in the eight tones), the poetry is thrilling—not rhyme and rhythm, which are mostly stripped out by the time it arrives in English, but the weaving of words and ideas into illuminating juxtaposition.

I mentioned before how the homilies and explanations in the Lives of Saints joyously illumine the Christmas season. All of this is amplified, magnified in the services. But look here. In the weeks *before* the Nativity

---

[1] [*The Synaxarion*, see above.]

of our Lord, the *Menaion* has Christmas hymns—in festive, forward-looking melodies—sprinkled through the services. What a delightful anticipation! A sort of living Advent calendar.

And saints every day. It quickly becomes clear, dear Valentine, that we worship not only pictures and pieces of wood, but *dead people*. Every day, every service, several times each service, we honor the saints, praise their achievements, and ask for their intercession. (I might add here that Saint George's battle with the dragon is not mentioned in his service, but many times he is praised for vanquishing the *spiritual* dragon, that is, the devil and his demon horde—which is certainly how to approach his icon ... and children's books. Come to think of it, the services must be torture to those in the Church who believe that the saints and Church teachings are fabulous hocus-pocus....)

One *Menaion* introduction describes itself like this:

> The holy *Menaia*, beloved Christians, are a divine school wherein we are taught the dogmas of the Church, the witness of the holy Martyrs and Confessors, and the accomplishments of the Saints. Throughout the centuries, before seminaries and so-called theological schools were established, both the clergy and the laity were schooled in the teachings of the Church through the liturgical books, i.e., the *Octoechos* (*Paracletike*), the *Triodion*, the *Pentecostarion*, and the *Menaia*.[1]

Saint Cyril of Jerusalem [†386] and all the catechists exhort their wards to attend the services, to listen and to learn: a sort of pre-school. Yet Elder Porphyrius [†1991] and many others call the services the "University of the Church." How can this be?

> By attending to the sacred hymnology, we almost unconsciously are schooled in the mind of the Fathers and their understanding of Holy Scripture, the Feasts of the Church, and the accomplishments of the Saints.[2]

Rest assured, Valentine, that the "communion of saints" is not some academic abstraction or wishful thinking, but a living wonder. To read their lives, to greet their icons, to pray to them, and to praise them in their canons and services, to *commune* with the saints is a great joy.

---

1 [*The Menaion*, translated from the Greek by Holy Transfiguration Monastery (Boston: Holy Transfiguration Monastery, 2005), 1:5. Copyright © Holy Transfiguration Monastery, Brookline, MA, used by permission. All rights reserved.]

2 [Ibid., 12.]

The Source

A contemporary letter from our files. Used with permission.

Miscellanea

A Reason for Reading

It is extremely profitable to bring to mind those who have suffered for Christ, for the very thought of their passion is able to stir up our minds to the love of God and gives, as it were, wings to our strivings for virtue, inciting us to bear spiritually the sufferings which they bore in the flesh, for the sake of a future reward.[1]

— Saint Demetrius of Rostov

Parent Friendly

Reading the Orthodox Lives of Saints with children (you read to them, they read to you—besides your own reading for yourself) grounds them (and you) in basic understanding of the Church, instills morals, ethics, spiritual understanding, a sense of history, and it (re)introduces them to real friends and helpers. The same Holy Spirit that acts in the Holy Scriptures acts also in the Lives of Saints.[2] Reading the Lives can lead to a lifelong and ever deepening love of God, the saints, and sanctity.

Troublesome Concepts

As the letter to Valentine alludes to the "tollhouses," an additional note may be useful. The tollhouses and what happens after death are not dogmatized by the Church, but references and descriptions are found in much of the Church's literature. Like other spiritual realities described with human language, they are not to be interpreted in the strictest *literal* sense.[3] Human

1 St Demetrius of Rostov *The Great Collection of the Lives of the Saints*, trans Fr Thomas Marretta (House Springs, MO: Chrysostom Press, 1995), 2:200. Used with permission.
2 See *Elder Barsanuphius of Optina* by Victor Afanasiev (Platina, CA: St Herman Press), 497.
3 For one thing, coming upon the tollhouses in person will be intensely more terrifying than any written description.

language and understanding are not sufficient to comprehend spiritual realities. For a further, thoroughly patristic discussion of the tollhouses—and much else—see *Life after Death* by Metropolitan Hierotheos of Nafpaktos,[1] who explains, characteristically, that this topic is found in the whole biblico-patristic tradition and that it behooves us to consider it in order to prepare for death.

Saint Symeon the New Theologian addresses the difficulty of using physical images to convey spiritual realities in a homily on Chapter 10 of Saint John's Gospel, where Jesus describes Himself as "the door."

> But beware as you hear these things, that you do not take the images of literal houses and doors and permit the physical pattern to be imprinted on your minds, so that your soul falls into doubt and blasphemy. You must reflect on all these images in a proper way, in a manner that befits God, if you are able, according to the rule and standard of the spiritual interpretation, and so you will find the right interpretation of them all. But if you are incapable of so understanding them in a manner that befits God, then receive them by mere faith and refuse all curious inquiry.[2]

This is not to deny in any way the reality of the miracles recorded in the Lives of Saints, which are not spiritual description but actual fact. Despite the grumbling of Valentine's correspondent about Saint George and the dragon, the point is not to "spiritualize" *everything*. The saints truly work miracles, as our Lord Jesus Christ promised and predicted: "Verily, verily, I say unto you, he that believeth on Me, the works that I do shall he do also; and greater works than these shall he do; because I go unto My Father" [Jn 14:12].

1 Trans Esther Williams (Levadia, Hellas: Birth of the Theotokos Monastery, 1996).
2 Symeon the New Theologian [†1022, March 12], *The Discourses*, trans C.J. deCatanzaro (New York: Paulist Press [The Classics of Western Spirituality series], 1980), 343. Used with permission.

9. Annunciation Canon

"The Communion of Saints" (chapter 7) explained what *we believe about the saints and Mary's special place in Creation. "Valentine" described what we do about it—getting to know the saints by reading their lives, honoring them by greeting their icons, praying their canons, and asking for their help and intercession—the* how *we believe. The services, then, especially of the Great Feasts, are the what and how* in action.

The Annunciation Canon, sung at Matins on the Feast of the Annunciation [Mar 25], was written by **Saint John of Damascus** *[†c.749, Dec 4]. As we pray the canon, we see how greatly God honors the Theotokos, and how highly she is revered by angels as well as men. It is not a quick read. In a monastic service, each troparion would be repeated two or three or four times in succession, a sort of Orthodox-style meditation: "Let these sayings sink down into your ears" [Lk 9:44]. The services are not just a "memorial" of the celebrated event, but an actual participation in it. Reading the service beforehand enhances that participation and elevates one's experience of it.*

Canticle One

Irmos: I shall open my mouth and the Spirit will inspire it, and I shall utter the words of my song to the Queen and Mother: I shall be seen radiantly keeping feast and joyfully praising her conceiving.

Refrain: Most holy Theotokos, save us.

Troparion: Let thy forefather David sing to thee, O Lady, striking upon the harp of the Spirit: 'Hearken, O Daughter, to the glad voice of the Angel, for he discloses to thee joy past telling.' [Ps 44:11]

The Angel

In gladness I cry to thee: incline thine ear and give heed unto me, as I tell thee of God's conception without seed. For thou, O Most Pure, hast found grace before the Lord such as no other woman ever found.

The Theotokos

O Angel, help me to understand the meaning of thy words. How shall what thou sayest come to pass? Tell me clearly, how shall I conceive, who am a virgin maid? And how shall I become the Mother of my Maker?

The Angel

Thou dost think, so it seems, that I utter words deceitfully; and I rejoice to see thy prudence. But take courage, O Lady: for when God wills, strange wonders are easily accomplished.

Katavasia: I shall open my mouth.... [same as irmos]

Canticle Three

Irmos: O Mother of God, thou living and plentiful fount, give strength to those united in spiritual fellowship, who sing hymns of praise to thee: and on this feast of thy holy conceiving vouchsafe unto them crowns of glory.

The Theotokos

There is no more a prince from Judah's line, but the time is at hand in which Christ, the hope of the Gentiles, shall appear. But do thou make plain to me how I, being a virgin, shall bear Him? [Gen 49:10]

The Angel

O Virgin, thou dost seek to know from me the manner of thy conceiving, but this is beyond all interpretation. The Holy Spirit shall overshadow thee in His creative power and shall make this come to pass.

The Theotokos

My mother Eve, accepting the suggestion of the serpent, was banished from divine delight: and therefore I fear thy strange salutation, for I take heed lest I slip.

The Angel

I am sent as the envoy of God to disclose to thee the divine will. Why art thou, O Undefiled, afraid of me, who rather am afraid of thee? Why, O Lady, dost thou stand in awe of me, who stand in reverent awe of thee?

Katavasia: O Mother of God, thou living and plentiful....

Sessional Hymn

The Word of God is now come down upon earth. The Angel stood before the Virgin and cried aloud: 'Hail, blessed Lady, who alone among women hast preserved the seal of thy virginity, while yet receiving in thy womb the pre-eternal Word and Lord, that He as God may save mankind from error.'

Glory to the Father and to the Son and to the Holy Spirit, both now and ever and unto ages of ages. Amen.

Repeat: The Word of God is now come down....

Canticle Four

Irmos: He who sits in glory upon the throne of the Godhead, Jesus the true God, is come in a swift cloud, and with His pure hand He has saved those who cry: Glory to Thy power, O Christ. [Is 19:1]

The Theotokos

I have learnt from the Prophet, who foretold in times of old the coming of Emmanuel, that a certain holy Virgin should bear a child. But I long to know how the nature of mortal men shall undergo union with the Godhead. [Is 7:14]

The Angel

The bush that burnt with fire and yet remained unconsumed, disclosed the secret mystery that shall come to pass in thee, O pure Maiden, full of grace. For after childbirth thou shalt remain ever-Virgin. [Ex 3:2]

The Theotokos

O Gabriel, herald of the truth, shining with the radiance of Almighty God, tell me truly: how shall I, my purity remaining untouched, bear in the flesh the Word that has no body?

The Angel

I stand before thee in fear, as a servant before his mistress, and in awe I am afraid to look at thee now, O Maid. In His good pleasure shall the Word of God descend upon Thee, as dew upon the fleece. [Judg 6:38; Ps 71:6]

Katavasia: He who sits in glory....

Canticle Five

Irmos: The whole world was amazed at thy divine glory: for thou, O Virgin who hast not known wedlock, hast held in thy womb the God of all, and hast given birth to an eternal Son, who rewards with salvation all who sing thy praises.

The Theotokos

I cannot understand the meaning of thy words. For there have often been miracles, wonders worked by the might of God, symbols and figures contained in the Law. But never has a virgin borne child without knowing a man.

The Angel

Thou art amazed, O all-blameless Virgin; and amazing indeed is the wonder that comes to pass in thee: for thou alone shalt receive in thy womb the King of all who is to take flesh. It is thou who art prefigured by the utterances and dark sayings of the prophets and by the symbols of the Law.

The Theotokos

How can He whom nothing can contain, upon whom none can gaze, dwell in the womb of a virgin whom He Himself has formed? And how shall I conceive God the Word, who with the Father and the Spirit has no beginning?

The Angel

He who promised to thy forefather David that of the fruit of his body He would set upon the throne of his kingdom, He it is that has chosen thee, the only excellency of Jacob, as His spiritual dwelling-place. [Ps 131:11, Ps 46:5]

Katavasia: The whole world was amazed....

Canticle Six

Irmos: Prefiguring Thy three-day burial, the prophet Jonah cried out in the belly of the whale: 'Deliver me from corruption, O Jesus, King and Lord of hosts.' [Jonah 2]

The Theotokos

Receiving thy glad tidings, O Gabriel, I am filled with divine joy. For thou dost speak to me of joy, a joy without end.

The Angel

Divine joy is given to thee, O Mother of God. All creation cries unto thee: 'Hail, O Bride of God.' For thou alone, O pure Virgin, wast foreordained to be the Mother of the Son of God.

The Theotokos

May the condemnation of Eve be now brought to naught through me; and through me may her debt be repaid this day. Through me may the ancient due be rendered up in full.

The Angel

God promised to our forefather Abraham that in his seed the Gentiles would be blest, O pure Lady; and through thee today the promise receives its fulfilment. [Gen 22:18]

Katavasia: As we celebrate this sacred and solemn feast of the Mother of God, let us come, clapping our hands, O people of the Lord, and give glory to God who was born of her.

Kontakion[1]

To thee, O Theotokos, victorious leader of triumphant hosts, we thy servants, delivered from calamity, offer hymns of thanksgiving. In thine invincible power, keep us free from every peril, that we may cry to thee: Hail,[2] thou Bride unwedded.

Ikos

A prince of the angels was sent from heaven to say to the Theotokos, 'Hail!' And seeing Thee, O Lord, take bodily form at the sound of his bodiless voice, he was filled with amazement and stood still, crying to her thus:

Hail, thou through whom joy will shine forth:
Hail, thou through whom the curse will cease.
Hail, thou restoration of fallen Adam:
Hail, thou redemption of the tears of Eve.
Hail, thou Height hard to climb for the thought of man:
Hail, thou Depth hard to perceive even for the eyes of angels.
Hail, thou that art the throne of the King:
Hail, thou who dost hold Him who holdeth all.
Hail, thou Star who dost make the Sun appear:
Hail, thou Womb of the divine incarnation.
Hail, thou through whom the creation is made new:
Hail, thou through whom the Creator becomes a newborn child.
Hail, thou Bride unwedded!

---

1 [This kontakion with its ikos are hymns by St Romanos the Melodist [†c.555, Oct 1]; they are the first kontakion and ikos of his Akathist service to the Theotokos. Cf. "To Thee, the Champion Leader" in chapter 12, "Weekday Hymnal," p 156.]

2 ["Hail" is more often translated "Rejoice," reflecting the Orthodox sense (and joy) of it.]

Canticle Seven

Irmos: The Holy Children bravely trampled upon the threatening fire, preferring not to worship created things rather than the Creator, and they sang in joy: 'Blessed art Thou and praised above all, O Lord God of our fathers.' [Dan 3:26–56 LXX]

The Theotokos

Thou dost bring me good tidings of divine joy, that the immaterial Light, in His abundant compassion, will be united to a material body; and now thou criest out to me: 'O All-Pure, blessed is the fruit of thy womb.'

The Angel

Hail, O Lady, hail, O most pure Virgin; hail, thou vessel wherein God is contained, hail, thou candlestick of the Light, the restoration of Adam and the deliverance of Eve, holy Mountain, shining Sanctuary, and Bridal Chamber of immortality.

The Theotokos

The descent of the Holy Spirit has purified my soul and sanctified my body: it has made of me a Temple that contains God, a Tabernacle divinely adorned, a living Sanctuary, and the pure Mother of Life.

The Angel

I see thee as a Lamp with many lights and as a Bridal Chamber made by God. As an Ark of gold, O spotless Maiden, receive now the Giver of the Law, who through thee has been pleased to deliver the corrupt nature of mankind.

Katavasia: The Holy Children bravely trampled....

Canticle Eight

Irmos: The offspring of the Theotokos saved the Holy Children in the furnace. He who was then prefigured has since been born on earth, and He gathers together all the creation to sing: O all ye works of the Lord, bless ye the Lord and exalt Him above all for ever. [Dan 3:57–88 LXX]

The Angel

'Hearken, O pure Virgin Maid: let Gabriel tell thee the counsel of the Most High that is ancient and true. Make ready to receive God: for through thee the Incomprehensible comes to dwell with mortal men. Therefore I cry rejoicing: O all ye works of the Lord, bless ye the Lord.'

The Theotokos

'All mortal thought is overwhelmed,' answered the Virgin, 'as it ponders the strange wonders of which thou tellest me. I am filled with joy at thy words, yet am afraid: I fear lest thou deceive me, as Eve was deceived, and lead me far from God. Yet lo, thou criest out: O all ye works of the Lord, bless ye the Lord.'

The Angel

'See, thy difficulty is resolved,' said Gabriel to this. 'Thou hast well said that this matter is hard to grasp. Obey, then, the words of thine own lips: doubt not as though it were deceitful, but believe in this thing as very truth. For I cry rejoicing: O all ye works of the Lord, bless ye the Lord.'

The Theotokos

'Childbirth comes from mutual love: such is the law that God has given to men,' said again she who is without reproach. 'I know not at all the pleasure of marriage: how then dost thou say that I shall bear child? I fear lest thou speakest in guile. Yet lo, thou criest out: O all ye works of the Lord, bless ye the Lord.'

The Angel

'O holy Virgin,' replied the Angel, 'thou speakest to me of the customary manner whereby mortal men are born. But I tell thee of the birth of the true God. Beyond words and understanding, in ways that He alone knows, He shall take flesh of thee. Therefore, I cry rejoicing: O all ye works of the Lord, bless ye the Lord.'

The Theotokos

'Thou dost appear to me to speak the truth,' answered the Virgin. 'For thou hast come as an angel messenger, bringing joy to all. Since, then, I am purified in soul and body by the Spirit, be it unto me according to thy word: may God dwell in me. Unto Him I cry aloud with thee: O all ye works of the Lord, bless ye the Lord.'

Katavasia: 'Hearken, O pure Virgin Maid....' [first troparion]

Canticle Nine

Before the irmos and the troparia we sing the megalynarion:
O earth, announce good tidings of great joy: ye heavens,
praise the glory of God.

Irmos: Let every mortal born on earth, carrying his torch, in spirit leap for joy; and let the order of the angelic powers celebrate and honour the holy feast of the Mother of God, and let them cry: Hail! Thou blessed and ever Virgin, who gavest birth to God.

Let no profane hand touch the living Ark of God, but let the lips of the faithful, singing without ceasing the words of the Angel to the Theotokos, cry aloud in great joy: Hail, thou who art full of grace: the Lord is with thee.

Having conceived God in ways past understanding, O Maiden, thou hast escaped from the ordinances of nature. For though by nature mortal, thou wast not subject to the established laws of motherhood. Therefore, as is meet, dost thou hear the salutation: 'Hail, thou who art full of grace: the Lord is with thee.'

How dost thou give milk, O pure Virgin? This the tongue of mortal man cannot make plain. For thou showest forth a thing unknown to nature, that utterly surpasses the usual laws of birth. Therefore, as is meet, dost Thou hear the salutation: 'Hail, thou who art full of grace: the Lord is with thee.'

The Holy Scriptures speak of thee mystically, O Mother of the Most High. For Jacob saw in days of old the ladder that prefigured thee, and said: 'This is the stair on which God shall tread.' Therefore, as is meet, dost thou hear the salutation : 'Hail, thou who art full of grace: the Lord is with thee.' [Gen 28:12]

The bush and the fire showed a strange marvel to Moses, the initiate in sacred things. Seeking its fulfilment in the course of time, he said: 'I shall observe it brought to pass in the pure Virgin. To her as Theotokos shall the salutation come: Hail, thou who art full of grace: the Lord is with thee.' [Ex 3:2]

Daniel called thee a spiritual mountain; Isaiah, the Mother of God; Gideon saw thee as a fleece and David called thee sanctuary; another called thee gate. And Gabriel in his turn cries out to thee: 'Hail, thou who art full of grace, the Lord is with thee.' [Dan 2:34; Is 7:14; Judg 6:38; Ps 95:6 and 131:8 (LXX); Ezek 44:2]

Katavasia: Let no profane hand touch.... [first troparion]

Exapostilarion

The captain of the angelic hosts was sent by God Almighty to the pure Virgin, to announce the good tidings of a strange and secret wonder: that, as man, God would be born a babe of her without seed, fashioning again the whole race of man. O ye people, announce the good tidings of the refashioning of the world (*twice*).

Glory to the Father . . . Both now . . . .

Hail, O Theotokos, deliverance from the curse of Adam. Hail, holy Mother of God; hail, living Bush. Hail, Lamp; hail, Throne; hail, Ladder and Gate. Hail, divine Chariot; hail, swift Cloud. Hail, Temple; hail, Vessel of gold. Hail, Mountain; hail, Tabernacle and Table. Hail, thou release of Eve. [Gen 3:15–17; Ex 3:2, 25:31; Gen 28:12, 17; Ezek 44:2; Is 19:1; Ex 16:33; Daniel 2:34–35; Ex 26:1, 25:23]

The Source

"Annunciation Canon," by St John of Damascus, from *The Festal Menaion*, trans Mother Mary and Metropolitan Kallistos Ware (Waymart, PA: St Tikhon's Seminary Press, 1998), 448–459. Reprinted with permission.

The Festal Menaion is an excellent resource for understanding the Great Feasts and for personal preparation for the services.

Miscellanea

Angelic Fear

The noetic hosts are terrified, beholding the Father's divine Effulgence inexplicably held in thine arms, and bearing a likeness to thee, to the end that He might deify mortals, O ever-virgin Mother, who knewest not wedlock.

Another translation:

The noetic armies are filled with awe, beholding the divine Effulgence of the Father ineffably held in thine arms and assuming our form, that He might deify mortals, O most immaculate Virgin Mother.[1]

The Festal Menaion

As a convenient subset of the (huge) *Menaion* (see below), *The Festal Menaion*, now published by St Tikhon's Seminary Press, contains the services for the "immoveable" Great Feasts, like Christmas and Theophany, Transfiguration and Exaltation of the Cross. This edition includes elucidating introductions to the Great Feasts and to the cycle of services throughout the year. It also breaks down the basic structure of the individual services, i.e., Vespers, Compline, Matins, and the Hours. It makes a handy primer for learning how the services work. For greater appreciation of the services in general, for deeper understanding of the Great Feasts in particular, and for personal preparation before these services of the Great Feasts, it is an indispensable resource.

Parent Friendly

Children naturally follow their parents' example and assume their attitudes. Teaching children early on about proper church etiquette makes Orthodoxy natural to them. The Holy Fathers say that external holiness, when practiced conscientiously—neither pharasaically nor robotically—leads to

1 Theotokion from the ninth ode of the Canon to Holy Martyr Sebastian (Dec 18). The first translation is from the Brookline *Menaion* (Boston: Holy Transfiguration Monastery, 2005), 4:142. The second is from the SJKP *Menaion*, trans Isaac E. Lambertsen (Liberty, TN: St John of Kronstadt Press, 2011), 4:243; www.SJKP.org. Used with permission.

internal holiness. Thus, the sign of the cross, bows and prostrations, fostering attentiveness and an awareness of God's presence—at home as well as in church—become a precious reality and way of life. Keeping children quiet and in the service until the end can be challenging, but anecdotal evidence (from a loving but no-nonsense matushka) suggests that there is great benefit from this extra effort. Children who are brought up in this way through high school are much more likely to return to the Church—after the rebellion of their teen years and beyond—than children who are allowed to do whatever they want.

Likewise, children should be taught the real prayers of the Church. Children who learn childish, dumbed-down prayers grow out of them, yet retain a sense that church and prayers and God are childish and dumb.

The Menaion

The *Menaia*, a separate volume for each month, contain the services for every calendar day of the year, that is, the changing parts of the services for the saints of the day and the immoveable feasts. The *Menaion* from Holy Transfiguration Monastery (Brookline) is a beautiful publication. It contains the ancient commemorations for each day, with many additions for more contemporary saints. In accordance with Greek practice, there is a brief synaxarion listing of the saints of the day between the sixth and seventh odes of the matins canons. The text generally is in large print for easier reading on the cliros. Many stichera and sessional hymns are metered to fit *prosomia* melodies, some of which are sampled in this Reader in chapter 12, "Weekday Hymnal." The book's format is streamlined to work with the monastery's *Great Horologion*. The Foreword and Introduction in the first volume (September) are greatly encouraging and edifying.

The *Menaion* from St John of Kronstadt Press is bulkier but with good reason. It contains many more Russian saints and a few more contemporary saints. It also conveniently repeats, in each of the twelve volumes, the Canon of Supplication to the All-holy Theotokos (the Paraclesis canon), the variable theotokia, and the common katavasiae.

Preference for either translation is a matter of personal taste. People who, for private devotions, want the complete canons for their patron or favorite saints may lean toward the St John of Kronstadt Press edition because it includes all of the irmoi for every canon. The canons in the edition from Holy Transfiguration Monastery are trimmed specifically for use in Matins. (One delightful workaround, however, is always to preface the patron canon with, for example, the Paraclesis Canon.)

Technical Books

For people getting deeper into the services, here are a couple of helpful books—both, however, with a Russian slant.

The Order of Divine Services According to the Usage of the Russian Orthodox Church by Peter Fekula and Matthew Williams, from St John of Kronstadt Press. This book describes the structures of and variations in Sunday services, weekdays, forefeasts, feasts, and afterfeasts, the *Triodion* and *Pentecostarion*. It especially helps in understanding how to perform the matins canons during Great Lent.

An Abridged Typicon, compiled and edited by Feodor S. Kovalchuk (3rd ed revised and updated 2013) from St Tikhon's Monastery Press. This volume is directed more toward clergy concerns and church order.

These books are for serious personal study of the services, not for harassing or henpecking priests.

Whenever we are found in prayer or hymnody or reading of the Scriptures, the Angels gather. Our holy Father Saint John of Kronstadt tells us that just at the mention of the name of a Saint, he is present. So it is with the holy icons—there is a real presence. So it is when the Dismissal Hymns of the Saints are chanted—they are present. They are especially present in a singular way on the day of their commemoration when their service is chanted and their feast is celebrated. What better way to spend our time in this life than in such a manner, in such company?[1]

The sacred hymnology therefore is a vehicle of grace and a mystical meeting-ground for communion with God and His Saints, according to His own word, "Where two or three are gathered together in My Name, there am I in the midst of them" [Mt 18:20], since its purpose is to draw our heart and mind out of the world and into the presence of God. And although the hymns do refer to the historical events of this or that Feast of the Master or life of a Saint, they do not aim primarily to give a complete and sequential narrative of them—the Scriptures and the Saints' lives do that—but to inspire us to worship, to praise, to imitation, to wonder, to love, and to draw us into mystical communion with those who are "invisibly present" whenever their praises are sung.[2]

[1] *The Menaion* (Boston: Holy Transfiguration Monastery, 2005), 1:7.
[2] Ibid., 12.

10. A Sower Went Out to Sow His Seed

This homily by ***Saint Gregory Palamas*** *[†1359, Nov 14 and Second Sunday of Great Lent] heralds the happy news that one need not be a scholar or a saint to understand the writings of this famous and glorious teacher: Saint Gregory is accessible to normal people. Homilies by the Holy Fathers are a good source for Orthodox explication of Scripture, Christian life, and a variety of spiritual considerations. The homily below describes an important element of Orthodox attitude: to seek diligently to understand holy teaching and to put it into practice.*

Our Lord Jesus Christ chose His disciples not from the wise, not from the noble, not from the rich or the famous, but from among fishermen and tentmakers and poor and illiterate men. This was to make clear to all that neither poverty, nor lack of learning, nor lowly origins, nor anything else of that sort is an impediment to acquiring virtue and understanding the divine sayings and the mysteries of the Spirit. But even the poorest and lowliest and least educated person, if he gives proof of eagerness and an appropriate inclination towards what is good, can not only come to know the divine teaching but also become a teacher himself through God's grace. And the things that hinder us from understanding and grasping the meaning of spiritual teachings are our own indifference and the fact that we cling with all our might to the fleeting concerns of this life. As a result, we do not allow space or time for listening and studying and recalling to mind what we have heard, nor do we care about the things which are to come and things eternal.

Nothing demonstrates this more clearly than today's Gospel reading [Lk8:5–15]. After the Lord had addressed the people using a parable, the disciples approached Him privately and sought to learn the purpose and meaning of the parable He had related on that occasion. They asked why He spoke to the people in parables which were not readily comprehensible. Then the Lord answered them, "Unto you it is given to know the mysteries of the kingdom of God: but to others in parables; that seeing they might not see, and hearing they might not understand" [Lk 8:10].

One might be so bold as to ask Him, "Why is this, Lord? You who are the only Guide of all men, the only universal Master and Provider, only Father and Saviour of all, the light of those lying in the darkness of ignorance, the light that 'lighteth every man that cometh into the world' [Jn 1:9], do You now only illumine Your chosen disciples, and speak obscurely to the rest, lest they should understand and be enlightened?" "Yes," replies the Lord, "man is the only living creature in this world that I wished to create with freedom of choice. I did not come into the world to destroy this handiwork of Mine which had been spoilt, but to rescue it. For that reason, I never draw anyone by force. According to My righteous judgment, only those people who choose, long and seek to put the knowledge of salvation into practice are worthy to be enlightened. 'For every one that asketh receiveth; and he that seeketh findeth; and to him that knocketh it shall be opened' [Lk 11:10]. In My surpassing love for mankind, however, I also address those outside this category, without making Myself clear, that I might give them motivation and encouragement to choose and learn how to search out My teaching in order to practice it. For in this way it will be granted to them too to know the mysteries of God's kingdom. This knowledge," He says, "has been given to you who seek more diligently on your own account to put into action what you have learnt. For it is not mere knowledge that is good, but knowledge translated into deeds, and action in accordance with reason. 'For not the hearers of the law', says the Scripture, 'but the doers of the law shall be justified'" [Rom 2:13].

Do you see, brethren, that the fact that we do not easily understand or grasp the holy teaching is due to our own inaction and indifference? I say this now to your charity, having been appointed as your teacher, for reasons known to the Lord. If anyone is unable to understand the meaning of my teachings in church in all respects, he should come and ask me privately, and with the help of God, who gives me utterance "at the opening of my mouth" [Eph 6:19], he will hear more clearly and will put what he hears into practice, on account of his persistence in asking.

Let us now look at the parable from the beginning. "A sower went out to sow his seed" [Lk 8:5]. The grace of the Spirit rightly ordained that this parable should be read in church in the hearing of all just at this time, for now is the season for sowing, and most people are striving to sow their land with seeds that originate from the earth. Anyone who sows crops every year is sowing perishable seed, which will not sprout unless it dies. Obviously, therefore, he will harvest and reap perishable things, temporary sustenance for the flesh that will soon come to nothing. Through this parable we shall teach you, however, what spiritual and imperishable seeds are, when it is time to sow them, who sows them, and what type of land is able to receive them, so that we may not toil merely in the hope of the harvest which nourishes us for a short time, but may do everything in the hope of that harvest which will provide us with eternal life. "A sower," it says, "went out to sow his seed." Who is he? The Lord Himself, who through the psalmist foretold concerning Himself, "I will open my mouth in parables" [Ps 77:2, Mt 13:35]. But whence did He come out, who is everywhere present? Whither did He come, who is absent from nowhere? Again He said of Himself, "I came forth from the Father, and am come into the world" [Jn 16:28]. Without being separated from the Father's bosom, He who is in the world and by whom the world was made [Jn 1:10] came out and entered the world. He who fills heaven and earth came down from heaven to earth. Consequently, the coming forth of the only-begotten Son of God, and His descent from heaven, represent nothing other than His manifestation in the flesh and His self-emptying, from the unutterable exaltation of divinity down to human nature at the other extreme.

He came out in this way "to sow his seed." What seed is this? The word of instruction, the words of eternal life, the commandments of immortality, the promise of restoration to life, and the gospel of the kingdom of heaven. These all belong to Him, for He said of Himself, "The words that I speak unto you, they are spirit, and they are life" [Jn 6:63]; and Peter told Him, "Thou hast the words of eternal life" [Jn 6:68]. Such seed is His alone and He alone ceaselessly sows it, showing in this way that He is God over all [Rom 9:5]. Every teacher, evangelist and preacher of godliness and pious living also sows the words of life, the word of evangelical and heavenly teaching, but once he has served God's will in his generation he departs, nor did he exist previously. Moreover, the word of salvation which he sows by teaching is not his own but belongs to God, who assists him and "gives utterance at the opening of his mouth."

Our Lord Jesus Christ, however, being true God, has this seed of eternal life as His own possession, and is always sowing it through the natural law in creation, through the law given in writing to the Israelites, through the prophetic word, and later through the gospel of grace. So the season for such sowing is the entire lifetime of every person, or rather, the whole period from the Lord's advent until the end of the world. Harvest time for this seed will be at the Lord's second coming and manifestation, which we await. That is why the apostle says, "He that ploweth should plow in hope" [1Cor 9:10], and "He that soweth to the Spirit shall reap life everlasting" [Gal 6:8]. Also the psalmist says, "They that sow in tears" now "shall reap in joy" at that time [Ps 125:5].

The Lord went out to sow His seed. Where? In people's hearts, for these are the fields which receive spiritual seeds. Some of them resemble a path, as they have been trampled down and pressed solid by evil thoughts and passions, and by the most wicked demons who oversee these things. Those who are like rocky ground are unable, on account of their faint-heartedness and hardness, to hold on to the seeds of teaching to the end, or to bear fruit through them for eternal life. As for those who resemble ground which brings forth thorns, they are intent on possessions and wealth, fleeting pleasures and what springs from these.

Since many differences can be observed between the hearts of men, "A sower," it says, "went out to sow his seed: and as he sowed, some fell by the wayside; and it was trodden down, and the fowls of the air devoured it" [Lk 8:5]. Some seed, it says, fell beside the path, meaning either into hearts which were outside the right way of the Lord [cf. Acts 13:10], in which case it was trampled underfoot by the evil demons who walk about in trackless places, or else into hearts on the demons' evil path, such that the birds, the evil spirits in the air, ate it up and destroyed it; and so it is as though these people never heard God's word at all. "Those by the wayside are they that hear; then cometh the devil, and taketh away the word out of their hearts, lest they should believe and be saved." "And some fell," it says, "upon a rock," though Matthew says, "upon stony places" [Mt 13:5], meaning, on a hard unyielding heart within which the word cannot develop, or take a vigorous hold, or put down roots. So "as soon as it was sprung up," it says, "it withered away, because it lacked moisture." That is to say, they endured for a while, and seemed to grow to some extent, then when temptations came upon them they disappeared, as they were incapable of bringing fruit to perfection, because of the weakness of their resolve. "They on the rock are they, which, when they hear, receive the word with joy; and these have no root, which for a while believe, and in time of temptation fall away." "And some fell among thorns," hearts entirely devoted to the fleeting material things of this life, and submerged in the concerns and delights which come from them. Once such thorns have grown up alongside the seed, they choke and obliterate it completely. "That which fell among thorns are they, which, when they have heard, go forth, and are choked with cares and riches and pleasures of this life, and bring no fruit to perfection."

In this way, the Lord casts out and rejects those who pay no attention to the divine Spirit's teaching (the ones who fall by the wayside), and those who take notice but only for a short time (those who resemble stony ground), and also those who accept and retain a knowledge of it, but are corrupted by wealth and glory and self-indulgence (these are the fields full of thorns). He then uses the parable to introduce and set before us those people well-pleasing to God, saying, "Other fell on good ground," that is to say, a soul with a good and noble disposition, which eagerly receives the word of instruction and holds on to it, without allowing itself to be used as a channel for the enemies of its salvation to pass through, and which patiently watches over it, resolutely holding fast to what it has heard, bearing temptations with fortitude. Rejecting a fleeting life devoted to money-making and enjoyment, it matures and bears fruit, which, in the words of the divine Mark, "sprang up and increased; and brought forth, some thirty, and some sixty, and some an hundred" [Mk 4:8].

It would be possible to call these categories servitude, work for wages, and sonship. When at first someone approaches God as a guilty man, he really is a slave on account of his former disobedience and defiance. Next, having served as a slave, he desires a recompense as well. Then, after making progress in love, he becomes a son, who is now in possession of virtue and submits as if by nature to the heavenly Father, without compulsion. Let us strive, brethren, either to lay claim to divine sonship by loving God and refraining from everything else, through continuous prayer and psalmody, and waiting upon Him without distraction, or else to be classed with the hired workers, who successfully achieve self-control in all aspects of the struggle, or else to be numbered among the slaves mourning their former sins. Anyone who does not fall into one of these three groups is not among those being saved.

"When he had said these things," it says, "the Lord cried, He that hath ears to hear, let him hear" [Lk 8:8]. This is not because some people do not have ears, but because not everyone has ears for the purpose of hearing the word of salvation. Since, as the saying goes, "It is the mind which sees and the mind which hears," those who have ears to hear are the ones who listen with their minds and with understanding. If it is also the case that "a good understanding have all they that do his commandments" [Ps 110:10], and the word is recognized through deeds, it is not simply the listener who has ears to hear, but the obedient man who puts what he hears into practice.

Before all else, brethren, I beseech you, let us hear with understanding that the Lord did not say that He went out to plough the human fields, or to break up the ground two or three times, dig up the roots of the weeds and smooth out the clods of earth, that is to say, to prepare our hearts for cultivation, but that He went out immediately to sow. Why? Because this preliminary work on our souls prior to sowing ought to be done by us. That is why the Forerunner of the gospel of grace, anticipating this fact, says with a loud voice, "Prepare ye the way of the Lord, make his paths straight" [Mt 3:3], and "Repent ye: for the kingdom of heaven is at hand" [Mt 3:2]. Our preparation and the starting point of repentance is blaming ourselves,[1] confession, and abstention from evil. He also issued a warning to those who had not made themselves ready in this way to bear fruits worthy of repentance [cf. Mt 3:8, Lk 3:8]. "Every tree which bringeth not forth good fruit is hewn down, and cast into the fire" [Mt 3:10]. The sentence God passes on unrepentant sinners is that they be cut off, that once they have been torn away from this present life and the life to come, they be despatched, alas, to unquenchable hell-fire.

Let us repent, brethren, and display fruits worthy of repentance. Let each of us abstain from his wicked ways, and let us learn to speak and do what is good. Let us prepare ourselves to receive the heavenly seed, the word of life. Let us restrain our tongue from evils (What sort of evils? Idle words, abuse, slander), and our lips from uttering oaths, lies and foolish speech. Perhaps these are the evil birds mentioned in the

---

1 Gk, αὐτομεμψία, *self-condemnation*, *self-accusation*, which is perhaps even better rendered as *self-hatred*, appears at first sight to be a rather heavy and somewhat discouraging term. In the Patristic tradition, however, it refers to that spiritual disposition, which is necessary if one is truly to deny one's self, take up one's cross, and follow Christ (cf. Mt 16:24, Mk 8:34, Lk 9:23). *Self-condemnation*, therefore, is the spirit of the Cross, the spirit of martyrdom and repentance. But far from being an occasion for sorrow and despair, it is the only way that can lead to salvation and eternal joy: "For behold, by the Cross is joy come into all the world." Without *self-condemnation*—that is to say, as long as we are still governed by the spirit of *self-love*—it is not possible for us to make a full and clean confession, and to be spiritually healed.

parable, who eat up the good seed and bring it to nought. For every word is like a flying bird, which is why some have referred to them as "having wings." An evil word let loose through the mouth from its nest in the evil treasure of a man's heart [cf. Mt 12:35] robs the soul of its sanctification. The Lord says elsewhere on this subject, "Those things which proceed out of the mouth defile the man" [Mt 15:18]. May no corrupt words come out of your mouth, but only such as are capable of giving edification to those listening.

None of you should be so engrossed in the concerns of this life that you are somehow turned into stone by them and cannot open your ears and heart to the dew of the words of the Spirit's teaching. Why is it that when the earth receives rain it is loosened, softened and enriched, but fired clay stays hard and dry and does not dissolve? Is it not because the earth is warmed but not burnt by the sun's rays, and so has its pores open to receive moisture, whereas the earthenware has been burnt through forcible contact with fire, and has its pores tightly closed and sealed deep down, so that it cannot let in even the finest rain? In the same way, when anyone is obsessed by the bodily, earthly cares of everyday life his heart is continuously and severely hardened. Deadened in his understanding even before he returns to the ground, he is incapable of any perception of divine teaching. On the other hand, he who deals with the world as though he had no dealings with it, according to the apostle's advice [1Cor 7:31], will be ready to seek heavenly things, listen to them with understanding, and zealously and eagerly act upon them. He will not merely hear, but retain inwardly and put into practice, that he may be called blessed by the Lord for being like the faithful and wise servant [cf. Mt 24:45–46]. "Whosoever heareth these sayings of mine," says the Lord, "and doeth them, I will liken him unto a wise man" [Mt 7:24].

If any of you amuses himself with gluttony, excessive drinking, self-indulgent pleasure and drunkenness, he should stop. Otherwise he receives the heavenly seed, the words of instruction, to no avail, and will not be shown to be a fruitful field for God. You all know that when sown fields are too wet they cannot produce crops. So how can a heart sodden with self-indulgence and wine-drinking display heavenly fruit? If anyone has fallen into any sort of impure fornication, let him turn back, give it up, and cleanse himself through repentance. "Shall he fall, and not arise? shall he turn away, and not return?" [Jer 8:4] If he wallows in this filth, how can he keep safe within him the holy myrrh which he receives, the pearl of great price [Mt 13:46], by which I mean the word of salvation. Pearls are not given to pigs [cf. Mt 7:6], and people in their right mind do not mix myrrh with mud. If someone poured out myrrh and mingled it with dung, and put it into a dirty container, he would make the myrrh useless and ruin it. Even though holy myrrh cannot be damaged, anyone who approaches it without abstaining from impurity can be sure of suffering the harm it would have suffered, had it been capable of being spoilt. Whoever is greedy for gain, let him be so no longer, but share what he has with those who have nothing. Unless he does so, he will not escape God's anger, and if he cannot get away from the divine wrath, how can he receive the holy seed? To those who asked John, the Lord's Forerunner, how to flee from the wrath to come, he replied, "He that hath two coats, let him impart to him that hath none; and he that hath meat, let him do likewise" [Lk 3:11].

In a word, let each one of you, through repentance, pull up by the roots the thorns and thistles of sin that you have nurtured in yourself through a life full of passions and pleasures. By so doing, you will cultivate your field and make yourself ready to receive the saving seed. Then once you have received it, you will bring to perfection the fruit of eternal life. Not only ought we to give up our physical desires for the sake of that life, but even, if need be, our soul, for thus we shall follow in the Master's footsteps, be partakers of the glory and kingdom which are in Christ, and live with Him for ever, glorified with Him.

Our irrefutable witness is the most excellent of martyrs, the wonderworker and myrrh-gusher Demetrius,[1] before whose icon kings and priests prostrate themselves and rejoice to be present, for he followed in the Lord's footsteps by the way he lived, by his words and his sufferings. Not just anyone will be acceptable to him as a participant in the festival and the ceremony which has already been announced, but only those who have already been initiated into repentance. Given that the saint left behind every material attachment and showed himself in his entirety to be, in Paul's words, "a sweet savour of Christ" [2Cor 2:15], to the point that, after his struggle, even his coffin became a fount of fragrant myrrh, how can he allow anyone to dance around him and sing to him who smells of the stuff of passions and reeks of the unhealed wounds of

---

1 [Holy Great-Martyr Demetrius the Myrrh-gusher [†c.306, Oct 26], patron saint of Thessalonica, where Archbishop Gregory was preaching. His relics give forth a fragrant, healing oil to this day.]

sin? "Praise is out of place on the lips of sinners," says the Scripture [Sir (Ecclus) 15:9]. As we celebrate the forefeast, let us also purify ourselves in advance of the appointed feast of the Greatmartyr, which is drawing near. Then, having rejoiced in spirit together with him at the memory of his struggles for Christ's sake, his Christlike life beforehand, and his rewards from Christ afterwards, may we receive this pledge of our hope to dwell in heaven with those who rejoice eternally.

May we all attain to this by the prayers of our city's patron saint and martyr for Christ, to the glory of the Father and the Son and the Holy Spirit, now and for ever and unto the ages of ages. Amen.

The Source

Homily 47, "On the Gospel for the Fourth Sunday of Luke Which Says, 'A Sower Went Out to Sow His Seed,'" from *Saint Gregory Palamas: The Homilies*, trans Christopher Veniamin (Dalton, PA: Mount Thabor Publishing, 2009), 366–374.

The extensive, scholarly footnotes were abridged for easier introductory reading.

Miscellanea

Cultivating the Field

Our soul has three parts or powers—the thinking, the desiring, and the excitable.[1] Owing to their corruption, these three powers give birth to three corresponding kinds of wrong thoughts and

1 [The "thinking" part of the soul is sometimes translated as the "intelligent" ("the intellect") or "reasoning" part; the irrational parts of the soul are the "desiring" part, also translated as "appetitive" or "concupiscible," and the "excitable" part, also translated as "incensive" or "irascible"—not limited to anger but vehement feelings generally.]

movements. The thinking power gives birth to thoughts of ingratitude to God and complaints, forgetfulness of God, ignorance of divine things, ill-judgment, and all kinds of blasphemous thoughts. The desiring power gives birth to pleasure-loving thoughts, thoughts of vainglory, love of money, and all their numerous ramifications, belonging to the domain of self-indulgence. The excitable power gives birth to thoughts of anger, hatred, envy, revenge, gloating, ill-will, and generally to all evil thoughts. You should overcome all such thoughts and impulses by the methods indicated above, trying on every occasion to arouse and establish in your heart good feelings and dispositions opposed to them: in place of unbelief—undoubting faith in God; in place of complaints—a sincere gratitude to God for everything; in place of forgetfulness of God—a constant deep remembrance of the ever-present and all-powerful God; in place of ignorance—a clear contemplation or mental examination of all the soul-saving Christian truths; in place of ill-judgment—faculties trained to discriminate between good and evil; in place of all blasphemous thoughts—praise and glorification of God. In the same way, in place of love of pleasure—every kind of abstinence, fasting, and self-mortification; in place of vainglory—humility and desire of obscurity; in place of love of money—contentment with little and love of poverty. Again, in place of anger—meekness; in place of hatred—love; in place of envy—rejoicing with others; in place of revenge—forgiveness and a peaceful disposition; in place of gloating—compassion; in place of ill-will—well-wishing.

In short, with Saint Maximus, I shall condense all this in the following propositions: adorn your thinking power with a constant attention to God, prayer, and knowledge of divine truths; the desiring power—with total self-denial and renunciation of all self-indulgence; the excitable power—with love. If you do this, then, I assure you, the light of your mind will never be dimmed and wrong thoughts will never find place in you. If you are active in setting up such good thoughts and dispositions in yourself morning, evening, and at all other hours of the day, invisible foes will never come near you.[1]

—*Unseen Warfare*

1 *Unseen Warfare*, the *Spiritual Combat* and *Path to Paradise* of Lorenzo Scupoli, edited by St Nicodemus of the Holy Mountain [the Hagiorite, †1809, July 14] and revised by St Theophan the Recluse [†1894, Jan 10], trans E. Kadloubovsky and G.E.H.Palmer (Crestwood, NY: St Vladimir's Seminary Press, 1987), 105. Used with permission.

Faith Comes through Hearing

At a recent Great Feast service that happened to fall on a weekday, the priest's homily was about how good it is to attend the feasts. He was "preaching to the choir," as they say, to the few people in attendance. It would be more helpful if this sermonette were given to the much larger congregation on Sundays to encourage all to attend to the feasts.

This is not to place all the burden on the priests. Saint John Chrysostom, in fact, takes it a step further. In the cleverly titled sermon, "To Those Who Had Not Attended the Assembly," he does not chide those who are not in attendance—how could he? they're not there—but rather the few who show up for the regular services.

> How distressed am I, do you think, when I call to mind that on the festival days the multitudes assembled resemble the broad expanse of the sea, but now not even the smallest part of that multitude is gathered together here? Where are they now who oppress us with their presence on the feast days? [1]

He takes to task those who are assembled for not encouraging the others to attend.

> I did no good as it seems by the prolonged discourse which I lately addressed to you with a view to kindling your zeal for the assemblies here: for again our Church is destitute of her children. Wherefore also I am again compelled to seem vexatious and burdensome, reproving those who are present, and finding fault with those who have been left behind: with them because they have not put away their sloth, and with you because you have not given a helping hand to the salvation of your brethren.

It would be much easier for the laity to encourage one another to come to weekend Vespers and Matins and weekday feasts (and normal weekday services, if they existed) if the words of the services were intelligible. That is, when the services are incomprehensible, how can one invite people to come stand for two hours to listen to (and languish in) gibberish? If one cannot draw *Orthodox* people to the services—people who should understand what goes on in the services even if they cannot *hear* them—how can one possibly invite lapsed or slothful Orthodox? Or even

1 All quoted passages are from St John Chrysostom, "To Those Who Had Not Attended the Assembly," in *Nicene and Post-Nicene Fathers*, First Series (Peabody, MA: Hendrickson Publishers), 9:223–232.

non-Orthodox—people who are hungry for God but simply don't know any better?

> Even if we are earnest and well trained and have much zeal about hearing the holy scriptures, this does not suffice for our salvation. For the *deposit* must be doubled,[1] and it becomes doubled when together with our own salvation we undertake to make some provision for the good of others.

Simply by making the services intelligible with clear enunciation and disciplined singing in a language the congregation understands, how much continuing Adult Education is provided!—without any extra commitments of time, effort, or resources. How much catechesis for the young! How much missionary work is carried on!

The priests, then, along with the readers and chanters, are instrumental in ensuring the intelligibility of the services, but the laity are equally responsible for encouraging attendance. Naturally, it helps the laity when the priests take the lead.

> I have been anxious at any rate to know clearly, whether you continue to exhort your brethren, and if they remain all the time in the same condition of indolence: otherwise I would never have given you any trouble: as it is, I have fears that they may remain uncorrected in consequence of your neglect and indifference. For it is impossible that a man who continually has the benefit of exhortation and instruction should not become better and more diligent. The proverb which I am about to cite is certainly a common one, nevertheless it confirms this very truth. For "a perpetual dropping of water," it says, "wears a rock," yet what is softer than water? and what is harder than a rock? Nevertheless perpetual action conquers nature: and if it conquers nature, much more will it be able to prevail over the human will. Christianity is no child's play, my beloved: no matter of secondary importance. I am continually saying these things . . . .

Let the obvious be emphasized: nagging is counterproductive; self-righteousness, abominable. When attempting to encourage others (gently, *softly*), it might be helpful to mention *why* to attend or perhaps a tidbit of clarification regarding the feast or service; as Saint John says, "exhortation and instruction."

1 *Deposit* refers to the Master who gave his servants five talents, two talents, and one talent, Mt 25:14–30.

11. Glory Be to God!

We believe in God: Father, Son, and Holy Spirit, in Orthodox manner, as Christ taught the Apostles, as it has been passed down to us. To believe in *God is only the beginning. We must also* believe *God: that He truly loves us and cares for us at every moment; that keeping His commandments benefits* us, *is healing for us; that He knows everything about us and all those around us and directs—respecting our free will—all things for our good.*

Saint Ignatius Brianchaninov *[†1867, April 30], a contemporary of the first Optina Elders, a director of monks, and a spiritual writer, in the following essay considers and marvels at how, and how much, God loves us. With this kind of attitude, how can we do other than to continuously thank and praise and glorify God?*

Glory be to God! Glory be to God! Glory be to God! For all that I see in myself, in everyone, in everything—*glory be to God!*

And what do I see in myself? I see sin, incessant sin. I see the ceaseless violation of the most sacred commandments of my God, Creator, and Redeemer. And my God sees my sins; He sees them all, and sees their innumerable quantity. When I, a man, a limited being, in my feebleness like unto the grass and the flowers of the field, gaze clearly at my sins, they horrify me—both by their quantity and by their character. What must they be before the eyes of God, Who is all-holy and all-perfect?

And up to now, God has looked upon my stumblings with long-suffering! Up to now He has not given me over to the destruction I have long deserved and called upon myself! The earth does not open beneath me, and does not swallow the offender who has burdened it! Heaven does not cast down its fire, does not consume the violator of the heavenly commands! The waters do not overflow their reservoirs and rush upon the sinner, who has sinned openly before all creation. They do not seize him and bury him in the depths of their dark abysses! Hades is held back:

it is not given the victim it justly demands, over whom it has inarguable rights!

Reverently and with fear, I look upon God, Who looks upon my sins, Who sees them more clearly than does my own conscience. His wondrous long-suffering astonishes and confounds me: I give thanks to and glorify this *Ineffable Goodness*. My thoughts are at a loss. I am utterly overcome with gratitude and doxology. Gratitude and doxology have totally taken possession of me, and impose a reverent silence upon my mind and heart. I feel, think, and utter with my tongue only one thing: *Glory be to God!*

Whither art thou carried away, O my thought? Look steadfastly upon my sins; arouse mourning over them within me. I need cleansing through bitter weeping, washing through uninterrupted tears. My thought does not hearken, it flies—it is irrepressible—it takes its stand at an unbounded height! Its flight is like unto the racing of lightning, when in one instant it touches two extremities of the horizon. And my thought has risen to the height of spiritual contemplation, whence it looks upon an extraordinary, most vast spectacle; upon a most striking, most remarkable picture. Before it is the whole world, all of time, from the creation to the end of the world, all the events of the world—past, present, and future. Before it is the fate of each man, in its most minute detail. Above time, social events, and the destinies of every man, it sees God, the Fashioner of all creatures and their infinite Master, Who sees all and directs all, Who foreordains the ends of all things and gives them their purpose.

God permits man to observe His directing of all things. But the causes of destinies, the origins of God's decrees, are known to God alone. *For who hath known the mind of the Lord? Or who hath been His counsellor?* [Rom 11:34]. And the fact that man is permitted to be an observer of God in His providence, in His direction of creation, in His judgments—this is the greatest good for man, and yields abundant benefit for his soul.

By beholding the Creator and Lord of all visible and invisible creations, the observer is clothed with supernatural power. This vision is united with the recognition of the unlimited authority of the Almighty King of creation over His creation. The hairs of our heads—hairs that are so insignificant according to the feeble opinion of man—are numbered by that unlimited and all-embracing Wisdom, and are preserved by It [cf. Mt 10:30; Lk 21:18]. Even more so—without a sign from Wisdom, not a single incident, not a single upheaval can take place in human life.

A Christian who steadily looks upon God's providence preserves constant courage and unshakable steadfastness amidst the fiercest tribulations. He says, with the holy Psalmist and Prophet: "*I beheld the Lord ever before me, for He is at my right hand, that I might not be shaken* [Ps. 15:8]. The Lord is my helper: I will not be afraid of any kind of misfortune. I will not give myself over to despondency, nor will I sink into the deep sea of sorrow. For everything—*glory be to God!*"

Beholding God's providence instills unlimited submission to God. Do various and twisted afflictions surround the servant of God on all sides? This is how that servant consoles his wounded heart: "God sees all of this. If, according to reasons known to Him, the Wise One, these afflictions were not to my benefit and were not necessary, He, the Almighty, would have warded them off. But He is not warding them off: it is His all-holy will that they oppress me. Precious to me is His will, more precious than life! It is better for a creature to die than to reject the will of the Creator! In this will is true life. He who dies to fulfill the will of God enters into greater progress in life. For everything—*glory be to God!*"

When one beholds God's providence, profound meekness and immutable love for one's neighbor arise in one's soul, and no winds can agitate or trouble him. For such a soul there are no insults, no offenses, no crimes: all of creation acts according to the will or permission of the Creator. Creation is merely a blind implement. The voice of humility can be heard in such a soul, accusing him of numberless sins and justifying his neighbors as the instruments of *impartial providence*. This voice comforts amidst sufferings; it offers tranquility and consolation. It quietly says, "I am receiving the due reward of my deeds [cf. Lk 23:41]. It is better for me to suffer in this brief life than to suffer eternally in the everlasting torments of hell. My sins cannot go unpunished: God's justice requires this. In the fact that they are being punished in this brief earthly life I see God's ineffable mercy. *Glory be to God!*"

Beholding God's providence preserves and increases faith in God. He who sees the invisible, almighty hand that directs the world, abides undisturbed in the terrible storms that roil the sea of life. He believes that the life of society, the helm of the Church, and the fate of each man are held in the almighty and all-wise right hand of God. When he looks upon the fierce waves, the menacing storms, and the dark clouds, he contents and pacifies himself with the thought that God sees what is taking place. Proper to man—a feeble creature—is a quiet, humble submission, and a reverent awareness and contemplation of God's judgments. May everything be directed according to His foreordained ways, to the aims determined on high. For everything—*glory be to God!*

Not only temporal sorrows, but also those that await man at his entry into eternity, beyond the bounds of the grave, are unable to withstand the vision of Divine providence. They are blunted and destroyed by the grace-filled consolation that always descends upon a soul who denies himself in order to be submissive to God. In the face of selflessness, in the face of devotion to God's will, death itself is not terrible. The true servant of Christ entrusts his soul and his eternal lot into Christ's hands, entrusting them with firm faith in Christ, with unwavering hope in His goodness and power. When his soul parts from his body, and the rejected angels defiantly and impudently approach him, he strikes the dark and evil angels with his self-renunciation and turns them to flight. "Take me—take me!" he courageously tells them. "Cast me into the abyss of darkness and fire; cast me into the abyss of hell, if it is my God's will for you to do that, if such a determination has come from Him. It is easier to be deprived of the sweetness of Paradise, it is easier to bear the flames of hell, than to transgress the will and decision of the great God. I have surrendered myself to Him, and still surrender to Him! He is the Judge of my infirmities and sins, not you! You—even in the midst of your insane rebelliousness—are only the fulfillers of His determinations." The servants of the prince of this world will tremble and become astonished, seeing such courageous selflessness, such meek, total devotion to God's will! When they spurned that blessed obedience, they went from being radiant and good angels to being dark and utterly malicious demons. They will back away with shame, and that soul, without hindrance, will direct his course to where his treasure is—to God.[1] There he will see, face to face, Him Who is seen here through faith in His providence, and he will eternally exclaim: *Glory be to God!*

Glory be to God! What mighty words! Amidst sorrowful circumstances, when the heart is beset and surrounded by thoughts of doubt, faintheartedness, dissatisfaction, and murmuring, it must force itself to the frequent, unhurried, attentive repetition of the words: *Glory be to*

---

1 Cf. St John of Karpathos, "One Hundred Texts for the Encouragement of the Monks of India Who Had Written to Him," Chapter 25, in *The Philokalia: The Complete Text*, (London: Faber & Faber, 1983), 1:303–4.

God! He who with simplicity of heart believes the advice that is offered here, and actually tries it when he encounters need, will see the wondrous power of the glorification of God. He will rejoice over the acquisition of such beneficial, new knowledge. He will rejoice over the acquisition of such a powerful and advantageous weapon against his noetic foes. From the sound alone of these words, uttered at the amassing of dark thoughts of sorrow and despondency; from the sound alone of these words, uttered with compulsion, as it were with the lips alone, as it were merely into the air—the princes of the air will tremble and turn to flight. All dismal thoughts will be scattered, like dust by a strong wind. Burdens and tedium will recede from one's soul, and lightness, tranquility, peace, consolation, and joy will draw near to it and make their abode within it. *Glory be to God!*

Glory be to God! What triumphant words! Words that are a proclamation of victory! Words that are joy to all God's faithful servants, and fear and defeat to all His enemies, and the destruction of their weapon. That weapon is sin; that weapon is the fleshly mind and fallen human wisdom. This wisdom arose from the fall, and has sin as its initial cause—it is rejected by God, it is at constant enmity with God, and it is continually repudiated by God. In vain do all the wise of the world gather before one who is wounded by sorrow. In vain will they try to heal him with treatments of eloquence and philosophy. Futile is the labor of the infirm one himself, if he wants to untangle the twisted net of sorrows by the efforts of his own intellect. Very often, almost always, the intellect becomes utterly lost in this twisted net! It often sees itself ensnared, and confined on all sides! Deliverance, and consolation itself, often no longer seem possible! And many perish under the unbearable weight of fierce sorrow; they perish from the deadly wound, the wound of grief, having found no remedy on earth powerful enough to cure that wound. Earthly wisdom has appeared with all its remedies, but they all turn out to be powerless and worthless. Beloved brother: spurn what is rejected by God! Set aside all the weapons of your own reason! Take up the weapon that is given to you by the boldness of the preaching of Christ! Human wisdom smiles derisively when it sees the weapon offered by faith. Fallen reason, by its characteristic of enmity against God, will not be slow to offer the cleverest objections, full of educated skepticism and irony. Pay no attention to them—they are rejected by God, and are God's enemies. In your sorrow, say from your soul, without any deliberation, the words:

Glory be to God! You will see a sign; you will see a miracle. These words will drive away sorrow and summon consolation into your heart. They will accomplish what the reason of the rational and the wisdom of the wise of this world could not accomplish. That kind of reason and wisdom will be put to shame—they will be put to shame. And you—delivered, healed, and believing with a living faith, proven to you within yourself—will offer up *glory to God!*

Glory be to God! Many of God's saints loved to repeat those words often: they tasted the power concealed within them. When Saint John Chrysostom spoke with his spiritual friends and brothers about any circumstances, in particular about those that were sorrowful, he would always set down, as the foundation stone, as the fundamental dogma of his discourse, the words: *Glory be to God for all things!* According to his custom—which has been preserved by Church history for posterity—striking the index finger of his right hand against the outspread palm of his left hand, he would always begin his talk with the words: *Glory be to God for all things!*

Brethren! Let us, too, train ourselves in the frequent glorification of God. Let us resort to this weapon in our sorrows. By the unceasing glorification of God, let us repulse and shake our invisible foes, especially those of them that try to cast us down through sorrow, faintheartedness, murmuring, and despondency. Let us purify ourselves with tears, prayer, and the reading of Holy Scripture and the Patristic writings, so as to become beholders of the providence of God, Who sees all, rules over all, governs all, and directs all by His unsearchable judgments to the aims known to God alone. Having become beholders of the Divine governance, let us—in reverence, in inviolable peace of heart, in total submission and firm faith, astonished at the greatness of the ineffable God—send up glory to Him both now and unto the ages of ages.

It is meet and right for creation to unceasingly glorify Thee, O God the Creator, Who hath brought us forth into being from nothingness by Thine endless, ineffable goodness; Who hath adorned us with beauty, with the glory of Thine image and likeness; Who hath led us into blessedness and the delight of Paradise, for which no end hath been appointed.

How have we rewarded our Benefactor? What has the dust, brought to life by the Creator, offered Him in thanksgiving?

We have come to an agreement with His enemies, with the angels who rebelled against God, with the captain of evil. We have hearkened to words of blasphemy against our Benefactor. We have dared, in envy, to be suspicious of our Creator, of all-perfect Goodness.

Alas, what darkness! Alas, what a fall of the mind! From the height of the vision of God and of theology, in an instant, our race—in the person of our first parents—fell into the abyss of eternal death....

In the first place, Satan fell. The radiant angel was made into a dark demon. Not having a body, he sinned in mind and word. Instead of glorifying God, the Benefactor, in innocent gladness with the rest of the holy angels, he came to love blasphemy. Barely had he conceived his dark, death-bearing thought, barely had he carried out his pernicious word, like unto the most evil venom, when he became dark, was changed, and was cast down from the height of heaven to the earth with indescribable speed. The Pre-eternal Word witnesses to the speed of his fall: *I beheld Satan as lightning fall from heaven* [Lk 10:18].

Just as rapid was the fall of man, who followed the fallen angel, having begun his fall with the acceptance of a dark blasphemous thought, after which followed the transgression of God's commandments. That transgression had already been anticipated by concealed disdain and rejection of God.

Alas, what blindness! What a terrible sin! What a terrible fall! In the face of this sin, in the face of this fall, how negligible the punishment was: banishment from Paradise, the gaining of our daily bread in the sweat of our face, the pain of bearing children, and our return to the earth, from which our bodies had been taken by the Creator.

But Thou—what dost Thou do, O immeasurable Goodness? How dost Thou reward us for the reward we accorded Thee for Thy first benefactions? How dost Thou reward us for disobeying Thee, for our lack of faith in Thee, for our acceptance of terrible blasphemy against Thee—against Thee Who art Goodness itself, Perfection itself?

Thou rewardest us with new benefactions, greater than the first. In One of Thy Divine Persons Thou takest on humanity. With the exception of sin, Thou takest on all our infirmities, that adhered to human nature after its fall. Thou appearest before our eyes in human flesh, concealing the unbearable glory of Thy Divinity. Being the Word of God, Thou proclaimest to us the word of God in the sounds of human words. Thy power is the power of God. Thy meekness is the meekness of a lamb. Thy Name is the name of a man. This all-holy Name makes heaven and earth to turn. How consoling and great Thy Name sounds! As it enters into our hearing, as it proceeds from our mouth, it enters and proceeds like a priceless treasure, like a priceless pearl. *Jesus Christ!* Thou art the Lord of man, and Thou art Thyself a man. How wondrously and gracefully Thou unitest Divinity with mankind! How wondrously Thou actest! Thou art both God and man! Thou art both Master and slave![1] Thou art both Priest and sacrifice! Thou art both the Savior and the future impartial Judge of the whole world! And Thou healest all infirmities! And Thou visitest and receivest sinners! And Thou raisest the dead! And Thou commandest the waters of the sea and the winds of heaven! And Thou dost increase bread in Thy hands, and grant a thousandfold harvest—sown, reaped, baked, and broken, at one and the same time, in one instant! And Thou dost hunger, so as to deliver us from famine! And Thou dost thirst, that our thirst might be quenched. And Thou dost journey throughout the land of our exile, tiring Thyself, so as to give us back our tranquil heavenly nature, filled with delights, which we have lost! And Thou pourest out Thy sweat in the Garden of Gethsemane, that we might cease to pour out our sweat in the gaining of bread for our belly. We have learned to pour out our sweat in prayer for the worthy communion of Heavenly Bread. Thou didst receive the thorns, brought forth for us by the earth because of the curse, upon Thine own head. Thou didst crown and wound Thine all-holy head with thorns! We were deprived of the paradisal Tree of Life and its fruit, which gave immortality to those who tasted of it. And Thou, being stretched out upon the tree of the Cross, becamest for us the Fruit that granteth eternal life to Thy communicants. And both the fruit of life and the tree of life appeared on earth, in the land of our exile. That fruit and that tree are superior to those of Paradise; the latter imparted immortality, but the former impart immortality and divinity. By Thy sufferings Thou didst pour forth sweetness into our sufferings. We reject earthly delights and choose suffering as our lot, if only we might be made partakers of Thy sweetness! As a foretaste of eternal life, it is sweeter and more precious than temporal life! Thou didst fall asleep in the sleep of death, which could not hold Thee in eternal sleep—it could not hold Thee, Who art God! Thou didst arise, and didst grant us to wake from that sleep, from the fierce sleep of death—Thou didst grant us blessed and glorious resurrection! Thou didst raise up our nature to heaven, and didst seat it at the right hand of

1 Cf. Blessed Theophylact of Ohrid and Bulgaria, *The Explanation of the Holy Gospel according to St Luke* [Lk 14:17] (House Springs, MO: Chrysostom Press, 2007), 182–83.

Thy Pre-eternal Father, Who is co-eternal with Thee! Thou madest Thy Father our Father! Thou didst open to us the path to heaven! Thou didst prepare habitations for us in heaven. Thou guidest to those habitations, and receivest, consolest, and grantest peace to all the tired earthly wanderers who believed in Thee, called upon Thy holy name, kept Thy commandments, served Thee in Orthodoxy and piety, bore Thy Cross, and drank Thy cup courageously, with thanksgiving to Thee, with doxology to Thee!

Glory to Thee, Thou Creator of those who did not previously exist! Glory to Thee, Thou Redeemer and Savior of the fallen and the lost! Glory to Thee, our Lord and God! Grant us, both on earth and in heaven, to glorify, bless, and exalt Thy goodness! Grant us to openly gaze upon Thy fearful, unapproachable, magnificent glory, to gaze upon it eternally, to worship it, and to enjoy blessedness therein. Amen.

The Source

St Ignatius Brianchaninov [†1867, April 30], "Glory Be to God!" in the periodical *The Orthodox Word* (Platina, CA: St Herman Press) 50 nos 1–2 (294–295): 43–52 (January–April, 2014). Used with permission.

Miscellanea

Really Big God

The popular morning prayer below is sometimes attributed to Saint Philaret, Metropolitan of Moscow [†Nov 19, 1867] and sometimes to the Optina Elders [Oct 11]. If we are persuaded by the previous essay by Saint Ignatius, if we believe, if we *trust* that all things are in God's hands, that He directs all things for our own personal good—all the while completely respecting our free will (which He gave to us)—and that everything works for good to those who believe [Rom 8:28], then the prayer may take on fuller meaning. (Emphasis added.)

> O Lord, *grant* me to greet the coming day in peace. *Help* me in all things *to rely upon your holy will.* In every hour of the day *reveal your will* to me. *Bless* my dealings with *all who surround me. Teach* me to treat *all that comes to me throughout the day* with peace of soul and with firm conviction that *Your will governs all.* In all my deeds and words, *guide* my thoughts and feelings. In unforeseen events, *let me not forget* that *all are sent by You. Teach* me to act firmly and wisely, without embittering and embarrassing others. *Give me strength* to bear the fatigue of the coming day with all that it shall bring. *Direct* my will, *teach* me to pray, and You Yourself *pray in me.*

Public Display of Affection

Some Americans are uneasy with public display of affection, whether by other people or—God forbid!—themselves. Yet this is exactly what veneration of icons, quiet reverence in the temple, prostrations and the like happen to be. It can make "reverence in the temple" uncomfortable. Intensifying this reluctance is the instilled politeness or correctness not to make a show of one's religion. The American casual attitude, irrepressible geniality, and quick, clean efficiency can also add difficulties.

Further discomfort may come from ignorance and uncertainty. Orthodox who left the Church and have returned may not remember the churchy protocol of their youth. Or, if the only church they can attend is of a different jurisdiction, they may hesitate at the local practices. Or, influenced by heterodox experiences, they may no longer be sure of how they feel about the "orthodox" way of doing things. Then again, there are the many converts entering the Church who are mostly untrained (no yia-yia[1]), unexposed to "best practices," and left to their own devices.

> Despite the importance of some rules of Church etiquette, we should remember that the meaning of Christian life is not in following rules, but in a closer union with God. Rules merely serve a supportive, utilitarian role. The meaning of a saw or hammer is not in owning and caressing them, but in the building that can be built with their help. . . . If you notice that someone has broken a rule of Church etiquette out of ignorance, do not take a whip and chase that person out of the temple, especially if you are an older person, and the man or woman whom you plan to drive out is much younger than you. First, learn to heal and raise from the dead, only then to drive out of temples. It is absolutely unacceptable to take upon yourself the role of a Church policeman: teaching and correcting parishioners' mistakes is the job of a bishop or a priest, to whom the bishop delegated this responsibility in a particular parish.[2]

Some people are just way too pious, and others aren't nearly pious enough. Alas and alack, however, for those bishops and priests who are supposed to teach these American parishioners. It puts the clergy on the receiving end of that quintessential American trait: the bristling, quick-to-take-offense, "You can't tell me what to do!"

1 Orthodox grandmother.
2 Fr Sergei Sveshnikov, "On Church Etiquette," in the periodical *Orthodox Life* (Jordanville, NY: Holy Trinity Monastery) 61 no 1 (Jan-Feb 2010): 25–26. Used with permission.

12. Weekday Hymnal

"Be filled with the Spirit; speaking one to another in psalms and hymns and spiritual songs, singing and making melody with your heart to the Lord." [Eph 5:19]

Hymns and praises belong not only in Sunday church services but in our hearts and daily life. They are a source of instruction, consolation, and joy. Moreover, they counteract the worldly soundtrack that pervades our lives, the **noise** *that insidiously nests and endlessly spawns in our hearts and minds: inane and often perverse popular songs, advertising jingles, verbal, visual, and musical clichés from movies, TV, the Internet barrage.*

*This weekday hymnal follows the Church's sanctification of the days of the week, that is, commemorating the Holy Angels on Monday, Saint John the Baptist on Tuesday, the Cross and Theotokos on Wednesday and Friday, and on Thursday the Apostles and Saint Nicholas. The hymns are from various services and make use of special melodies. The letters above the staff indicate the ison, the base [*sic*] note that supports the melody. It is not really necessary for our present purpose, but is provided for those with special interest. The tempo of each tune is a little less than three quarter notes per second (about 160 on the metronome), a very natural pace.*

"Learn to sing psalms, and thou shalt see the delightfulness of the employment. For they who sing psalms are filled with the Holy Spirit, as they who sing satanic songs are filled with an unclean spirit. What is meant by 'with your hearts to the Lord'? It means, with close attention and understanding. For they who do not attend closely merely sing, uttering the words whilst their heart is roaming elsewhere."[1]

For those who can't sing or read music, the words themselves provide cheerful meditation.

---

1 St John Chrysostom, Homily XIX on Ephesians, *Nicene and Post-Nicene Fathers*, First Series, (Peabody, MA: Hendrickson Publishers), 13:138.

Monday :: The Holy Angels

Tone 4, *Thou Who wast raised up*

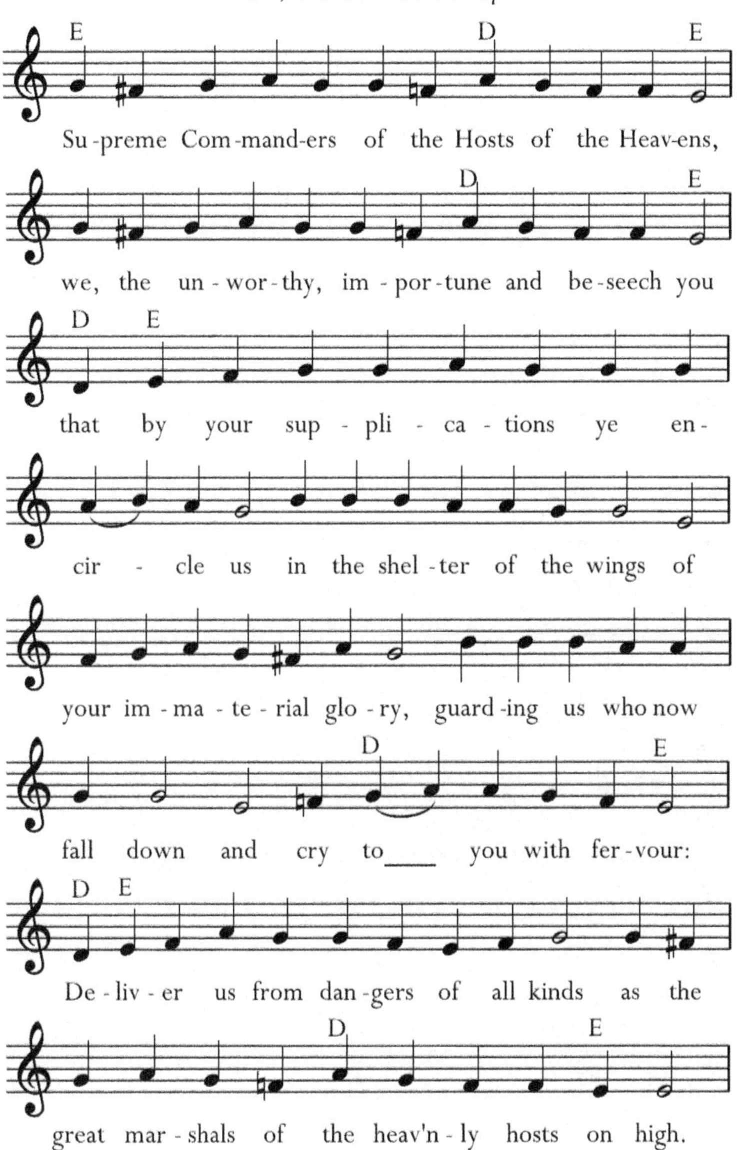

This troparion is sung every Monday for the Holy Angels and also at the Synaxes of Holy Archangels Michael (Nov 8) and Gabriel (Mar 26 & Jul 13).

Tuesday :: Saint John the Baptist

Tone 5 (Plagal of First Tone), *Let us worship the Word*

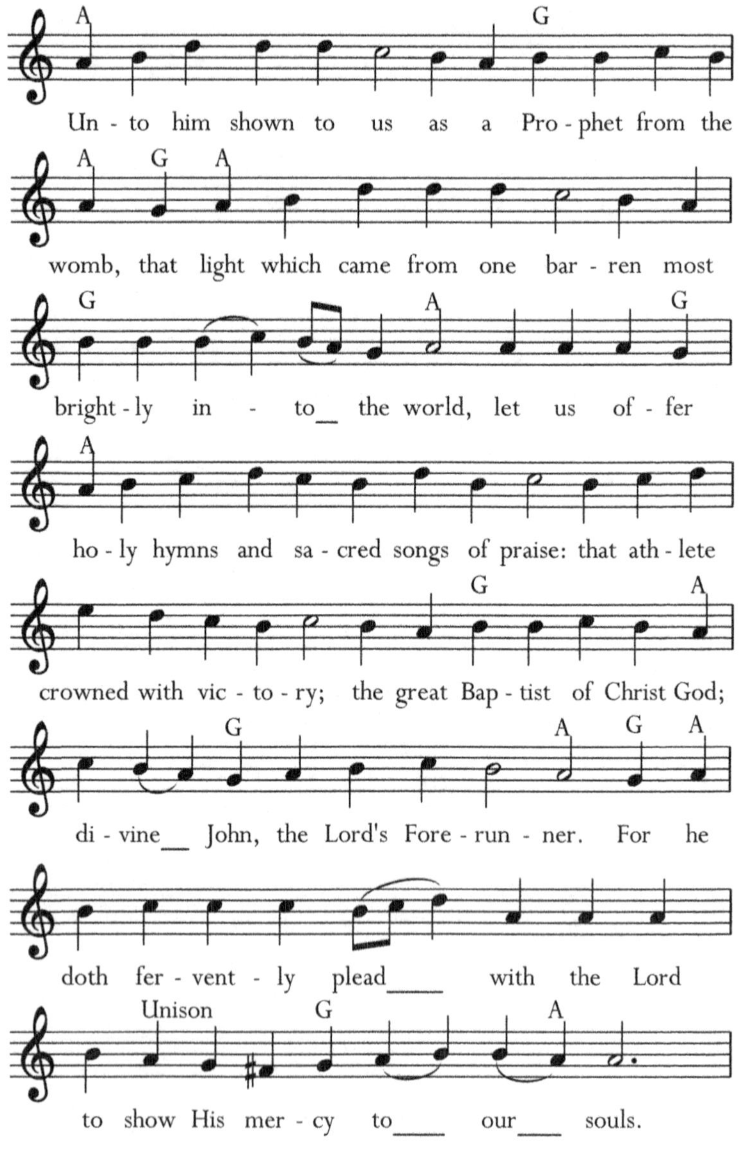

Matins sessional hymn from the Beheading of the Holy and Glorious Prophet, Forerunner, and Baptist John (Aug 29).

Wednesday :: The Holy Cross

Tone 3, *The power of Thy Cross*

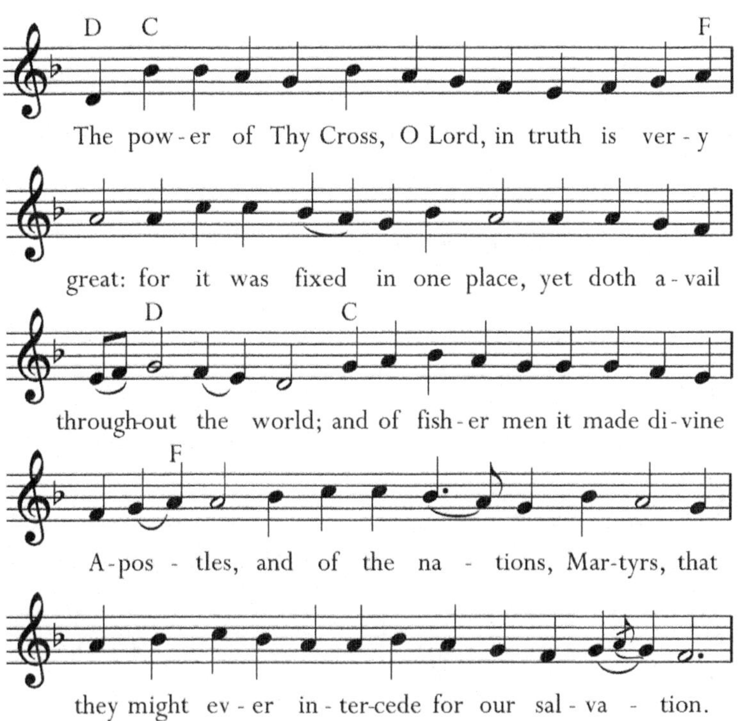

From the Sunday and Monday Vespers aposticha in Tone Three of the *Octoechos*.

The Source

Angels, Baptist, Apostles, Nicholas, and Protection: text from *The Menaion* (2005); music from *Byzantine Prosomia: The Chanter's Companion* (2005). Power of Cross text and music from *Byzantine Prosomia*. 'Champion Leader' and 'Awed by the Beauty' from *Selected Byzantine Hymns* (1986). All of the above from Holy Transfiguration Monastery.

The monastery also offers a CD recording of prosomia hymns sung by the monks. This chapter can be printed out from www.OrthodoxReader.com.

'Rejoice Life-giving Cross' is public domain. Russian choral arrangements can be found at www.orthodoxchurchmusic.org and elsewhere.

Wednesday :: The Theotokos

Tone 8 (Plagal of Fourth Tone), *To thee, the champion leader*

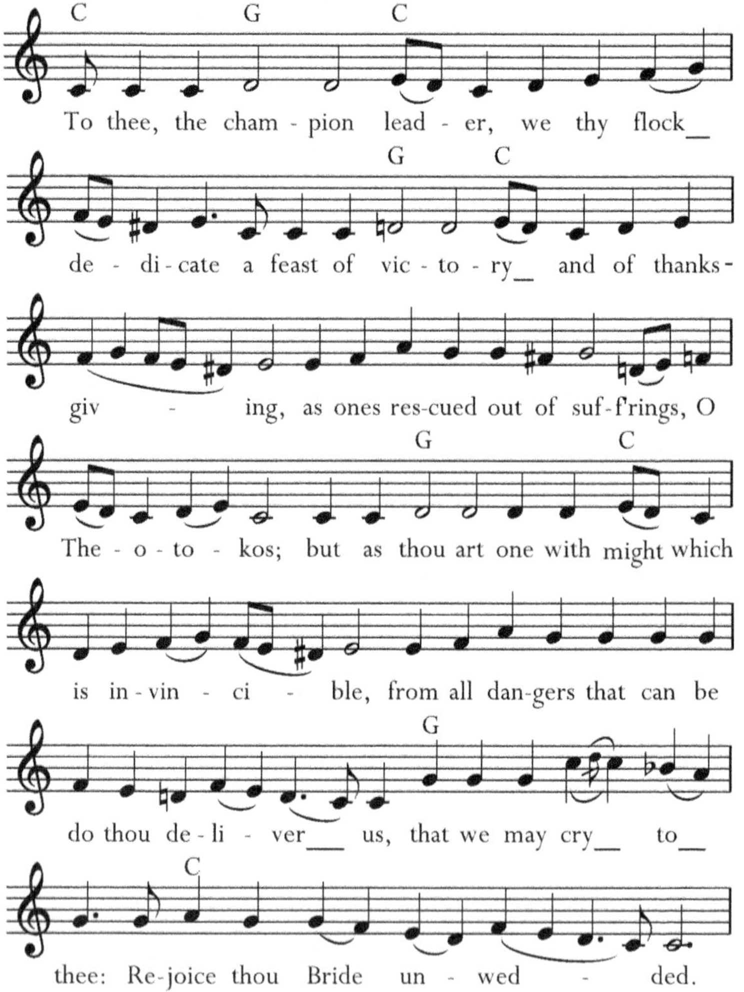

This kontakion by St Romanus the Melodist (†518, Oct 1) is from his *Akathist Hymn to the Most Holy Theotokos* and appears also in the *Annunciation Canon* (Mar 25, see chapter 9, p 120). In some typica it is sung daily at the end of First Hour or Compline or both.

Thursday :: The Holy Apostles

Tone 4, *As one valiant*

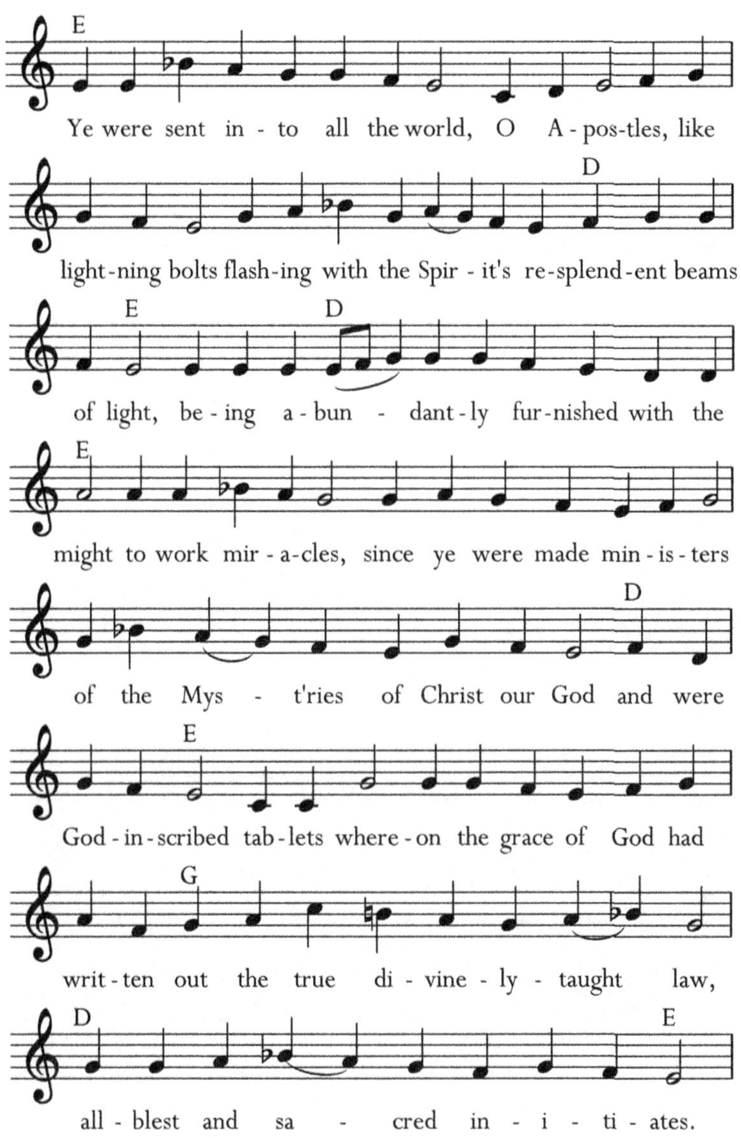

Vespers sticheron from the Synaxis of the Holy Twelve Apostles (June 30).

If the beginning interval is too strange, first think (sing) a C-dominant 7th chord (C-**E**-G-**B-flat**).

Thursday :: Saint Nicholas

Tone 3, *On this day the Virgin*

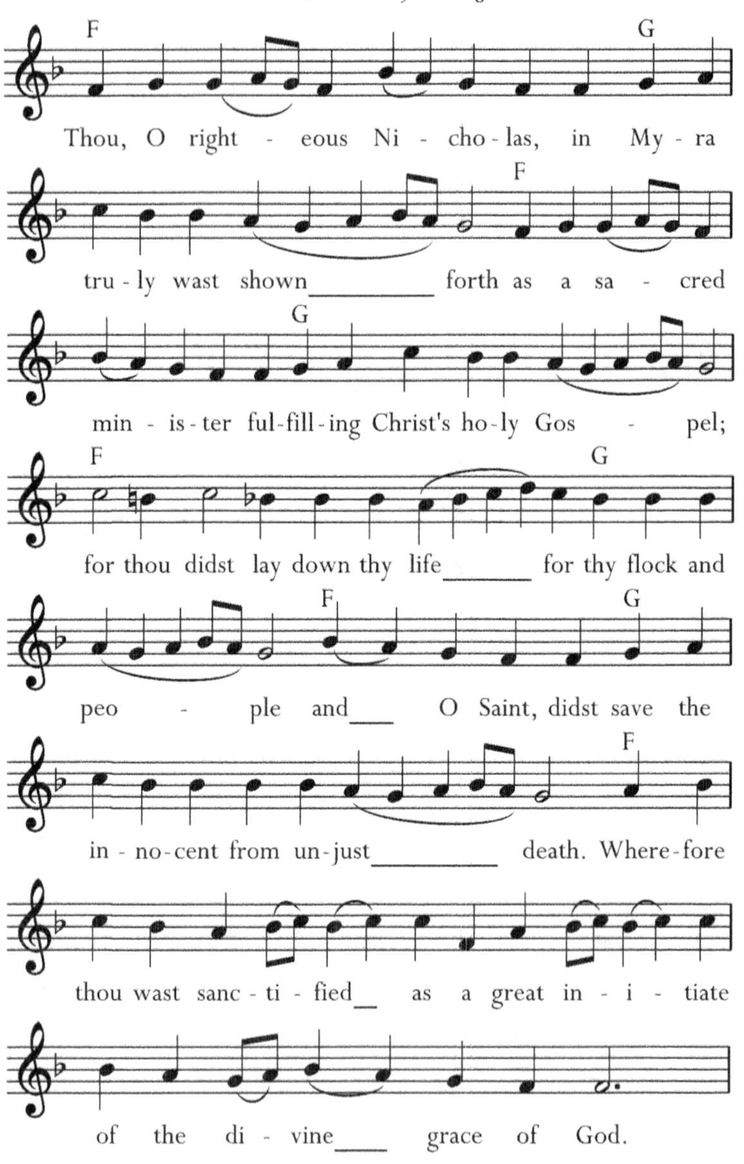

Kontakion of St Nicholas (Dec 6): same melody as the Christmas kontakion: "On this day the Virgin beareth the Transcendent in essence; * to the Unapproachable, * the earth doth offer a small cave; * Angels join in choir with shepherds * in giving glory; * with a star the Magi travel upon their journey; * for our sakes is born a young Child, * He that existed * before the ages as God."

Friday :: The Holy Cross

Russian Special Melody

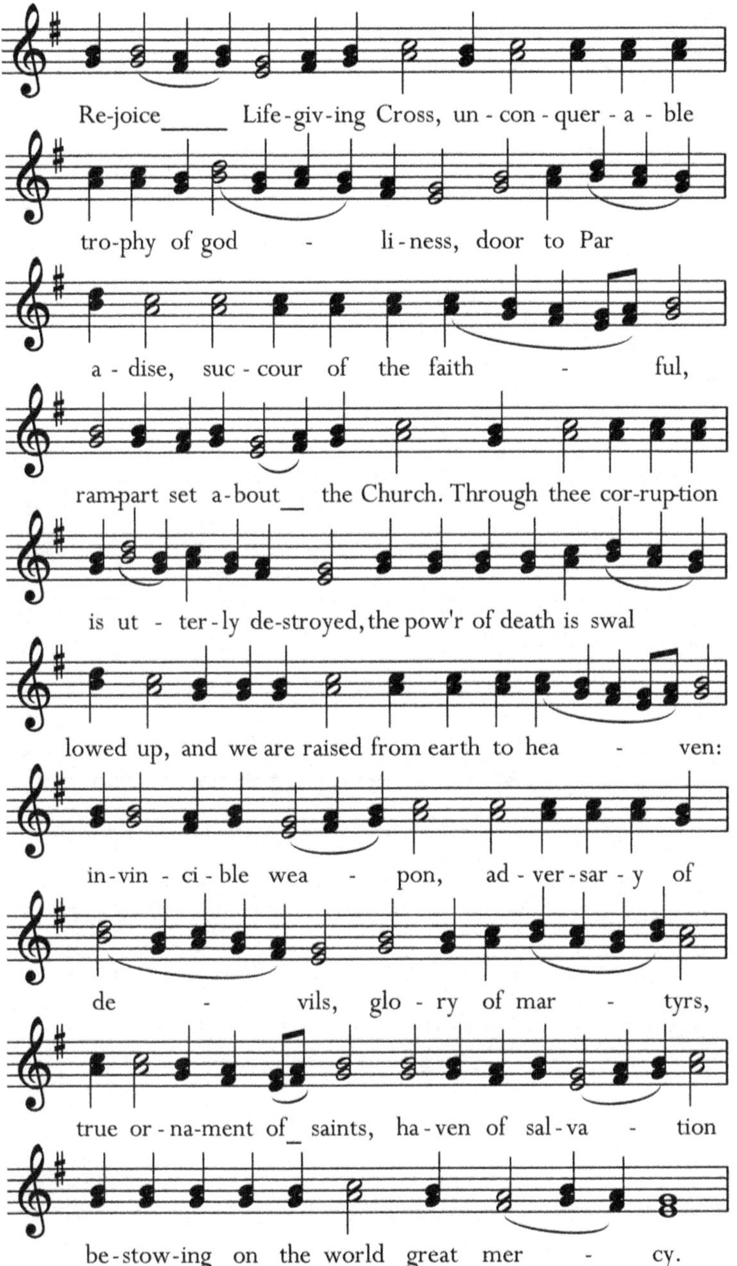

Friday :: The Theotokos

Tone 1, *While Gabriel was saying*

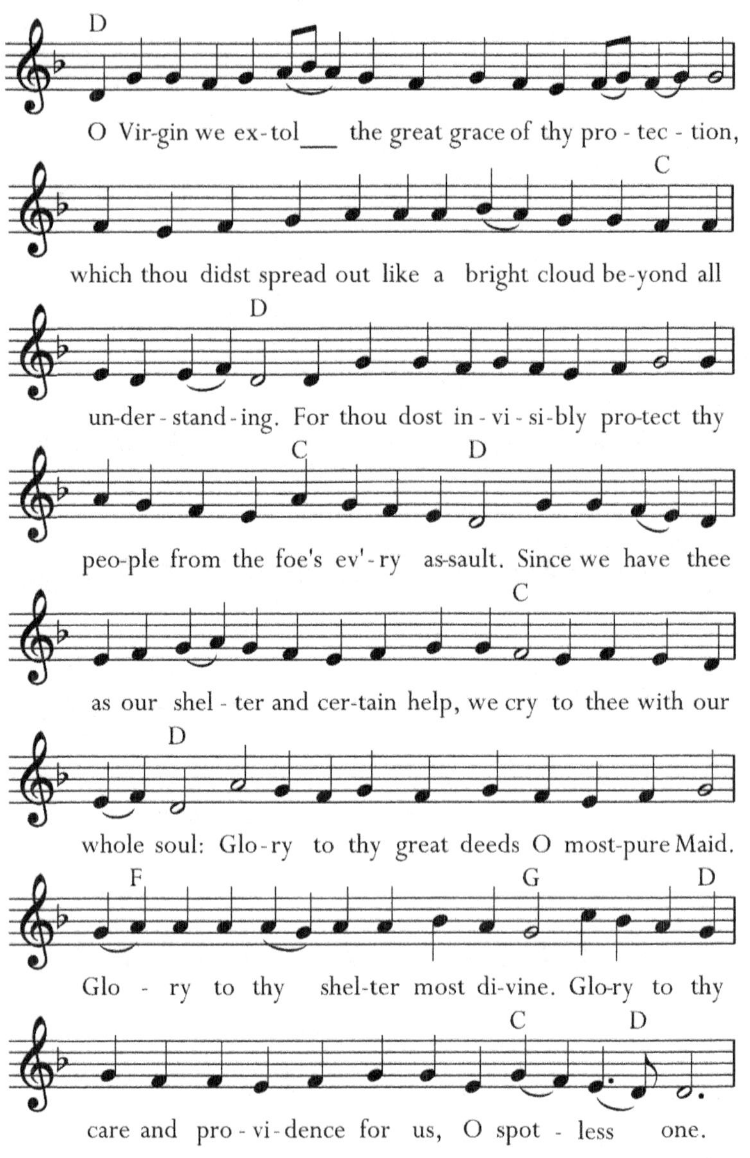

This page: troparion from Protection of the Most Holy Theotokos (Oct 1).

Previous page: from Vespers aposticha of the Elevation of the Holy Cross (Sep 14). Note that the melody is in the lower voice, upper voice is harmony.

Miscellanea

Bedtime Bonus! Every day of the week!

"Awed by the beauty" is sung daily at Compline and in other services throughout the year. (Slav variant: "To thee, the Champion Leader")

Tone 3, "Awed by the Beauty"; c. 2 beats per second (metronome 120)

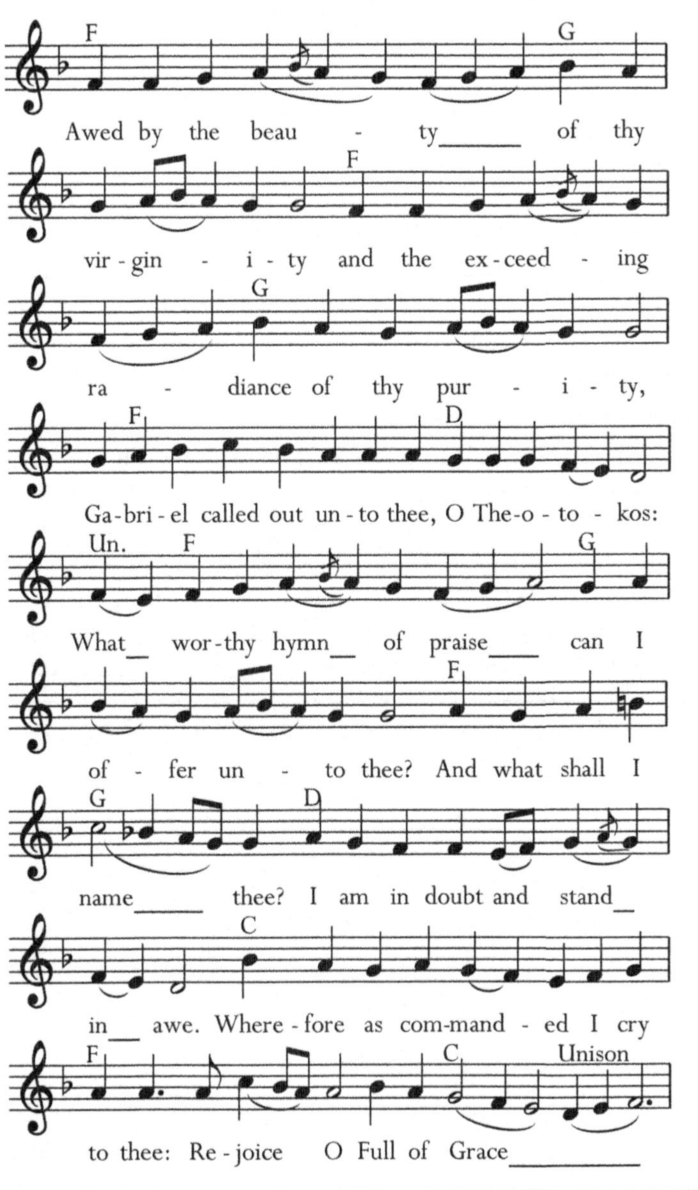

Parent Friendly

Children love to sing. These hymns could be sung before school, added to mealtime blessing or thanksgiving, used with bedtime prayers or even in the car when things get rambunctious. The Protection of the Theotokos troparion (*O Virgin, we extol*, see Friday) would be good to sing before leaving home, while away from home, arriving home—or anytime.

Do you sing "O Joyous Light" from Vespers every evening? If not, perhaps you could learn the tune sung in your home parish.

Chant Recordings

Church music recordings from various local traditions are available both in English and in their native languages. Worth special mention, perhaps, is a series by Vassilis Hadjinicolaou. Seeking a traditional form suitable to the New World, he chants in traditional Greek style (in English) but adds—sparingly, sensitively—pleasing yet completely non-distracting harmonies.

Chant Attitude

These hymns are neither art songs nor Protestant pep rally broadsides. Chant is a different animal.

> There are actually some simple folk among us who, though they believe the words [of the Psalms] to be inspired, yet think the reason for singing them is just to make them more pleasing to the ear! This is by no means so; Holy Scripture is not designed to tickle the aesthetic palate, and it is rather for the soul's own profit that the

Psalms are sung. This is so chiefly for two reasons. In the first place, it is fitting that the sacred writings should praise God in poetry as well as prose, because the freer, less restricted form of verse, in which the Psalms, together with the Canticles and Odes, are cast, ensures that by them men should express their love to God with all the strength and power they possess. And, secondly, the reason lies in the unifying effect which chanting the Psalms has upon the singer. For to sing the Psalms demands such concentration of a man's whole being on them that, in doing it, his usual disharmony of mind and corresponding bodily confusion is resolved, just as the notes of several flutes are brought by harmony to one effect; and he is thus no longer to be found thinking good and doing evil . . . . And it is in order that the melody may thus express our inner spiritual harmony, just as the words voice our thoughts, that the Lord Himself has ordained that the Psalms be sung and recited to a chant. . . . [They] who do not chant the Divine Songs intelligently but simply please themselves, most surely are to blame [i.e., incur blame], for praise is not befitting in a sinner's mouth.[1]

— Saint Athanasius the Great

This is not intended to take all the enjoyment out of singing, but rather to understand and approach it in a different way. As they say in Alaska: the opposite of pleasure is not pain, but joy.[2] Still, there must be some *fun* in learning ancient chant....

1 St Athanasius the Great [†373, Jan 18], "The Letter of St Athanasius to Marcellinus on the Interpretation of the Psalms," appended to *On the Incarnation*, trans and ed by a Religious of C.S.M.V. (Crestwood, NY: St Vladimir's Seminary Press, 1996), 114–115. Used with permission.

Also available in *Athanasius: The Life of Antony and The Letter to Marcellinus* (New York: Paulist Press [Classics of Western Spirituality series], 1980).

Also available in *A Psalter for Prayer*, 2nd ed (Jordanville, NY: Holy Trinity Publications, 2011).

2 See Michael J. Oleksa, *Orthodox Alaska: A Theology of Mission* (Crestwood, NY: St Vladimir's Seminary Press, 1992), 55.

Many people, not understanding the Divine services, especially the All-night Vigil, are bored in church and can't wait until it's over. In order to take delight in services one must understand them; and for this it's good, although more difficult, to read through something—the Canon, for example—at home before services. I knew one man of high rank who, before church services, would usually gather his whole family and read and explain to them the Canon, the kathismata, and those prayers which are sung at a Vigil. All those who listened to him would then stand in church with great attention and the service would go by quickly. You too should try to enter thoroughly into the services of the Orthodox Church, and they will open up to you a fount of such consolation that you will hasten with joy to God's temple. *I was glad because of them that said unto me: Let us go into the house of the Lord* [Ps 121:1] said David, and that's what you too will say, setting out for church. Amen.[1]

[From a different perspective: If you are bored in the services, it may be that you are in your head and not in your heart.]

1 St Barsanuphius [†1913, Synaxis of Optina Elders Oct 11], quoted in Victor Afanasiev, *Elder Barsanuphius of Optina* (Platina, CA: St Herman of Alaska Brotherhood [St Herman Press], 2000), 357. Used with permission.

13. Treatise on Prayer

The Orthodox Morning Prayers are taken from the monastic Midnight Office. In the following treatise by ***Saint Symeon, Archbishop of Thessalonica*** *[†1429, Sep 15], the description of the ritual and symbolism within the Midnight Office and Matins can provide a deeper context for one's morning prayers. Additionally, there are short explications of the Trisagion Prayers, the Our Father, and the Gloria, which may refresh one's understanding of these prayers.*

Prayer should be unceasing and tireless, as it is with the angels, since this is all that God asks of us: that we keep his memory always in our souls, that we should be with him and seek him only, to love him and behold him clearly and directly. However, since this unceasing prayer is impossible because of our veil of flesh and bodily needs, and is granted only rarely to very few "equal-of-the-angels" as a gift of God, the Church has, therefore, of necessity, set certain times for prayer, at which times it is indispensable that all the faithful should pray.

* * *

Beginning of the Midnight Office

If there is no priest, the first of the brothers—or one of them—begins, but does not give the blessing, since he does not have this grace. Instead he calls on Christ to have mercy through the prayers of the Fathers ["Through the prayers of our Holy Fathers, Lord Jesus Christ our God, have mercy on us. Amen"], humbling himself in Christ and not trusting in himself but in the prayers of the Fathers he invokes. Among them are bishops and priests, but also the whole choir of saints who are called Fathers. Then they call upon the Holy Spirit who makes prayers perfect, to come and dwell in us, to cleanse and save us ["Heavenly King, Comforter, Spirit of Truth ..."]. For we do not know how to pray as we should, unless we are guided by the Holy Spirit: "For we live in him and pray through him," Paul says, "and in him we cry Abba, Father" [Rom 8:15]. Then, in imitation of the angels, they recite the Trisagion, "Most-holy Trinity," for the mercy of the Holy Trinity and as praise similar to that of the angels, and confession of the one God in Trinity.

Then they add the God-given prayer ["Our Father"] which we will expound in another place, although many have interpreted the divine wisdom relating to this, especially Gregory of Nyssa.[1] Finally, when the priest has recited the prayer as doxology, "Lord, have mercy" is said twelve times—for the twelve-hour periods of the night and day. Then they say: "Come let us fall down ..." [Ps 94:6] three times, as David sang and as Athanasios the Great recommended be said as an introduction to the services; for he alone is our king and our eternal Christ, with the Father and the Holy Spirit, and by falling down we show our servanthood and subjection. Then they add the psalms according to custom.

* * *

Why the Symbol of Faith is recited morning and evening

The Confession of Faith is said immediately after these psalms in accordance with patristic tradition, since the Fathers tell us: "Arise and praise God, then proclaim the faith." This most holy creed is the faith. Another of the venerable Fathers says that we should proclaim the faith morning and evening, so that if Death comes he will find us confessing. After the Confession of Faith we recite again the Trisagion and "Our Father," since we should praise the Holy Trinity always at every hour—at the beginning, in the middle and at the end—as the source of all things, and because everything is done through him and we are thereby perfected and purified.

Then "The Bridegroom Comes at Midnight" indicates the aim of the Midnight Service of Praise. After this, "Lord, have mercy" is recited forty times, this number signifying that we offer as a sacrifice to God a tithe of all the days and hours of our life. We do this at all the services, invoking the mercy of God before all things, for he alone can save us, since we have need of mercy. For we sin continually and cannot be saved by any other means than the mercy of God alone, not having anything in ourselves to propitiate him. We provoke him incessantly by our deeds, our words, our thoughts, so that we are not worthy even to thank him

1 [St Gregory of Nyssa [†c.395, Jan 10], *The Lord's Prayer, The Beatitudes*, trans Hilda C. Graef (New York: Paulist Press [Ancient Christian Writers series], 1954), vol 18.]

or praise him, nor to petition him for anything—but only to say "Lord, have mercy," hoping only in our merciful God.

After this, we invoke the Mother of God as "truly more honored than the Seraphim," for she is a powerful intercessor above all others. Then immediately the priest's prayer: "God have mercy upon us ..." as the seal and completion, this prayer having been said by Moses to Aaron by divine command [Num 6:22f]. The divine ancestor David also wrote it more clearly in Psalm 66.

* * *

Then the Dismissal takes place. It is necessary for us to commemorate the dead, since we also will die, and to commemorate them especially at the Midnight Office, for at this hour the resurrection of the dead is expected. We ought also to pray for our departed relatives and members of our household, and in general for all, as a work of charity. Then the common petition for all and the prayer, the priest beginning and the others continuing: "For faithful rulers, for Orthodox bishops, for the father abbot, for the brotherhood in Christ, and all other Christians...." Then again for our fathers and brothers who have died in the Orthodox faith.

It is most necessary that we commemorate all at the end of the prayers, since in this way we all pray for each other everywhere, and so it happens that we are healed and saved willy-nilly. The leader sets the seal on the common prayer, calling on Christ our God for mercy with "Through the prayers of our Holy Fathers...."

The Service of Matins

Thus, when the Midnight office is ended, the doors of the nave open like the heavens and we enter as from the earth, just as Christ's chosen will be taken up in clouds and be forever with the Lord. Like a cloud also the incense is offered, symbolizing the Holy Spirit and the transmission of his divine grace and fragrance. Then, when we have all entered—the leader through the Royal Door, which is closed to us, symbolizing the Theotokos [Ezek 44], and which he opens to us like the gates of heaven, since he typifies Christ; the others from the sides, as his servants and under his wing—the priest as the minister of Christ gives the blessing from the sanctuary, blessing him with the Father and the Holy Spirit before his throne and his saints.

Then all sing the Trisagion and the God-given prayer, hymning the Holy Trinity with the angels. Regarding the prayer of the Trisagion, we should remind you in brief that this is an ancient prayer compiled by the early Fathers. For this reason the Church sings the Trisagion continually, both in the Holy Liturgy and at the end of the services, anathematizing certain heretics who made an addition to this hymn, while the Church—as from heaven through the boy taken up there—continually sings this heavenly and sweet melody.

The Trisagion and the whole prayer with it refers to the Holy Trinity, our only God, and derives both from the angelic hymn and from David—from the angels because they sing holy, holy, holy [Is 6]; from David: "My soul thirsted for the Lord, the strong and living one" [Ps 41:3]—who also cries "have mercy upon me" in the 50th Psalm. This hymn proclaims continually the trinity of persons and the unity of the nature. Similarly also, "Most-holy Trinity, have mercy upon us" teaches the simultaneous trinity and unity: "Lord be merciful ..." refers to the Father; "Master, forgive ..." to the Son; "Holy One, visit ..." to the Holy Spirit. The indivisibility is expressed in saying "for thy name's sake." We rightly say to the Father "Be merciful," inasmuch as we have been reconciled to him through the Son; we rightly say to the Son "forgive," since he became human like us, suffered for us and all mankind, although provoked and grieved by us, the very people who have put him on in baptism and myron and have been united with him in Communion and the other sacraments. Again, we rightly say to him "forgive," for he himself granted the power to loose and to bind, and established forgiveness. We rightly say "visit" to the Holy Spirit, for he gives us life and strengthens us, and without his power and gift there would be no good in us.

"Lord, have mercy" also proclaims the Holy Trinity, for the Holy Trinity is One Lord, and in repeating it thrice we testify and request mercy. Similarly also, "Glory to the Father and to the Son and to the Holy Spirit" is a clear confession and doxology of the same Holy Trinity, sung perpetually to God. For this reason we sing it continually, at the start and the finish of the hymns. Similarly also, "Our Father"—even though it is addressed to the Father and was given to us by the Son. Since, however, the Holy Trinity is indivisible and there is one name of the Father and of the Son and of the Holy Spirit, and one God—because the Father is the father of lights, of the Son and of the Holy Spirit, and is in the Son and the Holy Spirit, and the Son and Holy Spirit in the Father—therefore this prayer is addressed to God, and in saying "Father" it calls to mind the Son and the Holy Spirit also. The Church also witnesses to this in saying: "For yours is the kingdom, of the Father and of the Son and of the Holy Spirit."

Let us return now to our subject. When, as we said, the priest has given the blessing, he censes the sanctuary, the nave and all present, since all things are sanctified—the things he censes, as being holy; the people present, to sanctify them. Thus, beginning at the Holy of Holies, the sanctuary, he censes everything in order. However, he does not cense them simply as by chance, but he seals and sanctifies and offers the sanctification to Christ, so that it may become acceptable in heaven, and that the grace of the all-holy Spirit may be sent upon us. For this reason let nobody neglect the censing, since through it he receives the grace of the Holy Spirit.

* * *

The Lauds Psalms and The Great Doxology

Then the Lauds Psalms [Ps 148–150] are added, calling all creation, the angels and all creatures to the praise of the Creator, and witnessing that all creatures are the works of God, created in word and spirit. "For he spoke and they were created," it is written, "He commanded and they were made" [Ps 148:5]. "Spoke" here means through the Word [the Son]; "commanded" means through the operation of the Holy Spirit.

After the appropriate hymns to the Lauds Psalms and "Glory be to the Father …" and "Now and ever …" in honor of the Holy Trinity, the Great Doxology is performed. . . . Here it is sung by all more fully and with melody, for the mystery was revealed to the whole world and not to the shepherds only, but to all the nations as well. Therefore we say: "We praise you, we bless you, we worship you, we glorify you, we thank you for your great glory," because heaven is full of his glory and so is earth. Whose glory?—that of God in Trinity. Thus the Church theologizes in crying: "O Lord, King, heavenly God, Father almighty; O Lord, only-begotten Son Jesus Christ, and Holy Spirit…." See that it has preached the three persons in one Divinity; in saying "we praise you" it manifests the unity of God who is on high, while by the number it proclaims the persons. Then we solemnly praise the incarnation of God, chanting: "O Lord God, Lamb of God," taking this from Isaiah and the Forerunner because of his passion and sacrifice; "Son of the Father"—from the Gospel; "who takes away the sin of the world, have mercy upon us, you who take away the sins of the world, and receive our prayer"—this also from Isaiah; "You who sit at the right of the Father, and have mercy upon us"—this gleaned from the Gospel; "receive" and "have mercy" from David; "For you alone are holy, you alone are Lord, Jesus Christ, in the glory of God the Father, Amen."—from Paul; "Every day I will praise you and extol your name forever and ever"—from the divine David. The remainder is made up of petitions and prophetic verses.

As we said above, this hymn was originally composed by the holy Fathers and is called Great Doxology. Each of the faithful should study and learn and recite it every morning and evening to God, since it is both a confession and doxology of the Holy Trinity, the one God, and a commemoration of the incarnation and dispensation, crucifixion and resurrection of one person of the Holy Trinity, of the Word of God; an acceptable prayer that we may be preserved sinless all day and night; that we may be made worthy of the divine mercy, as we hope; that He may have pity on us; therefore we cry with David: "Have mercy and heal my soul, for I have sinned against you" [Ps 40:5]—behold the confession; and "for I took refuge with you" (the refuge of all) and "teach me to do your will, for you are my God" [Ps 142:9–10], the Father together with the Son and the Holy Spirit. For this reason is added "with you is the spring of life" (the Holy Spirit), "in your light" (i.e., in your Spirit) "we shall see light" (that is, the Son), "Extend your mercy to those who know you" [Ps 35:11]—you, the true God and Father with the Word and your Holy Spirit through the incarnation of your Son.

The Trisagion

Finally, the Trisagion Hymn is added, being the seal and completion of every hymn, since it refers to the one God, to the Holy Trinity: "Holy God, holy and mighty, holy and immortal, have mercy upon us." The Trisagion Hymn is sung by the angels, as we have learnt from Isaiah, in the following way: "Holy, Holy, Holy, Lord of Sabaoth: heaven and earth are full of your glory" [Is 6]. As we have learnt from Athanasios the Great and the other Fathers, the meaning is this: the Father is holy, the Son is holy, the Holy Spirit is holy—behold the three persons; "Lord of Sabaoth"—behold the unity of the Godhead, the uniqueness of the nature and the oneness of the glory. "Holy" is said three times because of the three persons, "Lord" once because of the one Divinity, and "heaven and earth are full of your glory" because of the knowledge of the Holy Trinity, the thrice-holy God. This knowledge was granted by divine dispensation, through the angels and apostles of Christ; and heaven and earth became full of this dispensation. The hymn states "full of your glory" in the singular, for there is one glory of the Holy Trinity, one power, one will, one movement and operation, and one God alone in Trinity.

Therefore, the Fathers originally received from the angels the "Holy, Holy, Holy," and from David the remainder, where he glorifies God in Trinity saying: "My soul thirsted for God, the mighty One, the living One" [Ps 41:3], and rightly and most appropriately composed the Trisagion Hymn. As a mark of petition they added—again from David—the "have mercy upon us." So they say "Holy God ..."—the "holy" from the angels, the "God" from David; "Holy (and) Mighty"—similarly the "holy" is angelic, the "mighty" Davidic; "Holy (and) Immortal"—"holy" from the angels, while they took the "immortal" from David instead of "living"; the "have mercy upon us" similarly from David, for he also spoke in the Holy Spirit, as the Savior witnesses: "David said in the Spirit" [Mt 22:43]. Consequently, they applied the "God" to the Father, since he is the spring and root of the divinity and source of the Son and the Holy Spirit; the "mighty" was applied to the Son as arm and power of the Father personified—"For Christ is the power of God and the wisdom of God," says Paul [1Cor 1:24]; the "immortal" was applied to the Holy Spirit, since life belongs to the Holy Spirit—"The Spirit is the life-giver," it is said; and since God is mighty and living, both his power is mighty and his life immortal.

Against Peter the Fuller

A great and foolish attack has been made by the heretics through a certain person of ill-fame, Peter the Fuller, who wished to add to this hymn to the Holy Trinity, who is incapable of suffering: "who was crucified for us." Such an addition was extremely blasphemous, since the Holy Trinity is incapable of suffering, infinite and incorporeal. Only one person of the Trinity, God the Word, suffered—not in his divinity, but in the flesh, since the divinity remained incapable of suffering and uncrucified; just as when iron is beaten and suffers while incandescent, the fire does not suffer with it, nor is it changed, but it illumines and fires the iron, as Saint Basil says. However, this heresy—after lighting fiery temptations for the Church for a long time—was quenched again by the power of God through a miracle which took place in the Christ-loving city of Constantine during the reign of Theodosios the Younger. While the Church was holding a procession, a boy was caught up into midair and came down crying that the angels recite it "Holy God, Holy and Mighty, Holy and Immortal: have mercy upon us," and then died.[1] You see therefore that the Church received this Trisagion Hymn not only from the prophets, but also from its children in the Holy Spirit. God the Trinity witnessed also that this hymn is sung ceaselessly by the angels to the same Trinity.

For this reason, having received it from God, who settled the upheaval on earth by the correct formulation of the hymn, the Church always sings it with the angels at all times of prayer, especially with divine melody as in the Great Doxology at the end of Matins and in the Holy Liturgy. The Great Doxology is, therefore, sung daily, on feasts, and commemorations of saints—according to the Typikon; on other days it is read penitentially by one person, with the prayer of the Trisagion afterwards. . . .[2]

"Glory be to the Father" and by whom it was composed

Another hymn composed by the Fathers is sung to the glory of the Holy Trinity, as some say by Meletios and Flavianos the patriarchs of Antioch among the saints. "Glory be to the Father and to the Son and to the Holy Spirit, both now and forever and to the ages of ages, Amen." This was piously composed against Arios and Sabellios, the "Glory" being aimed against the Arians, since the glory of the Holy Trinity is one and the Trinity is consubstantial, while "to the Father and to the Son and to the Holy Spirit" was composed against Sabellios, who blasphemously claimed that there is one person in the Holy Trinity; and "both now and forever ..." because it is so and will be so forever.

* * *

Brief exposition of the most holy prayer, "Our Father"

"Our Father": We call the God of heaven "Father" as maker and creator, since he formed us from nothing; and he is our Father, indeed, by grace, since his Son—only-begotten by nature—became man for our salvation.

"Who are in heaven": Being holy, as he is called in the sacred Scriptures, God is pleased and rests in his saints. The angels in heaven are

1 [Greek Synaxaria commemorate this event on Sep 25, Slav in the Life of St Proclus, Nov 20.]

2 [The version of the Doxology used on non-feast days is known as the Small (or Lesser) Doxology: same text but slightly rearranged, and no Trisagion, which comes afterward, i.e., after the aposticha. It is said daily in Compline.]

holier than we humans, and heaven is purer than earth; therefore, God is mentioned in heaven rather than on earth.

"May your name be hallowed": Since you are holy, O God, sanctify your revered name among us also, and sanctify and cleanse us from every stain, so that we may be sanctified and become your own through our purity; and preach your holy name, so that it may be glorified always through us and not be cursed by us humans.

"May your kingdom come": May you be king over us because of our good and virtuous works, and not your enemy the Devil because of our evil and lawless works. And may your heavenly kingdom come, i.e., the last day of the world, since you will then reign over all—even over your enemies. And may your kingdom be eternal, as it is now. May it be a spring of grace for those who are worthy, virtuous and prepared for the time of your kingdom with their good works, but also punitive towards your foes.

"May your will be done, on earth as it is in heaven": Like the angels, make us perform it among us as your will is among them. Let not our will be done, since we are passionate and human, but your own dispassionate will, just and holy. Since by the incarnation of your only-begotten Son you united the heavenly and earthly spheres, may your heavenly wishes be executed in us also who are on earth.

"Give us today our daily bread": Even though we have sought the heavenly work, since the whole hope of us Christians is towards the heavenly life, yet being mortal and human we also seek the sustaining bread to support our life, while knowing well that it can only be given by your hand; you alone are self-sufficient, whereas we are subject to needs and necessity. Since we have confidence and hope in you alone, we do not seek something superfluous in seeking that bread, but only what satisfies our current needs and necessity; for we have been taught in the Gospels not to take thought for the morrow, since you who are provident for us today will also be so tomorrow and forever. "Give us today our essential bread" signifies also the living, heavenly bread, the most holy body of the living Word, our Savior Christ. It is called essential because it strengthens both our souls and bodies. Whoever does not eat this has no life in Christ, but whoever eats of it will live the heavenly and unaging life forever.

"And forgive us our debts, as we forgive our debtors": In this is contained all the wisdom and power of the sacred gospel, for it was primarily to forgive our sins and trespasses that the Word of God, our loving Savior, came into the world and became incarnate, sharing all the things of mankind except sin, and finally shed his pure blood. For this reason he gave us the sacrament of Holy Communion for forgiveness of sins, teaching us and legislating clearly, "If you forgive, you will be forgiven" [Mt 6:14]. For this reason also he said to Peter when he asked him: "How many times a day should I forgive my brother?" [Mt 18:21]. He replied up to seventy times, i.e., unceasingly. In this sacred prayer God appoints the person praying to be his own judge. If we make peace with whoever has grieved us, God also will make peace with us: "... he forgave and it will be forgiven him" [cf. Lk 17:3]. We must not bear grudges or want revenge at all costs against our brothers who have offended us, for this is the will of our Lord and Savior; we being all similar as humans, subject to error and granting little forgiveness to sinners because of our self-love, although we receive much from God and are forgiven often. If we forgive other humans, we also are forgiven by God.

"And lead us not into temptation": This is said because there are many who tempt us, full of envy and enmity, and many are the temptations that come—from the demons, from mankind, from the body, from negligence, in short from spiritual sloth. These temptations afflict both the careful and the careless, the virtuous and the wicked. The only difference is that the temptations of the righteous have more reward from God, because they occur to test and exalt us, as with Job, and also because these righteous persons have greater need of patience, since they are afflicted more by being envied and hated in the world: Their "spirit is willing, but the flesh is weak" [Mt 26:41]. There are also other temptations, such as rejecting and neglecting your brother in tribulations, persecuting him, oppressing him, and neglecting or despising the divine things. So, whatever sins and faults we may have committed against God and our brother, we need only beg mercy from God, have mercy and forgive others, driving temptations and evil away from us—immediately we enjoy forgiveness and mercy. However, if somebody is righteous, he should, nonetheless, not have confidence in himself, because being righteous consists primarily in humbling oneself and in being merciful and forgiving to others.

"But deliver us from evil": Save us from evil, from the Devil who is our mortal and untiring enemy, possessed by a mania, for without God's grace we are powerless against him, since he is a spirit of subtle nature and cunning, inventing and devising a myriad of evils against us daily. If you, the Creator and Master of All—of the wicked Devil and other evil powers also, as you are of the angels and us humans—if you did not snatch us away from the temptations of the Devil, who else could save us? Since we have no power to resist an incorporeal enemy who is always so envious, crafty and scheming, you alone save us from him!

"For yours is the kingdom and the power and the glory forever, Amen": Who could hurt us and afflict us, when we are ruled by you, the God and king and lord of all, the commander of the angels themselves? Or who could oppose your power? Nobody since you created us and protect us all. Or who could contradict or dare to do anything against your glory, when this glory commands the furthermost limits, and heaven and earth are filled by it, being more ancient than the heavens and the angels, for you alone existed always and are eternal. May your glory—of the Father and of the Son and of the Holy Spirit—and your kingdom and power be eternal, amen. For you are truly and confessedly the king, the mighty and glorified One forever.

This is, in brief, the power of the Trisagion and the sacred prayer "Our Father." Every Orthodox Christian should know this prayer—no excuses!—and offer it to God, both when he leaves his house and when he enters the holy temple of God, before and after meals, and in the evening when going to sleep, because this prayer of Trisagion and "Our Father" contains confession and glorification of God, humbling of the person praying, revelation of his sins, requesting of forgiveness, hope in heavenly benefits to come, requesting of necessary things and renunciation of unnecessary ones, hope in God and the wish that temptation may be driven from us, that we may be saved from evil and execute God's holy will, and be his children—as we are by grace—and may finally be made worthy of his kingdom. This is why the Church offers this prayer to God many times each day. You see that we have discussed this in detail as best we could—now we must add the conclusion of Matins, in Christ.

Why we request mercy in the prayers

On feasts after the Great Doxology, or on ordinary days after the prayer of the Trisagion and the Lord's Prayer, the priest performs the intercession, in which firstly and principally we request God's mercy and divine pity from our merciful God, saying: "Have mercy upon us, O God, according to your great mercy, we beseech you," etc. This intercession is appropriate, since we should not ask for anything except for mercy, as we have neither boldness nor access to offer anything as our own, nor to request anything as such, since everything is from God and of God, nor can we think that we have not sinned.

So, as sinners and condemned through sin we cannot, nor dare not, say anything to our loving Master except "have mercy." For we have grieved him and grieve him every day, so much that we cannot cry anything except "have mercy," both priest and people together, while the priest says: "Have mercy upon us, O God, according to your great mercy: we beseech you, hear and have mercy." What does this mean, "we beseech you, hear and have mercy?" We cry that we are not worthy to be heard and pitied, because of the multitude of our faults, so we beseech you, i.e., we ask you to hear our prayers and have mercy upon us. As mediator, the priest stands before God and says "we beseech you" and "hear us," while the people add the petition "Lord, have mercy." For it is your great love for mankind, O God, that you have mercy, and the fitting petition and request of us sinners is the "Lord, have mercy." For this reason before every other prayer the priest says: "Let us beseech the Lord," i.e., let us beg of the Lord. Those present show that this is a petition for the divine mercy by crying: "Lord, have mercy," at the same time assisting the priests, for the petition of the righteous has great power with God.

You see then the humble wisdom and order of our Church? You see how it sets in order and offers its children to God through penitence and humility? We do not perceive this, brethren, nor do we understand these lofty meanings, but only speak with our lips by habit, and are in a hurry to shake off prayer as a burden. Others out of indolence do not say the "have mercy," nor do we attend with our mind when it is recited, and therefore do not receive God's mercy. Ponder and reflect on the aim of the Church, however, and attend to this aim—both you and other pious persons so that you may receive mercy from God.

Cleric: I understand, holy master, and surprised at your words I shrink, because although we have been made worthy of such gifts beyond our merits we do not appreciate them at all.

Archbishop: May God, who adorned mankind with wisdom, grant us understanding, strengthen us and have mercy upon us. Know that in the evening services and in the Holy Liturgy the Church does not refrain from teaching and inciting us to understand, which is why it adds: "Let us all say … with all our mind let us say …," etc.

Significance of "Wisdom," "Let us attend"

"Let us all say …" and what follows is an incitement and teaching, as is "Wisdom," "Let us attend" and "Wisdom, be upstanding," i.e., all be upstanding in wisdom, for what is said and done is the wisdom of God, and belongs to God's living wisdom. Since "The fear of the Lord is the beginning of wisdom" [Prov 1:7] let us be with wisdom and piety when we see and hear the divine things; let us attend to them with the fear of God; let us stand upright in wisdom, both in body and soul, upright in faith and thoughts. Do you understand how much wisdom the details of the Church contain, which seem trifling to us?

Cleric: I understand and am amazed, master.

Archbishop: Do not be amazed, brother, because the Church is the dwelling of the living wisdom of God personified, which is why "Wisdom has built herself a house" [Pr 9:1]—the sacred body of the Church. This is why those details of this Church which seem trifling are full of wisdom; and the smaller some people think them, the greater the knowledge and understanding required. For the things of God which seem foolish to mankind are very wise, and those which seem weak are very strong, and the living wisdom of God is one and simple. In it are to be found all the treasures of wisdom and knowledge.

The Source

St Symeon of Thessalonike, *Treatise on Prayer: An Explanation of the Services Conducted in the Orthodox Church*, trans Harry L.N. Simmons (Brookline, MA: Hellenic College Press, 1984), 18–44, abridged.

This book also addresses the Jesus Prayer, the ancient Cathedral Rite, and the Presanctified Liturgy.

Miscellanea

Parent Friendly

Something that makes long services seem much shorter (for adults as well as children) is a growing familiarity with the services. Helpful in this regard is the *Service Book* by Isabel Hapgood.[1] It contains not only the Divine Liturgies and the festal offices (Matins, Great Vespers, Great Compline), but also the services of Naming a Child (eighth day after birth), Churching the Mother (fortieth day), Baptism, Marriage (Crowning), and Burial, and the occasional services of Moleben (prayer service), Panikhida (memorial service), and Anointing of the Sick. The book provides the text of the services, the rubrics (what the clergy are doing), and the complementary *why* these things are done and the meaning of certain words and actions. These extra explanations are necessarily basic—otherwise the book would be thousands of pages—but a very good start for understanding the services and being able to explain to children the explicable parts. The goal, naturally, is not simply to know about but to participate in the services, the spiritual realities.

A basic book that deals with the broader Orthodox culture is *These Truths We Hold* from St Tikhon's Seminary Press (Waymart, PA). One might prefer to keep it handy as a reference book. It includes a brief history of the Church from the Apostles through the Councils to today and worldwide; descriptions of the temple, servers, and furnishings; the services, feasts, and fasts; monasticism, dogma, icons, sacraments, prayer, and Scripture. It is replete with icons, illustrations, and photos.

Orthodoxy a la Mode

Some people view traditional Christian spirituality as outmoded; others feel that it is constrictive. In search of contemporary, relevant, omni-pan-ecumenical ways of worship, they embrace the New Age and world religions. They combine beliefs and practices into a spiritual crazy quilt: flashy, even artful, but full of holes, affording neither warmth nor protection.

Gabriel Bunge, a former Benedictine monk, found his way to Orthodoxy by studying and practicing the teachings of the Holy Fathers. His book, *Earthen Vessels: The Practice of Personal Prayer According to the Patristic Tradition*,[2] demonstrates that the ancient Christian practices and forms of prayer are neither arbitrary nor haphazard but exactly suited to Christian life and spirituality. Standing, kneeling, bowing, prostrating, raising hands and eyes

1 *Service Book of the Holy Orthodox-Catholic Apostolic Church*, 7th ed (Englewood, NJ: Antiochian Orthodox Christian Archdiocese of North America, 1996).

2 Ignatius Press, San Francisco, 2002.

to heaven, the Sign of the Cross—these are the most effective mode of expression for progress and understanding in the Orthodox faith.

Holistic Experience

The life and practice of the Orthodox Church form a cohesive whole with the doctrine, official prayers, Scriptures, creeds, and canons that both enshrine and regulate her life. Within the Church there is a seamless connection between what is prayed and what is believed, and this holistic experience means that, under most circumstances, it is not necessary for anyone to make a distinction between religion and spirituality. . . .

Religion and spirituality are two allied concepts, yet each has a different focus:

- Religion is concerned with the Person of God; spirituality is concerned with what God does.
- Religion has an important historical dimension; spirituality is most concerned with the present moment.
- Religion often has a speculative quality; spirituality is entirely practical.
- Religion focuses on God's relationship with humankind; spirituality focuses on a person's relationship with God.
- Religion is concerned with God's relationship with the universe; spirituality is focused on the way a person sees his own place in the universe.[1]

Excesses on the Right and on the Left

Among the modernists, be cautious of anyone who emphasizes that the Canons [laws of the Church] are outmoded, that the message of the Fathers is outdated and irrelevant, and that Orthodox Christianity must move out of the "Dark Ages." Orthodox tradition is a living force that has survived the vicissitudes of every age. Those who teach to the contrary are dangerous and know nothing of Orthodox spirituality. Be wary, too, of Priests who violently oppose fasting, regular confession and Communion, and proper, modest dress both for the clergy and laity. They are usually suffering from an excessive love of our modern age. Christians are called to be *in* the world, but not *of* it, as Saint Paul tells us.

1 Father Meletios Webber, *Steps of Transformation: An Orthodox Priest Explores the Twelve Steps*, (Ben Lomond, CA: Conciliar Press/Ancient Faith Publishing, 2003), 81–82. Used with permission.

Among the traditionalists, avoid anyone who attacks the catholicity (universality) of the Church and who, in the name of Tradition, excludes ailing Orthodox from the ranks of the Church. A genuine traditionalist wishes to cure those who are ill, not to revile or exclude them. Be careful, too, of gurus and false "Elders" who create small enclaves of Orthodox who begin to think that all other Orthodox are evil and that, since the end of the world is at hand, one can retreat from service to the world. A true Christian works all the more diligently for Christian union and the conversion of mankind when the world's end seems near.

Finally, where you find vicious gossip, malevolence directed against other people, a denial of the forgiveness offered by the Church to those who err, and such illogical things as hatred for Orthodox brothers in the face of ecumenical love for the heterodox (a widespread modernist disease), exercise caution.

In the face of the modernist–traditionalist division in Orthodoxy today, no Christian acts rightly by breaking up communities and causing undue confusion. If the situation in which you find yourself is in violation of your conscience, state your case succinctly, politely, and without condemning anyone. Then be on your way, never forgetting to pray for those in error and never forgetting that your good example, in serving your conscience properly, may bring others to their senses. An attack upon a clergyman or parish that you may leave because of matters of Faith will compromise both your Christianity and that of those whom you leave. All will suffer. And your own example will have been spoiled.

Traditionalist, modernist, Old Calendarist, New Calendarist, or whatever—we are still all Orthodox. The Church is still essentially one. Once more, if we follow the dictates of the Church and our consciences in fleeing error and innovation, it is for the purpose of preserving Holy Tradition, which has always been the force and criterion by which Orthodox are restored to unity in times of trial. We must not forget this. The "true" Orthodox Christian is such only when he is true to his ailing Orthodox brother.[1]

1 Archbishop Chrysostomos, Bishop Auxentios, and Archimandrite Akakios, *Orthodox Insights: A Collection of Short Questions and Answers on Orthodox Theological, Pastoral, and Ecclesiastical Concerns* (Etna, CA: Center for Traditionalist Orthodox Studies, 2009) 2:70–71. Used with permission.

14. Short Hours

As Saint Symeon of Thessalonica explains, the Church has set certain times for prayer to help us toward our goal of unceasing prayer. The following prayers have been called the "Short Hours." They are short enough that any or all could be prayed even in the busiest workplace. We bring God to our remembrance, and we remember ourselves, as it were, to God. First Hour roughly corresponds to 6:00 a.m. (not to replace one's morning prayers); Third Hour, 9:00 a.m.; Sixth Hour, noon; Ninth Hour, 3:00 p.m. Along with the Hours, one might remember the saint(s) of the day.

First Hour

Monday, Tuesday, Thursday

The most glorious Mother of God, more holy than the holy angels, let us hymn unceasingly with our hearts and mouths, confessing her to be the Theotokos, for truly she gave birth to God incarnate for us, and prayeth unceasingly for our souls.

Wednesday, Friday

Hasten to our aid, ere we be enslaved to the enemies that blaspheme Thee and threaten us, O Christ our God. By Thy Cross, destroy them that war against us. Let them learn the might of the Orthodox Faith; through the intercessions of the Theotokos, O only Lover of mankind.

Third Hour

Blessed art Thou, O Christ our God, Who hast shown forth the fishermen as supremely wise, by sending down upon them the Holy Spirit, and through them didst draw the world into Thy net. O Lover of mankind, glory be to Thee.

Glory.

Grant speedy and steadfast consolation unto Thy servants, O Jesus, when our spirits are become despondent. Depart not from our souls when they be in afflictions, nor be Thou afar from our minds when they be in tribulations, but do Thou ever go before us. Draw nigh unto us, draw nigh, O Thou Who art everywhere present: even as Thou wast ever with Thine apostles, so also do Thou unite Thyself to them that long for Thee, O Compassionate One, that, being one with Thee, we may praise and glorify Thine All-holy Spirit.[1]

Both now.

The hope and protection and refuge of Christians, the unassailable battlement, the storm-free haven of the weary art thou, O immaculate Theotokos. But as thou art one that savest the world by thine unceasing intercession, remember us also, O all-hymned Virgin.

Sixth Hour

Thou hast wrought salvation in the midst of the earth, O Christ God; Thou didst stretch out Thine immaculate hands upon the Cross, thereby gathering all the nations that cry to Thee; O Lord, glory be to Thee.

Glory.

We worship Thine immaculate icon, O Good One, asking the forgiveness of our failings, O Christ God; for of Thine own will Thou wast well-pleased to ascend the Cross in the flesh, that Thou mightest deliver from slavery to the enemy those whom Thou hadst fashioned. Wherefore, we cry to Thee thankfully: Thou didst fill all things with joy, O our Saviour, when Thou camest to save the world.[2]

Both now.

Monday, Tuesday, Thursday

As thou art a well-spring of pity, count us worthy of compassion, O Theotokos. Look upon a sinful people; show forth, as always, thy power. For hoping in thee, we cry Rejoice to thee, as once did Gabriel, the Supreme Commander of the Bodiless Hosts.

---

1 The first two troparia of the Third Hour are the troparion and ikos of Pentecost.

2 This troparion, "We worship Thine immaculate icon," and the Theotokion, "As thou art a well-spring of pity," are the prayers that clergy use when greeting the icons as they enter the Church. It is a good practice for laity as well.

Wednesday, Friday

Most glorified art thou, O Virgin Theotokos; we praise thee, for by the Cross of thy Son, hades was cast down and death slain. Having been put to death, we were raised up, and were deemed worthy of life. We received paradise, the ancient bliss. Wherefore, in thanksgiving, we glorify Christ our God, since He is mighty and alone abundant in mercy.

Ninth Hour

Seeing the Author of life hanging on the Cross, the thief said: Were it not God incarnate Who is crucified with us, the sun would not have hid its rays, nor would the earth have quaked and trembled. But do Thou Who endurest all things remember me, O Lord, in Thy Kingdom.

Glory.

In the midst of two thieves, Thy Cross was found to be a balance of justice; for the one was borne down to Hades by the weight of his blasphemy; the other was raised up from his sins to the knowledge of theology. O Christ God, glory be to Thee.

Both now.

When she who bare the Lamb and Shepherd and Saviour of the world beheld Him on the Cross, she said with tears: The world rejoiceth at receiving redemption, but my bowels burn as I see Thy crucifixion which Thou endurest for all, O my Son and my God.

The Source

These so-called "Short Hours" are the kontakia of the Hours during Great Lent, but are appropriate to read year-round. This translation is taken from *The Unabbreviated Horologion or Book of the Hours* (Jordanville, NY: Holy Trinity Monastery, 1997), 90, 117, 128, 178–9. Reprinted [and placed on the Internet] with permission.

A one-page version of this chapter can be printed out from www.OrthodoxReader.com.

Miscellanea

Parent (and Other Busy People) Friendly

The times for prayer set by the Church, mentioned by Saint Symeon of Thessalonica in the previous chapter, are the offices of Vespers, Compline, Midnight Service (Nocturns), Matins, First, Third, Sixth, and Ninth Hours. An extremely portable and abbreviated (do-able) version of these offices is *A Manual of the Hours of the Orthodox Church*. Compiled by Archimandrite Cherubim of the Monastery of the Paraclete, Attica, Greece, it is available from Holy Myrrhbearers Monastery in Otego, New York. At 4½" x 5½" and less than five ounces, this booklet is intended specifically as a help for busy people who desire this godly connection through the day and night. These shortened services, in modern English, might also be a good starting point for children. Although it uses non-Septuagint Psalm text and numbering, it is a good beginning guide and help.

The Horologion

On the other end of the scale (from less than five ounces to right at five pounds, from modern English to Elizabethan) is a full-size Horologion, a "Book of Hours." Holy Transfiguration Monastery (Brookline, MA) publishes *The Great Horologion*. It contains all of the offices throughout the day (not the Divine Liturgy) from the Midnight Service to Compline and provides for seasonal variations. In addition, it supplies short lives of saints and their troparia and kontakia for every day of the year (an especial blessing for one's daily rule). There are also prayers and explanatory notes for the moveable feasts of the Triodion and Pentecostarion periods, the various theotokia and katavasiae, and the standard (and more) canons and akathists.

The Unabbreviated Horologion or Book of Hours from Holy Trinity Monastery (Jordanville, NY) seems more monastery specific. It includes all of the offices (plus Divine Liturgy), festal and weekday troparia and kontakia, and standard canons and akathists.

The Gift of Literacy

We might also advise those who are literate to read more often. Besides the morning and evening prayers, in which the poverty of our spirit is very well expressed, they could also read the Great Canon of Saint Andrew of Crete,[1] the canons and akathists to the Savior and the Mother of God,[2] the canon to the Guardian Angel, and the canons for every day of the week.[3] It goes without saying that we should not leave out the Gospel and the Psalter, which are the best teachers of humility.[4]

—Saint John of Kronstadt

1 Available in *The Lenten Triodion* from St Tikhon's Seminary Press as well as in a softcover edition with the Life of St Mary of Egypt from Holy Trinity Monastery; et al.

2 Available in the personal prayer books from Holy Trinity Monastery, Jordanville, NY; Holy Transfiguration Monastery, Brookline, MA; and St Tikhon's Monastery, Waymart, PA (all also include the canon to the Guardian Angel).

3 Available in the *Octoechos*; as this homily was given just before Great Lent, perhaps he suggests the daily canons in *The Lenten Triodion* (and, in English, the *Triodion Supplement*); or for every day of the year from the *Menaion*.

4 St John of Kronstadt [†1908, Dec 20], *Ten Homilies on the Beatitudes*, trans Professor N. Kizenko-Frugier (Albany, NY: Cornerstone Editions/La Pierre Angulaire, 2003), 29. Used with permission.

15. Vesper Hymns

The Octoechos *(Book of Eight Tones, sometimes called* Parakletike*) provides the hymns of Vespers and Matins that relate to the days of the week (Sunday through Saturday) in an eight week cycle (one tone per week). That is, these are the words of the Church that one would hear every day at prayer. In America, weekday services are nearly unheard of, and at Vespers and Matins before Sunday Divine Liturgy, it is too often the case that the words cannot be heard or understood.*

In the excerpts below, the Saturday evening hymns are provided for those who want to know what they are missing. Following that are hymns from Monday evening, which convey the contrast in mood and emphasis from day to day. It has been advised and assumed since the Apostles that Christians attend church services twice every day. It may not be possible to pray every day at *the church, but with* The Octoechos, *one can pray every day* with *the Church.*

Eve of Sunday Vespers

On "Lord, I have cried ..." [Psalms 140, 141, 129, 116], ten Resurrectional Stichera in Tone III:

Stichos: Bring my soul out of prison, that I may confess Thy name. [Ps 141:8]

By Thy Cross hast Thou destroyed the might of death, O Christ our Savior, and hast set at naught the deception of the devil. And the human race, saved by faith, ever offereth a hymn unto Thee.

Stichos: The righteous shall wait patiently for me until Thou shalt reward me. [Ps 141:8]

All things have been illumined by Thy resurrection, O Lord; paradise hath again been opened, and all creation, praising Thee, ever offereth a hymn unto Thee.

Stichos: Out of the depths have I cried unto Thee, O Lord; O Lord, hear my voice. [Ps 129:1]

I glorify the power of the Father and the Son, and I hymn the authority of the Spirit: the indivisible and uncreated Godhead, the consubstantial Trinity, Who reigneth unto the ages of ages.

Stichos: Let Thine ears be attentive to the voice of my supplication. [Ps 129:2]

We bow down before Thy precious Cross, O Christ, and we hymn and glorify Thy resurrection; for by Thy stripes have we all been healed.

Stichos: If Thou shouldst mark iniquities, O Lord, O Lord, who shall stand? For with Thee there is forgiveness. [Ps 129:3,4]

We hymn the Savior incarnate of the Virgin; for, crucified for our sake, He arose on the third day, granting us great mercy.

Stichos: For Thy name's sake have I patiently waited for Thee, O Lord, my soul hath waited patiently for Thy word, my soul hath hoped in the Lord. [Ps 129:5]

Descending, Christ proclaimed the glad tidings to those in hades, saying: "Be of good cheer! Now have I triumphed! I am the resurrection! And, breaking down the gates of death, I will lead you up!"

Stichos: From the morning watch until night, from the morning watch let Israel hope in the Lord. [Ps 129:6]

Standing unworthily in Thine all-pure house, O Christ God, we send up our evening hymnody, crying out from the depths of our souls: O Thou Who lovest mankind, Who illumined the world with Thy resurrection on the third day, rescue Thy people from the hands of Thine enemies.

And these stichera of the all-holy Theotokos, the composition of Paul of Amorium, which are chanted when there is no Menaion, or at Litia. In Tone VII: Special Melody: "Today Judas keepeth watch..."—

Stichos: For with the Lord there is mercy, and with Him is plenteous redemption; and He shall redeem Israel out of all his iniquities. [Ps 129:7,8]

O Virgin, thou hast shown thyself to be merciful, kind and right heedful to me who truly invoke thy divine grace in all that befalleth me; for on thee have I set all the hope of my soul, and in all things I trust in thy divine foreknowledge. Do thou vouchsafe me divine life and the glories which are to come.

Stichos: O praise the Lord, all ye nations; praise Him all ye peoples. [Ps 116:1]

The burning coals of my passions have been kindled within me, O Theotokos, by wrath and anger, by drunkenness and fornication, by greed, hardness of heart and grievous mortification, by despondency and vexation, by vainglory and the trampling down of my conscience. From these things, I pray thee, deliver my soul, and save me, O Mistress.

Stichos: For He hath made His mercy to prevail over us, and the truth of the Lord abideth forever. [Ps 116:2]

With pure conscience let us all fall down before the Theotokos, crying out unceasingly from within our hearts: O holy Mistress, save us all from wrath and misery, from misfortunes and falls; for, saved by thee, we have acquired thee as a rampart and support, having recourse to thy shelter.

Glory..., from the Menaion.

Now & ever...: The dogmatic theotokion, in Tone III—

How can we not marvel at thy giving birth to the God-man, O all-honored one. For without having accepted the temptation of a man, O all-immaculate one, without a father thou gavest birth in the flesh to a Son Who was begotten without a mother before the ages, without His undergoing change, confusion or division, yet preserving intact the character of both essences. Wherefore, O Virgin Mother and Mistress, entreat Him, that the souls of those who in Orthodox manner confess thee to be the Theotokos be saved.

The Aposticha stichera, in Tone III—

O Christ Who by Thy suffering didst darken the sun, and with the light of Thy resurrection hast illumined all things: Accept our evening hymnody, O Thou Who lovest mankind.

Stichos: The Lord is King, He is clothed with majesty. [Ps 92:1]

Thy life-bearing resurrection hath illumined the whole universe, O Lord, and restored corrupted creation. Wherefore, loosed from the curse of Adam, we cry out: O almighty Lord, glory be to Thee!

Stichos: For He hath established the world which shall not be shaken. [Ps 92:1]

Though Thou art God immutable, yet suffering in the flesh Thou wast altered. Creation, unable to bear the sight of Him hanging [on the Cross], fell prostrate in fear and groaned; and it hymneth Thy long-suffering. Having descended into hades, Thou didst arise on the third day, granting life and great mercy to the world.

Stichos: Holiness becometh Thy house, O Lord, unto length of days. [Ps 92:5]

Thou didst endure death, O Christ, that Thou mightest deliver our race from death; having risen from the dead on the third day, Thou didst raise with Thyself those who acknowledged Thee as God; and Thou hast enlightened the world. O Lord, glory be to Thee!

Glory..., from the Menaion, if there is a doxasticon provided. If not, Glory..., Now & ever...: Theotokion—

Through the divine Spirit, by the will of the Father, without seed thou didst conceive the Son of God Who hath existed without mother from before the ages, and for our sake thou gavest birth in the flesh unto Him Who came forth from thee without father; and thou didst nurture Him on milk as a babe. Wherefore, cease not to pray that our souls be delivered from tribulations.

Eve of Tuesday Vespers

On "Lord, I have cried ...", 3 stichera of repentance, in Tone IV:[1]

Stichos: If Thou shouldest mark iniquities, O Lord, O Lord, who shall stand? For with Thee is forgiveness.

Emulating the Canaanite woman, O my soul, touch Christ from behind, and cry out repeatedly: Have mercy on me, O Master! My body, like her daughter, is possessed by evil spirits, and it flaileth about. Quench the burning of my flesh, I pray; and, causing the disorderly seizures thereof to cease, mortify it by the fear of Thee, through the supplications of her who conceived and gave Thee birth, and of all the saints, O greatly merciful Benefactor. [Mt 15:22]

Stichos: For Thy name's sake have I patiently waited for Thee, O Lord; my soul hath waited patiently for Thy word, my soul hath hoped in the Lord.

Thou didst once send Jonah to the sinful Ninevites to preach to them, O Christ, and, repenting, they transformed their anger into kindliness, delivered from pernicious wrath. Wherefore, send also Thy mighty help unto me, who am unworthy, O Thou Who lovest mankind, that I may turn away from my countless offenses and be guided to the path of

1 [The change of tone here is due to editorial selection of hymns. Normally, the tone of Sunday is used until the following Saturday Vespers.]

repentance; for I weep, groaning bitterly, to be delivered by Thy mercy from my many transgressions.

Stichos: From the morning watch until night, from the morning watch let Israel hope in the Lord.

O Compassionate One, Who camest into the world to save sinful men and call them to repentance: In that Thou art full of lovingkindness, have pity on me who have angered Thee more than all other men, save me in Thy goodness, guide me to the way of repentance, and grant me thought of compunction, in Thy goodness making my heart steadfastly humble, simple, meek and guileless, O my Savior, in that Thou art full of lovingkindness.

Then the stichera of the holy & great John the Forerunner.

Stichos: For with the Lord there is mercy, and with Him there is plenteous redemption; and He shall redeem Israel out of all his iniquities.

O Forerunner, who hast boldness before the Lord, and who dost surpass all born of women: Unceasingly entreat Him in behalf of those who pray to thee with faith, that He grant us conversion and a beginning to repentance, that, saved, we may ever hymn thee.

Stichos: O praise the Lord, all ye nations; praise Him, all ye peoples.

Thou wast called a prophet from thy mother's womb and a preacher from her belly, O Forerunner and Apostle of the coming of the Lord. I have given myself over to the demons and am become an industrious slave to sin. As a mighty warrior cure me of both these sins, that I may proclaim thy speedy help.

Stichos: For He hath made His mercy to prevail over us, and the truth of the Lord abideth forever.

As the winnowing-fan of the divine Spirit, winnow away like weeds the ways of my heart, gathering divine deeds from me to store like grain in the granary of God, that, enriched by thee, my mediator, I may become food fit for the Master, O blessed one who baptized Christ.

Glory..., Now & ever...: Theotokion

Grant me tears from the depths of my heart, sighing from the depths of my soul, O Maiden, and contrition and confession of the transgressions I have committed in this life, that by thy help, O most pure one, I may pass my life in repentance and receive surcease.

Aposticha stichera of repentance, in Tone IV

I desired to erase the record of my transgressions with tears, and to please Thee well by repentance for the rest of my life; but the enemy deceiveth me and wageth war on my soul. Before I perish utterly, O Lord, save me!

Stichos: Unto Thee have I lifted up mine eyes, unto Thee that dwellest in heaven. Behold, as the eyes of servants look unto the hands of their masters, as the eyes of the handmaid look unto the hands of her mistress, so do our eyes look unto the Lord our God, until He take pity on us. [Ps 122:1,2]

Who is tempest-tossed, yet fleeth to Thy haven, O Lord, and is not saved? Who is sick and, falling down before Thy healing power, is not cured? O Lord, Creator of all and Physician of the infirm: Before I perish utterly, save me!

Stichos: Have mercy on us, O Lord, have mercy on us, for greatly are we filled with abasement. Greatly hath our soul been filled therewith; let reproach come upon them that prosper, and abasement on the proud. [Ps 122:3,4]

Martyricon: O Thou Who lovest mankind, and Who hast accepted the patience of the holy martyrs, through their supplications grant us great mercy.

Glory . . ., Now & ever . . .: Theotokion:

Deliver us from our needs, O Mother of Christ God, who gavest birth to the Creator of all, that all of us may cry out to thee: Rejoice, O only intercession for our souls!

The Source

Reprinted with permission from *The Octoechos: The Hymns of the Cycle of the Eight Tones for Sundays and Weekdays*, vol 2 (Tones III & IV), trans Reader Isaac E. Lambertsen (Liberty, TN: Saint John of Kronstadt Press, 1999), 4–5, 101–102; SJKP.org. Psalm verses from *The Psalter of the Seventy* (Boston: Holy Transfiguration Monastery, 1974).

Miscellanea

Sweeter than the Psalms

Saint John of Damascus [†c.749, Dec 4] received an extraordinary education in all the branches of learning of his day with his stepbrother, Saint Cosmas [Bishop of Maiuma, Oct 14 Greek, Oct 12 Slav]. They both excelled in poetry and music. John became a valued counsellor to the ruling caliph in Damascus. When the iconoclast Roman Emperor Leo the Isaurian began his assault on the Church and the icons, John wrote letters that were disseminated throughout the empire defending the true faith and the veneration of icons. In revenge, the emperor sent to the caliph forged letters as if by John that encouraged the emperor to invade Damascus. The caliph believed the fraud and ordered John's right hand cut off. In great pain, John prayed and wept before the icon of the All-Holy Mother of God, and she restored the hand to his arm. In grateful remembrance, he always wore on his head the bandage in which he had wrapped his severed hand.[1]

Saint John left Damascus and entered the monastery of Saint Sabbas near Jerusalem. He was put under the care of an elder who, though knowledgeable and experienced in spiritual life, was not formally educated. He prohibited John from philosophy, music, and poetry, but as the quickest path to obedience and humility (and thus to heaven), assigned him to menial tasks. John was diligent and uncomplaining. When one of his monastic brothers lost a parent, he begged John to compose a hymn for consolation. Though loathe to disobey his elder's instruction, John finally relented and wrote hymns for the grieving monk—hymns that are used today in the funeral service.[2]

The elder, upon hearing of this disobedience, refused to have John any longer as a disciple. The other elders pleaded on John's behalf, and eventually the elder agreed to take John back if he cleaned all the latrines and chamber-pots in the monastery. This John did with eager and grateful obedience, with the very hand that the most holy Theotokos had restored to him. The Mother of God then appeared to the elder, asking him to lift the prohibition he had placed on John. The hymns and poetry that John would write, the Theotokos explained, would surpass the Psalms of David and the Odes of the prophets in beauty and sweetness.

John went on to compose a great many hymns, still in use today, that incorporate the theology and wisdom of the greatest holy Fathers. He wrote

1 This is seen in his icons. See also the Icon of our Most Holy Lady the Theotokos "Of the Three Hands" [Greek June 28, Slav July 12].

2 See the funeral services, available in Hapgood, *Service Book*.

the Paschal Canon and canons and hymns for many of the Great and lesser Feasts in the *Menaion* (see his "Annunciation Canon" in this book, chapter 9). He also composed most of the hymns for the Resurrection in the *Octoechos*. He reviewed and edited his many homilies and theological expositions to the end of his life so that no error would remain in them.

Octoechos, Triodion, Pentecostarion

Since Sunday always celebrates the Resurrection of the Lord, the Divine Liturgy may seem very much the same year-round. To those who limit their church attendance to Divine Liturgy—and for all who attend Vespers or Matins where the canons are skipped and the stichera are unintelligible—the Sundays before and after Pascha may seem ho-hum. "What's the big do-to?" Reading the services, however, makes very clear the gravity (*Triodion*) and the joy (*Pentecostarion*) of these Sundays and all the days in between. Add to these the *Octoechos* and *Menaion*, and every day of the year is bright, joyous, festive.

The Octoechos provides the hymns for the days of the week. For Vespers, as we have seen, are the stichera for "Lord, I have cried" and the aposticha. For Matins are the sessional hymns, the canons, and the aposticha. These continue for most of the year in the eight tone/eight week cycle. With an *Octoechos*, ordinary services can be read even without a *Menaion*.

A complete *Octoechos*[1] (every day of the week) is published by St John of Kronstadt Press. In addition to the stichera and canons for Vespers and Matins, it includes the Trinity canons of Sunday Nocturns (Midnight Office) and a canon to the Theotokos every night for Compline.

A weekday version, the *Parakletike*, translated by Mother Mary and (now Metropolitan) Kallistos Ware, is published by the Monastery of the Veil of Our Lady, Bussy-en-Othe, France (available from American book dealers). A church library might want both versions to provide alternative translations when meanings seem murky.

The Lenten Triodion makes its appearance on the Sundays before Great Lent: Publican and Pharisee, Prodigal Son, Last Judgment, Forgiveness Sunday; it takes over completely, every day of the week, during Great Lent. The texts for all of the Sundays, the First Week of Lent, and Holy Week are contained in *The Lenten Triodion* from St Tikhon's Seminary Press. The other Lenten weekdays (including Cheese Week as a sort of warm-up),

1 Perhaps it is more correct to say, "The *Octoechos* hymns combined with the *Parakletike*"?

which continue the meditations of the previous Sunday, are in *The Lenten Triodion Supplement*, also from St Tikhon's.

The Pentecostarion begins with Matins of Pascha and carries the services through Pentecost and Sunday of All Saints. *The Pentecostarion* is available from Holy Transfiguration Monastery (Brookline) as well as from St John of Kronstadt Press. The latter edition also includes the Compline Triodia—for which reason the Slavs call the *Pentecostarion* the *Flowery Triodion*. Additionally, this edition provides more rubrics that explain the Pascha-through-Pentecost order of services.

What a different understanding these books bring about! What marvellous sermons they might inspire!

Synaxaria

A synaxis is an assembly, a meeting, a coming together of the faithful to praise and worship God, to commemorate His saints, to participate in spiritual events (e.g., the occasions of the Great Feasts), and to engage in podvig (spiritual labor or struggle).

The what, why, and when of these synaxes are provided for every calendar (immoveable) day of the year for both saints and feasts in *The Synaxarion: The Lives of the Saints of the Orthodox Church.*[1] As discussed in chapter 8 ("Valentine"), it is recommended that this *Synaxarion* be used in concert with the St Demetrius of Rostov *Great Collection of the Lives of the Saints*:[2] St Demetrius for depth, *The Synaxarion* for breadth.

For the moveable commemorations of Great Lent through Pentecost, there is the single-volume *Synaxarion of the Lenten Triodion and Pentecostarion.*[3] From the Sunday of Zaccheus to the Sunday of All Saints of North America, a brief (two to six pages) but edifying explanation is given for every Sunday and the major Saturdays and weekdays, plus a one- or two-page homily for each occasion from the Holy Fathers. Great information in a trim package.

Convert English to Orthodoxy

The on-going complaints that English is not Orthodox—"Slavonic is so deeply Orthodox!" "Greek is the only Orthodox language!"—Pish! Posh! From the beginning Christianity has challenged humans to communicate spiritual concepts in human language. Even after three hundred years of

1 Hieromonk Makarios of Simonos Petra, *The Synaxarion: The Lives of the Saints of the Orthodox Church* (Mt Athos, Greece: Holy Monastery of Simonos Petra, 1998–2008).
2 St Demetrius of Rostov [†1709, Oct 28], *The Great Collection of the Lives of the Saints*, trans Fr Thomas Marretta (House Springs, MO: Chrysostom Press, 1994–2012).
3 Edited by Father David (Kidd) and Mother Gabriella (Ursache), Rives Junction, MI: HDM Press, 1999.

Christianity in Greek, the Holy Fathers strained to force new meanings into/out of existing Greek words (e.g., *homoousios*). When the Slavs were converted to Christianity, they were presented—from the start—with native language translations from Saints Cyril and Methodius [†869, 885, May 11]. Still, they had yet to grasp new understanding of existing words that had been given different, fuller meaning. Slavonic indeed *became* an Orthodoxy-saturated language, having steeped in Orthodox culture for nine hundred years, but it also became (*is*) unintelligible to the average Russian.

> In the church I had rather speak five words with my understanding, that by my voice I might teach others also, than ten thousand words in an unknown tongue ... Else when thou shalt bless with the spirit, how shall he that occupieth the room of the unlearned say Amen at thy giving of thanks, seeing he understandeth not what thou sayest? [1Cor 14:19,16].

At Pentecost, the Holy Spirit clearly demonstrated that God is to be praised in all languages. The Russian missionaries on their first voyage to Alaska were already translating Church texts into the native language. The reason ancient Greek and Slavonic are Orthodoxy-saturated is because they are taught and transmitted that way.

Make English Orthodox! Teach Orthodox concepts—in sermons, yes! in classrooms, in personal conversations—and explain how the Orthodox understanding of certain words differs from the worldly, Protestant, or Roman Catholic meaning. Preach an Orthodox world view so that those words—and their hearers—live in a natural, compatible, organic context. Explain, expand, expound—and repeat!—the Orthodox understanding, the mind of the Church. Don't complain about how ignorant, how "stupid" parishioners are and then hide yourself away in "Orthodox" languages, lest you and the incomprehensible cantor/choir be likened to the sons of Eli the priest, "causing the people not to serve God" [1Kgs 2:24[1]]. Equip the people—in their native language, *broaden* their native language—to be able to live in an Orthodox manner and to be an Orthodox influence and persuasion in this dark world.

1 Scripture taken from the St Athanasius Academy Septuagint™.

Once a visiting priest came to us (we did not yet have our own at that time) and served the All-night Vigil. The Vigil lasted only forty-five minutes. We were scandalized. So much had been omitted that we decided to report it to Vladika [Saint John of Shanghai and San Francisco] in hopes that he would chastise the priest into proper observance of the church rubrics. But Vladika only smiled and said, "Well, there's no way to satisfy you! I serve too long (on Holy Saturday, services began at 9 a.m. and by 4 p.m. they hadn't yet reached Communion; after that Vladika shortened the service), and the other serves too short!" We felt so ashamed that we had judged the priest, and even Vladika. To judge anyone is terrible, but especially the clergy. And how kindly and humbly Vladika gave us this lesson! [1]

1 *Man of God: Saint John of Shanghai & San Francisco*, trans from Russian edition and compiled by Archpriest Peter Perekrestov (Richfield Springs, NY: Nikodemos Orthodox Publication Society, 1994), 53. Used with permission.

16. Prologue of Ohrid

The Prologue of Ohrid[1] *was compiled by our American* ***Saint Nikolai Velimirovic*** *[of South Canaan, of Zhicha, of Ochrid, †1956, March 5]. While Bishop of Ohrid (Serbia), he composed it specifically as daily reading for clergy and laity. It provides just a few pages for each day of the year, a workable bit of reading even for busy Americans. Whether or not one reads* The Prologue, *Saint Nikolai's prescription for daily reading bears consideration: Scripture, lives of saints, hymns, and homilies—with time for reflection.*

JULY 4

1. Saint Andrew, Archbishop of Crete

Andrew was born in Damascus of Christian parents, and he was mute from birth until the age of seven. When his parents brought him to church and he received Holy Communion, he began to speak. Such is the power of Divine and Holy Communion. At age fourteen, Andrew went to Jerusalem and was tonsured in the Lavra of Saint Sava the Sanctified. By his understanding and asceticism, he surpassed many of the older monks and was an example to them. After a while the patriarch took him as his personal secretary. But when the Monothelite heresy—which held that the Lord Jesus did not possess a human will, but only a divine will—began to rage, the Sixth Ecumenical Council was convened in Constantinople, in the year 681 during the reign of Constantine IV. Theodore, the Patriarch of Jerusalem, was unable to attend the council but sent Andrew (at the time an archdeacon) as his representative. There Andrew displayed his splendid gifts, his oratory,

1 "The Prologue is a centuries-old reader of the Orthodox people.... 'Prologue'—a Preface or Introduction to the profound and wonderful system of Christian knowledge—is a word that our Slavic fathers substituted for another Greek word, *Synaxarion*."—from author's Preface.

his zeal for the Faith, and his rare prudence. Having assisted in strengthening the Orthodox Faith, Andrew returned to his duties in Jerusalem. Later he was elected and installed as Archbishop of Crete. As archbishop, he was greatly loved by the people. Andrew was very zealous for Orthodoxy and vehemently resisted all heresies. Through his prayers he worked miracles, including driving the Saracens off the island of Crete. Andrew wrote many books of instruction, hymns and canons, of which the most renowned is the Great Canon of repentance, read on the Thursday of the fifth week of Great Lent. His outward appearance was such that, "seeing his face and hearing his words flowing like honey, everyone found delight and mended their ways." Finally, while returning from a sea journey to Constantinople, Andrew foretold that his death would occur before he arrived in Crete. And so it happened. As the ship sailed near the island of Mitylene, this beacon of the Church finished his earthly life and his soul took up habitation in the Kingdom of Christ, in the year 712.

2. Saint Martha

Martha was the mother of Saint Simeon of the Wonderful Mountain [May 24]. Dedicated with all her soul to the Faith, she did not think of marriage. When her parents betrothed her to a young man, Martha thought of leaving the home of her parents and withdrawing from the world. Then Saint John the Baptist appeared to her and counseled her to fulfill the will of her parents by entering into marriage, which she did. From this marital union, the wondrous Saint Simeon, ascetic of the Wonderful Mountain, was born. Saint Martha had the regular habit of rising at midnight for prayer. With great compassion she helped the poor, visited the orphaned, and served the sick. A year before her death she saw a multitude of angels with candles in their hands, and learned from them the time of her death. Upon learning this, Martha dedicated herself to prayer and good works with even greater zeal. She died peacefully in the year 551, and was buried near the pillar of her son, Simeon the [New] Stylite. After her death, she appeared many times to instruct people and to heal the sick. Her most significant appearance on record was to the abbot of Simeon's monastery. Following the burial of Saint Martha, the abbot placed a lamp on her grave, with the understanding that it should never be extinguished. But after a certain time, people became lazy, and the lamp went out. Then the abbot became ill, and the saint appeared to him and said: "Why do you not burn a lamp on my grave? Know that

I am not in need of the light from your candles, since I have been found worthy before God, the Eternal Heavenly Light—but you need it. When you burn a light on my grave, you prompt me to pray to the Lord for you." It is obvious from this that the goal of our veneration of the saints is to prompt them, as those worthier than we are, to pray to God for us and for our salvation.[1]

HYMN OF PRAISE
The divine providence of God

The Lord is miraculous in His divine providence;
He gave a clear voice to Andrew the mute,
And made the mute His audible trumpet
As once He made Saul the pillar of His Church.
In vain did the holy Martha shun marriage;
To the will of God she had to bow down.
To marriage God's providence led Martha—
To bear a saint for God and for mankind!
Whoever gives himself to God gives to the Best,
And overcomes his human will by that of God.
My child, plan nothing without the Lord,
That your plans be not fruitless.
All the threads of your life and all your desires
Are held in the hands of the Creator Almighty.
His are the fields, His are the slopes,
His are the elements—the foundations and the threads.
His is the soul, His is the body,
And the spirit of everything, and its attire.
In His field, with His tools,
Whose will shall we fulfill, except His?

REFLECTION

If your entire life has passed smoothly and without cares, then weep for yourself. For the Gospel and human experience assert with one accord that, without great pain and suffering, no one has left behind any great

---

[1] [Among the many reasons for burning candles, consider St Seraphim of Byritsa [†1949, March 21/April 3], who suggests that we light a candle, at least once in our lives, for all to whom we have done ill.]

or beneficial work on earth or been glorified in the heavens. If, however, your earthly sojourn has been completely bathed with sweat and tears—to attain justice and truth—rejoice and be exceedingly glad, for your reward will be truly great in the heavens. Never succumb to the insane thought that God has abandoned you. God knows exactly how much each one can endure and measures the sufferings and pains of each accordingly. Saint Nilus of Sora says: "When even men know how much weight a horse can carry, how much a donkey, and how much a camel, and thus load them according to their strength; and when a potter knows how long to leave the clay in the kiln, so that it will neither be shattered nor over-baked—how could God not know how much temptation a soul can bear to make it ready and fit for the Kingdom of Heaven?"

CONTEMPLATION

Contemplate all the miracles that the Lord performed at the hands of Moses and Aaron in the land of Egypt [Ex 7–10]:

1. How great and awesome were those miracles;
2. How the heart of Pharaoh remained obstinate before all the miracles of God;
3. How my heart is also hard before the countless miracles of God—in my life and around me—and how I need to repent before the end befalls me and I face eternal punishment.

HOMILY
on the salvation of a soul as the end of faith

Receiving the end of your faith, even the salvation of your souls [1Pet 1:9].

Brethren, what is the end of faith? The salvation of the soul. What is the goal of faith? The salvation of the soul. What is the fruit of faith? The salvation of the soul. Therefore, we do not adhere to faith for the sake of faith, but rather for the salvation of our souls. No one travels for the sake of the road, but because of someone or something that awaits him at the end of the road. No one throws a rope into the water in which someone is drowning for the sake of the rope, but for the sake of the one drowning. God gave faith to us as a road, at the end of which the travelers will receive the salvation of their souls. And like a rope, God extended faith to us who are drowning in the dark waters of sin, ignorance and vice, so that we, through the help of faith, might save our lives.

That is the purpose of faith. Whoever knows the price of a human soul must admit that there is nothing in this world more necessary or more beneficial than faith. A merchant who carries precious stones in an earthen vessel preserves the vessel carefully and cautiously; he hides it and keeps watch over it. Is it because of the vessel that the merchant exerts such effort and concern? No, but because of the precious stones which are in the vessel. Our entire earthly life is like an earthen vessel in which a priceless treasure is hidden. That priceless treasure is our soul. A vessel is cheap, but a treasure is precious. First, one must have faith in the value of the human soul; second, in the future radiance and life of the soul in the Kingdom of God; third, in the Living God, Who waits for the return of the soul, which He Himself gave us; and fourth, in the possibility that a soul can be lost in this world. Whoever has faith in these four things will know how to protect his soul, and will further know that the salvation of his soul is the end of his road—the goal of his faith, the fruit of his life, the purpose of his existence on earth, and the justification of his sufferings.

We believe for the sake of the salvation of our souls. Whoever has a true faith must know that faith is for the sake of the salvation of the soul. He who thinks that his faith serves a purpose other than salvation does not have a true faith—nor does he know the value of his soul.

O All-gracious Lord Jesus, Who has given us a shining and victorious faith, strengthen and maintain that faith in us, that we may stand unashamed before Thy judgment with our pure and shining souls.

To Thee be glory and praise forever. Amen.

The Source

The Prologue of Ohrid: Lives of Saints, Hymns, Reflections and Homilies for Every Day of the Year, by Saint Nikolai Velimirovic, trans Fr T. Timothy Tepsic (Alhambra, CA: Serbian Orthodox Diocese of Western America, 2002), 2:16–20. Reprinted with permission.

An earlier English translation of this work is published in four volumes by Lazarica Press, Birmingham, England, 1985.

Miscellanea

Prayer Books

A prayer book is meant to be worn out. *A Prayer Book for Orthodox Christians* is available from Holy Transfiguration Monastery (Brookline, MA), and *Prayer Book* from Holy Trinity Monastery (Jordanville, NY). They both contain the standard canons and akathists,[1] daily and festal troparia, excerpts from the Divine Liturgy, and the pre- and post-Communion prayers.

As for their morning and evening prayers, the Jordanville book is more monastic; the length, style, and repetition of the prayers, without guidance from a spiritual director, could be overwhelming for someone just beginning this sort of prayer rule. The Brookline book, by contrast, offers standard morning prayers of reasonable (do-able) length. For evening prayers, Brookline recommends and provides the service of Small Compline. The Jordanville Prayers before Sleep might assume that Compline has been read previously, but that service is not provided in the book.

Jordanville gives "Selections" from Vespers and Matins, whereas Brookline provides the entire services—except, of course, for the changeable parts from the *Octoechos*, etc. Having the full services available helps in learning the services and even *doing* the services, as far as one is able. For beginners, however, Jordanville's "Selections" may be a more practicable, less cluttered initiation into and assimilation of these services. In more recent editions, Jordanville has adopted, with small changes, the Brookline translations.

A thinner prayer book, *Orthodox Daily Prayers*, is available from St Tikhon's Seminary Press. Its morning and evening prayers are nearly the same as Jordanville, although they add the service of Compline. They provide the Canons of Repentance, to the Theotokos, and to the Guardian Angel (pre-mixed), and the pre- and post-Communion prayers.

The Psalter — The Original Prayer Book

The Psalter is the hymnal of Israel. Christ and His Apostles sang the psalms, as have Christians ever since. All of the Church services abound with psalms, and the psalms provide spiritual nourishment, help, and consolation in the daily life of every Christian.

Monastics read through the entire Psalter every week—twice a week during Great Lent—in addition to the thirty-some psalms that they chant every day in the services. Lay people are not expected to psalmodize like monastics, but even a small amount every day rewards the effort. People

1 Canons to Our Lord and God and Savior Jesus Christ, the Most-Holy Theotokos, one's Guardian Angel; akathists to Jesus Christ and the Theotokos.

who are not familiar with the Psalms may at first find them a little strange, but they quickly become near and dear.

Psalter Considerations. Liturgical Psalters are divided into twenty sections, each called a "kathisma" (plural *kathismata*). Each kathisma is further divided into three sections, each called a "stasis" (plural *stases*) or "Glory." At the rate of one stasis per day, the reader would progress through the entire Psalter once every two months; or, let's say, one stasis in the morning and one in the evening, the entire Psalter once a month.

Memorization is a valuable practice ("In my heart have I hid Thy sayings" Ps 118:11), including psalms and other scriptures and prayers. Psalm 50 (51) may be a good start.[1] At first it may be easiest to memorize short and favorite psalms. Then one might choose the psalms in the Divine Liturgy, Matins, Vespers, and the Hours.

> No other book so glorifies God as does the Psalter. It profits the soul; it glorifies God together with the angels, and exalts and extols with a powerful voice, and imitates the angels. At times, it flogs the demons and drives them out, and causes them much weeping and injury. It prays to God for kings and princes, and for the whole world. With the Psalter you can pray to God even for yourself, for it is the greatest and most exalted of books.[2]
>
> —Saint Basil the Great

Liturgical Psalters

The Psalters below follow the Septuagint and include the nine Biblical Odes.

The Psalter of the Seventy from Holy Transfiguration Monastery, Brookline, MA (1974). The monastery also provides a pocket-size version—very convenient—but this smaller version does not include the Biblical Odes.

The Psalter of the Prophet and King David from the Center for Traditionalist Orthodox Studies, Etna, CA (2008), compiled by Michael Asser from the King James and Douai versions, translated to conform to the Septuagint; it is adorned with many brightly colored icons and illustrations.

A Psalter for Prayer from Holy Trinity Publications, Jordanville, NY, (2nd edition, 2011), based on the Miles Coverdale translation (1535) and conformed to the Septuagint. Emulating the traditional Church Slavonic "Augmented"

1 Psalm 50 is considered of such moment that the offices employ it four times a day (Midnight, Matins, Third Hour, Compline).

2 St Basil the Great [†379, Jan 1], quoted in *A Psalter for Prayer*, 2nd ed (Jordanville, NY: Holy Trinity Publications, 2011), 42. Used with permission.

Psalter, it includes instructional material from the Holy Fathers, special prayers following each kathisma, and "The Rite for Singing the Twelve Psalms."

The Orthodox Psalter from Holy Apostles Convent/Dormition Skete, Buena Vista, CO (2010) includes patristic commentary on the psalms. As with their translation of the New Testament, they precisely render verb forms. For example, the familiar Mt 7:7 Ask, Seek, Knock translates "Keep on asking ... Keep on seeking ... Keep on knocking."

Psalms for the Dead

When an Orthodox Christian dies, it is traditional to read the Psalter over the body before the funeral. A person wishing to do this for the departed would coordinate with the priest or, more likely, the funeral director. The prayer that is read for the departed after each kathisma is included in *The Psalter of the Seventy*. *A Psalter for Prayer* also provides this prayer, with additional short prayers that are read after each stasis ("Glory").

> The body feels nothing then; it does not see its close ones who have assembled, does not smell the fragrance of the flowers, does not hear the funeral orations. But the soul senses the prayers offered for it and is grateful to those who make them and is spiritually close to them.[1]

Arrangements also should be made for the commemoration of the newly reposed person for the forty days following death, at churches or monasteries where the Divine Liturgy is performed daily. Almsgiving in the name of the reposed is also especially helpful for the departed soul.

1 St John of Shanghai and San Francisco [†1966, Jun 19/Jul 2], "What Can We Do for the Dead?" in the pamphlet *The Dead Urgently Need Our Help* (Marrickville, NSW, Australia: Orthodox Monastery of the Archangel Michael). Used with permission.

17. An Odd Chapter

Many books and authors are "hidden away" in expansive (and expensive) multi-volume sets of books, a mere glimpse of which wrests a gasp of dismay, dread, despair. Fear not! They are not as formidable as they appear. One is not required to read the whole thing. *Or to* buy *the whole thing. Volumes can be purchased individually or borrowed from a library.*

The lists below emphasize how much material is available in English. Not all are saints, not all are Orthodox. It is often helpful to read the Life of a saint before reading his works to get a better idea of the context of the writings and their place in the Church.

A cautionary note. These translations are produced by Roman Catholics, Protestants, and Western academics with their various distortions. The translations themselves are fairly reliable, but it may be best to skip the introductions, overviews, and elucidations, and to read with one's thumb over the notes.

Ancient Christian Writers Series (Paulist Press)

Arnobius of Sicca
The Case Against Pagans, 2 vols
Athanasius
The Life of Antoni
Athenagoras
Embassy for Christians
Resurrection of the Dead
Augustine
First Catechetical Instruction
Faith, Hope and Charity
The Lord's Sermon on the Mount
The Greatness of the Soul; Teacher
Against the Academics
Sermons for Christmas and Epiphany
The Problem of Free Choice
On the Psalms, 2 vols
Literal Meaning Of Genesis, 2 vols
Faith and Works

Cassiodorus
Explanation of the Psalms, 3 vols
Clement of Rome
Epistles (w/Ignatius of Antioch)
Cyprian of Carthage
The Lapsed, The Unity of the Catholic Church
Letters, 4 vols
Early Epistles
Didache & Barnabas, Polycarp, Papias, Diognetus
Egeria
Diary of a Pilgrimage
Evagrius Ponticus
Ad Monachos
Firmicus Maternus
Error of Pagan Religions

Ancient Christian Writers Series – cont'd

Gregory of Nyssa
The Lord's Prayer, The Beatitudes
Gregory the Great (the Dialogist)
Pastoral Care
Ignatius of Antioch
Epistles (w/Clement of Rome)
Irenaeus of Lyons
Proof of the Apostolic Preaching
Against the Heresies, 3 vols
Isidore of Seville
De Ecclesiasticis Officiis
Jerome
Commentary on Ecclesiastes
Letters, Vol 1
John Cassian
The Conferences
The Institutes
John Chrysostom
Baptismal Instruction
Julian of Toledo
Foreknowledge of the world to come
Julianus Pomeruis
The Contemplative Life
Justin Martyr
The First and Second Apologies
Marcus Minucius Felix
Octavius
Maximus of Turin
Sermons
Maximus the Confessor
Ascetic Life, Four Centuries on Charity
Methodius
Symposium, Treatise on Chastity
Origen
Prayer, Exhortation to Martyrdom
Song of Songs, Commentary and Homilies
Treatise on the Passover, Dialogue with Heraclides
Homilies 1–14 on Ezekiel
Palladius
Lausiac History
Dialogue on the Life of John Chrysostom
Patrick Secundinus
Works of, Hymn of Patrick
Paulinus of Nola
Letters, 2 vols
Poems
Prosper of Aquitaine
The Call of All Nations
Defense of Augustine
Quodvultdeus of Carthage
The Creedal Homilies
Rufinus
Commentary on the Apostles Creed
Tertullian
Treatises on Marriage and Remarriage
Against the Hermogenes
Treatises on Penance
Theodoret of Cyrus
On Divine Providence

Cistercian Publications

Bede the Venerable
Commentary on Acts of the Apostles
Commentary on 7 Catholic Epistles
Homilies on the Gospels I–II
Besa
The Life of Shenoute
Cyril of Scythopolis
Lives of the Monks of Palestine
Dorotheus of Gaza
Discourses and Sayings
Evagrius Ponticus
Praktikos and Chapters on Prayer
Gregory the Great (the Dialogist)
Forty Gospel Homilies
Handmaids of the Lord
Harlots of the Desert
John Moschos
The Spiritual Meadow
Lives of the Desert Fathers
Nil Sorsky
The Authentic Writings
Paphnutius
Histories/Monks of Upper Egypt
Sayings of the Desert Fathers
Symeon the New Theologian
The Theological and Practical Treatises & The Three Theological Discourses
Theodoret of Cyrrhus
A History of the Monks of Syria

Classics of Western Spirituality Series (Paulist Press)

Athanasius: The Life of Antony and The Letter to Marcellinus
Augustine of Hippo: Selected Writings
Bede the Venerable: On the Song of Songs and Selected Writings
Ephrem the Syrian: Hymns
Gregory of Nyssa: The Life of Moses
Gregory Palamas: The Triads
John Cassian: Conferences
John Climacus: The Ladder of Divine Ascent
Maximus the Confessor: Selected Writings
Nicodemos of the Holy Mountain: A Handbook of Spiritual Counsel
Nil Sorsky: The Complete Writings
Origen: Selected Writings
Pseudo Dionysius:Complete Works
Pseudo-Macarius: The 50 Spiritual Homilies and The Great Letter
Symeon the New Theologian: The Discourses

Fathers of the Church Series
(The Catholic University of America Press)

Ambrose of Milan
Hexameron, Paradise, Cain and Abel
Letters, 1-91
Seven Exegetical Works
Theological and Dogmatic Works
Andrew of Caesarea
Commentary on the Apocalypse
Apostolic Fathers
The Apostolic Fathers
Augustine
Against Julian
Catholic & Manichaean Ways of Life
Christian Instruction; Admonition and Grace; The Christian Combat; Faith, Hope and Charity
Commentary on Sermon on Mount
Confessions
Eighty-Three Different Questions
Four Anti-Pelagian Writings
Letters, 6 vols
On Genesis
Sermons on the Liturgical Seasons
The City of God, 3 vols
The Happy Life; Answer to Sceptics; Divine Providence and the Problem of Evil, Soliloquies
The Immortality of the Soul; The Magnitude of the Soul; On Music; The Advantage of Believing; On Faith in Things Unseen
The Retractations
The Teacher; The Free Choice of the Will; Grace and Free Will
The Trinity
Tractates on the First Epistle of John
Tractates on Gospel of John, 55-111
Treatises on Marriage et al
Treatises on Various Subjects
Barsanuphius and John
Letters, 2 vols
Basil the Great
Against Eunomius
Ascetical Works
Exegetic Homilies [*contains* Hexameron and Psalms]
Letters, 2 vols
Caesarius
Sermons, 3 vols
Clement of Alexandria
Christ the Educator
Stromateis, Books 1-3
Cyprian
Letters, (1-81)
Treatises
Cyril of Alexandria
Comment on the 12 Prophets, 3 vols
Festal Letters, 1-12
Letters, 2 vols
Cyril of Jerusalem
The Works of, 2 vols
Didymus the Blind
Commentary On Zechariah
Ephrem the Syrian
Selected Prose Works
Eugippius
Life of St. Severin
Eusebius Pamphili
Ecclesiastical History, 2 vols

Fathers of the Church Series – cont'd

Fulgentius
Fulgentius and the Scythian Monks: On Christology and Grace
Selected Works

Gregory of Nazianzus (the Theologian)
Funeral Orations
Select Orations
Three Poems

Gregory of Nyssa
Ascetical Works

Gregory Thaumaturgus (the Wonderworker)
Life and Works

Gregory the Great (the Dialogist)
Dialogues

Hilary of Poitiers
Commentary on Matthew
The Trinity

Iberian Fathers
Braulio of Saragossa and Fructuosus of Braga
Martin of Braga, Paschasius of Dumium, and Leander of Seville
Pacian of Barcelona, Orosius of Braga

Jerome
Commentary on Galatians
Commentary on Matthew
Dogmatic and Polemical Works
Homilies, 1 (1-59 on the Psalms)
Homilies, 2 (Homilies 60-96)
On Illustrious Men

John Chrysostom
Apologist
Commentary on John Homilies, 2 vols
Discourses Against Judaizing Christians
Homilies on Genesis, 3 vols
On Repentance and Almsgiving
On Incomprehensible Nature of God

John of Damascus
Writings [Fount of Knowledge: *contains* On the Orthodox Faith]

Justin Martyr
The First Apology, The Second Apology, Dialogue with Trypho, Exhortation to the Greeks, Discourse to the Greeks, The Monarchy of the Rule of God

Lactantius
Minor Works
The Divine Institutes, Books I-VII

Marius Victorinus
Theological Treatises on the Trinity

Nicetas
Writings; Commonitories; Grace and Free Will

Novatian
The Trinity, The Spectacles, Jewish Foods, In Praise of Purity, Letters

Oecumenius
Commentary on the Apocalypse

Origen
Commentary on John, 2 vols
Commentary on Romans, 2 vols
Homilies on Genesis and Exodus
Homilies on Jeremiah and I Kings 28
Homilies on Joshua
Homilies on Judges
Homilies on Leviticus, 1-16
Homilies on Luke

Pamphilus
Apology for Origen

Paulus Orosius
The Seven Books of History Against the Pagans

Peter Chrysologus and St Valerian
Selected Sermons; Homilies

Peter Chrysologus
Selected Sermons, 2 vols

Pontius
Early Christian Biographies

Pope Leo I
Letters
Sermons

Prudentius
Poems, 2 vols

Salvian
The Writings of Salvian, the Presbyter

Tertullian
Disciplinary, Moral, Ascetical Works

Tertullian; Minucius Felix
Apologetical Works: Tertullian; Minucius Felix; Octavius

Theodore of Mopsuestia
Commentary on the 12 Prophets

Theodoret of Cyrus
Commentary on the Psalms, 2 vols
Eranistes

Ante-Nicene Fathers Series

Volume 1

Clement of Rome
First Epistle to the Corinthians
Mathetes
Epistle to Diognetus
Polycarp of Smyrna
Epistle to the Philippians
Encyclical Epistle of Smyrna
Ignatius of Antioch
Epistles to the Ephesians, Magnesians, Trallians, Romans, Philadelphians. Smyrnaeans, Polycarp
Appendix: Syriac Version
Spurious Epistles
Martyrdom of Ignatius
Barnabas – Epistle
Papias – Fragments
Justin Martyr (the Philosopher)
First Apology
Second Apology
Dialogue with Trypo, a Jew
Hortatory Address to the Greeks
On the Sole Government of God
On the Resurrection - Fragments
Lost Writings
The Martyrdom of the Holy Martyrs
Irenaeus of Lyon
Against Heresies
Fragments from Lost Writings

Volume 2

Hermas, Shepherd of (Pastor of)
Book First – Visions
Book Second – Commandments
Book Third – Similitudes
Tatian
Address to the Greeks
Theophilus of Antioch
Theophilus to Autolycus
Athenagoras
Plea For the Christians
On the Resurrection of the Dead
Clement of Alexandria
Exhortation to the Heathen
The Instructor
The Stromata, or Miscellanies
Fragments
Who is the Rich Man that Shall Be Saved?

Volume 3

Tertullian (see also vol 4)
The Apology
On Idolatry
The Shows, or De Spectaculis
The Chaplet, or De Corona
To Scapula
Ad Nationes
Appendix: Fragment
Answer to the Jews
The Soul's Testimony
On the Soul
Prescription Against Heretics
Against Marcion
Against Hermogenes
Against the Valentinians
On the Flesh of Christ
On the Resurrection of the Flesh
Against Praxeas
Scorpiace
Appendix: Against All Heresies
On Repentance
On Baptism
On Prayer
Ad Martyras
Passion of the Holy Martyrs Perpetua and Felicitas
Of Patience

Volume 4

Tertullian (see also vol 3)
On the Pallium
On the Apparel of Women
On the Veiling of Virgins
To His Wife
On Exhortation to Chastity
On Monogamy
On Modesty
On Fasting. In Opposition to the Psychics
On Fleeing Persecution
Appendix
Minucius Felix
Octavius
Commodianus
Instructions in Favour of Christian Discipline, Against the Gods of the Heathens
Origen
Prologue of Rufinus
Origen de Principiis
Letter to Origen from Africanus About the History of Susanna
Letter to Africanus
Letter to Gregory
Against Celsus

Ante-Nicene Fathers Series – cont'd

Volume 5

Hyppolytus
- Refutation of All Heresies
- Extant Works and Fragments

Cyprian, Bishop of Carthage
- Life and Passion of Cyprian
- Epistles
- Treatises
- Seventh Council of Carthage
- Treatises Attributed to Cyprian on Questionable Authority

Caius – Fragments

Novatian
- On the Trinity
- On the Jewish Meats

Appendix
- Acts and Records of the Famous Controversy About the Baptism of Heretics
- Against the Heretic Novatian
- On Re-Baptism

Volume 6

Gregory the Wonderworker
- Declaration of Faith
- Metaphrase of the Book of Ecclesiastes
- Canonical Epistle
- Oration and Panegyric Addressed to Origen
- Sectional Confession of Faith
- On the Trinity
- Twelve Topics on the Faith
- On the Subject of the Soul
- Four Homilies
- On All the Saints
- On the Gospel of Matthew

Dionysius, Bishop of Alexandria
- Extant Fragments
- Exegetical Fragments

Julius Africanus – Extant Writings

Anatolius of Alexandria
- Determining the Date of Pascha
- Fragments: Books on Arithmetic

Alexander of Cappadocia
- Epistles

Theognostus of Alexandria
- Hypotyposes or Outlines (excerpts)

Pierius of Alexandria
- Fragment of a Work on 1 Corinthians
- Writings

Theonas, Bishop of Alexandria
- Epistle to Lucianus

Phileas, Bishop of Thmuis
- Fragments: To the People of Thmuis
- Epistle to Meletius, Bishop of Lycopolis

Pamphilus
- Exposition of the Chapters of Acts

Malchion of Antioch
- Epistle
- Fragments
- From the Acts of the Disputation Conducted by Malchion Against Paul of Samosata

Archelaus
- Acts of the Disputation with the Heresiarch Manes

Alexander of Lycopolis
- Of the Manichaeans

Peter, Bishop of Alexandria
- Genuine Acts of Peter
- Canonical Epistle
- Fragments

Alexander of Alexandria
- Epistles on the Arian Heresy

Methodius, Bishop of Patara
- Banquet of the Ten Virgins
- On Free-Will
- Discourse on the Resurrection
- Fragments
- Oration Concerning Simeon and Anna
- Oration on the Psalms
- Three Fragments from the Homily on the Cross and Passion of Christ
- Other Fragments

Arnobius
- Against the Heathen

Volume 7

Lactantius
- Divine Institutes
- Epitome of the Divine Institutes
- On the Anger of God
- On the Workmanship of God, or the Formation of Man
- Of the Manner in Which the Persecutors Died
- Fragments
- The Phoenix
- Poem on the Passion of the Lord

Venantius
- Poem on Easter

Asterius Urbanus
- Extant Writings

Ante-Nicene Fathers Series – cont'd

Victorinus
On the Creation of the World
Commentary on the Apocalypse of the Blessed John
Dionysius of Rome
Against the Sabellians
Didache: Teaching of the Twelve Apostles
Constitutions of the Holy Apostles
Clement
Homily Ascribed to Clement
Early Liturgies
Divine Liturgy of James
Divine Liturgy of the Holy Apostle Mark
Liturgy of the Blessed Apostles

Volume 8

The Twelve Patriarchs
The Testaments of the Twelve Patriarchs
Theodotus – Excerpts
Pseudo-Clementine Literature
Two Epistles Concerning Virginity
Recognitions of Clement
Epistle of Peter to James
Epistle of Clement to James
The Clementine Homilies
Apocrypha of the New Testament
Protevangelium of James
Gospel of Pseudo-Matthew
Gospel of the Nativity of Mary
History of Joseph the Carpenter
Gospel of Thomas
Arabic Gospel of the Infancy of the Saviour
Gospel of Nicodemus
Letter of Pontius Pilate
Report of Pilate the Procurator
Giving Up of Pontius Pilate
Death of Pilate
Narrative of Joseph
Avenging of the Saviour
Acts of the Holy Apostles Peter and Paul
Story of Perpetua
Acts of Paul and Thecla
Acts of Barnabas
Acts of Philip
Acts and Martyrdom of the Holy Apostle Andrew
Acts of Andrew and Matthias
Acts of the Holy Apostles Peter and Andrew
Acts and Martyrdom of St. Matthew the Apostle
Acts of the Holy Apostle Thomas
Consummation of Thomas the Apostle
Martyrdom of Holy Apostle Bartholomew
Acts of the Holy Apostle Thaddaeus
Acts of the Holy Apostle John
Revelation of Moses
Word and Revelation of Esdras
Revelation of Paul
Revelation of St John the Theologian
The Account of St John the Theologian
The Passing of Mary
The Decretals
Epistles of Zephyrinus
Epistles of Pope Callistus
Epistle of Pope Urban the First
Epistles of Pope Pontianus
Epistle of Pope Anterus
Epistles of Pope Fabian
Decrees of Fabian
Memoirs of Edessa
Relating to the Earliest Establishment of Christianity in Edessa and the Neighbouring Countries
A Canticle of Mar Jacob the Teacher on Edessa
Extracts from Various Books Concerning Abgar the King and Addaeus the Apostle
Ancient Syriac Documents
Teaching of Addaeus the Apostle
Teaching of the Apostles
Teaching of Simon Cephas in Rome
Acts of Sharbil
Further, the Martyrdom of Barsamya
Martyrdom of Habib the Deacon
Martyrdom Of the Holy Confessors
History of Armenia
Homily on Habib the Martyr
A Homily on Guria and Shamuna
Bardesan
A Letter of Mara, Son of Serapion
Ambrose
Remains of the Second and Third Centuries
Quadratus, Bishop of Athens
Aristo of Pella
Melito, the Philosopher
Hegesippus

Ante-Nicene Fathers Series – cont'd

Dionysius, Bishop of Corinth
Rhodon
Maximus Bishop of Jerusalem
Claudius Apollinaris, Bishop of Hierapolis
Polycrates Bishop of Ephesus
Theophilus Bishop of Caesarea in Palestine
Serapion Bishop of Antioch
Apollonius
Pantaenus The Alexandrian Philosopher
Pseud-Irenaeus
Letter of the Churches of Vienna and Lugdunum to Asia and Phrygia

Volume 9

Recently Discovered Additions
Gospel According to Peter
Synoptical Table: 4 Canonical Gospels & Gospel According to Peter
Diatessaron of Tatian
Apocalypse of Peter
Vision of Paul
Apocalypse of the Virgin
Apocalypse of Sedrach
Testament of Abraham
Acts of Xanthippe and Polyxena
Narrative of Zosimus
Epistles of Clement
Aristides - Apology
Passion of the Scillitan Martyrs

Origen
Letter to Gregory
Commentary on the Gospel of John
Commentary on the Gospel of Matthew

Volume 10

Bibliography, Indices

Nicene and Post-Nicene Fathers, FIRST Series

Volume 1 (First Series)

Augustin
The Confessions of St. Augustine
Letters of St. Augustine

Volume 2 (First Series)

Augustin
The City of God
On Christian Doctrine

Volume 3 (First Series)

Augustin
On the Trinity
The Enchiridion
On the Catechising of the Uninstructed
On Faith and the Creed
Concerning Faith of Things Not Seen
On the Profit of Believing
On the Creed: for Catechumens
On Continence
On the Good of Marriage
Of Holy Virginity
On the Good of Widowhood
On Lying
Against Lying
Of the Work of Monks
On Patience
On Care to Be Had for the Dead

Volume 4 (First Series)

Augustin
Anti-Manichaean Writings
Anti-Donatist Writings

Volume 5 (First Series)

Augustin
On the Merits and Remission of Sins, and on the Baptism of Infants
On the Spirit and the Letter
On Nature and Grace, Against Pelagius
Concerning Man's Perfection in Righteousness
On the Proceedings of Pelagius,
On the Grace of Christ, and on Original Sin
On Marriage and Concupiscence
On the Soul and Its Origin
Against Two Letters of the Pelagians
On Grace and Free Will
On Rebuke and Grace
On the Predestination of the Saints
On the Gift of Perseverance

Nicene and Post-Nicene Fathers, FIRST Series – cont'd

Volume 6 (First Series)
Augustin
- Our Lord's Sermon on the Mount
- The Harmony of the Gospels
- Sermons on Selected Lessons of the New Testament

Volume 7 (First Series)
Augustin
- Homilies on the Gospel of John
- Homilies on the First Epistle of John
- Soliloquies

Volume 8 (First Series)
Augustin
- On the Psalms

Volume 9 (First Series)
John Chrysostom
- On the Priesthood
- To Theodore after His Fall
- Letter to a Young Widow
- Homilies on St Ignatius and St Babylas
- Concerning Lowliness of Mind
- Instructions to Catechumens
- Three Homilies Concerning the Power of Demons
- Against Marcionists and Manichaeans
- On the Paralytic Let Down Through the Roof
- To Those Who Had Not Attended the Assembly
- Against Publishing the Errors of the Brethren
- On Eutropius, Patrician and Consul
- To Prove that No One Can Harm the Man Who Does Not Injure Himself
- Letters to Olympias
- Correspondence with Innocent, Bishop of Rome
- On the Statues

Volume 10 (First Series)
John Chrysostom
- Homilies on Matthew

Volume 11 (First Series)
John Chrysostom
- Homilies on the Acts of the Apostles
- Homilies on Romans

Volume 12 (First Series)
John Chrysostom
- Homilies on First Corinthians
- Homilies on Second Corinthians

Volume 13 (First Series)
John Chrysostom
- Homilies on Galatians
- Homilies on Ephesians
- Homilies on Philippians
- Homilies on Colossians
- Homilies on First Thessalonians
- Homilies on Second Thessalonians
- Homilies on First Timothy
- Homilies on Second Timothy
- Homilies on Titus
- Homilies on Philemon

Volume 14 (First Series)
John Chrysostom
- Homilies on John
- Homilies on Hebrews

Nicene and Post-Nicene Fathers, SECOND Series

Volume 1 (Second Series)
Eusebius Pamphilus
- Church History
- Life of Blessed Emperor Constantine
- Oration of Constantine
- Oration in Praise of Constantine

Volume 2 (Second Series)
Socrates Scholasticus
- Ecclesiastical History

Sozomen
- Ecclesiastical History

Volume 3 (Second Series)
Theodoret of Cyrrhus
- Ecclesiastical History
- Dialogues
- Demonstrations by Syllogisms
- Letters

Jerome and Gennadius
- Lives of Illustrious Men
- Gennadius' Additions

Rufinus
- Prefaces
- Letters

Nicene and Post-Nicene Fathers, SECOND Series – cont'd

Jerome (see also vol 6)
Apologies in Answer to Rufinus

Volume 4 (Second Series)

Athanasius the Great, Bishop of Alexandria
Against the Heathen
On the Incarnation
Deposition of Arius
Council of Nicaea
Statement of Faith
On Luke X. 22
Encyclical Letter
Apology Against the Arians
Defence of the Nicene Council
Defence of Dionysius
Life of Antony
To the Bishops of Egypt
Apology to Emperor Constantius
Defence of His Flight
History of the Arians
Against the Arians
Councils of Ariminum and Seleucia
To the People of Antioch
To the Bishops of Africa
Festal Letters
Personal Letters

Volume 5 (Second Series)

Gregory of Nyssa
Against Eunomius
Answer to Eunomius' Second Book
On the Holy Spirit against Macedonius
On the Holy Trinity
On "Not Three Gods"
On the Faith
On Virginity
On Infants' Early Deaths
On Pilgrimages
On the Making of Man
On the Soul and the Resurrection
Great Catechism
On Meletius
On the Baptism of Christ
Letters

Volume 6 (Second Series)

Jerome (see also vol 3)
Letters
Life of Paulus the First Hermit
Life of St Hilarion
Life of Malchus, the Captive Monk
Dialogue Against the Luciferians
The Perpetual Virginity of Blessed Mary
Against Jovinianus
Against Vigilantius
Against John of Jerusalem
Against the Pelagians
Prefaces

Volume 7 (Second Series)

Cyril of Jerusalem
Catechetical Lectures
Gregory Nazianzen (the Theologian)
Orations
Letters

Volume 8 (Second Series)

Basil the Great
On the Holy Spirit
Hexaemeron
Letters

Volume 9 (Second Series)

Hilary of Poitiers
On the Councils, or the Faith of the Easterns
On the Trinity
Homilies on Psalms 1, 53, 130
John of Damascus
An Exact Exposition of the Orthodox Faith

Volume 10 (Second Series)

Ambrose, Bishop of Milan
On the Duties of the Clergy
On the Holy Spirit
On the Death of His Brother Satyrus
Exposition of the Christian Faith
On the Mysteries
On Repentance
Concerning Virgins
Concerning Widows
Letters

Volume 11 (Second Series)

Sulpitius Severus
Life of St. Martin
Letters
Dialogues
Doubtful Letters
Sacred History
Vincent of Lerins
Commonitory (Aid to Memory)

Nicene and Post-Nicene Fathers, SECOND Series – cont'd

John Cassian
Institutes of the Coenobia
Conferences
On the Incarnation of the Lord, Against Nestorius

Volume 12 (Second Series)

Leo the Great
Letters
Sermons

Gregory the Great (the Dialogist)
Book of Pastoral Rule
Epistles

Volume 13 (Second Series)

Gregory the Great (the Dialogist)
Epistles

Ephraim the Syrian
Nisibene Hymns
Hymns on the Nativity
Hymns for the Epiphany
Hymns on the Faith (The Pearl)
Three Homilies

Aphrahat
Of Faith
Of Wars
Of Monks
Of the Resurrection of the Dead
Of Pastors
Of Christ the Son of God
Of Persecution
Of Death and the Latter Times

Volume 14 (Second Series)

The Seven Ecumenical Councils
and related local councils and canons

Within the Public Domain, the Ante-Nicene Fathers *and the* Nicene and Post-Nicene Fathers *series can be found on-line in the Christian Classics Ethereal Library at* www.ccel.org.

This list can be printed out from www.OrthodoxReader.com.

Miscellanea

Keep Them Honest

One need not be a scholar to appreciate the books in the foregoing lists. Simply in the course of reading, references to these books come up again and again. For example, a reader frequently runs across attention-catching ancient quotes. The source may be available in English translation, and the reader could follow up. On the other hand, contemporary authors may "quote" the ancients in a dubious way. Sometimes it is good to check their references just to keep them honest.

An Introduction to Orthodox Theology

Before looking into this huge collection of books, the reader may want an introduction to Orthodox Patristic Theology. An excellent overview is *Patristic Theology* by Father John S. Romanides [†2001].[1] It is surprising and surprisingly understandable.[2] It consists of informal lectures for university freshman, easily within the grasp of laymen. At times one may need to hang on to the saddle horn, but it is foundational, enlightening, and encouraging. Like Saint Symeon the New Theologian, he exhorts: This is *real!* His very first topic: What is the *nous*?

The Library

Books from these multi-volume sets can be purchased individually. But wouldn't it be nice to have the entire sets handy in the church library?

Translations

Some of the translations in the above lists may seem stilted, especially when the translation is into an older English. Part of the difficulty is that often the translators aim for a precise rendering of the Greek text rather than a more mellifluous English—and realistically, some translators are just better than others.

Robert Charles Hill, for his part, produces comfortably readable and accurate translations. Readers who would like to read Saint John Chrysostom and prefer to start with a smoother (modern English) translation might begin with Hill's translation of the *Genesis* homilies[3] in the Fathers of the Church series or Saint Chrysostom's *Commentary on the Psalms* from Holy Cross Orthodox Press. The caveat applies in any case to read with one's thumb over the notes. In constant battle with Saint Chrysostom in the footnotes, Hill is quite vexed, for example, that the saint is too barbaric to understand the (obvious!) modern academic theory of conflated texts in *Genesis*. He gnashes his teeth!

Just read Saint Chrysostom; the translations are reliable.

1 *Patristic Theology: The University Lectures of Fr. John Romanides*, prepared by Monk Damaskinos Agioreitis, trans Hieromonk Alexios (Trader) (Thessaloniki, Greece: Uncut Mountain Press, 2008).

2 It may be a little too surprising when he mentions the *Ninth* Ecumenical Council (referring to 1351, when St Gregory Palamas quashed Barlaam and the Scholastics) —an enumeration not to be dismissed out of hand. Read without reservation.

3 Unless you are a speed-reader, do not plan to get through these homilies in their entirety alongside the *Genesis* readings of Great Lent. However, reading *occasional* homilies parallel to the lectionary might be worth a try.

Speaking of Translations....

Masoretic Text—the "reformed" Hebrew text adopted in the West	*Septuagint Text—the Greek translation used by the Church*
Psalm 144	**Psalm 143**
11 Rescue me and deliver me from the hand of foreigners, whose mouth speaks lying words, and whose right hand is a right hand of falsehood—	11 Deliver me and save me from the hand of the sons of foreigners, Whose mouth speaks empty things, And their right hand is a right hand of wrongdoing,
12 That our sons may be as plants grown up in their youth; that our daughters may be as pillars, sculptured in palace style;	12 Whose sons are like new plants Matured in their youth, Their daughters beautified, Adorned like a temple;
13 That our barns may be full, supplying all kinds of produce; that our sheep may bring forth thousands and ten thousands in our fields; 14 That our oxen may be well-laden; that there be no breaking in or going out; that there be no outcry in our streets.	13 Their storehouses are full, Bursting forth with abundance on all sides; Their sheep give many births, Multiplying in their streets; 14 Their oxen are fat; There is no gap in their fence or passage, Nor outcry in their streets.
15 **Happy are the people who are in such a state; happy are the people whose God is the LORD!** [1]	15 **They call the people blessed, whose lot this is;** **But rather, blessed is the people** **Whose God is the Lord.** [2]

1 Scripture taken from the New King James Version®. Copyright © 1982 by Thomas Nelson, Inc. Used by permission. All rights reserved. Emphasis added.
2 Scripture taken from the St Athanasius Academy Septuagint™. Copyright © 2008 by St Athanasius Academy of Orthodox Theology. Used by permission. All rights reserved. Emphasis added.

Thou art running for thy soul. . . . Shew in ascetic exercise that thy heart is nerved. Cleanse thy vessel, that thou mayest receive grace more abundantly. For though remission of sins is given equally to all [in baptism], the communion of the Holy Ghost is bestowed in proportion to each man's faith. If thou hast laboured little, thou receivest little; but if thou hast wrought much, the reward is great. Thou art running for thyself, see to thine own interest. . . . Attend diligently to the Church assemblies. . . . Wrestle for thine own soul, especially in such days as these. Nourish thy soul with sacred readings; for the Lord hath prepared for thee a spiritual table; therefore say thou also after the Psalmist, *The Lord is my shepherd, and I shall lack nothing: in a place of grass, there hath He made me rest; He hath fed me beside the waters of comfort, He hath converted my soul.*[1]

A knowledge of Divine enjoyments which is not linked to devotion to, and love of, God is not able to coax the mind to disdain material things. Such knowledge is similar to a simple thought about a perceptible thing. For this reason, it is easy for us to find many who are distinguished for their knowledge, but who nonetheless wallow in their passions, like pigs in the mud. These types, having for a short time exercised care to cleanse their mental world of the passions and evil thoughts, come to knowledge of God; however, by their negligence they come to be like Saul, who, while initially worthy of kingship was, however, afterwards removed as king by the wrath of God for having conducted himself unworthily [1Kgs 9–31].[2]

---

1 St Cyril of Jerusalem [†386, Mar 18], First Catechetical Lecture, found in *Nicene & Post-Nicene Fathers,* Second Series, 7:7.

2 St Maximos the Confessor [†662, Jan 21], quoted in *The Evergetinos: A Complete Text*, trans Archbishop Chrysostomos, et al (Etna, CA: Center for Traditionalist Orthodox Studies, 2008), Book IV:277. Used with permission.

18. Self-Restraint

The Evergetinos, *from which the following selection is taken, is a distillation of ascetic wisdom of the early fathers compiled in the eleventh century by Paul, founder and abbot of the Monastery of the Most Holy Theotokos. The monastery was also called "of the Evergetis," that is, of the Benefactress; hence, Evergetinos. Its four books were edited and prepared for publication by* ***Saint Nikodemos the Hagiorite*** *["of the Holy Mountain" (Mount Athos), †1809, July 14] at the request of Saint Macarios, Bishop of Corinth [†1805, Apr 17].*

This selection considers fasting, which is always a challenge. It discusses the how as well as the why, offering general strategies rather than specific rules. It emphasizes the royal road: neither too little nor too much.

Hypothesis XVIII
How we should care for the body and what constitutes proper asceticism and restraint.

* * *

Saint Evthymios the Great said that perfect restraint is that which keeps a man from reaching satiation, even if we feel the need to eat and there is still food before us. This means that we should eat less than that which we feel we need.

B. From the Life of Saint Synkletike

The Blessed Synkletike said that not every act of asceticism is genuine; for there is asceticism which the Enemy of our souls intensifies, as indeed his disciples also do. How, then, do we distinguish Divine and kingly asceticism from that which is tyrannical and diabolical? Assuredly, by its measure. Let the standard of your fasting be for all times; do not simply fast for three or four days and then destroy the power of fasting by eating a great deal on other days. Do not use all of your weapons at once, so as not to chance finding yourself naked in battle and easily captured by the Enemy. Our weapons are the body and our soul the soldier; one must attend to both in meeting his needs.

When you are young and healthy, fast, for old age and illness will come. To the extent that you can, put away staples that you can use when you are unable to find them. Fast with discretion and exactness; take care, lest the Enemy of your soul should enter in secretly by way of your spiritual work of fasting. Become a skilled money changer, as the Lord says [Mt 25:27], and become well acquainted with the image of the king. For there are forged coins. And while the substance of the gold in various gold coins is the same, they differ one from the other (in value) by virtue of the image engraved on them. Now fasting, restraint, and almsgiving are the gold. But the children of the Greeks (philosophers and idolaters) also engrave their seals on gold coins, and the heretics also take pride in such things. However, you should avoid these coins as forgeries and continually watch that you are not harmed by this and do not, without giving sufficient thought, become involved in their work.

C. From the *Gerontikon*

1. Abba Joseph asked Abba Poimen how one should fast, and the latter replied: "I prefer a monk to eat daily, but to eat a little, so that he does not feel satiated."

Abba Joseph asked him further: "Abba, when you were young, did you not eat one day and then fast for two days?"

"In fact," the Elder answered, "I even fasted for three and four days, if not a whole week. But all of these things the Fathers found to be severe, coming to the conclusion that it was better to eat every day, but just a little. They thus bequeathed to us the royal path of moderate fasting; for light burdens are also profitable."

2. The same Abba said that all immoderation is from the demons.

3. There was in the desert a certain hunter of wild animals who saw Saint Anthony bantering with the brothers. The Elder, wishing to show this man that we must from time to time show leniency to the brothers, said to him: "Put an arrow on your bow and draw it taut." The hunter did just this, drawing his bow taut. "And draw it further," Abba Anthony told him. The hunter drew it more tightly. Then the Elder told him a third time, "Draw it tighter." "But if I draw it any tighter than it should

be," the hunter objected, "the bow will break." Thereupon, the Elder said to him, ending the exchange: "And so it is with the work of God. If I should ask of the brothers austerity beyond good measure, they would shortly lose heart. One must then—when the circumstance demands—show leniency to the brothers."

4. Abba Isaac once visited Abba Poimen; when he saw him washing his feet in a little water—since he was bold before him—he said: "How is it, Elder, that so many are so severely hard on their bodies?"

And Abba Poimen replied to him: "We have not been instructed to put the body to death, but to put the passions to death."

5. A brother consulted Abba Sarmatas: "My thoughts tell me: 'Do not work, but eat, drink, and sleep.'"

The Elder answered him: "When you are hungry, eat; when you are thirsty, drink water; when you are sleepy, sleep."

The brother departed.

By coincidence, another Elder happened to encounter this brother; so, the brother related to the latter what Abba Sarmatas had told him. Upon hearing this, the Elder said to the brother: "The things that Abba Sarmatas told you have the following meaning: when you are so very hungry and are so thirsty that you cannot stand it anymore, then you should eat and drink. And when you have gone for some time without sleep and are tired, then you should sleep. When, however, you do not feel great need, you should do none of this."

6. An Elder said: "There are some men who eat a lot and are still hungry; there are others who eat little and are satisfied. A man who eats a lot and restrains himself, remaining hungry still, will have a greater reward from God than the man who eats little and is satisfied."

7. Another time, the same Elder said: "If your body is given to illness, in accordance therewith satisfy your needs, so that you do not by chance become ill and have to be fed by the person looking after you, thus inconveniencing him."

8. Of Abba Netras, the disciple of Abba Silouan, it is said that he sat in his cell, atop Mount Sinai, and lived moderately, without excess, as regards his bodily needs. When he became the Bishop of Pharan, however, he practiced great austerity in his daily living.

His disciple said to him: "Elder, when we were in the desert, you did not engage in such severe asceticism."

The Elder replied: "There I had the desert, silence, and poverty, and I wanted to look after my body in such a way that I would not become ill and have need for that which I did not have. This, however, is an inhabited place and there are opportunities (for sinful thoughts); and moreover, if I should fall ill here, there are those who will help me, so that I will not have to give up my monastic practices."

9. Abba Megethios the Younger, who lived on Sinai, was visited by one of the Elders, who asked him: "How are you doing, my brother, in this desert?"

"I fast two days," the former replied, "and on the third day I eat a little bread."

The Elder then told him: "If you care to heed me, eat half that amount of bread, but daily."

The brother did so and found rest.

10. A brother asked an Elder: "To what extent should I fast?"

And the Elder answered him: "Do not attempt to go beyond what is appointed; for many individuals, wishing to fulfill more than what is appointed, have failed at fulfilling even the least."

D. From Antiochos (author of the *Pandects*)

Fasting is not simply to eat only between long intervals, but to eat sparsely. Asceticism is not for one to eat every two or three days but to avoid eating different kinds of foods. That is, a meal with only one kind of poor food constitutes asceticism. Moreover, fasting is foolish if, though one observes the appointed fasting period, when the time for meals comes around he unrestrainedly rushes to the table and focuses his mind on the pleasure of the food found on the table.

E. From Isaiah the Anchorite

When you are living in your hermitage, arrange your life such that you take only enough food to meet your bodily needs and to sustain you in fulfilling your duties, and so that you need not to venture out. If the demons put it into your mind that you should undertake ascetic labors beyond your strength, do not listen to them; for they urge a man on to every thing which he cannot attain, so that he might fall into their hands and they might rejoice at having conquered him.

Therefore, give your body the food which it needs, then get up, even though you may wish to eat more. Do not eat anything for pleasure's sake or on account of your tastes, whether good or bad. If the need arises to drink wine, take only up to three small glasses, and do not break this rule for the sake of friendship. Do not be a glutton, so as not to awaken within you your past sins. Do not drink wine to the point of inebriation, so that you forfeit the joy of God. The ascetic labor of the soul is to abhor the distraction of one's attention by divers things and to deprive the body. To distract your attention with divers things is to make the soul impotent; but its restoration is occasioned by silence and (Divine) knowledge. If, then, brother, you wish to offer repentance before God, avoid too much wine, for much wine arouses the passions and dispels the fear of God from the soul.

F. From Abba Mark

Those living the ascetic life, when they begin their ascetic labors, must be able to bring them to fruition; thus, both those young and old who have a strong body, and do not fear hardship, should eagerly undertake the most useful and advantageous kind of fasting. They should carefully weigh how much bread they eat and should drink moderate amounts of water at sparse intervals, so that they may depart from their meals without having completely consumed all of their food and water, not having been impeded by the pleasure of the stomach in carrying out their duties to God. If we desire to take our fill of food, soon we will be lax in our attentiveness and will turn to some other desire; and should we also satisfy that desire, then we will abandon it, too, like the first. Indeed, it is impossible to remain satiated when, in order to satisfy ourselves, we fulfill whatever desire we can concoct.

What food is sweeter and more exquisite than manna? Yet, when Israel ate from this and was filled, even though it could want nothing better, it brought to mind what was inferior: that is, onions and garlic.

Within abundance, there dwell new desires. So if, by taking our fill of bread, we want yet other things, let us then not eat it to satiation, lest we still be hungry and need more to eat to be filled. In this way, we will avoid the harm brought on by our desires and will find benefit from the virtue of restraint.

But perhaps some from among such individuals, who are not greatly inclined towards fasting, will say: "Could it be that it is a sin for a man to eat?" But even we do not advise that one refrain from food because it is a sin, but because food sometimes accompanies sin. And Israel did not sin by desiring food, but showed impiety by virtue of complaining against God [Ps 77:17–21]. That is, the Jews said: "Cannot God furnish a table in the wilderness?" And having prepared a table for them, the wrath of God was then raised up against them and their mighty were slain, so that they should not again seek and desire other food and blaspheme against the Most High, in this way bringing destruction upon their offspring [Num 11:1–35]. It is difficult for one to bridle a voracious belly, for it becomes a god to those who are conquered by it—and one who cannot bear with it cannot be saved.

Danger lies, however, not only in satiation, but also in exhaustion. When we spend too many days completely without food, then exhaustion and depression will have occasion to rise up and war against us. And our nightly vigils, as well, will occasion sleep, while our daytime prayer will lead us into lustful thoughts, with the result that our sleep will be of no benefit at all, and we will be very greatly harmed by these lustful thoughts. For we will begin to take pride that we have subjected ourselves to greater asceticism than others and to disdain the lesser, which is the greatest of all other errors. That is, just as a farmer, though he may spend a great deal of money to cultivate his fields, will, if he does not plant seeds in them, come to ruin, so it is with us; if we subdue our flesh attentively, but do not capture within our souls the blessing of prayer, so that we pray unceasingly, we well may work against ourselves.

Now, however, someone may say: "Where there is prayer or, in general, virtue, is there a need for fasting?" Of course—the greatest need. That is to say, precisely as a poor farmer, if he seeds a fallow field without first cultivating it, will reap thistle instead of wheat at harvest time, so it is with us; if we do not exhaust our flesh with fasting, we cannot bring to fruition the words of prayer in our hearts, wherefore we will harvest sin instead of virtue. For this flesh comes from that earth. If we do not then show to the flesh the same care that we show to the earth, the fruit of virtue will never germinate.

We say all of this, not to impede those who may benefit from fasting, but to counsel those who do not wish to come to harm. For just as he who undertakes fasting with foresight derives benefit, so, on the contrary, one who is not prudent in its application comes to ruin. Thus, those who are interested in being benefited would do well to protect themselves against such harm; that is, the vainglory which it can create. The bread which we eat in the course of fasting, which we apportion for ourselves, let us distribute throughout our fast days, so that we eat a little daily. In this way, we will bind our fleshly mind and have our hearts fixed on prayer, which will better aid to safeguard us, by the power of God, from boasting and to pass all of our days in humility, without which no one can please God.

G. From Saint Diadochos

Just as variety in foods burdens the body and makes the mind timorous and slow, by the same token, contrarily, when one is enfeebled by too much restraint, the contemplative part of the soul becomes surly and loquacious. One must, then, in keeping with the condition of the body, regulate one's food so as to suffer privation while fasting, when possible, and at times, when one is ill, to strengthen himself by a relaxation of his fast. For a struggler should not lose bodily strength when fasting, but should have the strength necessary to struggle, such that the soul is also cleansed by the strengthening and combative effort of the body.

Fasting is praiseworthy in itself, but not before God; for it is like an implement which directs those who so wish to prudence. Strugglers after piety, thus, should not become proud from fasting, but should simply await, with faith in God, the fulfillment of our goal. Indeed, not even craftsmen, who know a certain art, are quick to show pride over their tools, alone, in producing their art; but each one expects the kind of work that he does to demonstrate his ability in his art.

Just as soil, when it is regularly watered, makes the seeds which fall upon it to burst forth with a great yield, yet, when it is flooded by too much rain, produces thorns and thistles, such is the soil of the heart. If we take wine in measure, then the heart yields its natural seeds in a pure way and those which are sown therein by the Holy Spirit it makes to blossom most beautifully and to bring forth many fruits; if, however, these seeds are washed away by great amounts of drink, all of the thoughts which are formed in it will truly be thorns and thistles.

When our minds are flooded by the wave of much drink, then they not only passionately turn to those idols which the demons form in our minds during sleep, but the same also create, moreover, various beautiful images from these dream fantasies, and the mind puts them to use like lovers with burning passion; for, the sexual organs having been excited by the warmth that wine promotes, there of necessity arise passionate spectres which occasion pleasure.

One must, therefore, use wine in moderation, so as to avoid harm from its improper use. For when the mind is not seized by pleasure, which leads it to embrace evil, then it is free from demonic fantasy and fleshly desires.

H. From Abba Cassian

The Fathers have not handed down to us only one rule of fasting, or a specific diet, or permission for everyone to eat freely, since all do not have the same strength, whether because of age or illness or because they have not yet subjected their bodies to a firm regimen. To all, however, the Fathers have appointed one goal: to avoid too much food and not to let our stomachs reach satiation. On the basis of vast experience, they ascertained that daily temperance in eating, that is, a little fasting, is far more beneficial than extensive fasting that lasts three or four days or for the period of an entire week. For, as they say, he who undertakes fasting without moderation often also partakes of food without moderation.

Thus, sometimes, from excessive starvation, one weakens the body and becomes lazy in spiritual works; yet another time, he burdens himself from great quantities of food, inviting sloth and indolence. From their vast experience, the Fathers have also determined that vegetarian foods are not appointed to everyone—that is, not to the healthy but to the weak (in faith) [Rom 14:2]; nor are legumes for everyone; nor can everyone use dried bread for sustenance (only the healthy, but not the ill). The Fathers note that one person can eat two pounds of bread and still be hungry, while another person may be sated by one pound and six ounces of bread. To everyone, as we have observed, one rule of self-restraint applies: not to be beguiled by the desire to fill our stomachs or to be led astray by the pleasure of the gullet; for, not only does the qualitative difference in foods ignite the fiery darts of immorality, but often the quantity of food, too.

When the belly is full from any food whatsoever, the seeds of debauchery are generated. And furthermore, not only does the immoderate drinking of wine bring inebriation to the mind, but much water and excessive eating lull the mind into sleep and cause it to feel drowsy. The Sodomites were not destroyed by the dizziness of too much wine or a variety of foods, as the Prophet says, but by the "fulness of bread" [Ezek 16:49].

Illness of body does not come into conflict with purity of heart, when we are careful to give our bodies whatever illness demands and not that which pleasure desires. We should eat food in moderation, in the amount that is required to live, and not become slaves to the assaults of evil desires. The moderate and logical use of food insures the health of the body; it does not detract from holiness. This is the rule of self-restraint which the Fathers have handed down to us: while eating, that one should stop while he is still hungry, without persisting until he is completely satiated. Indeed, the Apostle Paul, when he said, "and make not provision for the flesh, to fulfill the lusts thereof" [Rom 13:14], did not mean to impede the necessary governance of our lives, but forbade sensual attention thereto.

I. From the *Gerontikon*

1. There was once held an oblation (Feast) on Abba Anthony's mountain. Now, a small container of wine was left there. So, one of the Elders took it, put it in a glass, and offered it to Abba Sisoes. He drank it. He was also given a second glass, and drank it. When he was offered a third glass, however, he did not take it, but said: "Stop, brother. Or are you not aware of the existence of Satan?"

2. A confused life derives from an unruly life; moderation and propriety in one's life enlighten the mind and cast out confusion. A confused mind, which is born of disorder, brings confusion to the soul, on account of which purity slowly disappears and there comes about, thereafter, turmoil. Whereas order arises out of peace and from peace light is born in the soul, and from the light of peace a pure wind blows through the mind. To the extent that the heart can draw near to wisdom, it receives Grace from God.

If you wish, then, to approach God with your heart, demonstrate this desire to Him in bodily things; that is, in the control of needs, by the moderate consumption of one kind of food, and with similar bodily asceticism and hardships undertaken with discretion and moderation. It is on this that the Lord established the foundation of perfection, since He began His work by suffering in the desert [Mt 4:1–11]. It is thus, then, that you should also rise up to greater and more perfect things and approach God noetically, with the help of Divine Grace.

3. A humble and undisturbed way of life, which abides in stability, is a great power; for it can open up a cave in a hard rock. Do not think, brother, that outside thoughts are blocked in any other way, save by making our bodies accustomed to a defined order.

* * *

Hypothesis XXXII
How great is the work of contrition, what the manifold forms of contrition are, and what the different kinds of tears are.

* * *

From the *Gerontikon*

On another occasion, when the Elder saw that the brother was weighed down from over-eating (for some people had come to visit them the evening before), he said to him in private: "Do you not know that contrition is a small lamp, which, if you light it and do not cover it carefully, is quickly extinguished and goes out? So, too, contrition is extinguished by large amounts of food and impeded by much sleep; slander destroys it; and loquacity and, in general, all bodily respite, drives it away and obliterates it. He who loves God and desires to preserve a feeling of contrition should, in every task that he performs, dedicate one part of it to Christ."

"What do these words mean, Father?" asked the brother. And the Elder replied: "Do you wish to learn how one can set aside a part for Christ in everything that he does? Pay attention: when, for example, some quality bread comes your way, put it aside for another brother to eat; and as for yourself, for the sake of Christ eat some moldy bread. If, again, you are given some good wine, mix it with a little vinegar, for the sake of Christ, Who drank vinegar. Do not gorge (when you eat), but leave a little food aside and say: 'Here is a portion for Christ.' If you find a soft pillow, put it aside and use a rock, for the sake of Christ.

"If you feel cold when you sleep, endure it and say: 'Other people are not sleeping at all.' If you are cooking food for yourself to eat, spoil it a little and say: 'Others, though they deserve it, do not even eat bread, while I, who am unworthy, eat cooked food—whereas I ought to be eating dust and ashes on account of my unclean deeds.' To put it simply, mingle a little affliction in all that you do and live humbly, keeping in mind how the Saints lived. In this way, when the hour of death comes, we, too, will have experienced a certain amount of affliction and distress and will thereby attain rest in the next life."

* * *

An Elder said: "Discussing matters of faith and reading books about dogma cause a man's compunction to wither and disappear; by contrast, the lives and sayings of the Elders enlighten the soul, filling it with spiritual tears."

* * *

We asked him: "How is one to preserve compunction when it does come?" The Elder replied to us: "On that day, or as long as one's contrition of soul lasts, he should be careful not to visit anyone. He should also guard himself from gluttony and haughtiness, so that he does not imagine that he is weeping at all and so that he does not judge anyone; and he should persist in prayer and reading. At the same time, when (Godly) contrition enters into our soul, it will teach us which kinds of things are conducive to it and preserve it, and which hinder it.

"I know a brother who was sitting in his cell, weaving a basket, when contrition was suddenly born in his soul. Then, as soon as tears began to come, he arose to pray and they ceased at once. So he resumed his weaving and collected his mind, and once more tears came. The same thing happened to him at the time of reading; while he was reading, he was overcome by compunction; but no sooner did he arise to pray than the tears stopped. But when he looked closely at the book, he began to weep again. The brother then understood the reason for this difference and said inside himself that the Fathers were right in saying that contrition is our teacher; for it teaches a man all that is to his benefit.

"I am of the opinion that contrition left the brother's soul during prayer for two reasons. The first is that he had not yet acquired prayer that was pure and free from distraction. His mind was running hither and thither out of anxiety and he was not preserving his former compunction, which was produced within him while he was engaged in handiwork and reading, since he concentrated his mind more on these activities. Secondly, this happened so that he might not suppose that he had managed to attain contrition by his own effort and prayer, but so that he could understand that it had been granted to him by the mercy and Grace of God, and might, therefore, be moved to thank God and acquire greater humility, whereby the contrition within him would be further strengthened. Should something similar ever happen to us, that is, should we experience compunction of heart and fervent tears, let us immediately disregard everything else and have recourse to prayer, persevering in it, until we feel the flame of the heart being kindled within us; for we might otherwise not find a similar opportunity."

* * *

From Saint Barsanouphios

A brother asked an Elder: "How is it possible for me to suppress loquacity and control my tongue?" "With contrition," answered the Elder. "And how can I preserve contrition," the brother asked again, "when I associate with people and look after my duties? Furthermore, how can there be contrition in the heart without tears?"

To these questions the Elder replied: "Contrition does not come from tears, but tears come from contrition. If one lives among men, yet cuts off his own will and pays no heed to the faults of others, he acquires contrition. As a result of this, he gathers his thoughts together and, when they are thus collected, they produce Godly sorrow [2Cor 7:10] in his heart, and this sorrow then engenders tears."

The Source

The Evergetinos: A Complete Text, trans Archbishop Chrysostomos, et al (Etna, CA: Center for Traditionalist Orthodox Studies, 2008), Book II: 138–148, 249, 254–258. Used and abridged with permission.

Miscellanea

Body Talk

Gluttony is hypocrisy of the stomach. Filled, it moans about scarcity; stuffed, and crammed, it wails about its hunger. Gluttony thinks up seasonings, creates sweet recipes. Stop up one urge and another bursts out; stop that one and you unleash yet another. Gluttony has a deceptive appearance: it eats moderately but wants to gobble everything at the same time. A stuffed belly produces fornication, while a mortified stomach leads to purity. The man who pets a lion may tame it but the man who coddles the body makes it ravenous.

The Jew celebrates on Sabbaths and feast days. The gluttonous monk celebrates on Saturdays and Sundays. He counts the days to Easter, and for days in advance he gets the food ready. The slave of the belly ponders the menu with which to celebrate the feast. The servant of God, however, thinks of the graces that may enrich him.

If a visitor calls, then the slave of gluttony engages in charitable acts—but for the reasons associated with his love of food.[1] He thinks that by allowing relaxations for himself, he is bringing consolation to his brother. He thinks that the duties of hospitality entitle him to help himself to some wine, so that while apparently hiding his virtuous love of temperance, he is actually turning into a slave of intemperance.

Vanity and gluttony sometimes vie with one another and they struggle for the poor monk as if he were an acquired slave. The one tells him he should take it easy and the other suggests that he ought to emerge virtuously triumphant over his urge to gratify his appetite. A sensible monk, however, will avoid both vices, using one to repulse the other.

As long as the flesh is in full vigor, we should everywhere and at all times cultivate temperance, and when it has been tamed—something I doubt can happen this side of the grave—we should hide our achievement.[2]

— Saint John Climacus [of the Ladder]

1 [He calls off his fast in order to serve (and partake of) rich and plentiful foods for his guest.]

2 St John Climacus [†Seventh Century, Mar 30], *The Ladder of Divine Ascent,* trans Colm Luibheid and Norman Russell (Mahwah, NJ: Paulist Press [Classics of Western Spirituality series], 1982), 165–166. Used with permission.

Also available from Holy Transfiguration Monastery, Brookline, MA, 1979.

Habits/Addictions

Dead bodies do not sin. They have no attachments, no desires, no habits. Souls do. It is said that souls with addictions on earth carry them into eternity—where there is no way to satisfy them.

Christ says: judge no one but yourself. Contemporary America says: treat all with supportive tolerance. In what way supportive? In what manner tolerant? These are important distinctions that are often lost. For example, it is confusing to hear in Confession: "Drunk? Noah got drunk. Don't worry about it." "Smoking? Saint Nektarios smoked. Don't worry about it."

Don't worry about it? Most strikingly, it is deeply troubling that this is how the lives of saints are used "to comfort" and "to edify" the laity. But to the point: one should not condemn the person, but neither should one condone bad behavior (sin).

> Kindness and sympathy are very often the most pernicious gifts that can be offered to an alcoholic. Both tend to give the message that the drinker need not have a sense of responsibility, given the circumstances of his life. The alcoholic picks up such sentiment as if he had a hidden short-wave radio tuned in just to that sort of statement. In the thinking of the alcoholic, any excuse for his drinking allows him to drink. In much the same way, any excuse for the overeater allows him to over eat, for the sex addict to act out, for the gambler to gamble, or the overspender to overspend. Any relaxation of the notion of total responsibility is enough to create a reason to wriggle through and do the behavior—not for its own sake—but for the feeling of relief it brings. It is not so much the taste of the alcohol, or even the effect of the alcohol that is so intoxicating. Rather, it is the freedom to "indulge"—to act without responsibility—which is more tempting than the human frame can bear.[1]

"Take heed to yourselves, lest at any time your hearts be overcharged with surfeiting and drunkenness" [Lk 21:34]. "Drunkenness" (or overeating or sex or gambling or overspending, or the like) "is self-imposed possession,

1 Father Meletios Webber, *Steps of Transformation: An Orthodox Priest Explores the Twelve Steps*, (Ben Lomond, CA: Conciliar Press/Ancient Faith Publishing, 2003), 47. Used with permission.

the emptying of thought, a calamity of derision, a disease worthy of ridicule, a voluntary demon."[1]

What about "innocuous" activities? A drunk once spent nine months watching television in the evening instead of drinking. He said of the experience: "It's just like being drunk! Only the hangover's a little different."

Helpful books:

Breaking the Chains of Addiction: How to Use Ancient Eastern Orthodox Spirituality to Free Our Minds and Bodies from All Addictions, Victor Mihailoff (Salisbury, MA: Regina Orthodox Press). Even for non-addicts, this book offers good suggestions for how and why to ramp up one's spiritual life.

Steps of Transformation: An Orthodox Priest Explores the Twelve Steps, Father Meletios Webber (Ben Lomond, CA: Conciliar Press, 2003). The Twelve Steps of Alcoholics Anonymous have proven successful when applied to many kinds of addiction. The author demonstrates that the Twelve Steps and Orthodoxy are compatible and complementary. His explanations also expand the understanding of the twelve step program for non-alcoholic, non-addict Orthodox who wish to follow the steps as an alternative path of repentance or spiritual tune-up.

Alcoholics Anonymous (known as "The Big Book") and *Twelve Steps and Twelve Traditions* might be helpful for those who have a problem, for those who think they might have a problem, and for those who are adamant that they do *not* have a *problem*. It is also helpful for family members and acquaintances of those with addictions.

For still others, these books may shed new light on the Mystery of Confession and the need for ongoing self-examination, constant vigilance (attentiveness to one's thoughts, feelings, actions), and lifelong repentance. The Big Book chapters "How It Works" and "Into Action" describe the passions as natural instincts gone awry—a useful beginning concept—and discuss the destructive influence of the most commonplace things, like self-centeredness, self-pity, and resentments (remembering wrongs, real or imaginary).

1 St John Chrysostom, Homily on the Resurrection, quoted in *Journey to Heaven* by St Tikhon of Zadonsk, trans Father George D. Lardas (Jordanville, NY: Holy Trinity Monastery), 85. Used with permission.

Traditional Remedies

When one feels the need for extra help—for self-control, for example, or in times of sickness or difficult situations—traditional remedies are available. Canons and akathists are always in season: said or sung privately, with another person or persons, or in church with a priest. The Small Supplicatory Canon to the Most Holy Theotokos is read most often (in Russian prayer books, this is the standard canon to the Mother of God). The canon can be read by itself,[1] as part of a service, or as its own service.[2] Some Greek churches have a regularly scheduled Paraklesis (as the service is also known) during fasting periods or year-round.

Some Orthodox consider that the only "real" akathist, the only akathist that matters, is the one by Saint Romanus the Melodist [†c.555, Oct 1] to the Most Holy Theotokos. For those who disagree, there is the *Book of Akathists* (two volumes) from Holy Trinity Monastery (Jordanville, NY). It includes several akathists for Our Lord Jesus Christ, the Most Holy Mother of God, and various saints and icons.

The Russian Church has its own special prayer service, said in the church or on a priest's visit to a parishioner's home, called a Molieben. It seems to have fallen into infrequent use in America. It is a powerful tool (weapon) and comes in various flavors. A favorite is the Thanksgiving Molieben, which says, essentially, "Thank you, O God, for your help. Please keep helping!"

Parent Friendly

The women monastics of St Paisius (Velichkovsky) Monastery (Safford, AZ) publish many canons and akathists that "hit home" with immediate domestic concerns. A short list: to the Mother of God, "Nurturer of Children"; to Righteous Joachim and Anna for Blessed Married Life; to the Lord for a Sick Child; and to the Mother of God, "Healer of Cancer."

For strugglers there is Saint Mary of Egypt, "Humble Victor over Carnal Passions," and for combatting alcohol and other addictions, the Mother of God, "The Inexhaustible Cup."

Converts to Orthodoxy might be interested in the "Akathist to Martyr Varus, Holy Intercessor for Family Members Who Reposed Outside the Orthodox Faith."

1 Said with the usual prayers before and after; see "Canon Basics" in the appendix.

2 This service is provided in *A Prayer Book for Orthodox Christians* from Holy Transfiguration Monastery (Brookline, MA) as well as in their *Great Horologion*. They also provide a Byzantine chant version: *The Service of the Small Supplicatory Canon to the Most Holy Theotokos*. It is written in western notation and does not require special training —although one might eventually want to learn about the variously third-of-a-flatted "A" in Second Tone. It is published and distributed by St Nectarios Press (Seattle).

19. The War of Thoughts

A major part of Orthodox struggle is against thoughts. We do not struggle against "reason"—indeed, we must keep our wits about us. Rather, we struggle to control our thoughts, so that our thoughts do not control us.

This interview with **Saint Paisios the New of Mount Athos** *[†1994, July 12] explains that spiritual life is based on thoughts. Purification and healing require the cultivation of good thoughts, the expelling of evil thoughts, and constant vigilance.*

The Power of Good Thoughts[1]

Geronda,[2] in the Old Testament, in the book Maccabees IV, it is written: For devout thought does not uproot the passions but is their antagonist [cf. 4Mac 3:5]. What does this mean?

The passions are deeply rooted in us, but the good, devout thought helps us to not become enslaved to them. When man brings only good thoughts to mind and establishes a strong and healthy spiritual state, then the passions lie dormant, and it is as if they did not exist. In other words, devout thoughts do not uproot the passions altogether, but combat them and can defeat them. I think the author is describing what the Holy Seven Young Men, their mother Saint Solomone and their teacher Saint Eleazar[3] were able to endure by having good and devout thoughts [cf. 4Mac 5:1f.], and thus is indicating precisely the extent of the power of good thoughts.

---

1 The term *logismos* (reason, thought) in the ascetic writings denotes either a simple thought that passes through the mind, or an emotion of the soul directed toward good or evil, or even a good or evil tendency, which has been acquired with the help of the mind, the conscience, the emotions and the will. Since a thought precedes every action, for this reason the struggle of every believer, but primarily of every monastic, to be authentic, requires constant vigilance and examination of these thoughts in order to cultivate the good and discard the evil.

2 [*Geronda* = Elder. The *Gerontikon* of the previous chapter is the Book of the Elders.]

3 [IV Maccabees expands on II Maccabees 6:18–7:42; commemorated on August 2.]

One good thought is equal to a very long vigil! It is very powerful. Similar to how certain new weapons can intercept a missile at its base by using laser beams and prevent it from being fired, so good thoughts can also anticipate and immobilize evil thoughts at the devil's "airports," where they are launched from. This is why you must struggle as much as you can—before the tempter devil has a chance to plant evil thoughts in your mind—to plant good thoughts and transform your heart into a flower garden, so that your prayer will be enriched by the divine fragrance of your heart.

When we hold even the slightest grudge, a small bad thought about anyone, any ascetic discipline we may undertake, such as fasting, vigils and so forth, will be in vain. What will be the use of such ascetic disciplines, if one does not struggle concurrently to prevent and reject all evil thoughts? Why not first empty the vessel of any impure residue oil, which is only good for making soap, before putting in the good oil; why should we mix good oil with filthy residue?

A single good and pure thought has more power than any ascetic exercise. For example, a young man is tempted by the devil and has impure thoughts, and he undertakes vigils and three-day fasts in order to be rid of his impure thoughts. But one single good and pure thought which he manages to bring to mind can have greater effect than the vigils and the fasts; it can be of more positive help to the young man in overcoming his problem.

Geronda, when you say "pure thought", are you referring to specific matters or to more general ones?

I am also referring to more general matters. For when man can see all things with good thoughts, he is purified and filled with the Grace of God. With evil thoughts one condemns and wrongs others, impedes the coming of divine Grace, and then the devil comes to do his evil work to us and in us.

In other words, Geronda, do we give the devil the right to attack us just because we condemn someone?

Yes. Everything starts from good thoughts. This is what elevates a person and changes him for the better. One must reach a point of being able to see all things in purity. It is as Christ said: *Judge not according to the appearance, but judge righteous judgment* [Jn 7:24]. And having acquired this, man can reach the point of seeing everything with spiritual eyes, not physical eyes. All things can be justified, in the good sense of the term.

We must be careful not to accept the devil's evil messages, so as not to pollute *the temple of the Holy Spirit* [cf. 1Cor 6:19, 3:16], thereby banishing the Grace of God and bringing spiritual darkness to our soul. When the Holy Spirit sees our heart in purity, He comes and dwells in us, because He loves purity—this is why He manifests Himself as a dove.

The Greatest Disease: Evil Thoughts

Geronda, I am anxious and can't sleep when I have a problem to deal with.

Your basic problem is your many thoughts. If you didn't have all these thoughts, you would be able to accomplish much more in your assigned duties and in your spiritual life. Here is one way to avoid all these thoughts: When you think of something that, let's say, needs to be done tomorrow, tell yourself, "This work is not for today, I will think about it tomorrow." Also, when you have to make a decision, do not trouble yourself with the thought of how to make the best decision, and thus end up constantly procrastinating. Make a decision and move on; then let God take care of the rest. Try to avoid being overly meticulous and scholastic about too many details, which will only confuse your mind. Do whatever you are able to do with *philotimo*,[1] simplicity and, above all, with great trust in God. This way we "oblige" God, in a manner of speaking, to help us, when we place our hopes and our future in His hands. Even a healthy person will become useless with too many thoughts running through his mind. One who is sick and suffering can justifiably have worrisome thoughts. But one who is healthy and yet becomes confused and suffers from sinister[2] thoughts, deserves a straitjacket! To be healthy and yet tormented by one's thoughts is a terrible sickness!

In our times, one of the greatest illnesses is the vain thoughts of worldly people. People can have all the good things in life except good thoughts. They are tormented simply through not facing up to things in a spiritual manner. For example, someone sets out to go somewhere but has a little car trouble and is a little late getting to his destination. If he has a good thought, he will say, "Perhaps the Benevolent God brought

---

1 *Philotimo*, according to Elder Paisios, is the spontaneous, self-sacrificing love shown by humble people, from whom every trace of self has been filtered out, full of gratitude towards God and their fellow men. *Philotimo* comes from a deep, abiding connection with God, so that one is constantly moved to do and seek that which is good, right, and honorable. Out of spiritual sensitivity, such people try to repay the slightest good which others do for them.

2 That is, to have a thought "from the left side," an evil thought.

this delay in order to prevent a possible accident. How can I thank You, my God, for this?" So he praises God for the delay. On the contrary, if he does not have a good thought, he will not face the incident in a spiritual manner; he will curse and blame God: "What a misfortune, what a useless delay! And where is God in all this?"

When we accept whatever happens to us with a good and positive thought, we are helped; while on the contrary, we are tormented and come apart at the seams emotionally and physically when negative and evil thoughts prevail.

* * *

Whoever Has Good Thoughts Sees Good in Everything

Some people tell me that they are scandalized because they see many things wrong in the Church. I tell them that if you ask a fly, "Are there any flowers in this area?" it will say, "I don't know about flowers, but over there in that heap of rubbish you can find all the filth you want." And it will go on to list all the unclean things it has been to. Now, if you ask a honeybee, "Have you seen any unclean things in this area?" it will reply, "Unclean things? No, I have not seen any; the place here is full of the most fragrant flowers." And it will go on to name all the flowers of the garden or the meadow. You see, the fly only knows where the unclean things are, while the honeybee knows where the beautiful iris or the hyacinth is....

As I have come to understand, some people resemble the honeybee and some resemble the fly. Those who resemble the fly seek to find evil in every circumstance and are preoccupied with it; they see no good anywhere. But those who resemble the honeybee only see the good in everything they see. The stupid person thinks stupidly and takes everything in the wrong way, whereas the person who has good thoughts, no matter what he sees, no matter what you tell him, maintains a positive and good thought.

* * *

Spiritual Life Is Based on Thought

Geronda, I read that during the Italian war the Greeks first attempted to destroy the fortifications of the enemy and then went on the offensive.

This is what the devil does, too. Just as the enemy, before going on the offensive with the infantry, will use the air force to bomb the fortifications and destroy them, in the same way the devil will first bomb a person with thoughts and then attack him directly. He will not attack until he has managed to break down the man's thoughts, because a person can defend himself with good thoughts, which are his basic protective trenches.

A sinister thought is a foreign substance that a person must try to reject. This is a battle that all of us have the power to undertake. No one is justified in saying that he is weak and unable to wage such a battle. These are not heavy tools that one may not be able to raise and work with because his hands are weak and shaking. I don't think it's a difficult thing to see and take everything in a positive way. For example, why should I attempt to examine other people's peculiarities? It is quite possible that what someone is doing is not peculiar, but something that he does intentionally in order to humble himself.

Geronda, I am troubled because I constantly have sinister thoughts. I do struggle, but I cannot make myself think aright.

Being able to recognize which thoughts are not pure, being troubled by them, and struggling to dispel them, is progress in itself. If you wish to make spiritual progress, when the devil attacks you with sinister thoughts and seeks to draw you to himself, turn the steering wheel hard away from him and ignore him. Try to have good thoughts about both the younger and the older Sisters, who are carrying on an inner struggle without fanfare, because the evil one is distracting your thoughts in order to delay your spiritual progress. If you hadn't persisted in your thoughts, you would have made great spiritual strides by now. All spiritual life is based on thoughts. Progress in spiritual life depends upon our thoughts.

Geronda, how can I be helped in the struggle against these sinister thoughts?

With vigilance and unceasing prayer. If you are vigilant, then you are attentive to good thoughts. For example, you look upon a glass or cup and you recall the sacred Chalice, the Last Supper, Christ and so forth; whereas if you are not vigilant, your mind may wander off to consider non-spiritual things or even wretched things. For this reason, try not to gather useless thoughts, which you will later struggle to get rid of. Concentrate and say the Jesus Prayer. And if your mind wanders, call it back again and again. Do not allow your mind to wander. For even if the mind is not always preoccupied with evil things, but merely neutral things, these too, nevertheless, will neutralize the mind with useless and wasteful distractions. In fact, the thoughts created from such distractions can be more insidious than the outright evil ones, because we do not always directly recognize them so as to dispel them.

Geronda, my thought tells me, "You have not made any progress after all these years in the monastery."

Tell me, what else does your thought tell you? It seems you pay a lot of attention to the devil who whispers things to you and tries to deceive you! Why do you believe the evil one? Why do you confuse yourself? Be at peace. You worry in vain and torment yourself without reason. The demon presents things in a confused and tangled manner. He fogs your mind with pessimistic thoughts in order to waste your time and distract you from prayer and attention to your daily tasks. Even if you are only a little confused, just enough to take away your desire to fight him, this alone is enough for him to be promoted to a higher rank. When working alone, try to follow this rule: Sing psalms, doxologies, and verbal or silent prayer of the heart, in order to avoid the murmur of thoughts. In other words, try to turn your thoughts to God. Since the devil changes the subject of our thoughts in order to deceive us, why shouldn't we do the same thing? I've told you this before. When I'm speaking with someone and am about to say something which may be useful to him, someone else will come to interrupt, or there will be some distracting sound or something else that forces me to stop. If the tempter the devil devises such machinations against us, why should we not similarly devise our own defensive mechanisms? You must be intelligently vigilant in outsmarting the little devil.

Geronda, I am troubled by sorrow, by listlessness ... I am tormented by it.

This is martyrdom before the martyrdom! You are placing too much trust in yourself. Self-confidence. Certain sinister thoughts have become entrenched in you and this is why you are being thus tormented. You need to think straight. You have to remove the worn-out machinery of your mental factory and install good machinery. The best enterprise is for someone to establish a factory of good thoughts. Then, even bad thoughts will be transformed into good ones by his mind. For example, when you look upon a person as a soul, as an angel, you can ascend angelically to Heaven and your life becomes a festival. But if you look upon a person in a carnal way, you descend into hell.

Geronda, sometimes when I think of something good and positive, a sinister thought will soon come to destroy everything for me. Could it be that I don't do this from my heart?

The goal is to do it from your heart and, if you have a sinister thought, say, "This thought is a stranger; I must send it away. I have signed the eviction; it's gone, it's out of my mind."

Geronda, when I have taken great effort in expelling a bad thought, how is it that it returns again after it's been dealt with?

Yes, the subject may have been dealt with, but the little devil has not finished. The devil never dies. An elder monk used to say, "If you kick a dog a couple of times, it will go away. But the devil does not go away; he persists with his attacks, here, there, everywhere!" I light a candle to the Saints of our *Kelli* to make him go away, and the demons ask me, "Did you light the candle for us?" "You trash, why would I light a candle for you? I lit it for the Saints." "Yes, but it was we who made you light it," they tell me.

Geronda, when a misfortune happens to someone and he begins to say, "Why, O God, has this happened to me?" can that person be helped?

How can he be helped? The first thing is for a person to interpret everything with good and positive thoughts; only then can he be helped. Some people have a good machine, many prerequisites for a spiritual life, but their steering wheel is faulty and leads them in the wrong direction. If they turn the steering wheel in the direction of good thoughts, then they can proceed steadily in the right direction.

Cultivating Good Thoughts

Geronda, do good thoughts come on their own, or do I have to cultivate them?

You must cultivate them. Observe yourself, scrutinize yourself and, when the enemy sends you bad thoughts, try to expel them and replace them with good thoughts. When you struggle in this manner, the disposition of your soul will be cultivated and become positive and good. Then God, seeing your good disposition, will condescend to help you, and the evil thoughts will find no place in you to dwell. The evil thoughts will be expelled and then you will naturally have good thoughts. You will acquire a habit toward what is good, goodness itself will come into your heart, and then you will provide hospitality in your heart for Jesus Christ Himself. But this does not happen overnight; it takes time and a constant struggle for the soul to receive the crown of victory. Eventually the war will end for good, because such battles result from our disorderly inner state, which is exploited by the propaganda of the enemies.

Geronda, does this mean that those who have good thoughts have achieved this spiritual state-of-being through struggle?

It depends. Some people have good thoughts from the start of their spiritual life and can thus advance readily. Others, on the contrary, while they may have good thoughts at the beginning, later on are not careful and vigilant, and start to have bad thoughts. Others, again, have sinister thoughts at first, but by being carefully observant of themselves and seeing how often they have fallen, lose their self-confidence and begin to have good and positive thoughts.

* * *

The Purification of the Mind and the Heart

Geronda, how does one achieve purification of the mind and the heart?

I have told you that in order to purify the mind and the heart one must not accept the cunning thoughts brought by the devil, nor have any cunning thoughts of one's own. One must always try to have good thoughts, to avoid being scandalized easily, and to view the faults of others with leniency and love. When good thoughts are multiplied, a person is cleansed spiritually, behaves with authentic devotion, becomes peaceful, and lives a life of Paradise. Otherwise, he sees everything with suspicion and his life becomes hell. He himself turns his life into hell.

We must work to achieve purification. We may recognize our wretchedness, but that is not enough. If we stop accepting cunning thoughts, and we ourselves do not think cunningly, but instead have only good thoughts about what we are told and what we see, then our mind and heart will be purified. Of course, the tempter will continue to send us, from time to time, a cunning telegraph message. Even if we get rid of our own thoughts, the devil's temptations will persist; but they will not stick if our heart is pure.

Geronda, doesn't prayer help in the purification of the mind?

Prayer alone is not enough. It's of no benefit to burn pounds of incense while we are praying if our mind is filled with evil thoughts about others. The evil telegraph message is transmitted from the mind to the heart and turns a person into a beast. God wants us to have *a clean heart* [Ps 50:12]; and our heart is clean when we do not allow a bad thought about others to pass through our mind.

Geronda, does a person first have a good thought, and then God helps?

A person is entitled to divine help only when he has good thoughts. With good thoughts, he purifies his evil heart, because *out of the heart proceed* all evil things [Mt 15:19]. And *out of the abundance of the heart his mouth speaketh* [Lk 6:45]. Most certainly, God will reward us for the good thoughts we have.

We Must Not Be Suspicious

Geronda, what will help me to dispel my suspicions?

Are things always the way you see them? Since you usually see everything in a negative way, place a big question mark after every single one of your thoughts, and spare a good thought for others, in order to avoid being wrong in your judgments. It's better if you place two big question marks, and even better if you place three. This way you calm yourself and benefit, but you also benefit others. Otherwise, with your sinister thoughts you will become all steamed up, troubled and upset, in which case you suffer spiritual harm. But when you confront whatever you see with good thoughts, after a while you will see that everything was indeed as you saw them with your good thoughts. I will tell you of an incident, to show you what a sinister thought can do.

One day a monk came to my *Kalyvi* and told me, "Elder Charalampos is a sorcerer and I saw him practicing magic!" "What a silly thing to say! You should be ashamed of yourself!" I told him. "Indeed, I saw him one night when there was a full moon, pouring something from a glass jug into the bushes and saying 'm, m, mmm…'." One day I went to Elder Charalampos and asked him, "Father Charalampos, how are you? Is everything all right with you? Someone saw you pouring something from a jug into the bushes and making an 'mmmm' sound." "Oh, there were some beautiful irises in the bushes and I went down to water them," he explained. "As I watered them, I chanted to each one of them, *Rejoice, O Bride Unwedded!*" Do you see what he was doing? And yet the other monk took him to be a sorcerer! . . .

Another time, someone who had a sick child came to see me. I took him into the Chapel to talk. After listening to his problem, in an effort to help, I told him, "You yourself must do something for the child to be helped. Since you do not do prostrations, you do not fast, and you have no money to offer charity, you must say to God, 'My God, I have nothing good to sacrifice for the health of my son, but at least I will try to break my habit of smoking cigarettes.'" The poor fellow was moved, and he promised me that he would do it. I went to open the door for him to go out, and he left his lighter and the cigarettes in the Chapel, under the Icon of Christ. I did not notice this at first. After him, another young man entered the Chapel to speak to me; and when he went out, he started to smoke. I had to tell him, "Young man, it is not proper to smoke here; go a little further away." But he retorted by saying, "Is it permitted to smoke in the Chapel?" He apparently had seen the lighter and the cigarettes left behind by the father of the sick child and imagined that I smoked. I allowed him to leave with his negative thought. After all, even if I did smoke, would I be smoking in the Chapel? Do you see what it is to have negative thoughts?

* * *

Geronda, what happens if a suspicious thought about someone proves to be true?

Even if such a thought proves to be right, does this mean that such thoughts will always be true? And how can you then be sure that God did not permit such a thought to be proven true in order to test you and provide you with a spiritual lesson in humility?

Certainly one must be careful not to give cause for others to draw the wrong conclusions. For example, someone may have a sinister thought about you simply because he is spiteful; but you, too, may very easily give him cause by your own behavior. But if even though you have been careful not to give cause, someone still thinks something negative about you, then you should give glory to God and pray for that person.

Conversing With Thoughts

Geronda, when a proud thought comes to me, I suffer over it.

Do you hold it within you?

Yes.

Why do you hold it within you? You should shut the door to it. You harm yourself by keeping it inside. The thought comes like a thief—you open the door, you let him in, you strike up a conversation with him, and then he robs you. Do you ever strike up a conversation with a thief? Not only do you not start talking with him, but you shut the door to prevent him from entering. You may not talk with him, but why allow him to enter in the first place? Let me give you an example. I am not implying that you have these thoughts, but let's assume that the thought comes to you that you could become the Abbess. Now, the thought has come to you. As soon as it comes, say to yourself, "Very well. Do you want to be the Abbess? First become Abbess to yourself." This way you immediately cut off any conversation. After all, are we going to hold a conversation with the devil? You see, when the devil went to tempt

Christ, He told him, *Get behind me, satan* [Lk 4:8]. Since Christ Himself sent the devil away, who are we to converse with him?

Geronda, is it bad for me to examine a sinister thought in order to see where it comes from?

The bad thing is that you are not talking with the thought, as you imagine, but with the devil. You may pass the time pleasantly, but later you are tormented. Do not by any means strike up a conversation with such thoughts. Pick up the hand grenade and throw it back to the enemy to kill him. It takes two or three minutes for the hand grenade to blow up. It's the same with sinister thoughts; they cannot harm you if you dispel them immediately. But sometimes you are not vigilant, you are not saying the Jesus Prayer and you cannot defend yourself. The devil's message comes from the outside, you receive it, you read it, you read it over again, you believe it and you file it away. Those files the devil will present on Judgment Day in order to condemn you.

When is the attack of a sinister thought a sin?

When the thought comes and you dispel it immediately, this is not a sin. When it comes and you talk with it, this is sin. It comes, at first you accept it and then you send it away. This is a half sin, because by now harm has already come to you, because the devil has polluted your mind. In other words, it is like the devil has come and you told him, "Good morning, how are you? Sit down, let me give you something to drink. Oh, you are the devil? Now go away." Since you saw he was the devil, why did you ever allow him to come in? You gave him a treat and now he will want to come again.

* * *

In other words, Geronda, when do we actually give our consent to these thoughts?

When you suck on them like they're candy. You must struggle not to suck on these thoughts that are sugar-coated on the outside but poison inside, causing you to despair. To have bad thoughts pass through us is not a cause for worry; only the Angels and those who are perfect have no bad thoughts. There is reason to worry when a person levels out a part of his heart to make a landing strip and accepts the little devils that come to him. And if this too happens once in a while, then go directly to Confession, plough up the landing strip, the mind and the heart, and plant fruit-bearing trees, to turn the heart again into Paradise.

The Source

Elder Paisios of Mount Athos, *Spiritual Counsels,* vol III: *Spiritual Struggle*, trans Reverend Father Peter Chamberas (Thessaloniki: Holy Monastery "Evangelist John the Theologian," 2001), 19–23, 29–30, 62–76, abridged and reprinted with permission.

Other volumes in this series include vol I: *With Pain and Love for Contemporary Man*; vol II: *Spiritual Awakening*; and vol IV: *Family Life.*

Miscellanea

Parent Friendly

A child needs to be surrounded by people who pray and pray ardently. A mother should not be satisfied by giving her child a physical caress, but should also coddle it with the caress of prayer. In the depths of its soul the child senses the spiritual caress that its mother conveys to it and is drawn to her. It feels security and certainty when its mother mystically embraces it with constant, intense and fervent prayer and releases it from whatever is oppressing it.

Mothers know how to express anxiety, offer advice and talk incessantly, but they haven't learned to pray. Most advice and criticism does a great deal of harm. You don't need to say a lot to children. Words hammer at the ears, but prayer goes to the heart. Prayer is required, with faith and without anxiety, along with a good example.

* * *

Pray and then speak. That's what to do with your children. If you are constantly lecturing them, you'll become tiresome and when they grow up they'll feel a kind of oppression. Prefer prayer and speak to them through prayer. Speak to God and God will speak to their hearts. That is, you shouldn't give guidance to your children with a voice that they hear with their ears. You may do this too, but above all you should speak to God about your children. Say, "Lord Jesus Christ, give Your light to my children. I entrust them to You. You gave them to me, but I am weak and unable to guide them, so, please, illuminate them." And God will speak to them and they will say to themselves, "Oh dear, I shouldn't have upset Mummy by doing that!" And with the grace of God this will come from their heart.

* * *

Children are not edified by constant praise. They become self-centered and vain. All their lives they will want everyone to be praising them constantly, even if they are being told lies. Unfortunately, nowadays all people have learned to tell lies and the conceited accept those lies as their daily sustenance. "Say it, even if it's not true, even if it's ironical," they say. God does not want this. God wants truth. Unfortunately, not all people understand this and they do the very opposite.[1]

—Saint Porphyrios the Kapsokalivite

Anger vs. Peace

You have filled Yourself with peace, O Glory of the realms on high, and the anger of all lands cannot confound Your peace.

Among mortals peace is scarce, therefore anger has become arrogant.

In the bosom of arrogance anger makes its nest, and in the bosom of anger lies murder.

All sins lead to murder, but none stands so close to murder as anger.

The one-eyed laws of the world do not punish anger, because they do not see that anger kills. But Your clairvoyant law, O Glory of the realms on high, calls anger murder.

I strove, in sunlight and moonlight, to penetrate the mystery of Your law. And once my striving began to wear away all my worldly aspirations, I began to perceive how the anger of my neighbors was killing me.

The children of anger are slaves, while the children of peace are sons. Therefore Your Wisdom vociferates and reiterates to people, telling them to be sons!

For a son looks into the face of his father, and directs his own face toward the face of his father. And when he sees peace in the father's face, how can he disfigure his own face with anger, without diverting his gaze away from his father?

1 St Porphyrios was canonized by the Ecumenical Patriarchate of Constantinople on Nov 27, 2013. The book: Elder Porphyrios [†1991, Dec 2], *Wounded by Love: The Life and Wisdom of Elder Porphyrios*, ed Sisters of the Holy Convent of Chrysopigi, Chania, Crete (Limni, Evia, Greece: Denise Harvey (Publisher), 2005), 199–200, 203, 208. Used with permission.

Anger brings infirmity into both the one who is angry and the one against whom the anger is vented. And infirmity is the predecessor of death.

A wonderworker does not work miracles among the children of anger, for the children of anger bring infirmity into him.

My neighbors: why do you feel stronger among those who love you, and weaker among those whom your presence angers? Is it not because the former lengthen your life with love, and the latter shorten your life with anger?

Therefore I enjoy being constantly with You, O Glory of the realms on high. For only in Your presence am I neither murdering, nor being murdered by them.

Just as drop after drop of water erodes even the hardest stone, so does anger erode the life of two people.

Like a murderer waiting in ambush with a knife, so does anger lurk in a haughty heart.

Truly, arrogance knows that it is guilty; therefore it places anger at the gates, to act as its sentry.

Arrogance knows that it is sinful; therefore it has found itself an advocate in another sin.

Fill my heart with serenity, O Glory of the realms on high, with the serenity of the angels before Your throne. For serenity has no abode or resting place for anger.

Grant me the serenity of a son, and I shall be ashamed to become angry at slaves or to kill slaves. Armor me with Your peace, which the anger of the children of anger will not be able to confound.[1]

— Saint Nikolai Velimirovich

1 St Nikolai Velimirovich [†1956, Mar 5], *Prayers by the Lake*, no LXXI, trans and annotated Rt Rev Archimandrite Todor Mika, STM and Very Rev Dr Stevan Scott (Grayslake, IL: Diocese of New Gracanica and Midwestern America, 2010), 135–136. Used with permission.

For more about anger and spiritual life, see Gabriel Bunge, *Dragon's Wine and Angel's Bread: The Teaching of Evagrius Ponticus on Anger and Meekness*, trans Anthony P. Gythiel (Crestwood, NY: St Vladimir's Seminary Press, 2009).

For more poetic prayers and hymns, see *A Spiritual Psalter or Reflections on God*, excerpted by Bishop (St) Theophan the Recluse from the works of our Holy Father Ephraim the Syrian, trans Antonina Janda, (Liberty, TN: St John of Kronstadt Press, 1997).

20. Life of Saint Stephen the New

Temptations to deny Christ take many forms. For example, in the life of Saint Sebastian [†c.300, Dec 18], two fearless champions of Christ, having preserved their faith under extreme physical torture, are subsequently brought to the brink of apostasy by the tears of their unbelieving parents, wives, and children—until Saint Sebastian brings them back to their senses.

This excerpt from the Life of **Saint Stephen the New** *[†766, Nov 28] is from the Lives of the Saints by* ***Saint Demetrius of Rostov*** *[†1709, Oct 28]. There are several things to observe. The reader absorbs its theological and spiritual instruction almost unconsciously. The Iconoclast Period transforms from mental abstraction to frightening reality. The Life clarifies the issues, demonstrates the inestimable value as well as the cost of Orthodoxy, bought with blood, and reveals that icons are much more about substance than about "pretty." One becomes more chary of the taint, frivolousness, and danger of heterodoxy.*

As his disciples multiplied, the blessed Stephen saw that the silence he so loved was being lost. Troubled over this, he summoned Marinus . . . and entrusted to him the direction and care of the monastery. Then he moved to another place on the mountain, where he built for himself a roofless hut. Stephen was forty-two years old when he secluded himself in this cell. . . . The good report of Stephen's holy life spread everywhere, and the Orthodox came to him in great numbers, like bees drawn to honey. Much benefited by the example of his austere life and by his instructive discourses, they were guided by him on the path of sorrows that leads to eternal life. Moreover, it was not only men who sought out the saint but women as well. Among the latter there was a renowned noblewoman named Anna, a young, childless widow. Having sold all her possessions and distributed the money to the poor, she came to the godly one, who tonsured her in the angelic schema and sent her to the Trikhinarion [a nearby convent].

After the death of the Emperor Leo the Isaurian, his son Constantine Copronymus came to the throne. Casting the sacred icons out of the churches and burning them, he proved to be an even crueller persecutor of the Church of God than his father. He was accused of heresy by many eminent and wise monastics, who proved his beliefs to be in error, so he rose up in savage, unbridled fury against the monks. He referred to the monastic habit as the robe of darkness and called the monks themselves idolaters since they defended the veneration of the holy icons with much zeal. Moreover, the iniquitous one assembled a great multitude of ignorant people, and placing before them holy crosses, sacred Gospel books, and the divine Mysteries of the Body and Blood of Christ, he had them swear that they would not revere the icons but would call them idols. He also made them declare under oath that they would neither receive Communion from the hands of monks nor associate with them in any way. As a result, whoever chanced to come upon a monk would throw stones at him, calling him a benighted son of darkness, a fool, or an idolater.

When the impious Anastasius—who was elevated by the Emperor Leo to the patriarchal throne after Saint Germanus—reposed, Copronymus raised to the rank of patriarch a monk called Constantine, a man who shared one name and mind with him. This he did on his own authority, without the consent of a council, leading his candidate to the ambo and placing the omophorion on him with his own hands, declaring that this Constantine alone was worthy of the patriarchal dignity. The Emperor and Patriarch then took counsel together and published a decree throughout the Empire summoning the bishops to the Imperial City to meet in council to condemn the holy icons. At that time shameless, godless deeds were wrought in Byzantium, and even the sacred vessels used for the celebration of the divine Mysteries were trampled underfoot because images of the Lord and His saints were depicted on them. The holy icons themselves were tossed into the mud or hurled into the sea, consumed by fire, or hacked in pieces with axes. Beautiful icons on the walls of churches were either scraped off with instruments of iron or covered with whitewash. The wicked Copronymus did not spare even the magnificent and glorious Church of the Most Pure Theotokos in the Blachernae, the walls of which were covered with mosaics set against a background of gold, portraying the entire earthly life of Christ from His Incarnation to His Crucifixion and Resurrection. Divesting the church of its iconographic decoration like an empress of her robe of purple, he stripped the walls of the golden tessarae and precious stones that adorned its mosaics, from top to bottom. In place of the holy icons, he ordered that the walls be covered with depictions of trees, beasts, and birds, so that the words of David were fulfilled: *O God, the heathen are come into Thine inheritance, they have made Jerusalem as it were the hut of an orchard-keeper* [Ps 78]. In addition to this, they removed the incorrupt relics of the saints from the churches, committing them to flames and casting them into the sea, dragging them out of the city and hurling them from mountains into ravines and thickets; *they made the dead bodies of* the Lord's *servants to be food for the birds of heaven, the flesh of* His *saints for the beasts of the earth*. Those who bravely defended the holy icons were put to torture and given over to a bitter death by the iconoclasts, who spilt their blood like water and left their bodies without burial, to become food for beasts and birds of prey. Great were the afflictions that befell the Orthodox, and especially the monks in those days, a tribulation such as was never seen since the beginning of the world!

Many monks fled to Mount Auxentius, seeking good counsel and spiritually profitable teaching from the venerable Stephen, and he did not fail to console them, instructing them to remain steadfast in piety, even if this should lead to the shedding of their blood. Those who lacked the strength for this and feared torments he told to flee to other lands where the iconoclasts would be unable to persecute them. All the monasteries of Byzantium were abandoned, and not a monk remained to be seen in the Imperial City: some of them were slain for their stand for Orthodoxy, while others, wishing both to preserve their lives and to remain firm in their confession of the true faith, fled to foreign countries.

In the year 754 after the Nativity of Christ, the fourteenth year of the rule of Copronymus, the iconoclasts convened a council in the Imperial City. It was attended by 338 bishops from the East, but no patriarch was in attendance, other than the false Patriarch of Constantinople, the heretic and confederate of the Emperor. The site appointed for the council was the most glorious Church of the Theotokos in the Blachernae, now stripped of its iconographic adornment and resembling a barren waste or a robber's den. After lengthy deliberations and debates, the Emperor prevailed upon all the bishops to adhere to the godless blasphemy he espoused. Although many of them clearly understood that the Emperor and Patriarch had fallen into error and were bringing much harm upon the Church, they were terrified and dared not withstand them, fearing lest new evils befall the Orthodox. Only later, at the true Seventh Council, held during the reign of Constantine the Younger and his mother Irene, did they repent and return to the true faith. At the false council the following impious doctrines, hateful to God, were formulated. First, the holy icons were proclaimed idols by all present. Secondly, those who revered icons, beginning with the Patriarch Germanus, were anathematized. The iniquitous heretics, being themselves accursed, did not hesitate to pronounce the anathema against a holy and righteous man, but God's blessing remained upon him, in fulfillment of the Scriptures: *They will curse*, but *Thou wilt bless* [Ps 108]. Thirdly, all professed that not only the saints but even the Mother of God are unable to aid us by their intercessions after their repose. Fourthly, it was forbidden to refer to the holy apostles, martyrs, confessors, virgins, and other holy persons as saints. Finally, the council included itself with the six councils preceding it among those numbered as ecumenical, calling itself the Seventh Ecumenical Council. Those who did not accept this council were anathematized with Arius, Nestorius, Eutychius, Severus, and Dioscorus. After the Patriarch, chief among the bishops of the council were Theodosius, Bishop of Ephesus; Constantine of Nicomedia; Nicholas of Nacolia; Sisinius; and Basil. Concluding their iniquitous work at the council, the bishops signed its decrees, so that the words of the Scriptures were fulfilled: *Wickedness came from Babylon, from the elders and judges of the people* [Dan 13 (History of Susanna)], and *Many shepherds have destroyed My vineyard, they have trodden my portion under foot, they have made my pleasant portion a desolate wilderness* [Jer 12]. When the council's sessions ended, the bishops had the people proclaim with solemn joy: "Today salvation has come to the world, for by your efforts, O Emperor, we have been delivered from idols!"

Meanwhile the wicked Emperor heard report of our venerable father Stephen, who was struggling in asceticism on Mount Auxentius. Learning that he was a man of virtue, well acquainted with the divine Scriptures, a zealot for the holy icons who taught all to revere the sacred images, whose fame was such that he was glorified as the equal of the holy fathers of old, the Emperor plotted how he might lead Saint Stephen astray. Certain that if the godly one accepted his beliefs, the impious doctrines of iconoclasm would be much strengthened, he summoned one of his firmest supporters among the patricians, his first councilor

Callistus, who was skilled and tried in the art of rhetoric. This man he commanded to go to the venerable Stephen and proclaim to him that it was the Emperor's will that he give his consent to the decrees of the council which had condemned the veneration of icons, and that he sign the acts of the council. Moreover, the Emperor sent with Callistus gifts for the venerable one; not gold or silver, because he knew that the saint had no need of these things, but various foods which the godly one ate: dates, almonds, and figs.

Arriving at Stephen's cell, Callistus offered him the Emperor's gifts and related to him Copronymus's message. Spreading out the cunningly woven net of his words, referring often to the sacred Scriptures, he harangued the saint for a very long time in the hope that the blessed one would submit. The saint endured Callistus's lengthy tirade, wisely answering his every point, and at the end declared to him fearlessly, "I will not sign the decrees of your council, which are full of lies and deceit, nor do I praise them. It is not my custom to call bitter sweet or darkness light [Is 5], since I do not wish to bring upon my head the prophet's curse. I am ready to die for the holy icons and have no fear of the Emperor's threats!" Then Stephen stretched out his arm, and cupping his hand, said, "If I had within me only as much blood as can be held in my hand, I would not hesitate to offer it to be shed for the icon of Christ. Take back the gifts you have brought me from the Emperor; I am in no need of them. With the divine Scriptures I say, *As for the oil of the sinner let it not anoint my head* [Ps 140]. Let my throat not delight in food given me by a heretic!"

Vanquished by these words, Callistus returned to the Emperor and told him everything Stephen had said. The Emperor became very angry and sent the nobleman back to Mount Auxentius, accompanied by brutal soldiers. The Emperor had commanded them to drag the godly Stephen from his cell, to take him to the Convent of Trikhinarion, which stood at the base of the mountain, and to imprison him there. The soldiers therefore broke down the door of the blessed one's cell and mercilessly dragged him away to the convent. There they locked up the saint and all his disciples. The soldiers remained on guard, awaiting further orders from the Emperor, but from within the saint could be heard chanting with his monks, "We bow down before Thine all-pure image, O Good One!" They remained imprisoned for six days, tasting no food whatsoever, and on the seventh an order was received from the Emperor commanding that Stephen be returned to his cell. At that time, the

Emperor unexpectedly received word of an incursion of the Scyths. Forced to turn his attention to the invasion, he put aside for a time his intent to persecute the venerable Stephen.

Meanwhile, Callistus, whose hatred and malice against the godly one were no less than the Emperor's, secretly summoned one of Stephen's disciples, the previously mentioned Sergius. Leading Sergius astray with beguiling words and much gold and silver, Callistus persuaded him to make slanderous accusations against the godly Stephen, which he hoped would be readily believed since the false monk lived with the saint and knew well his manner of life. Like a second Judas, that lover of money betrayed his teacher and began to consider how he might weave a net of deceit to ensnare his innocent and holy father. No more able to find a blemish in his way of life than on the radiant sun, he departed from Stephen's monastery like a lost sheep wandering away from its flock. He found a man as evil as himself, an imperial official named Aulicalamus, who was responsible for the collection of taxes in Nicomedia, and struck up a friendship with him. Together they devised accusations against the saint and prepared a written oath containing their slanders. They began by alleging that Stephen had reviled the Emperor as a heretic and was stirring up the people who came to him to revolt against the imperial authority. To this they added many other charges, which we shall not repeat, both to avoid loquacity and because they were nothing but falsehoods. They also accused Stephen of going by night to the Convent of Trikhinarion and committing fornication with the blessed Anna, who was previously mentioned as having forsaken the world and all its vanities and having received the tonsure into the angelic schema at the hands of the godly one. A maidservant of the holy nun was persuaded to witness to the truth of this charge and in return was promised her freedom, a great quantity of gold, and marriage to one of the noblemen serving in the imperial court. The document containing these slanders and the false testimony of Anna's maid was taken by a soldier to the Emperor, who was by that time in Scythia.

Constantine rejoiced when he read the accusations and sent a letter to his viceroy in the Imperial City, commanding him to go immediately to the Trikhinarion. The viceroy was ordered to remove the nun Anna from the convent and to send her to the Emperor without delay. The viceroy set off at once, accompanied by a troop of armed soldiers as though he were going to war. Entering the convent, they found the nuns assembled in church, chanting the Third Hour. The unexpected appearance of soldiers, their weapons drawn, filled the nuns with terror, and some of them ran into the altar where they hid themselves beneath the holy table. Others made haste to flee into the mountains, but all were seized by the soldiers. Their aged abbess went out boldly to meet the soldiers and demanded, "What business do you have here, you false Christians? Why do you affront the brides of Christ, who do you no evil?"

"Hand over to us Anna, Stephen's mistress," said they. "The Emperor demands that you surrender her!"

The abbess called for Anna and another nun, Theophania, and after exhorting them to guard themselves carefully from the enemy's temptations and to defend fearlessly the innocence of their holy and venerable father, she entrusted them to God's protection and sent them off with the troops.

The soldiers took the nuns to the Emperor without delay, and Copronymus commanded that they be kept apart. After a short time he had Anna brought before him and said to her, "I believe without any doubt that the things said to me concerning you are true; therefore, I have had you brought here so that you may tell me plainly what sort of magic the wicked sorcerer Stephen employed to compel you to give up your rich estates, to reject your noble lineage, and to submit to being clothed in black garments. It is clear that his purpose was to have you as his mistress. What charm do you find in this fellow that you permitted yourself to be seduced by him and fornicate with him shamelessly?"

Hearing the Emperor speak so vilely, the chaste Anna replied, "Do not imagine, O Emperor, that I have forsaken the inheritance I received from my parents, my noble estate, and the good things of this world to enslave my soul to the lusts of the flesh and fornication, as you say! As for those who have slandered me, they have *whetted their tongue like that of a serpent; the venom of asps is under their lips*, as David says [Ps 139]. My flesh is under your power, and you may torture it with fire or instruments of iron, but as long as my spirit remains in the body, you shall hear nothing from me but that Stephen is a holy, righteous man, the cause of my salvation!"

The Emperor marvelled when he heard this and fell silent. He then ordered that Anna be led away under guard and Theophania be sent back to the convent. Theophania related to the abbess and the godly Stephen everything that had occurred. A short time thereafter, the Emperor returned from battle to Constantinople. He ordered that the nun Anna be imprisoned in a dark, gloomy dungeon and sent his chamberlain to her with the following message: "Take pity on yourself, O woman, and lay aside your black garb. Return to an honorable life and you shall live with the Empress in the palace. Tomorrow when you are brought to me for questioning, speak the truth before all, for there is a servant woman who knows everything about your doings with Stephen, and she is prepared to speak. If you attempt to conceal anything, she will expose you. Then I, as a righteous judge and defender of the truth, will make you understand that it is impossible to defy the imperial authority. You will be forced to admit that Stephen has only brought you woe, for I shall cut your body to pieces. But if you heed my good counsel and openly confess the sorcerer's deeds of fornication, you will be deemed worthy of high honors."

Anna sighed deeply, wept, and said, "Do as you wish, but I will not lie about my righteous father. May the Lord's will be done!"

The following morning, the Emperor left the palace, and taking his seat in a public building, had the people assemble. The chaste Anna was brought from prison and stripped naked in the sight of all. Before her was borne the fasces,[1] symbol of the Emperor's magisterial authority, and she was preceded by the perjured witness, her handmaiden. As the innocent woman stood disrobed before the eyes of all, shame alone was her garment. During her questioning, she remained silent, emulating her Lord, Who gave no reply to His unjust judges. Meanwhile, the iniquitous maidservant bore false witness, not hesitating to swear that Stephen had sinned with Anna. The nun, however, remained like a lamb dumb before its shearer and did not open her mouth [Is 53].

Angered by her silence, the persecutor gazed wrathfully upon the blessed Anna and called her a whore, commanding that she be stretched out upon the ground and beaten with staves. Four powerful soldiers struck her back and belly for a long time. As she was being flogged, she said only: "I have never sinned with Stephen. Lord have mercy!" Nevertheless, the soldiers continued to beat her until she was almost dead. Seeing this, the persecutor arose from his throne and quickly returned to the palace, utterly defeated. He commanded that Anna be imprisoned in one of the city's abandoned monasteries where,

[1] A bundle of rods.

some time later, she reposed in holiness and departed unto the Lord.

The Emperor continued to ponder how he might ensnare Stephen and find some means to execute him as a criminal. He summoned a youth named George, a faithful servant in his palace, for whom he had great affection. Taking him aside, he asked, "George, how great is your love for me?"

"It is boundless," the young man replied.

The Emperor asked, "Are you prepared to die on account of your love for me?"

"Most certainly!" answered George.

The Emperor then kissed him joyfully, saying, "Behold, a new Isaac!" Then he added, "I do not intend to have you die for me, nor do I desire that you suffer for my sake. I ask only one thing of you. Go quickly to Stephen of Mount Auxentius, a man of whom I am loathe even to think, and beseech him to tonsure you into the monastic order and to number you among his disciples. After this, return here with all haste." The youth at once gave his consent and departed for Mount Auxentius.

Arriving by night at the monastery of the godly one, the young man cried out pitiably, "Have mercy on me! Have mercy on me, Christians! Have mercy on me, for I have lost my way and am afraid that I shall fall over a cliff or be devoured by wild beasts!" The compassionate Stephen sent for the monk Marinus to bring the youth into the monastery. George fell at the feet of the venerable one and asked his blessing. Seeing that the young man was not a peasant, Stephen questioned him as to who he was and whence he had come. George did not conceal the fact that he was from the palace but said that it was because the Emperor had departed from the path of truth and was leading those who followed him to perdition that he left the imperial service. "As soon as I came to my senses," said he, "I hastened to come to you, in the hope that you might clothe me in the angelic schema, which I greatly desire. I beg you, reverend Father, do not reject me as unworthy!" Fearing difficulties with the Emperor, the blessed Stephen at first refused to accept the young man, but the youth insisted that the Emperor would not be offended by his tonsure and continued to beseech the saint to number him among his disciples. "God will require you to answer for my soul if you do not tonsure me this day!" he cried.

Our venerable father was moved by these words, and failing to perceive the wiles of the devil, answered, "Child, I see that you have come here full of zeal for salvation. I do not wish to transgress the commandment of the Lord by driving you away." He began to instruct George, had him remove his secular garb, and put on him the robe of a novice. Then he ordered the youth to prepare himself to receive the full monastic habit, in which he clothed the young man three days later. Immediately after he was tonsured in the angelic schema, the deceiver fled to the Emperor.

Copronymus was happy to see George clad in monastic garb, not because he loved monks but because he would now be able to accuse Stephen of having tonsured his servant. The next morning he presented the newly tonsured monk to the assembled people and began to rail against monastics and especially against Stephen. He accused the saint of leading the people astray, saying, "Stephen deludes all the people just as he deceived my beloved servant!"

At this, the crowd cried out, "Death to the wicked deceiver!"

The Emperor commanded that George be stripped of his habit, which was cast to the ground, and the people trampled underfoot the monastic garb, blaspheming and reviling monasticism as they did so. Then the Emperor had water brought and ordered that George be washed, as if to cleanse him of his monastic rank. He was clothed in the uniform of a soldier, a helmet was put on his head, and he was appointed a guardsman in the cavalry. When these things were done, Copronymus dispatched a large company of troops to Mount Auxentius to destroy Stephen's monastery.

Like wolves attacking a flock of sheep, or robbers, the soldiers scattered the monks and set fire to the monastery and church. They dragged the godly Stephen from his cell and took him to Chalcedon. On the way they subjected him to every sort of indignity, tormenting him mercilessly. They dragged him cruelly along the ground, beat him with their fists upon the back and head, spat in his eyes, and otherwise abused him in ways best left undescribed. At Chalcedon the soldiers put the saint in a ship which bore him to the Monastery of Philipicus at Chrysopolis, close to Constantinople. There the saint was loaded with chains and put in custody, remaining for seventeen days without food. Even when the Emperor did send him food, Stephen refused to taste it and sent it back.

At that time, the Emperor and Patriarch sent to the monastery where the saint was imprisoned leaders of the iconoclastic heresy: Theodosius, Bishop of Ephesus; Constantine of Nicomedia; Nicholas; Sisinius;

Basil; the aforementioned Callistus; and other rhetoricians, commanding them to debate with Stephen concerning the faith. These men had the blessed Stephen brought before them, fettered in irons so heavy that he could neither walk nor stand without support on either side. Theodosius, the Bishop of Ephesus, began by asking, "On what basis do you number us among the heretics, setting yourself above emperors, patriarchs, bishops, and all other Christians? Are we all in error, destined for perdition?"

"Hearken to what the divine Scriptures relate concerning Elijah," Saint Stephen replied in a meek voice. "The prophet said to Ahab, King of Israel: *I have not troubled Israel; but thou and thy father's house* [3Kings 18]. Likewise, it is not I who trouble the Church, but you who violate the traditions of the Holy Fathers of old and introduce new dogmas into her, for Basil the Great says, 'Everything handed down from antiquity by the Holy Fathers is worthy of esteem, but what is recently established is worthless and untrustworthy.'[1] Such are your decrees against the veneration of the holy icons, which were promulgated not by sons of the Catholic Church but by godless adulterers. Certain is the prophet's saying: *The rulers* of the people *were assembled together* [Ps 2] with false shepherds and hirelings against Christ and His precious icon!"

At this, Constantine, Bishop of Nicomedia, rose from his seat and kicked Stephen (who was sitting on the floor) in the face. Then one of the guards began to kick the saint in the belly. The blessed one fell over, and the guard proceeded to trample upon his chest. Seeing these disgraceful deeds, the patrician Callistus became indignant and ordered them to cease. Then he addressed Stephen thus: "The choice lies before you, Stephen: either sign the acts of the council or be put to death as one who rejects the decisions of the divine fathers. Decide quickly."

The God-inspired Stephen said boldly, "Pay heed to my words, my lord! With the great Apostle Paul I declare that for me *to live is Christ, and to die* for his precious icon *is gain* [Phil 1]. I have told you once and now repeat: if I had within me only as much blood as can be held in my cupped hand, I would not hesitate to offer it to be shed for the icon of Christ. Nevertheless, order that the decrees of your council be read. I wish to learn why you renounce the divine icons."

Constantine, Bishop of Nicodemia, straightway took up the book entitled *The Tradition of the Holy Seventh Ecumenical Council* and began to read.

---

[1] From Basil the Great's First Homily on Fasting.

As soon as the title was announced, Saint Stephen gestured him to silence and cried, "What falsehood! You have built an unstable building upon a weak foundation indeed! How is it that you call your council holy? Have you not denied the title 'holy' to all the saints, forbidding the faithful to call either the apostles, prophets, martyrs, or any of the other saints holy? How can your council be holy when it defies and tramples upon all that is holy? Moreover, you call your council an ecumenical council, but how can it be ecumenical when not one of the patriarchs or their representatives attended it? None of them has sent out epistles expressing their consent to its decrees. Your council should not be called ecumenical, but a false council. You also call it the seventh council, but how can it be the seventh council when it rejects the six that came before it? If it were the seventh council, it would confirm the sixth, the fifth, and other previous councils. Your council should not be called the seventh, but the first: the first to reject the traditions of all six councils preceding it!"

To this the bishops protested, "What tradition handed down by the first six councils have we rejected? We accept both the earlier councils and their traditions."

"Were not those councils held in holy churches magnificently adorned with icons?" said the saint. "The first council took place in the great cathedral of Nicea, the second in Constantinople, in the Church of Holy Peace. The third was held in Ephesus, in the Church of Saint John the Theologian, the fourth in the cathedral church of Chalcedon. The fifth and sixth councils met in Constantinople, one in the Church of Holy Wisdom, the other in the palace church of Trullo. Were not all these churches adorned with holy icons? Not one of these councils denounced the icons as has your council! What answer have you to this?"

Astonished by his words, all the bishops fell silent, except for one, who exclaimed, "Indeed, Stephen has spoken the truth!"

The godly Stephen then lifted up his eyes and hands to heaven, and sighing from the depths of his heart, cried with a loud voice, "Let him be anathema who refuses to venerate the Lord Jesus Christ depicted upon the icons according to His human nature, and may his lot be with those who cried, *Away with Him, away with Him, crucify Him*!" [Jn 19]

Since they could not prevail over the saint in debate, the bishops ordered that he be imprisoned again. In shame, they returned to the Emperor, who enquired about their mission. The bishops did not wish to tell him of their defeat; Callistus, however, related to the Emperor the whole truth, saying, "We have been vanquished, O Emperor, overcome by Stephen, a wise man, most wise indeed. His words are full of ineffable power and his heart is fearless. He is afraid neither of threats nor death itself."

Enraged, the Emperor ordered that the venerable Stephen be banished to the island of Proconnesus in the Sea of Marmara. Before departing, the saint healed the abbot of the Monastery of Philipicus, who was very ill and near death. Stephen laid his hand upon the abbot and prayed for him, after which he arose from his bed. Then Stephen boarded the ship prepared for him and sailed to his place of exile. On the island, he began to wander through the wilderness until he found a beautiful cave, called Cissudas by those who lived nearby. In it there was a chapel to Saint Anna, the grandmother of the Lord according to the flesh and the mother of the most holy Theotokos. The saint rejoiced greatly, and erected a cell for himself near the cave, where he lived for God alone, sustaining himself on roots and wild herbs.

Meanwhile, Stephen's disciples, driven away when their monastery on Mount Auxentius was destroyed, were scattered like sheep which have lost their shepherd. However, when they heard that their father and teacher had been exiled to Proconnesus, they all gathered around him, save the two disciples who had fallen away from the flock, as did Judas from Christ or Demas and Hermogenes from Paul [2Tim 1:15, 4:10]. These two were Sergius, who had compiled the list of false accusations against our venerable father, and Stephen, who was once a priest in the world but later tonsured by Saint Stephen. Having renounced both his monastic rank and God Himself, he dressed himself in worldly garb, went to the Emperor, and declared, "O Emperor! You delivered me from the mouth of Satan! I have cast off my dark robes and clothed myself in bright array!" The Emperor was delighted, and to show Stephen his favor, assigned the fallen monk a position in the Sophia Palace. Whenever Copronymus saw him, he called Stephen "the father of his joy" although in truth the wretch was worthy of lamentation. Thus did Sergius and Stephen perish, having fallen from the choir of the godly Stephen's disciples, but the others gathered around the venerable one and erected a monastery. Saint Stephen's mother and sister also came to him and built a convent near his cell, where they lived a life of virtue, ever taking delight in the sweet teaching of their instructor. Later, the godly one erected a pillar for himself and on it built a little hut. He was forty-nine years of age when he took up his dwelling there.

God granted the saint the gift of working miracles, and Stephen opened the eyes of a blind man, drove an evil spirit out of a possessed youth, and healed by his prayer a woman with an issue of blood. Many times he calmed the waves of the sea, saving numerous ships from foundering. Sailors often saw him walking on the waters, piloting vessels, or unfurling their sails. Such were the miracles worked by the saint while he lived on Proconnesus . . . .

At that time there was a soldier, Armenian by origin, who fell grievously ill, half of his body withering up: he was completely enfeebled by his infirmity. His name, like the saint's, was Stephen. He had heard that the venerable one could heal every disease, so he came to him from the Empire's provinces in Europe, although the journey was almost beyond his strength. Falling down before the saint, he tearfully entreated him to have mercy on him. The godly Stephen had him venerate the icons of Christ and the Theotokos, and when he did this, he was at once made whole. When the soldier returned to his friends, they asked him how he had recovered his health. He did not conceal God's mercy but said, "When I bowed down before the icons of Christ and the Theotokos, as commanded by the monk Stephen, who lives in exile on the island of Proconnesus, I was healed of my infirmity."

The soldiers reported this to their commander, who had authority over Thrace, and he summoned the Armenian. Learning that the soldier became well after venerating the holy icons, the General sent him at once to the Emperor, who after questioning the man, began to call him an idolater, angrily reviling him as though he had committed some terrible, godless deed. Out of shame and fear the soldier repented of having bowed down before the icons and denounced their veneration, vowing never again to revere them. The iniquitous Armenian thus won the Emperor's favor and was promoted to the rank of centurion, but as he was leaving the imperial palace and mounting his horse, the beast began to buck wildly, throwing him to the ground and trampling him to death. Thus the ungrateful apostate was punished, perishing miserably.

This miracle and the many others worked by Saint Stephen filled the Emperor with yet greater anger, because he realized that even in banishment on Proconnesus the godly one did not cease to work glorious miracles and to teach the people to venerate the holy icons. He resolved therefore to put the saint to death and ordered him returned from exile. First Copronymus had Stephen fettered, put in stocks, and locked in the gloomy dungeon of Phial, and then, several days later, had him brought to the lighthouse of the palace of Iliatsos where he awaited him with two of his chief officials.

As the blessed Stephen was being brought to the Emperor, he passed a pious traveller. The saint asked this man to give him a coin bearing the image of the Emperor, which he hid under his veil. When Stephen entered, Copronymus immediately began to cry, "O woe, woe! What I must endure from this man, who reviles my authority and counts me as nothing!" The saint stood silently, looking down as the Emperor, breathing out wrath like fire, continued to rebuke him. Finally, the Emperor concluded, "Have you nothing to say for yourself, wicked one?"

"If it is your intention to put me to death, do so now," the blessed Stephen answered meekly. "If, however, you have brought me here to question me, then lay aside your anger and speak calmly. When you have brought yourself under control, we may converse."

The Emperor demanded, "Tell us why you number us among the heretics. Which traditions of the Fathers have we violated?"

"You have impiously commanded that the holy icons be cast out of the churches, although the God-bearing Fathers of ancient times delivered to us the tradition that we are to venerate them," replied the saint.

The tyrant said, "Do not call the images holy icons, but idols! What does that which is holy have in common with idols?"

To this the saint responded, "He that bows down before the image does not revere the material of which it is made: the honor he shows it passes on to its prototype, as Saint Basil says."

"Do you imagine that the Fathers would have us depict with material colors that which is dark and inaccessible to the mind and which no words can explain? And is it right to worship the physical depiction of a nature which no man can know?" the tyrant enquired.

Answered the saint, "What man of understanding would say that the immaterial nature of the Divinity, which surpasses all comprehension, can be depicted with material colors? How can that which the mind cannot even conceive be depicted with paints? When we portray Christ upon an icon, it is not His divinity that we depict but His appearance as the God-man in a form like unto our own. It was in this form that the apostles touched Him with their hands, as Saint John the Theologian said,

This is that which we have looked upon, and our hands have handled [1Jn 1]. If you cite the words of Moses: *Thou shalt not make unto thee any graven image, or any likeness of any thing that is in heaven above, or that is in the earth beneath* [Ex 20], I will answer that Moses himself made golden images of two cherubim, of which the divine Apostle makes mention, referring to them as *the cherubim of glory shadowing the mercy seat* [Heb 9]. Indeed, the altar itself, and the tabernacle, and the holy of holies are themselves likenesses of heaven, as the same Apostle says when he speaks of them as serving *unto the example and shadow of heavenly things* [Heb 8]. How then do we err, depicting Christ as a man on an icon and bowing down before Him? Do you suppose that when we bow down before the Cross, which is also made of a material substance, that we are worshipping matter? Likewise, our conscience makes no accusation against us when we show reverence for the sacred vessels, since we know that they have been sanctified by the invocation of the name of Christ. Would you also cast out of the Church the Body and Blood of Christ, which is mystically given us under the appearance of bread and wine? This mystery portrays the Body of Christ which suffered upon the Cross and now abides in heaven, and we bow down before it and kiss it and partake of it, thereby inheriting the blessing of holiness. But you make no distinction between what is holy and what is profane, considering an icon of Christ to be no different than an image of Apollo, and an icon of the Theotokos to be the same as a statue of Artemis. Therefore you do not hesitate to speak of the holy icons as idols, trampling them underfoot and burning them!"

To this the Emperor replied, "O blind fool, worthy of damnation! Do you imagine that Christ is trampled upon when we trample on these images?"

Then the divinely wise Stephen, intending, like a tried warrior, to wound the foe with his adversary's own weapon, turned Copronymus's words against him. Removing from his veil the coin bearing the image of the impious Emperor, he showed it to Copronymus and asked him in Christ's words, *Whose is this image and superscription?* [Mt 22]

The Emperor answered, "Whose can it be, but mine?"

Again the saint asked, "What would befall a man were he to cast this image to the ground and to trample it underfoot? Would he not be punished?"

"He would suffer a severe punishment for dishonoring the Emperor's image," said the others present.

Then the saint sighed deeply and cried with pain of heart, "How great is your foolishness and blindness! If you would punish a man severely for dishonoring the image of an earthly emperor, subject to death and corruption, what punishment do you suppose awaits you, who have dared to trample underfoot and burn the images of the Son of God and His most pure Mother?" With this, Stephen spat upon the coin, and throwing it to the ground, began to trample on it. The two officials hurled themselves upon him angrily, intending to drag him from the palace and to drown him in the sea, but the Emperor, feigning meekness (although his heart was ablaze with wrath), forbade them to do Stephen any harm, because he did not wish it to appear that he was unable to control his anger. Instead, he had the saint bound, taken to the common prison, and locked in a cell.

As he entered the prison, Saint Stephen exclaimed, "Lo, this is my place of rest for the remainder of my life! Here shall I dwell till my last breath; this place of sojourn is my reward for my faithfulness to the icon of Christ." Confined in the most remote cell of the prison, the blessed one found 342 monks from various monasteries and lands, imprisoned for venerating the holy icons. Some had their noses cut off, others their ears, others had their eyes gouged out, while the hands of still others had been removed. This last cruelty was reserved for those who had written books in defense of the veneration of icons. Many bore wounds on their bodies that had not yet healed completely; the faces of some had been smeared with pitch and set afire; the heads of others had been shaved in mockery. Seeing these men, who had suffered so many tortures, the venerable one blessed their patience and struggles and adjudged himself worthy of tears and lamentation because he had not been deemed fit to endure such grievous torments. As for the holy fathers, when they saw the godly Stephen, they crowded around him, embracing him affectionately, and chose him as their guide and teacher. Thus the prison became, as it were, a monastery where the usual hymns and prayers were chanted according to the typicon.

During his stay in prison, the saint received food from a pious woman, the wife of one of the guards. Every Saturday and Sunday she brought a crust of bread and a little water, which she gave to him secretly. At first the blessed one did not wish to take the food, until he made sure that she held to the Orthodox faith and venerated the holy icons, for the saint had a great aversion to heretics and did not want to accept anything from them; but the woman provided him with certain testimony to her piety, for she brought him two icons that she kept hidden, one of the most pure Theotokos and the other of the holy chief apostles Peter and Paul. She bowed down and kissed them in his presence and then gave them to Stephen to keep, begging him to remember her in his holy prayers.

One day, the saint was sitting with the other holy fathers, and they began to speak of the various tortures which the wicked Emperor's evil viceroys, proconsuls, and governors had inflicted on the pious. One of the prisoners, Anthony the Cretan, related the story of the martyrdom of the monk Paul. Theophanes, the Eparch of Cyprus, surnamed Lardotirus, set on the ground before Paul an icon of the Crucifixion of Christ on one side, and on the other, instruments of torture, and said to him, "Choose one or the other, Paul. Either agree to trample underfoot the icon of Christ and you shall live, or choose the instruments that will be used to subject you to a cruel death."

The courageous Paul cried out with a loud voice, "May I never trample upon Thy holy icon, O my Lord Jesus Christ, the only-begotten Son of God!" Then he knelt down and kissed the depiction of Christ's Crucifixion, showing thereby that he was not afraid of the tyrant's threats, and was prepared to die for the icon of Christ. Inflamed with wrath, the persecutor ordered that Paul be fastened to two iron plates and had the blessed one hung head downward. Paul's whole body was raked with an iron claw, and then a roaring fire was kindled beneath him. Consumed by the flames, the valiant Paul became a sweet-smelling sacrifice unto the Lord. All the fathers shed fervent tears as Anthony spoke.

After this, another prisoner described the sufferings of an old man named Theosterictus. He was a presbyter by rank, and his nose had been cut off and his face burned with boiling pitch for his faithfulness to the holy icons. "On Holy and Great Thursday of the week of the Passion of Christ," said the prisoner, "soldiers under the command of the persecutor Lachanodraconus fell without warning upon our monastery of Pelikitas as the Bloodless Sacrifice was being celebrated. Brazenly entering the altar, Lachanodraconus ordered that the chanting cease and threw the holy and life-giving Mysteries of Christ to the floor. He took forty-two of the monks and loaded them down with chains, and the rest he subjected to cruel torments, tearing their flesh to shreds. The beards and faces of some he smeared with pitch and set alight, and he cut off the noses of others. I was subjected to both these tortures. Then he burned down the whole monastery. The forty-two holy monks he had chained were led away to the furthest region of the province of Ephesus, where he imprisoned them in an old bathhouse, sealing off the entrance to the building and starving them to death."

The godly Stephen wept as he heard these accounts, and encouraged the brethren to display courage and endurance like the blessed martyrs. Then he told the others of a man named Peter, who lived in the quarter of the Blachernae in Constantinople. This Peter was mercilessly flogged with straps in the presence of the Emperor for a long time, but such was his patience that he neither groaned nor cried out, and it appeared that he felt no pain. It even seemed that it was he who inflicted the greater suffering on the Emperor, wounding him with the sharp blade of his words and calling him a second Julian the Apostate. Stephen then spoke of another man, John, whom the tyrant was also unable to force to trample upon the icons of Christ and the Theotokos. Copronymus had this man sewn in a sack, to which a large stone was fastened. The sack was thrown into the sea, and thus John drowned.

These accounts kindled in the hearts of the blessed fathers, prisoners of Jesus Christ, a great desire to suffer manfully for the holy icons. Each one strengthened the others, saying, "Let us endure, brethren, for the Lord's sake, and suffer for Him till our last breath. If we endure with Him, we shall also be glorified, because *the sufferings of this present time are not worthy to be compared with the glory which shall be revealed in us*" [Rom 8].

The godly Stephen remained in the dungeon for eleven months. Forty days before his repose, God revealed to him when he would die. After this, when the wife of the guard came to bring him food, he said to her, "May the Lord reward you for the good you have done me! You have shown me great kindness, but there is no need for you to continue to bring me earthly food and drink." When she heard this, the woman was taken aback, thinking the saint was spurning her. Seeing her response, Stephen explained to her, "I shall die in forty days and wish to redouble my monastic labors during the time left me, remaining without food and drink and so preparing myself for death."

During that time a number of eminent citizens who continued to hold the true faith secretly came to receive the saint's blessing. Gaining admittance to his cell by clothing themselves in rags, they hearkened with great delight to his edifying teaching of the Orthodox faith.

When the thirty-eighth day dawned, the saint summoned the woman who had provided him food and said to her in the presence of the fathers, "May God reward you a hundredfold for the compassion you have shown me! May He look down upon you from the heights of heaven with His merciful eye, for you have shown yourself to be a true disciple of Him Who said, *Inasmuch as ye have done it unto the least of these My brethren, ye have done it unto Me* [Mt 25], and *He that receiveth a righteous man in the name of a righteous man shall receive a righteous man's reward* [Mt 10], and *Whosoever shall give you a cup of water to drink in My name shall not lose his reward* [Mk 9]. By serving me you have done all these things, and the Lord will not deprive you of your recompense." Then Stephen returned to her the holy icons she had brought him, and said, "Take your precious treasures! They will serve to defend you against every evil and witness to your Orthodoxy both in the present age and in that to come." Having said this, the blessed one sighed deeply and added, "In two days I shall depart this life for another world where I shall stand before the heavenly King." Weeping bitterly, the woman took her icons and received a final blessing from the saint. Then she wrapped the icons in a towel and returned home, lamenting over her separation from her great father and teacher, but the godly one passed the remainder of that day and the entire night chanting God's praises with his fellow prisoners.

On the morning of the thirty-ninth day, the Emperor and his third wife Eudoxia began their celebration of the heathen festival called the Brumalia, a feast of the ancient Greeks held in honor of the pagan god Dionysus [Bacchus]. During this festival, the observance of which was not the least of the evils of which the heretical and God-hating Emperor was guilty, several iconoclasts accused Stephen of turning the dungeon in which he was imprisoned into a monastery. Many, they said, were going there to hear his teaching, whereby he led them to worship idols, as they called the holy icons. The Emperor became enraged and immediately sent an executioner to take Stephen out of the city and to behead him; but as Stephen was being led to execution, Copronymus began to regret what he had done, and said, "What could be more desirable to Stephen than for his life to be ended quickly by the sword?" He decided to put him to death in a crueler fashion, and ordered the saint returned to prison. That evening the Emperor held a great supper for his nobles and those of like mind with him, and they danced and made merry to the sound of musical instruments and the fanfare of trumpets. In the midst of this revelry, Copronymus remembered Stephen and said to two youths who stood at his side, handsome young men distinguished for their bravery, who were also twin brothers: "Go to the common prison and tell Stephen of Mount Auxentius the following. The Emperor says, 'Do you see what concern I have for you? Behold, I have returned you from the gates of death and granted you life. How long, then, will you remain disobedient?' I know that he will not submit but will revile me even more than before. When he does this, seize him and beat him mercilessly until he dies."

The two men went to the prison, but when they saw Stephen's face, they were put to shame by his evident holiness, for the saint's countenance was like that of an angel's. Falling at his feet, they asked his blessing and prayers and then returned to the Emperor, to whom they said, "The monk refused to submit, so we beat him without mercy, leaving him scarcely alive. So severely did we thrash him that we doubt he will live till morning."

The Emperor's mind was put at rest when he heard this, and he continued to dine with his companions, but Stephen remained at prayer through the entire night, preparing himself for death. At the appearance of the morning star, he called the godly fathers with whom he was imprisoned and said to them, "Fathers and brethren, I wish to give you a final kiss, because the hour of my death has arrived and the crown of martyrdom awaits me. Remain steadfast in Orthodoxy unto the end!"

The venerable fathers wept bitterly when they heard this, bathing their faces with tears. Then Stephen began to remove his robes. His companions said, "It would be better if you met death clothed in the sacred garb of monasticism, Father."

But the divinely inspired Stephen replied, "It is the custom for wrestlers to enter the contest naked; moreover, it is not fitting that the holy monastic habit be trampled beneath the feet of iniquitous men." Thus he undressed, leaving only a leather cloak to cover himself, and sat down with the holy fathers to await the hour of death.

That night, as the Emperor was resting on his couch after supper, the demon who was ever by his side informed him that the youths he had sent to Stephen had done the saint no harm but had bowed down before him and taken his blessing. When the Emperor awoke, at the second hour of morning, he hurried to another part of his palace and began to roar like a lion, crying, "O woe! O the great misfortune into which I have fallen! I have no helper; not one faithful servant remains to me! All hold me in contempt, and I do not know what to do with those men of whom I am loathe even to speak!" This is how he was accustomed to refer to monks.

Hearing the Emperor's cries, everyone in the imperial palace was troubled and ran to Copronymus with haste. Gazing up at them, the Emperor asked, "Where are you going? Whom do you seek?"

"We have come to you, our good lord and Emperor," they replied meekly.

Then Copronymus shouted, "I am not your lord! I am not your Emperor! You have another sovereign, another lord, at whose feet you fall down, entreating his blessing and prayers! Not one of you is willing to obey me or to serve me faithfully, helping me to destroy my enemy and to find peace of soul!"

With troubled hearts the courtiers asked whom he meant. Copronymus answered, "It is not I who am Emperor but Stephen of Mount Auxentius!"

As soon as he uttered these words, they all ran quickly to the prison, shouting and making a great tumult. There they demanded of the guard: "Give us Stephen of Mount Auxentius!"

The venerable Stephen hurried out of the prison to meet them with a joyful soul, his face radiant with gladness. "I am he whom you seek," he told them.

The Emperor's attendants fell upon the saint as wolves upon a lamb, hurling him to the ground, clapping his feet in irons, mercilessly trampling upon him, and beating him with staves. Then they pulled him through the outer gates of the prison and dragged him opposite the Church of the Holy Great Martyr Theodore. There Stephen placed his hands upon the ground, and bowing down his head as best he was able, made a last prostration to the holy martyr before his church. Thus he continued to perform acts of piety even while suffering cruel torments. Seeing this, one of those drinkers of blood, a man named Philommatius, took a large piece of wood and struck the saint's head with great force, cracking his skull. The venerable one surrendered his spirit into God's hands, and a demon suddenly attacked Stephen's murderer. Crying out with a fearful voice, the man fell down, shrieking terribly in the presence of all, thrashing about, writhing, and gnashing his teeth. The demon continued to torment him until finally he gave up his wretched soul.

The mob of enraged blood-drinkers did not cease, however, to mock the corpse of the saint, displaying the cruelty of ravenous dogs. They dragged the body of the venerable one through the streets, hurling stones at it. As they did this, his members were torn away and left to lie in the streets: here a finger, there an arm, there one of his inward parts. One of those wicked men lifted up a large stone with both hands and dropped it on the godly one. The saint's belly immediately burst open, and his intestines spilled out. The streets of the city were dyed red with the saint's blood, which poured out like water. Not only men, but women and little children, who ran out from their schools, hastened to throw stones at Stephen's desecrated body, for a proclamation was made in the Emperor's name declaring that anyone who did not stone the corpse of Stephen of Mount Auxentius would be regarded as the Emperor's enemy and punished by execution; therefore, the entire crowd of heretics, from the least to the greatest, rained stones upon the martyr. When the much-insulted body of the saint was dragged into the ox market, an innkeeper, who was cooking fish at the time, saw it, and thinking that the godly one was still alive, took a burning piece of firewood and struck the saint's head with it, dashing out his brains . . . .

Thus did our venerable father Stephen finish his course, departing this life on the twenty-eighth day of November. He was fifty-three years old. The day dawned exceedingly bright, and the sun cast its rays most brilliantly upon the earth, but at the third hour of the day, fiery clouds appeared in the east, in the direction of the mountain where the monastery of the godly one had stood. The sky above the city grew very dark, and the day turned to night. Then a tempest arose, accompanied by much hail, which fell throughout the Imperial City, causing the death of many. In the meantime, the Emperor sentenced to death for disobedience the two brothers whom he had sent to the prison to kill the blessed Stephen. He also executed the other holy fathers who had been imprisoned with the saint.

The Source

"The Life and Passion of the Holy Monastic Martyr and Confessor Stephen the New, Who Suffered for the Sacred Icons," *The Great Collection of the Lives of the Saints*, St Demetrius of Rostov, trans Father Thomas Marretta (House Springs, MO: Chrysostom Press, 1997), 3:627–659. Abridged and reprinted with permission.

Miscellanea

How do we honor the Saints?

Truly 'God is glorious in His saints' [Ps 67:36]. Let us call to mind the martyrs' superhuman struggles, how in the weakness of their flesh they put to shame the evil one's strength, disregarding pain and wounds as they struggled bodily against fire, sword, all different kinds of deadly tortures, patiently resisting while their flesh was cut, their joints dislocated and their bones crushed, and keeping the confession of faith in Christ in its integrity, complete, unharmed and unshaken. As a result there were bestowed on them the incontrovertible wisdom of the Spirit and the power to work miracles. Let us consider the patience of holy men and women, how they willingly endured long periods of fasting, vigil and various other physical hardships as though they were not in the body, battling to the end against evil passions and all sorts of sin, in the invincible inner warfare against principalities, powers and spiritual wickedness [Eph 6:12]. They wore away their outer selves and made them useless, but their inner man was renewed and deified by Him from whom they also received gifts of healing and mighty works. When we think on these matters and understand that they surpass human nature, we are filled with wonder and glorify God who gave them such grace and power. For even if their intentions were good and noble, without God's strength they could not have gone beyond the bounds of their nature and driven away the bodiless enemy while clothed in their bodies.

* * *

Let us too, brethren, give honour to God's saints. But *how* should we honour them? By imitating them and purifying ourselves 'from all defilement of flesh and spirit' [2Cor 7:1], and hastening towards holiness through abstaining from all evils. If we keep our tongue from swearing and making false oaths, as well as from speaking nonsense and abuse, and stop our lips from uttering lies and slanders, then we offer the saints sweet praise.[1]

—Saint Gregory Palamas

1 *Saint Gregory Palamas* [†1359, Nov 14 & Second Sunday of Great Lent]: *The Homilies*, Homily 25, "Delivered on the Sunday of All Saints," trans Christopher Veniamin (Waymart, PA: Mount Thabor Publishing, 2009), 199, 204–205. Used with permission.

Elders

Elders are those who have achieved (have received from God) spiritual vision (see Saint Niphon, next chapter). They can look at you and see your unconfessed sins—and everything about you. They can see the future (and the past). Healings come about through their intercession.

The Elders of Optina series by the St Herman of Alaska Brotherhood provides an impressive, awe-inspiring, encouraging study of eldership—and Orthodox culture. For nearly a century there was an unbroken line of elders at Optina, beginning with Elder Leonid in 1829.[1] They were the fruit of Saint Paisius Velichkovsky and his translation of hesychast texts from Mount Athos. The presence of the Elders and their publishing efforts were part of the Russian spiritual revival of that time.

The size of the Optina books or the series should not be frightening. You don't have to read the entire series or even an entire book. Instead of starting at page one, you might begin with the reminiscences of their spiritual children. (Hearing these accounts, one begins to ask, "How did that elder get that way?") Or begin with a chapter of their spiritual counsels. ("How does he know that?") Or if a monastery setting seems too unreal or unappealling, begin with Elder Sebastian, who, after Optina Monastery was closed by the Communists in 1923, worked in parishes, spent ten years in Communist prisons, and then led a remarkable parish in Kazakhstan until his death in 1966.

More recent Elders, short list: *Elder Paisios of Mount Athos* by Hieromonk Isaac,[2] see also Saint Paisios's *Spiritual Counsels*;[3] *Wounded by Love: The Life and Wisdom of Elder Porphyrios*;[4] *Our Thoughts Determine Our Lives: The Life and Teachings of Elder Thaddeus of Vitovnica.*[5]

1 The volumes include Elders Leonid, Macarius, Anthony, Ambrose, Barsanuphius, Nectary, and Sebastian (we have not yet seen Elder Anatole).

2 Chalkidiki, Greece: Holy Monastery Saint Arsenios the Cappadocian, 2004, 7th ed 2009.

3 See excerpt in chapter 19 of this Reader. Thessaloniki: Holy Monastery "Evangelist John the Theologian," 2001

4 See excerpt in chapter 19 Miscellanea. Edited by the Sisters of the Holy Convent of Chrysopigi; Limni, Evia, Greece: Denise Harvey (Publisher), 2005.

5 Platina, CA: St Herman of Alaska Brotherhood (St Herman Press), 2012.

In fact what belongs to God must by all means and at any cost be preserved for Him. If, then, on the one hand, the soul is unencumbered with superfluities and no trouble connected with the body presses it down, its advance towards Him Who draws it to Himself is sweet and congenial. But suppose, on the other hand, that it has been transfixed with the nails of propension[1] so as to be held down to a habit connected with material things—a case like that of those in the ruins caused by earthquakes, whose bodies are crushed by the mounds of rubbish; and let us imagine by way of illustration that these are not only pressed down by the weight of the ruins, but have been pierced as well with some spikes and splinters discovered with them in the rubbish. What then would naturally be the plight of those bodies, when they were being dragged by relatives from the ruins to receive the holy rites of burial, mangled and torn entirely, disfigured in the most direful manner conceivable, with the nails beneath the heap harrowing them by the very violence necessary to pull them out?—Such I think is the plight of the soul as well, when the Divine force, for God's very love of man, drags that which belongs to Him from the ruins of the irrational and material. Not in hatred or revenge for a wicked life, to my thinking, does God bring upon sinners those painful dispensations; He is only claiming and drawing to Himself whatever, to please Him, came into existence. But while He for a noble end is attracting the soul to Himself, the Fountain of all Blessedness, it is the occasion necessarily to the being so attracted of a state of torture . . . .

Then it seems, I said, that it is not punishment chiefly and principally that the Deity, as Judge, afflicts sinners with; but He operates as your argument has shown, only to get the good separated from the evil and to attract it into the communion of blessedness.[2]

---

[1] Propensity, inclination, tendency; the will's bias.

[2] St Gregory of Nyssa [†c.395, Jan 10], *On the Soul and the Resurrection* (a discussion with his sister, St Macrina [†c.380, July 19]), in *Nicene and Post-Nicene Fathers*, Second Series, 5:451.

21. Life of Saint Niphon

This final chapter is a review of the topics presented in this book as well as a re-viewing of the environment in which we live. The Life of ***Saint Niphon, Bishop of Constantia*** *[†c.350, Dec 23], again taken from Saint Demetrius of Rostov, demonstrates a different way of seeing and knowing, a different association and attitude. Divine Service is seen in a new way, along with the benefits of spiritual nurture and struggle (repentance). This different way reveals the real environment we inhabit, things beyond the visible, material realm.*

An explanatory caution. One does not look for facial expressions to change on icons, which would render oneself easy prey to delusion. On the other hand, one should be aware of the presence of angels and saints in the services and especially of the divine fire in the altar at the Divine Liturgy.

The venerable Niphon was born in Plagion, a city of Paphlagonia, and was the son of a nobleman named Agapitus. As a child he was entrusted to the care of General Sabbatius, who was sent from the city of Byzantium to Paphlagonia by Constantine the Great. Sabbatius had the keeper of his wardrobe take the boy to his wife in the capital to be educated. In the General's house there lived a presbyter, Peter, who became Niphon's teacher. Niphon studied diligently, and since he was quite intelligent, successfully mastered his lessons. At this young age he was good, quiet, meek, humble, and went to church frequently. Later, however, as a young man, he was gradually corrupted by bad companions; for if a youth is not kept under firm control, he readily goes astray. If even grown men of virtuous character can be ruined by wicked acquaintances (in accordance with the words of the psalmist: *With the perverse thou shalt be perverse* [Ps 17]), how much more easily can this happen with the young, who are naturally more inclined toward evil than good, as it is written: *The imagination of man's heart is evil from his youth* [Gen 8]. Niphon began leading an idle, lazy life, using foul language, engaging in useless conversations, and frequenting the shows of clowns. Soon he was defiling himself with unclean deeds, staying out the whole night with other young people working iniquity. He began to steal, and quarrelled and fought with everyone, becoming the leader of his companions, whom he initiated into every sort of transgression.

Niphon had a friend named Basil who constantly reminded him, "Woe to you, Niphon! Your body lives, but your soul is dead. You are nothing but a shadow walking about." Sometimes Niphon would ignore Basil, but sometimes his friend's words brought tears to his eyes, and he would lament his sins. Nevertheless, force of habit continued to steer him into vice as though he were bridled. Drowning in filthy deeds and in utter despair of his salvation, he would say to himself, "Since I am totally lost, and it is impossible for me to repent, I should at least do my best to enjoy the pleasures of this life." Little by little the devil hardened Niphon's heart to such an extent that it seemed a heavy stone lay on his chest, crushing his soul and preventing him from praying. Niphon's landlady saw what a dissolute life he led and would groan to herself, "Woe is me! How did my house ever become home to such a profligate?" Many times she scolded Niphon, quarrelling with him so violently they came to blows, but he remained incorrigible.

We have related this so that the reader may understand to what depths of infamy Niphon fell, and may marvel at the greatness of God's mercy when he learns how the Lord brought about the young man's rescue. Truly, our God makes sinners righteous and honorable, and there is no transgression that can prevail over His love for us! Having Saint Niphon as our example, let us never despair, for no matter what our failings may be, they can be corrected by repentance. He was a receptacle of iniquity, but contrition and self-amendment made him a vessel of the Holy Spirit, as we shall now explain.

Niphon had another friend, whose name was Nicodemus. One day, Niphon went to visit him, and when his friend saw him, he was aghast. Although Nicodemus said nothing, he could not hide the expression on his face, and Niphon asked him, "Why are you staring at me like that?"

"Believe me, brother," answered Nicodemus, "I have never seen you look like you do now. Your face is as black as an Ethiopian's."

Niphon shuddered and was filled with shame when he heard this. Covering his face with his hands, he went away grieving and telling himself, "Woe is me, a sinner! If in this life my soul and body are black, what will be my appearance on the day of judgement? How shall I dare present myself before the Lord? Woe is me, the evildoer! Where will you hide yourself, my soul? Woe is me! What can I do to escape my fate? Is it still possible for me to amend myself? Is there anyone who might instruct me in repentance and tell me whether I can hope to be saved? How can I say to God, 'Have mercy on me,' when I am guilty before Him of so many vile deeds?"

Repeating such things all the way home, Niphon retired for the evening, downcast, exhausted, and in turmoil. His conscience told him, "Spend the night praying, and God will deal with you as He wishes." However, this good thought was opposed by another, saying, "If you get up to pray, a demon will take possession of you. You will go mad, and everyone will laugh at you."

In this way the devil confused Niphon thoroughly and kept him for some time in a state of trepidation. After a while, though, Niphon summoned up a little courage and told himself, "While I was living an impure life, no evil befell me. Can it be that now, when I wish to turn to God, misfortune will be my lot? Rot in hell, you unclean, deceitful demon! May you perish with your damnable suggestions."

When the sun set, Niphon rose, and facing the east, began to weep and pray, beating himself on the breast and mourning, "Once I lived piously and virtuously, but sin wounded me grievously and slew my soul. But in Thee, O Lord my God, *have I put my hope; save me* from the devil, *lest at any time like a lion he seize my soul, when there is none to redeem me*" [Ps 7]. Suddenly, thick darkness enveloped him and prostrated him with weakness, affliction, and overwhelming terror. Niphon lay quaking on his bed till dawn, shedding bitter tears and lamenting. Then he ran to church, and raising his eyes to the icon of the most pure Theotokos and Virgin Mary, sighed, "O intercessor for Christians, whom the angelic messenger greeted, 'Rejoice!' Have mercy on me and help me, for great is thy compassion, and thou art the hope of the penitent."

At this, a gentle smile appeared on the face of the Mother of God. Niphon was astonished by the miracle, and his heart filled with gladness. "Oh, the depths of God's love for mankind!" he cried joyfully. "O Lord, great is thy forbearance towards sinners, to whom Thou hast granted Thy most pure Mother as mediatress before Thy dread majesty!"

After long prayer, Niphon kissed the icon of the Theotokos lovingly and left the church, saying to himself, "See, wretched soul, how God loves us? It is we who flee from Him. He has given us His most pure Mother as an intercessor, but we fail to resort to her aid."

Two days later, the devil appeared to Niphon in the guise of a young man who had been his companion in sin. The youth wore a sorrowful expression on his face, and Niphon inquired, "Why are you so dejected?"

"It has already been three days since your friend Nicodemus corrupted you. It grieves me greatly to see you pay me no heed," lamented the devil.

Niphon asked, "And just why does this make you so sad?" The devil gave no reply, but turned away. Niphon understood that the wicked spirit was downcast because of his repentance. He hurried to the church, where he again sent up supplication before the icon of the Theotokos. He remained at prayer, his eyes and mind uplifted to heaven, until he beheld a smile appear on the face of the Mother of God as before, filling his heart with divine sweetness.

One day, while on his way to church, Niphon saw a man on the street committing a sin, and judged him in his thoughts. Entering the temple, he lifted his eyes as usual to the icon of the Queen of Heaven, but this time her expression was angry and menacing. After a moment, the most pure Theotokos turned her face away. "Woe is me, a sinner," sighed Niphon, no longer daring to look up. "I had one joy in this life, thine immaculate image, O Lady, but now it turneth away its gaze, and I know not why." Then, reflecting a moment, he remembered that he had judged a sinner, and understood the reason why the Mother of the Lord had averted her face. From the depths of his heart he cried, "O God, forgive me, a sinner, for having assumed a prerogative that is Thine alone. I have dared to condemn my neighbor before Thou didst pass sentence upon him, but have mercy on me, Master, for my soul hopeth in Thee. Henceforth I will never judge my brother." Weeping bitterly, Niphon prayed like this for some time, then looked up and saw the icon smiling. Afterwards he was more careful to avoid condemning his neighbor. There were other occasions, too, when he sinned and the most pure Mother of God turned away her face, thereby reproving him and guiding him to correct his life.

It happened once that Niphon was drawing water, and the devil pushed him down the well. Grabbing the bucket, he shouted, "O Lady, help me!" The next thing he knew, he found himself standing on the beam that ran across the mouth of the shaft. Following this he never failed to have the name of his rescuer the Theotokos on his lips.

* * *

[After long, arduous struggles, and having become a monk,] the blessed Niphon's spiritual eyes were opened to such an extent that he could discern the secret thoughts of men's hearts, converse with angels openly as with friends, and see demons clearly. Once, returning from the Church of Saint Anastasia to his hut, he saw an angel weeping by the door of a harlot's house. The saint asked him why he was lamenting so bitterly, and received this reply: "I was entrusted with the duty of safeguarding the man sleeping with the whore who lives here. It grieves me greatly to see him defile himself. Indeed, how can I not weep when I behold God's image blackened?"

"Why do you not chastise him, so that he stops sinning?" wondered the saint.

"It is because I cannot get near him," answered the angel. "Since the time he became a slave to sin, he also made himself subject to the power of demons. I no longer have any authority over him. God made man with free will and allows him to choose either the narrow or the broad path."

Thereupon Niphon turned to his disciple and explained, "There is no transgression more vile than fornication; nevertheless, if the dissolute man repents, the Lord accepts him more quickly than He does other sinners, for carnal falls come from nature itself, at the instigation of the devil. This passion is banished by fervent prayer, strict fasting, and various mortifications of the flesh."

The saint could also see how the demons went about provoking people to judge, slander, and quarrel with their neighbors, keeping them in a state of perpetual discontent. One day, he saw a man at work, and presently a dark figure approached him and began whispering in his ear. Not far away another man was working, and the devil said something quietly to him as well. Abandoning their chores, they began arguing with one another. "Oh, how crafty are the demons! How much enmity they incite among us!" exclaimed the blessed one.

Once it happened that the demon of vainglory attacked Niphon, saying, "You will now begin to perform miracles, and your name shall be magnified throughout the earth, for you have pleased God."

"Yes, indeed," chuckled the blessed one. "Wait a moment, and you will not be disappointed." Then he issued this command to the rock that lay before him: "I order you to remove yourself to another place!" The stone remained where it was, and the saint turned back toward the evil spirit and spat in its face, saying, "This is for you, devil!" Presently Niphon began to pray, and the adversary disappeared.

At another time Niphon saw a clergyman walking along, followed by a demon that was instilling in him filthy and blasphemous thoughts. The man understood that the devil was planting disgusting notions in his heart, so he frequently turned around and spat at the tempter. The blessed one charged the wicked spirit to cease troubling God's servant, and asked, "What good does it do you if the soul of this man is damned?"

The demon replied, "It does me no good at all, but our king and princes have ordered us to assail men constantly. If they find out that we are hesitant to come to blows with the Christians, they beat us without mercy."

Again, the blessed one saw a monk walking by, whispering a prayer. Flame shot out of his mouth to heaven. Beside him walked an angel holding a fiery spear, which he used to drive demons away from his charge.

On the evening of Great Saturday, before the Paschal service, Niphon was standing in church with the people, and beheld a vision of the most pure Theotokos entering the building with the apostles and a multitude of saints. She gazed with motherly love upon the worshipers, and seeing some who were zealous to achieve salvation, she rejoiced; however, at the sight of those who were heedless, she shook her head and wept. Stretching out her arms, she prayed to God for one and the other alike, so that all might be saved. Witnessing how our protectress, the immaculate Mother of God, refused to abandon even sinful Christians, the saint was reassured that he had in her a special helper and defender.

One night, while Niphon was sleeping, a devil suddenly appeared with a weapon in its hand. The fiend threw itself upon the saint with the intention of killing him, but was quickly reminded how powerless it really was. Gnashing its teeth, it took to its heels, muttering, "O Mary, you never let me have my way with this brute."

It happened that a downcast brother came to ask advice of the godly one, who had the gift of knowing how to instruct and console the sorrowing. He asked, "What am I to do, Father? The evil spirits will not leave me in peace. Whether I am eating or drinking or praying, they implant in my heart heretical and blasphemous thoughts against the Lord Jesus Christ, His most pure Mother, and the holy icons. I am afraid that fire will rain from heaven and consume me."

"Take my advice, brother," the saint counselled. "When the sea is disturbed, waves arise and break against the rocks, but in the end return to the deep. Likewise, wicked suggestions capable of bringing about our destruction are stirred up by the devil and pound our souls; but if the warrior of Christ refuses to give way, especially if he actively opposes temptation, showing thereby that he despises the foul spirit, he will soon see the foe put to shame. It will not be long before he is granted his crown; therefore, child, endure, and combat the demon by prayer and fasting: he will turn tail before long. Flee slander and anger; they, more than anything else, evoke blasphemy." With this Saint Niphon let the brother depart in peace.

The venerable one also had the power to heal infirmities, and it happened that a woman with a toothache came to beg relief. He said to her, "Mother, I am a sinful, defiled man and cannot make you well unless God has mercy on you." With this Niphon left for church, where he prayed; and taking oil from the lamp that burned before the icon of the most holy Theotokos, he anointed the entire swollen area of the sufferer's face. The pain came to an end at once, and she departed, glorifying God. Another woman, who often brought him food, became sick and was near death, and he also healed her by prayer.

Saint Niphon was clairvoyant and could see souls after their departure from the body. Once, standing at prayer in the Church of Saint Anastasia, he raised his eyes and beheld the heavens open, and many angels, of whom some were descending to earth, and others ascending, bearing human souls. As he was looking at this, he noticed two angels going up with someone's soul. When they drew near the toll-house of fornication, the demonic tax collectors came out and shrieked, "That soul belongs to us. How dare you try to carry it by us!"

"And by what right do you claim it?" countered the angels.

"Before death, the man committed both natural and unnatural sins," the fiends replied. "Besides, he judged his neighbors, and what is more, expired without repentance. What do you say to that?"

"We know better than to believe you or your father Satan without confirming your accusations with the guardian angels of the deceased," said the heavenly spirits. When they took up the matter with the soul's angelic guardian, he told them, "It is true that the man sinned much, but then he fell ill, and wept and confessed his iniquities to the Lord. God's authority extends over all, and He knows when to forgive transgressions. Glory be to His righteous judgement!" Triumphant over the powers of darkness, the angels entered the celestial gates with the soul.

Shortly afterwards, the blessed one saw angels carrying another soul. As they did so, demons screeched, "You are taking away this soul without even knowing what sort of man it belonged to! He was a felon, avaricious and full of rancor."

The angels answered, "We know he was guilty of everything you say, but remember that he wept and lamented, confessed his iniquities, and gave alms. For this the Lord has forgiven him."

"If this soul is worthy of God's mercy, then take every sinner in the world! What is the point of our laboring?" wailed the unclean spirits.

"Every evildoer that confesses his sins humbly and with tears receives forgiveness, through God's compassion," said the angels, "but he who dies without repentance is judged by the Lord." Thus confounding their adversaries, the angels went on their way.

Again, the saint saw angels carrying the soul of a man who loved God, was chaste, merciful, and kind to all. Seeing it from afar, the demons gnashed their teeth, but the heavenly powers opened the gates on high and went out to meet it. They welcomed it and exclaimed, "Glory to Thee, O Christ God, Who didst not abandon this soul into the hands of the enemy, but hast delivered it from nethermost Hades!"

Presently the blessed Niphon saw demons dragging a soul off to hell. It belonged to a slave whose master had tormented him with blows and hunger. Rather than enduring this, the miscreant hanged himself. His guardian angel was following at a distance, and the demons were celebrating. The weeping angel was commanded by God to go to Rome and guard a newborn infant that was being baptised. The venerable one also saw another soul being carried through the air by holy angels, who were confronted by a throng of devils. They had not reached the fourth toll-house when the scornful demons snatched the soul and threw it into the abyss. This soul belonged to a cleric of the Church of Saint Eleutherius. He had incurred God's wrath by repeatedly committing fornication, by stealing, and by delving into sorcery. The man was the joy of the demons, and died suddenly and without repentance.

The saint built a church in Constantinople dedicated to the most pure Theotokos and had his dwelling beside it. He converted many unbelievers to the Christian faith. The devil, unable to endure the loss of so many souls without retaliating, set upon Niphon one night with about a thousand of his lackeys. The cell was full of demons eager to torture the blessed one, but with the sign of the Cross, Niphon turned the tables on them. Having the help of God and the assistance of a holy angel, he laid hold of the devils one by one and gave each a thousand blows, compelling them to promise they would keep their distance from any place the name "Niphon" was heard.

Conversing once with the brethren about matters beneficial to the soul, Niphon related this story:

"Here in Constantinople there lived a slave named Basil belonging to a certain patrician. He was a tailor by trade, and led a disreputable life, using foul language, disobeying his master, and acting like a buffoon. He wasted his time playing games of chance and consorting with women of the street. Nevertheless, the merciful Lord did not forget him, but wondrously brought about his salvation.

"Because of the sins of the people, God permitted a severe famine to occur. Masters chased away their slaves, since they did not have enough food for them, and Basil's lord also disowned him. That first day Basil sold his clothes so that he could buy something to eat, after which there was nothing left for him to do but to go naked begging alms. It was wintertime, and the wretch was shivering and freezing in the cold. Finally, he lay down exhausted in the street, and soon his toes froze off, then his feet also. Basil did not complain, but endured patiently, considering this as a chastisement for his iniquities, and saying nothing but, 'Glory be to God for all things.' For two months he lay there without anything to cover himself with, weeping for his sins. Then a man who loved Christ, Nicephorus by name, happened to pass by and see him. He commanded his servant to take him to his house. There Nicephorus made a bed for the cripple, fed him with his own hands, and gave him repose. Two weeks later, on a Saturday, Basil was heard to say, 'It is good that you have come, holy angels; rest a bit and we shall go.'

"They answered, 'No, come quickly; the Lord is calling you.'

"Basil said, 'Give me a little time, for I have a debt to pay. A friend loaned me ten copper pieces, and I must return them; otherwise, the devil may detain me in the air.' The angels waited until Basil collected ten coppers and sent them to his friend. After this the penitent surrendered his soul into God's hands."

"So you see, children," Niphon said in conclusion, "how remarkable are the means God employs to save sinners."

Once, the blessed one went with his disciple to the Divine Liturgy at the church adjoining the palace of Aponius. The Bishop was the chief celebrant, and the spiritual eyes of the saint were opened: he saw fire descend from heaven and cover the altar and the hierarch. During the Thrice-holy Hymn, four angels appeared and joined in the chanting. At the Epistle, he beheld the holy Apostle Paul standing behind the reader and watching. The words of the Gospel rose like lanterns into the heavens. When the gifts were transferred and the curtain was opened, the celestial realm was revealed. A marvellous fragrance wafted through the building, and angels descended, singing, "Glory to Christ God." They were carrying a splendid child on a paten, and surrounded the altar-table. As the Bishop stood before the precious Gifts, two seraphim and two cherubim hovered over his head, covering him with their wings, and when the time came for the Consecration, one of the most brilliant angels held up the Child and pierced Him with a knife. Blood spurted from the wound into the chalice; then the angel laid the Child on the paten and reverently returned to his assigned place. When the divine Gifts were imparted to the people, the blessed one witnessed how some partook with countenances bright as the sun, while the faces of others were black as those of Ethiopians. An angel stood there noting the condition of each communicant, crowning those who were deserving, but turning away in disgust from the unworthy. At the end of the holy service, Niphon saw that the Child's wound had disappeared. Held in the arms of angels, He returned to heaven. The saint related this to his disciple, who wrote it down for the benefit of many.

One day, the man of God was on his way to the Church of the Most Pure Theotokos which he had built, and he saw a very sorrowful Ethiopian walking by. This was a prince of the demons, and behind him were other devils. When they came nearer and heard the chanting in the church, the lesser demons berated their prince, saying, "Hear how the name of Jesus is glorified by those we once had in our power? Our strength is gone; our kingdom is at an end."

The evil prince did not long endure such scolding, but boasted, "Have no fear! I will soon arrange matters so that the Christians abandon Jesus and sing our praises."

A little way past the church, the devils met a group of thirty men, and the prince whispered in the ear of one them. The man's mind was darkened, and he began to utter profanities, dance, and sing shameful songs. Then along came a musician playing his instrument, and one of the Ethiopians bound all the men with a single rope and led them off. They followed happily, prancing down the street, and many people joined them, frolicking and singing bawdy songs. The demons roped them in also and led them away, having hooked them by the heart. Presently a certain wealthy man looked out of his house and paid the musician a copper coin to play for him. The musician put the money in his pocket, and the demons removed it and took it to Satan in hell, saying, "Rejoice, father! Our prince Alazion sends this. It is tribute offered by our enemies, the Christians."

"Strive, children," said Satan happily, "to conquer the Christians; may their offerings to us increase daily!"

Seeing this with his spiritual eyes, Niphon sighed, "Oh, woe to those whose amusements are oblations to the demons!" Later, he recounted this story to others, warning them to avoid listening to wild, filthy songs, which are inspired by the devil.

At another time the saint was in a state of ecstasy and saw a large, square field, on which stood a multitude of Ethiopians, divided into 365 regiments, one for each of the most serious sins. The blackest devil counted the warriors and arrayed them as if for battle. "Keep your eyes on me and fear nothing!" he shouted. "My power will be with you."

At this other demons began bringing large numbers of weapons of various kinds, distributing them among the regiments. When everything was ready, the devil conferred on his troops the power of sorcery, and ordered them to march against the Church of Christ and make war against it throughout the earth. Then suddenly the blessed one heard a voice exclaim, "Turn and look to the east, Niphon!"

Niphon turned around and saw another field, this one clean and splendid. On it stood hundreds of thousands of soldiers, a multitude greater in number than the Ethiopians. They were clothed in white robes and armed for battle. A man appeared, shining brighter than the sun, and announced, "The Lord of Sabaoth commands: disperse throughout the earth, help the Christians, and guard their lives." Seeing this, the venerable one glorified God, who succors His Church.

The Source

"The Life of Our Holy Father Niphon, Bishop of Constantia in Cyprus," *The Great Collection of the Lives of the Saints*, St Demetrius of Rostov, trans Father Thomas Marretta (House Springs, MO: Chrysostom Press, 2000), 4:438–454. Abridged and reprinted with permission.

Miscellanea

Visions

It is noteworthy that there is not a single Church prayer where it is said: "O Lord, grant me the gift of seeing visions." Rather, one encounters the following petitions: "O Lord, grant me humility, chastity, obedience, patience, and meekness. . . ." Saint Ephraim the Syrian prays to receive the following gifts (as a vision): "O Lord, grant me to see my own failings and not to judge my brother."[1]

—Archimandrite Seraphim Aleksiev

Confession and Communion

Saint Nikodemos the Hagorite says:

Gregory the Theologian says:

> When the most sacred body of Christ is received and eaten in a proper manner, it becomes a weapon against those who war against us, returns those to God who had left Him, strengthens the weak, causes those who are healthy to be glad, heals sicknesses, and preserves health. Through it we become meek and more willing to accept correction, more long-suffering in our pains, more fervent in our love, more

1 Archimandrite Seraphim Aleksiev, "Healthy and Unhealthy Mysticism," in *The Orthodox Word* 50, nos 1–2 (294–295):82 (January–April, 2014). Used with permission.

detailed in our knowledge, more willing to do obedience, and keener in the workings of the charismata.

* * *

Be resolved to prepare yourself next time with greater care and earnestness, so that you may receive Communion having confessed fervently, with contrition, having fulfilled your ascetical rule, and having fasted and watched over your thoughts (as much as possible), "with the fear of God, with faith, and with love," just as the priest calls out to you. This way you will serve the Lord and take greater benefit and fruit from the divine Mysteries. This is because, according to the greater or lesser preparation a man performs, so does he receive greater or lesser grace from the divine Mysteries.

It is obvious that the more frequently you prepare yourself and commune, the more frequently your soul receives benefit from the Mysteries, receiving them unto the healing of soul and body, unto the remission of sins, unto the further reception of His divine grace, unto the mortification of the passions, and unto the keeping of the commandments of Christ. For this reason, the divine Apostles in their Canons and the divine Fathers in their liturgies and teachings with one voice urge all Christians—both monastics and laypeople—who do not have an impediment from their Spiritual Fathers to prepare themselves in the manner we just described, and frequently partake of the divine Mysteries. For the longer they put this off and do not receive Communion, the more they are ruled by passions and sins.[1]

—Saint Nikodemos the Hagiorite

1 St Nikodemos the Hagiorite [i.e., of the Holy Mountain. †1809, July 14], *Concerning Frequent Communion of the Immaculate Mysteries of Christ*, trans Fr George Dokos (Thessalonica: Uncut Mountain Press, 2006), 210, 213. "Including a thorough explanation of the Lord's Prayer, an apology for frequent communion, answers to objections and clarifications of misconceptions, and two appendices on the Divine Eucharist." Used with permission.

He took the book out of his pocket and started reading a most beautiful story about one Agathonik, a devout man who from his childhood had been taught by pious parents to say every single day before the icon of the Mother of God the prayer which begins "Rejoice, God-bearing Maiden." And this he always did. Later, when he had grown up and started life on his own, he got absorbed in the cares and fuss of life and said the prayer but rarely, and finally gave it up altogether.

One day he gave a pilgrim a lodging for the night, who told him he was a hermit from the Thebaid and that he had seen a vision in which he was told to go to Agathonik and rebuke him for having given up the prayer to the Mother of God. Agathonik said the reason was that he had said the prayer for many years without seeing any result whatever. Then the hermit said to him: "Remember, blind and thankless one, how many times this prayer has helped you and saved you from disaster. Remember how in your youth you were wonderfully saved from drowning. Do you not recall that an epidemic of infectious disease carried off many of your friends to the grave, but you remained in health? Do you remember, when you were driving with a friend, you both fell out of the cart; he broke his leg, but you were unhurt? Do you not know that a young man of your acquaintance who used to be well and strong is now lying weak and ill, whereas you are in good health and feel no pain?" And he reminded Agathonik of many other things. In the end he said: "Know this, that all those troubles were warded off from you by the protection of the most holy Mother of God because of that short prayer, by which you lifted up your heart every day into union with God. Take care now, go on with it, and do not give up praising the Queen of Heaven lest she should forsake you."[1]

[1] Excerpt from pp 138–9 from *The Way of a Pilgrim and the Pilgrim Continues His Way*, trans R.M. French (New York: Seabury Press, 1965).

Epilogue

The selections in this Reader have emphasized *how* Orthodox believe, not with exacting rules and restrictions, but by exposure to various aspects of Orthodox life, by exhortation, and by example. Implementation rests with the individual—with complete dependence on God, within the context and community of the Church.

For example, consider Saint Benedict's "Instruments of Good Works."[1] The words are the same for everyone, the same Christian ideal. The application and expression of these "instruments," however, depend on each person's unique set of life circumstances, resources, talents, experience, situations that arise throughout the day, and specific people who become involved. Thoughts, words, actions, reactions, decisions, minute-by-minute choices can be brought into subjection unto Christ [cf. 2Cor 10:5], or not. Holy Scripture and the sources sampled in this book provide instruction, example, and encouragement.

Our Orthodox buffet overflows with spiritual delights and delicious everyday dishes. It is comfort food, food from home, our real home. Tastes vary. Some tastes are acquired. You have only to fill your plate. There will be temptations to bite off more than you can chew, and such distractions that you forget to eat at all.

Expect them. Meet them.

---

1 See Chapter 4 Miscellanea, "We're not Monks!" pp 60–1.

Appendix

The three short articles appended here address issues where our Orthodox lives, however diverse, directly intersect.

A Church Library *can be a meeting place of shared edification, interchange, and support.*

My Favorite Matins *considers communal prayer and perhaps anticipates answers for dispersed America's "commuter church."*

Canon Basics *provides help for private prayer.*

The Reading Calendar for **Saint Gregory Palamas: The Homilies** *is just really convenient.*

A Church Library

A church library is a blessing for the spiritual life of any congregation. Many churches have a bookstore, large or small. These are good, but they simply do not provide a library's exposure and accessibility either to material available only in multi-volume sets or to a larger, gradually accumulated collection of single-volume books, periodicals, CDs, etc. For free.

Many of the articles in this anthology are from multi-volume sets of books that an individual would naturally hesitate to purchase: because of their cost, the mystery of their contents, or the trepidation engendered by their bulk. Whatever the cause and despite their packaging, these books are not reserved for scholars, but are everyday reading for normal Orthodox.

Most individuals have a limited book budget. Worse, this budget can be quickly eaten up by hasty or sight-unseen purchases: books that turn out to be too advanced or too basic, too far afield from expectations or interests, or just plain rotten: un-Orthodox writing, bad translations, shameless drivel. So, even bad books have their place in the library: they can be investigated prior to purchase and remorse. Moreover, while any number of books may be worth reading, not all—from the perspective of personal budget, personal taste, personal shelf space—are "keepers."

A church library could also be useful for priests. Not only would it put greater resources at their fingertips for personal use, but it would also give them a ready repository for recommending to members of their flock specific titles or authors or broad topics, through sermons, confession, counseling, classes, individual instruction, or general encouragement.

A library can start small and build slowly. It is a long-term project. Enthusiasm can run high, and parishioners should be encouraged (not bullied) to reap the benefits. Expectations, however, should be kept low to avoid disappointment. Before major purchases, one might survey the interest level among more active parishioners to assess whether the books (CDs, etc.) would be utilized or sit idly on the shelf. To test the waters, to help identify common interests in certain topics or types of writings, one could start by circulating this Reader—not purchasing several copies, but simply loaning out the library copy.

Where to put a church library? Perhaps the best location is the parish hall where people meet for coffee hour. Because of the hustle and bustle of Sunday mornings, placing the library in the "educational wing" (usually a Sunday school classroom), even if right around the corner, renders it "out of sight, out of mind."

Making the library visible and easily accessible can serve several purposes. Shy visitors, while waiting for a friendly hello, could occupy themselves by looking at books. They might find something useful, or the titles alone might help them to discover and define their quandaries. For parishioners, it may spark godly conversation and sharing of books, insights, or experience. The sight of the library might even evoke a virtuous pride of common ownership. Being immediately accessible, it could give people time to browse titles and scan back-cover blurbs and tables of contents without missing out on coffee hour socializing. Including periodicals from the many Orthodox monasteries that produce them might remind people to pray for our monastic brothers and sisters; subscriptions would provide tangible support.

The obvious beneficiaries of a church library are priests, parishioners, visitors, and even our Orthodox monks and nuns. The benefit is an expanding, deepening, maturing Orthodox life and culture: not only for individuals, but for entire congregations; not "intellectual enhancement" for coffee hour chatter, but a knitting together and strengthening of the interdependent members of the Body of Christ. Pretty icons become beloved friends and helpers; the long list of saints in the Entreaty (Lity) becomes a deep yearning, urgent plea, and joy of fellowship. Services are no longer obligatory drudgery but eagerly anticipated visits to heaven. Tradition transforms from concept to personal heritage and way of life, the Church from social club to bulwark against the world, its mad desires, and demonic delusion.

My Favorite Matins

"Do your best, then, to meet more often to give thanks and glory to God. When you meet frequently, the powers of Satan are confounded, and in the face of your corporate faith his maleficence crumbles. Nothing can better a state of peaceful accord, from which every trace of spiritual or earthly hostility has been banished." [1]
—*Saint Ignatius of Antioch*

What is it that draws people to the services? Is it the fellowship? being with friends and allies? a return to the homeland? the gathering of angels and saints? Is it the quiet time with God? the feeling of peace within the temple? Is it the sensory luxuriance? the smell of incense and beeswax? the warmth and glow of lampadas and the lighting of candles? Is it the spaciousness of the temple? the pageantry? Is it the color and beauty of the icons? the music? the relief and therapy of singing? the joy of praising God and of hearing His Word? Is it the peace and sense of grace at the end of a long service? the pouring out of grief to God? the fervent supplications for help—for self, for situations, for loved ones? The comfort of being heard by God? or at least, in some way, drawing near to Him?

Planning a cross-country drive a few years ago, I searched the Internet for churches along the way. In one of the smaller metropolitan areas, there was a church with a weekly Wednesday Matins. I meandered accordingly.

The temple, a beautifully converted Protestant building, was close to downtown. The service began at 6:30 a.m., still dark at that time of year. It turned out to be a reader's service. After the initial Trisagion prayers, there were the Royal Psalms, the "Save, O Lord, Thy people" troparia, and the Six Psalms. Since there was no priest, the litanies

---

1 St Ignatius of Antioch [†c.110, Dec 20], "Epistle to the Ephesians," in *Early Christian Writings: The Apostolic Fathers*, trans Maxwell Staniforth (London: Penguin Classics, 1968, Revised 1987), 64. Copyright © Maxwell Staniforth, 1968. Reproduced by permission of Penguin Books Ltd.

Also available in *The Epistles of St. Clement of Rome and St. Ignatius of Antioch* (New York: Paulist Press [Ancient Christian Writers series]), 65.

throughout were "Lord, have mercy" repeated as required. Then came the Psalms, a sessional hymn, and Psalm 50. The Canon was complete, then the Exapostilarion, the Praises, Small Doxology, Aposticha, Trisagion, troparia, and done.

Done at 7:30. One hour. The downtown workers had plenty of time to get to their jobs.

What a way to start the day! to pray and praise God in His holy temple, with His people, as the Church prescribes. The service started on time—a necessary courtesy for American workers. It neither rushed nor dragged, but kept a prayerful rhythm. The words were clear and delivered naturally. The iconostas lampadas were lit, and the sun rose during the service to reveal the beautiful icons on the walls. It was a Matins full but not laborious, an excellent and very practical way to get to work.

All the parts of the service were done. The Psalm kathisma was actually only one stasis (that is, one Glory, one-third of a kathisma), but consider how often the kathisma(ta) is skipped altogether in our churches. It makes a significant difference in the shape of the office, and in any case, how pleasing to hear the psalms. The Canon was only one canon, the saint of the day, but done completely, with a sessional hymn after the third ode, kontakion and ikos after the sixth, and the full Magnificat sung with palpable joy. It is rare—and delightful—to *hear* a complete canon.

It may be worth another look to see what else made this Matins extraordinary.

First of all, the church website was accurate and up-to-date. It sometimes happens that a person shows up for a service ... and the doors are locked. The service was either cancelled "secretly" or happened to be on the calendar "by accident." This can be especially discouraging for someone making a special effort to get to church. The gumption to come again can dissipate entirely. On the other hand, it is discouraging to discover that services are being held, but that only "insiders" know about them. This is true not only for travelers like me passing through town, but also for local people from other churches who are eager to attend services, whether regularly or when they feel a special need. And why not inform and invite the other local [Orthodox] churches? As this particular church was close to downtown, it would be reasonable to assume that most of the suburban churches had members who worked downtown and might like to come to a weekday service. In fact, it might be worth surveying potential attendees to discover the best service times.

The readers were two lay women. They were obviously well trained in conducting services and had the blessing of the priest to lead these Matins services. They read articulately, naturally, reverently—no stumbling over unfamiliar texts—alternating back and forth rationally and rhythmically as fit the service. What a boon for clergy and congregation alike! Competent lay readers create more opportunity for holding services, and at the same time free both priest and choir director from the responsibility of "*I* have to do *everything*."

Some people may feel scandalized at non-official readers reading in the church, let alone *women*. Consider, however, America's Orthodox infancy: is it better to follow the canons to the letter and, consequently, to have no services at all? How canonical is that? And where are the men?

There is more to remark about these readers. They did not "sing." They either read straight out or chanted, that is, "intoned" on one or two or three notes. The result was that 99.8 percent of the words were crystal clear.[1] Anyone who has experienced this kind of clarity knows that it can turn a foot-throbbing, fiery-furnace, two- or three-hour service into a cool, dew-bearing breeze, seeming to pass in an easy forty-five minutes. It allows the congregation to focus, to fully participate in the service, to hear and understand, to comprehend and contemplate the teachings of the Church.[2]

This is not to advocate music-less services, but to insist on clarity. The words come first, the music is gravy. This is turned on its head, for example, in the concert-style Russian compositions ("war-horses") where the words exist merely to carry the tune. Even with the basic chants, so many singers get caught up—and tripped up—in the music, that services devolve into shambles. On the other hand, how many services are truncated, canceled, or simply never scheduled for lack of competent, talented, trained musicians? Even Great Feasts go without notice because they cannot be "done up big."

Another strange advantage of clarity, in ethnically diverse America, is that the words—the same across all of Orthodoxy—the *words* witness to and emphasize the *unity* of the Orthodox, despite their national

1 It is worth noting that these women were altos. Acoustics seem to require that soprano voices go just a little more slowly (that is, a little less fast) than their lower-voiced counterparts, perhaps a little more loudly, and with exceedingly clear articulation.

2 Clarity also greatly aids the congregation in memorizing scripture, hymns, and prayers—though of course, this requires consistent (and correct) translations.

differences and local variations. Every service of the Church proclaims the True Faith to its congregations and to the entire world ... when performed intelligibly. And what could be better than actually to engage the congregations by making it possible for them to *hear* the services?

Nor is this to advocate short services, but to insist that short services —done well, we hope, but even rough-edged—are better than none. They not only contribute to the improvement of the longer services, but also benefit individual souls and Church-life in general. Many saints have stressed the preeminence of common prayer, saying, for example, that reciting the Twelve Psalms individually is not worth a single *Kyrie eleison* sung communally in the church.[1] The services gather the Lord's people, they instruct and edify, they comfort and encourage, they pull down grace, they draw and befriend angels and saints, they prepare souls for the Eucharist, they honor the Lord, our God and King, and show Him that we *want* to rejoice in Him and to partake of Him and to receive His gifts.

A couple of practical notes may be useful.

Services can go at a pretty good clip, but they should always be comprehensible to the congregation. Some readers and even whole choirs go so fast that the words are completely unintelligible.[2] This is becoming to heathen, who think their prayer is heard for their many words [cf. Mt 6:7], but not for Orthodox Christians. Moreover, where entire services go on incomprehensibly, Orthodoxy is reduced to superstition: "If only we say these magic words at these particular times with these peculiar rituals...."

There is good reason for having two (or more) leaders for reader services. In case one leader is sick or otherwise detained, the other can carry on—an additional gumption-preserver for those non-readers who make the effort to come to the service. These leaders should be prepared, however, for temper flares and a thousand tiny annoyances—one way

---

1 See St Serapion of the Monastery of St Savior and St Eleazar at Pskov, [†1481, Sept 8], in Hieromonk Makarios of Simonos Petra, *The Synaxarion: The Lives of the Saints of the Orthodox Church*, trans Christopher Hookway, Mother Mary, et al (Mt Athos, Greece: Holy Monastery of Simonos Petra, 1998), 1:62–63.

2 Speed is not the only problem, but also an exaggerated rubato, speeding up and slowing down so quickly that the singers cannot find the beat to articulate the words together—producing aural mush—besides the disturbing, erratic, unprayerful rhythm of it. Even in straight-out reading, the speed should be held back enough for *comprehension*. That is, since the prayers and hymns allude to the Old and New Testaments and to the economy of our salvation, the mind needs time (only fractions of a second, perhaps, but time) to comprehend the words and to connect the allusions.

that Satan tries to destroy unity and good deeds. Also, readers need to become familiar with the texts and tunes before the service. Services are not rehearsals. The readers should have the texts available to them—in the correct translation—and, if necessary, practice at home. Stumbling is as bad as mumbling or incomprehensible speed. Moreover, they should find reliable people to "spot" for them—to listen from different parts of the church to make sure they maintain the right speed, volume, articulation, that is, to make sure they are easily understandable. This should be ongoing, since bad habits can creep in unnoticed.[1]

Was this my *favoritest* Matins? It was my favorite weekday Matins, and except for length, far exceeded almost every weekend Matins I have experienced. That it took place on a weekday was highly encouraging: a hope for the growth, maturation, and perhaps even bloom for Orthodoxy in America.

---

1 To the same end, individual choir members (and directors) might occasionally choose to experience a service as a member of the congregation, to hear how the services sound and to be inspired to aim for clarity. Some singers outside the choir loft discover bodily aches and pains and total mental distraction that they never experience when busy with the music in the loft. Welcome to the congregation!

Canon Basics

A canon is a form of liturgical poetry (different from the canons that are the "laws" of the Church[1]) that gained prominence in the Church in the eighth and ninth centuries.[2] Although the Canon of Preparation should be read before receiving Holy Communion, along with the other preparatory prayers, a surprising number of people are not familiar or comfortable with canons. This chapter provides a very basic introduction—enough to encourage, perhaps, the faithful to pray canons at home.

Basic Structure

Reading a canon from the small prayer books is straightforward where everything is written out. Things can become confusing, however, when refrains are missing or when combining two or more canons.

Generally speaking, a canon has (theoretically) nine odes.[3] However, except for Tuesdays in Great Lent and Saint Andrew's *Great Canon*, the second ode is omitted as being too heavily penitential. So, the usual order is **1**, **3**, 4, 5, *etc.* = 8 odes.

The first hymn of each ode is called the *heirmos* in Greek, *eirmos* or *irmos* in Russian, which means "link." It is the "link" between the original *biblical ode* (see below) and the ode of the canon. The heirmos usually summarizes or reflects the meaning of the biblical ode, but in the case of feast day canons, it more often relates to the feast.

The troparia that follow the hiermos (typically there are four) are each preceded by a refrain, for example, "Have mercy on me, O God, have mercy on me," said with the sign of the cross and a bow. Before

---

1 Canon Law should not be approached casually, especially for *ad hoc, ad hominem* attacks on priests, parish members, or pet peeves. It requires not only extreme humility, but also extensive knowledge of history, theology, law, scripture, lives of saints, etc. A possible introduction is *An Overview of Orthodox Canon Law* by Prof. Dr. Panteleimon Rodopoulos, Metropolitan of Tyroloë and Serention; Rollinsford, NH: Orthodox Research Institute, 2007.

2 See Lives of St John of Damascus (Dec 4) and St Andrew of Crete (Jul 4).

3 There are, for example, mon-ode and di-ode canons (canons with only one or two odes) and triodes (three odes, from which the Lenten *Triodion* gets its name), but this is a *basic* introduction.

the next-to-last troparion, the refrain is replaced by "Glory to the Father and to the Son and to the Holy Spirit"; before the last troparion, "Both now and ever, and unto the ages of ages. Amen." The last troparion usually is addressed to or in regard to the Mother of God and is called a "Theotokion."

After the third ode, there may be a Sessional ("Sitting") Hymn (*Kathisma* in Greek, *Sedalion* in Russian). If so, we preface it with "Lord, have mercy" thrice, "Glory to the Father and to the Son and to the Holy Spirit, Both now and ever, and unto the ages of ages. Amen."[1] After the Sessional Hymn, we continue with odes four, five, and six.

After the sixth ode, we say a litany: "Lord, have mercy" thrice, Glory, Both Now, and then the kontakion, ikos, and hymns (if any). Then we continue with odes seven, eight, and nine. (The *Song of Mary* before the ninth ode, interspersed with "More honorable than the Cherubim," is typically done only at Matins.[2])

At the end of the canon, we say, "It is truly meet to bless thee, O Theotokos ..." followed by a prostration. Then, if there is a concluding prayer for the canon—normally only the canons in the personal prayer books have these—it is said here.

The Biblical Odes

The Biblical Odes[3] are read with the canons in matins of Great Lent (except Sunday). If one so desires, however, they may be said anytime in private devotions. In any case, a familiarity with them is always helpful.

Ode One: *Song of Moses*, Exodus 15:1–19
[Ode Two: *Ode of Moses*, Deuteronomy 32:1–43]
Ode Three: *Prayer of Anna* (Hanna), 1 Kings 2:1–10 (in Western Bibles 1 Samuel 2:1–10)
Ode Four: *Prayer of Habbakuk*, Habbakuk 3:2–19
Ode Five: *Prayer of Isaiah*, Isaiah 26:9–20
Ode Six: *Prayer of Jonah*, Jonah 2:3–10 (in Western Bibles Jonah 2:2–9)

---

1 In a service in the church, this would be a Small Litany led by the deacon.

2 Also in Matins, the next-to-last refrain in the eighth ode, instead of Glory is, "We bless Father, Son, and Holy Spirit, the Lord," and before the katavasia we say, "We praise, we bless, we worship the Lord: praising and supremely exalting Him unto all ages." Note to the detail-voracious: the Magnificat is sung in the tone of the final canon. A vesperal extra: "Lord, I have cried" is sung in the same tone as the first sticheron.

3 The Biblical Odes are also available in liturgical psalters.

Ode Seven: *Prayer of the Holy Three Children,* Daniel 3:26–56 (in Western Bibles in the Apocrypha)

Ode Eight: *Song of the Holy Three Children,* Daniel 3:57–88 (in Western Bibles in the Apocrypha)

Ode Nine: *Song of Mary*, Luke 1:46–55, and *Prayer of Zacharias*, Luke 1:68–79

Praying a Canon by Itself

If one's normal Evening Prayers include Small Compline, a canon is usually read after the Symbol of Faith and before the concluding Trisagion.[1]

To pray a canon when not in conjunction with a service,[2] the order is as follows.

Prayers before the canon:

Through the prayers of our holy Fathers, Lord Jesus Christ our God, have mercy on us. Amen.

Glory to Thee, our God, glory to Thee.

Heavenly King... through Our Father...

Lord, have mercy. (12 times)

Glory. Both Now.

O come, let us worship...

Psalm 50

[Symbol of Faith]

The canon(s) [and/or Akathist]

Prayers after the canon:

It is truly meet to bless thee, O Theotokos...

Concluding Prayer of the canon (if there is one)

Trisagion through Our Father...

Lord, have mercy (3 times)

Glory. Both Now.

More honorable than the cherubim...

Through the prayers of our holy fathers, Lord Jesus Christ our God, have mercy on us. Amen.

---

1 Compline canons are provided in *The Octoechos* from St John of Kronstadt Press.

2 Although rarely done, a canon can be said at Vespers after the Song of Symeon and before the concluding Trisagion. It is read, not sung, straight through with the refrain before each troparion (and Glory, Both Now), and with the kontakion and oikos after the sixth ode, but without heirmoi, katavasiae, litanies, or additional hymns or prayers.

Praying More than One Canon

When canons are read together, the first ode of each canon is read: the first ode of the first canon, then the first ode of the second canon (etc., if more). Then the third ode of each canon is read: the third ode of the first canon, the third ode of the second canon (etc., if more). Glory and Both Now are said only before the next-to-last and last troparia of the *final* canon of each ode.

Details (see outline on next page). The first ode of the *first canon* is read: heirmos, refrain, troparion, refrain, troparion, etc. Before the last troparion of the first canon, which is almost always a Theotokion, the refrain is replaced with "Most Holy Mother of God, save us."[1]

Then we begin the first ode of the *second canon*. The heirmos of the second (and third) canon is omitted.[2] Start with the refrain of the second canon, then the first troparion and so on (if this is not the final canon, "Most Holy Mother of God, save us" before the Theotokion). If there is a third canon, read its first ode in the same way. Glory and Both Now are the refrains for the last two troparia of the final canon.

That completes the first ode of all the canons. All of the following odes are done in the same manner.

After the third ode: Lord have mercy (thrice), Glory, Both Now, then the kontakia (if any) from all but the first canon, then the sessional hymns (if any).[3] Then odes 4, 5, and 6.

After the sixth ode: Lord, have mercy (thrice), Glory, Both Now, then kontakion and ikos (if any) of the first canon.

Then odes 7, 8, and 9.

After the ninth ode: "It is truly meet" (with prostration), then all Concluding Prayers of the canons are read (if any).

If an Akathist is to be read with the canon, *all* of the kontakia are read after the third ode, and the entire Akathist is done after the sixth ode.

---

1 In the first canon, if the refrains are written out and the last two troparia are preceded with Glory, Both Now, ignore these, because the Glory and Both Now are said before the last two troparia, respectively, of the *final* canon.

2 Except in some feast day canons; special rubrics are provided in the books.

3 Some Slav sources put the sessional hymns before the kontakia.

Structure for Each Ode of Combined Canons

First Canon

Heirmos
Refrain of first canon
1st troparion
Refrain of first canon
2nd troparion
*** *etc.* ***
"Most holy Mother of God, save us."
Last troparion [Theotokion][1]

Intermediate Canon(s) (if any)

[Heirmos—not read]
Refrain of intermediate canon
1st troparion
Refrain of intermediate canon
2nd troparion
*** *etc.* ***
"Most holy Mother of God, save us."
Last troparion [Theotokion]

Final Canon

[Heirmos—not read]
Refrain of final canon
1st troparion
Refrain of final canon
2nd troparion
*** *etc.* ***
"Glory to the Father and to the Son and to the Holy Spirit."
Next-to-last troparion
"Both now and ever and unto ages of ages. Amen."
Last troparion

---

[1] In some canons, especially feast day canons to the Master, the last troparion is not a Theotokion, in which case the refrain of the canon is said instead of "Most holy Mother of God, save us."

Refrains for *Octoechos* Matins Canons

For those who wish to read the matins canons in the *Octoechos*, the refrains are shown below. (This will make sense when you have an *Octoechos* in front of you.) Same rules apply for Theotokia (preceded with "Most Holy Mother of God, save us") and Glory, Both Now (before the last two troparia of the final canon of each ode).

Sunday: *Canon of the Resurrection:*
Glory, O Lord, to Thy holy Resurrection.
Canon of the Cross and Resurrection:
Glory, O Lord, to Thy precious Cross and Resurrection.
Canon of theTheotokos:
Most holy Mother of God, save us.

Monday: *First Canon*
Have mercy on me, O Lord, have mercy on me.
O ye holy Martyrs, intercede for us.
Most holy Mother of God, save us.
Second Canon
O ye holy Archangels and Angels, intercede for us.

Tuesday: *First Canon*
Have mercy on me, O Lord, have mercy on me.
O ye holy Martyrs, intercede for us.
Most holy Mother of God, save us.
Second Canon
O holy Forerunner and Baptist of Christ, intercede for us.

Wednesday:*First Canon*
Glory, O Lord, to Thy precious Cross.
O ye holy Martyrs, intercede for us.
Most holy Mother of God, save us.
Second Canon
Most holy Mother of God, save us.

Thursday: *First Canon*
O ye holy Apostles, intercede for us.
Most holy Mother of God, save us.
Second Canon
Holy Father Nicholas, intercede for us.

Friday: *First Canon*
Glory, O Lord, to Thy precious Cross.
O ye holy Martyrs, intercede for us.
Most holy Mother of God, save us.
Second Canon
Most holy Mother of God, save us.

Saturday: *First Canon*
All ye saints, intercede for us.
Grant rest, O Lord, to the souls of Thy departed servants.
Most holy Mother of God, save us.
Second Canon: as indicated in text or
Wondrous is God in His saints, the God of Israel.
Grant rest, O Lord, to the souls of Thy departed servants.

Triadicon

When a troparion is marked as "Triadicon" or "To the Trinity," the refrain preceding it is "O Holy Trinity, our God, have mercy on us" or "O Holy Trinity, our God, glory to Thee"—unless it is the penultimate troparion of the final canon, in which case say, as usual, "Glory to the Father...."

Katavasiae

A katavasia is a concluding hymn for an ode. One would not normally worry about katavasiae in private devotions, but a word of explanation might be helpful.

The "katavasia" is a "going down" as the choirs of monks from each side of the church go down and meet in the center to sing the hymn together. In an ordinary matins, the katavasia is the irmos of the final canon of the ode, sung only after the third, sixth, eighth, and ninth odes. In a more highly ranked service, a katavasia is sung at the end of each ode; sometimes seasonal katavasiae are assigned. For festal services, they are of the feast or the season.

This canon primer can be printed out from www.OrthodoxReader.com.

Reading Calendar

for

Saint Gregory Palamas: The Homilies

Pre-Lent Homily

Canaanite Woman...........#43
Zacchaeus...........................62
Publican & Pharisee.............2
Prodigal Son.........................3
Last Judgment.....................4

Great Lent

1st Week (Wednesday)......6, 7
1st Sunday (Orthodoxy)....8, 9
2nd Sun (Palamas)..............10
3rd Sun (Cross)....................11
4th Sun (Climacus).............12
5th Sun (Mary of Egypt)......13
Palm Sunday.......................15
Holy Saturday.....................16

Pascha

2nd Sun (Thomas)...............17
3rd Sun (Myrrhbearers)......18
5th Sun (Samaritan)............19
6th Sun (Blind Man)...........20
Ascension.....................21, 22
7th Sun (1st Ec Council).......23

Pentecost............................24

All Saints............................25
3rd Sunday after.................26
3rd Sun (or 6th Tues)...........27
6th Sunday after..................29
7th Sunday after..................30
9th Sunday after..................32
11th Sunday after................36
12th Sunday after................38
14th Sunday after................41
17th Sunday after................43

Lucan Jump! Homily

2nd Sunday of Luke..............#45
3rd Sunday..............................46
4th Sunday..............................47
5th Sunday........................48, 13
6th Sunday..............................50
7th Sunday..............................51
12th Sunday............................61

Before Christmas

Nativity Fast..........................56
3rd Sunday before..................54
2nd Sunday before..................55
Sunday before Christmas......57

Homeless Homilies

(read ... whenever).......1, 39, 63

Immoveable Feasts

Sep 8 Nativity Theotokos...42
Sep 26 Apostle John............44
Oct 26 G-M Demetrius........49
Nov 21 Entry / Temple...52, 53
Dec 25 Christmas................58
Jan 5 Eve of Theophany.....59
Jan 6 Theophany...............60
Feb 2 Meeting of Lord..........5
Mar 25 Annunciation............14
Jun 29 Sts Peter & Paul........28
Aug 1 Cross Processn....31, 33
Aug 6 Transfiguration..34, 35
Aug 15 Dormition................37
Aug 29 John Bapt Behead....40

This calendar can be printed out from www.OrthodoxReader.com.

Author Index

Bold print indicates quoted source; italic page number indicates mention only.

Subject Index

If this book is useful to you, well and good, and glory to God! But don't dillydally. Move on to the sources.

Miscellanea

View to Salvation
- Reality Check
- Remember Death, Judgement
- Parent Friendly: Church/Bible Basics
- Digging Deeper
- Parent Friendly: Christian Upbringing
- Zeal
- Ascetic Shortlist
- Proof in Doing

Seeing
- Virtues, Vices, Passions
- Sin Oblivion
- THEM!
- We're Not Monks!
- Seeing in the Pentecostarion

Knowing
- Font of Tears
- Rogues' Gallery
- Christ is Preached?
- Believed Everywhere, Always, by All
- Immersion in Orthodoxy
- Magazines
- Saint Justin Books
- Environmental Interference
- Western Influence

Association
- Permanently Out-of-Print
- Church School/Congregation Friendly
- Prayers for the Dead
- Refreshing Courses
- A Reason for Reading
- Parent Friendly: Lives of Saints
- Troublesome Concepts
- Angelic Fear
- The Festal Menaion
- Parent Friendly: Natural Piety
- The Menaion
- Technical Books
- Blessed Hymnody

Attitude
- Cultivating the Field
- Faith Comes through Hearing
- Really Big God
- Public Display of Affection
- Parent Friendly: Singing
- Chant Recordings
- Chant Attitude
- Reading the Services

Divine Service
- Parent Friendly: Learning Orthodoxy
- Orthodoxy a la Mode
- Holistic Experience
- Excesses on Right and Left
- Parent Friendly: Short Offices
- The Horologion
- The Gift of Literacy
- Sweeter than the Psalms
- Octoechos, Triodion, Pentecostarion
- Synaxaria
- Convert English to Orthodoxy
- Services: Too Long, Too Short

Nurture
- Prayer Books
- Psalms
- Liturgical Psalters
- Psalms for the Dead
- Keep Them Honest
- Introduction to Patristic Theology
- Translations
- Running for Your Own Soul

Struggle
- Body Talk
- Habits/Addictions
- Traditional Remedies
- Parent Friendly: Canons & Akathists
- Parent Friendly: Praying for Children
- Anger vs. Peace
- How Do We Honor the Saints?
- Elders
- Nails of Propension

Re-View
- Visions
- Confession and Communion
- Protection of the Theotokos

CPSIA information can be obtained
at www.ICGtesting.com
Printed in the USA
BVOW08s0323030218
506826BV00001B/129/P